Religion and Law in Brazil

Religion and Law in Brazil

Thiago Magalhães Pires

This book was originally published as a monograph in the International Encyclopaedia of Laws/Religion Law

Founding Editor: Roger Blanpain
General Editor: Frank Hendrickx
Volume Editor: Wouter Druwé

Wolters Kluwer

Published by:
Kluwer Law International B.V.
PO Box 316
2400 AH Alphen aan den Rijn
The Netherlands
E-mail: lrs-sales@wolterskluwer.com
Website: www.wolterskluwer.com/en/solutions/kluwerlawinternational

Sold and distributed by:
Wolters Kluwer Legal & Regulatory U.S.
7201 McKinney Circle
Frederick, MD 21704
United States of America
Email: customer.service@wolterskluwer.com

ISBN 978-94-035-4881-4

e-Book: ISBN 978-94-035-4642-1
web-PDF: ISBN 978-94-035-4403-8

The Author

Thiago Magalhães Pires is a constitutional and public lawyer in Brazil. He is a graduate of the University of the State of Rio de Janeiro, where he received both a Master's and Doctoral degrees in Public Law. Professor Magalhães Pires is the author of *Entre a Cruz e a Espada: Liberdade Religiosa e Laicidade do Estado no Brasil* [Between the Cross and the Sword: Religious Freedom and State Laicity in Brazil], as well as other books and numerous articles on Constitutional Law and Public Law in general. He is a partner at *Barroso Fontelles, Barcellos, Mendonça Advogados* law firm, having served as a clerk at the Federal Supreme Court of Brazil and as a guest lecturer at the Judicial School of the State of Rio de Janeiro and the State Attorneys' Office of Rio de Janeiro.

Writing this monograph would not have been possible without the research assistance of Eloisa Chagas and Gabriel Carelli, brilliant undergraduate students at the University of the State of Rio de Janeiro. I would also like to thank my family – especially my parents, Heliane Magalhães and Sergio Pires, and my fiancée, Marjorie Buchi – as well as my dear friends Marisa Choeypant, Gabriel Accioly, Felipe Terra, and Juliana Beaklini for their love and support. I am also immensely grateful to all the great professors who have inspired me through the years – particularly Luís Roberto Barroso, Ana Paula de Barcellos, Carmen Tiburcio, Jane Reis, Daniel Sarmento, Patrícia Baptista, and Eduardo Mendonça – and to the amazing team of *Barroso Fontelles, Barcellos, Mendonça Advogados*.

The Author

Table of Contents

List of Abbreviations

AC	State of Acre
ACHR	American Convention on Human Rights
ADCT	*Ato das Disposições Constitucionais Transitórias* (Transitional Constitutional Provisions Act)
ADI	*Ação Direta de Inconstitucionalidade* (Direct Action of Unconstitutionality)
ADPF	*Arguição de Descumprimento de Preceito Fundamental* (Claim of Non-compliance with a Fundamental Precept)
ADRDM	American Declaration of the Rights and Duties of Man
AgInt	*Agravo Interno* (Appeal to reverse an in-chambers decision in appellate courts)
AgR	*Agravo Regimental* (Formerly existent appeal to reverse an in-chambers decision in appellate courts – replaced by *Agravo Interno*)
AI	*Agravo de Instrumento* (Appeal against interlocutory decisions of courts of first instance)
AL	State of Alagoas
ALEAM	*Assembleia Legislativa do Estado do Amazonas* (Legislative Assembly of the State of Amazonas)
ALECE	*Assembleia Legislativa do Estado do Ceará* (Legislative Assembly of the State of Ceará)
ALERGS	*Assembleia Legislativa do Estado do Rio Grande do Sul* (Legislative Assembly of the State of Rio Grande do Sul)
ALERJ	*Assembleia Legislativa do Estado do Rio de Janeiro* (Legislative Assembly of the State of Rio de Janeiro)
AM	State of Amazonas
AP	State of Amapá
Ap.	*Apelação* (Appeals against final decisions of courts of first instance)
ARE	*Agravo em Recurso Extraordinário* (Appeal to reverse the denial of an extraordinary appeal by a lower court)

List of Abbreviations

AREsp	*Agravo em Recurso Especial* (Appeal to reverse the denial of a special appeal by a lower court)
Arg. Inconst.	*Arguição de Inconstitucionalidade* (Incidental constitutionality review)
BA	State of Bahia
CA	Constitutional Amendment
CAJ	Court of Appeals Judge
CE	State of Ceará
CC	*Código Civil* (Civil Code)
CEM	*Código de Ética Médica* (Code of Medical Ethics)
CFM	*Conselho Federal de Medicina* (Federal Council of Medicine)
CLT	*Consolidação das Leis do Trabalho* (Consolidation of Labour Laws)
CM	*Câmara Municipal* (Municipal Chamber)
CNJ	*Conselho Nacional de Justiça* (National Council of Justice)
Const.	Constitution
CP	*Código Penal* (Penal Code)
CPC	*Código de Processo Civil* (Code of Civil Procedure)
CPP	*Código de Processo Penal* (Code of Penal Procedure)
CTN	*Código Tributário Nacional* (National Tax Code)
CRC	Convention on the Rights of the Child
Dec.	*Decreto* (Presidential Decree)
Dec. Leg.	*Decreto Legislativo* (Legislative Decree)
DF	*Distrito Federal* (Federal District)
DJ	*Diário da Justiça* (Judicial Gazette)
DREI	*Departamento Nacional de Registro Empresarial e Integração* (National Department of Business Registry and Integration)
EBC	*Empresa Brasil de Comunicação*
ECA	*Estatuto da Criança e do Adolescente* (Child and Adolescent Act)
ES	State of Espírito Santo
FCAJ	Federal Court of Appels Judge
GO	State of Goiás
ICCPR	International Covenant on Civil and Political Rights
ICESCR	International Covenant on Economic, Social and Cultural Rights
ICJ	International Court of Justice

Inter-Am. Comm'n HR	Inter-American Commission on Human Rights
Inter-Am. Ct HR	Inter-American Court of Human Rights
IURD	*Igreja Universal do Reino de Deus* (Universal Church of the Kingdom of God)
LDB	*Lei de Diretrizes e Bases da Educação Nacional* (Law on the Guidelines and Bases of National Education)
LGPD	*Lei Geral de Proteção de Dados* (General Data Protection Law)
MA	State of Maranhão
ME	*Ministério da Economia* (Ministry of Economy)
MG	State of Minas Gerais
MI	*Mandado de Injunção* (Petition for a Writ on an Unconstitutional Legislative Omission)
Min.	*Ministro/Ministra* (Minister – member of a higher court)
M. Seg.	*Mandado de Segurança* (similar to the *recurso de amparo* of other Latin-American countries)
MS	State of Mato Grosso do Sul
MT	State of Mato Grosso
OAS	Organization of American States
Org. Law	Organic Law
PA	State of Pará
PB	State of Paraíba
PE	State of Pernambuco
PI	State of Piauí
PR	State of Paraná
Proc.	*Processo* (Proceeding)
Rapp.	Rapporteur
RE	*Recurso Extraordinário* (Extraordinary Appeal)
Reg. Int.	*Regimento Interno* (Internal Rules of Procedure)
Rem. Nec.	*Remessa Necessária* (automatic and mandatory review of a decision)
REsp	*Recurso Especial* (Special Appeal)
REspe	*Recurso Especial Eleitoral* (Electoral Special Appeal)
RFB	*Secretaria da Receita Federal do Brasil* (Federal Revenue Department of Brazil)
RJ	State of Rio de Janeiro
RN	State of Rio Grande do Norte
RO	State of Rondônia
RR	State of Roraima

List of Abbreviations

RS	State of Rio Grande do Sul
SC	State of Santa Catarina
SE	State of Sergipe
SP	State of São Paulo
STF	*Supremo Tribunal Federal* (Federal Supreme Court)
SOUST	*Suprema Ordem Universal da Santíssima Trindade* (Supreme Order of the Holy Trinity)
STJ	*Superior Tribunal de Justiça* (Superior Court of Justice)
STM	*Superior Tribunal Militar* (Superior Military Court)
TJ	*Tribunal de Justiça* (Court of Appeals – e.g., TJAP: State Court of Appeals of Amapá)
TO	State of Tocantins
TRF	*Tribunal Regional Federal* (Federal Court of Appeals)
TSE	*Tribunal Superior Eleitoral* (Superior Electoral Court)
TST	*Tribunal Superior do Trabalho* (Superior Labour Court)
UDHR	Universal Declaration of Human Rights
UN	United Nations
UNRHC	United Nations Human Rights Committee

General Introduction*

§1. General Background of the Country

I. Basic Structure

1. The region that corresponds to modern-day Brazil was far from uninhabited when the first Europeans ventured ashore: a great number of Indigenous peoples lived in the territory, with estimates varying between 800,000 and 5 million people.[1] A Portuguese fleet arrived in 1500, commencing colonialism, which lasted until 1822. From the outset, the territory was divided into hereditary captaincies, however, they were later unified under the authority of a Governor-General (or Vice-Roy, as they came to be known). Fleeing the invasion of Portugal by Napoleon, the Portuguese Court settled in Rio de Janeiro and elevated the colony to the status of the realm, united with Portugal and Algarve.

2. Independence was declared in 1822, by Prince Regent Pedro – the son of King John VI, who had returned to Portugal. The Prince became a monarch, as Emperor Pedro I, and decreed the 1824 Constitution, being the first of independent Brazil. In 1831, the emperor abdicated and returned to Portugal to contest his brother for his daughter's claim to the Portuguese throne. As his heir was underage, a Regency was established, which prevailed until 1840, when the heir was declared of age and crowned as Emperor Peter II. His reign ended in 1889, with the Proclamation of the Republic. The former captaincies, which came to be the provinces of the Empire, were transformed into states under a new federal arrangement. The capital, Rio de Janeiro, became the new Federal District.

3. From 1889 to 1930, the country was administered by an oligarchic regime, centred around the wealthy rural elites, especially those emanating from the Southeast (São Paulo and Minas Gerais). In 1930, a revolution brought about the end of the regime and the beginning of the 'Vargas Age', named after the leader of the Revolution, Getúlio Vargas. Vargas served as President of the Provisional Government (1930–1934), President of the Republic (1934–1937), and dictator (1937–1945), under two constitutions (1934 and 1937). The fall of his regime led to

*. Except as otherwise specified, citations in Portuguese were freely translated into English by the author of this monograph.

1. Heloísa Pagliaro, Marta Maria Azevedo & Ricardo Ventura Santos, Demografia dos Povos Indígenas no Brasil: um Panorama Crítico, *in Demografia dos povos indígenas no Brasil*, 16 (Heloísa Pagliaro, Marta Maria Azevedo, & Ricardo Ventura Santos eds., 2005).

a new democratic era under the 1946 Constitution, and Vargas was popularly elected President for one more term, which then ended abruptly with his suicide (1954). A new capital, Brasília, was constructed in the centre of the territory and in 1960 it became the seat of the branches of the federal government. In 1964, the military seized power and installed a dictatorship that would last for twenty-one years. The first civilian President, Tancredo Neves, died before taking office, leaving his running mate, José Sarney, to be inaugurated as President, and a National Constituent Assembly was convened in 1986. In 1988, the current Brazilian Constitution was promulgated.

4. Under the 1988 Constitution,[2] Brazil is a federative republic. It is comprised of the *Union* (federal government), twenty-six states, the Federal District, and more than five thousand municipalities. The powers of government are divided between all of these entities, which are autonomous under the Constitution, bearing no political subordination, from one to the other. They all have directly elected legislative bodies and executive officials, with the Judiciary branch divided between the Union and the states.

5. The territory of Brazil encompasses over 8.5 million square kilometres (3.3 million square miles),[3] with its population being estimated to have surpassed 211,755,000 people in 2020.[4] Brazilian society is plural and vibrant, being constituted by people from different origins. The 2010 census employed five options as

2. In this monograph, the term 'Constitution', unqualified, as well as the phrases 'Federal Constitution' and the '1988 Constitution', is used as a reference to the 1988 Constitution of the Federative Republic of Brazil. State constitutions are expressly referred as such.
3. *Áreas Territoriais*, Instituto Brasileiro de Geografia e Estatística, https://www.ibge.gov.br/geociencias/organizacao-do-territorio/estrutura-territorial/15761-areas-dos-municipios.html?t=acesso-ao-produto&c=1 (last visited 17 Jan. 2021).
4. *Estimativas da População Residente no Brasil e em Unidades da Federação com Data de Referência em 1º de Julho de 2020*, Instituto Brasileiro de Geografia e Estatística, https://ftp.ibge.gov.br/Estimativas_de_Populacao/Estimativas_2020/POP2020_20201030.pdf (last visited 17 Jan. 2021).

'skin colour' or race[5] with which people were asked to identify themselves. Black or *pardos* were 50.7%,[6] 47.7% identified as white, 1.1% as 'yellow' (i.e., Asian-Brazilian), and 0.4% as Indigenous.

II. General Legal System

6. The 1988 Federal Constitution is an extended document of 250 articles, plus the 118 articles of the accompanying Act of Transitory Constitutional Provisions, many of which are subdivided and complemented by paragraphs and lists. Further to the six constitutional revision amendments of 1994, 116 constitutional amendments had been approved up until February 2022.

7. The first two parts of the Constitution address fundamental principles (Title I), e.g., sovereignty and human dignity, and fundamental rights (Title II), comprising civil, political, social, and economic rights. The Constitution also protects collective rights, including the right to a balanced environment (Article 225). Title III is dedicated to the political organization of the Republic in all levels of government, whilst Title IV deals with the branches of the federal government. Title V regulates the states of defence and siege, the Armed Forces, and public security

---

5. It would divert this monograph from its purposes to discuss the propriety of this use of the term 'colours'. One should note, nonetheless, that in Brazil, even though people do use them to describe the colour of their skin, they are actually a central part of a more comprehensive system of social 'markers', used to 'ascribe' people some places in society. 'Skin colours' interact with other elements – e.g., wealth, official capacity, fame, talent – to determine each person's status. Some of them, like race, are stronger than others, but they do not work as objective or inflexible standards. On the contrary, people may 'change colours', being more or less associated with one or another due to other 'markers'. Oracy Nogueira, in an important work on this field explains that, in places like Brazil, the threshold between the groups is indeterminate, so that it may change according to the specific characters of the observer and the other, as well as to the relationship between them (e.g., friendship of deference), but the physical appearance is still a strong limitation to all of this. Oracy Nogueira, *Preconceito Racial de Marca e Preconceito Racial de Origem: Sugestão de um Quadro de Referência para a Interpretação do Material sobre Relações Raciais no Brasil*, 19 Tempo Social 287, 293–294 (2006). Lilia Moritz Schwarcz reports an interesting case. In the nineteenth century, Saint Hilaire, a French traveller who came to Brazil, was puzzled when a soldier, asked about his troop's leader, pointed to a Black man. When he expressed his doubts, the soldier replied, 'he is not Black, for if he were, he would not be the leader'. *See* Lilia Moritz Schwarcz, *Do Preto, do Branco e do Amarelo: Sobre o Mito Nacional de um Brasil (Bem) Mestiçado*, 64 Ciência e Cultura 48, 49 (2012).
6. The closest translation of *pardo* may be 'brown'. The word is used both in popular and official discourse as a reference to people whose skin colour is thought to be lighter than that of Black individuals but do not see themselves (or are seen by others) as white. They are usually regarded as a result of miscegenation, and from a racial perspective, are placed in an apparently indefinite position, in which they frequently suffer the effects of racism, but also may not see themselves (or be seen by others) as part of a discriminated group. It is a category that clearly exemplifies the insidious way in which racism manifests in Brazil: by allowing people to be moved in and out of a marginalized condition, as it may fit the interests and prejudices of the dominant group, it sustains the illusion of a racial democracy in a structurally racist reality. Another element of complexity is the association of the word with a skin colour: since *pardo* refers to an individual who is neither white nor Black, it actually encompasses an impressive variety of groups, with quite different social conditions (e.g., people of Black, Indigenous, Middle-Eastern, Sinti and Roma descent).

(mainly, the police). Title VI establishes rules and principles regarding taxation and public finances, whilst Titles VII and VIII respectively deal with 'economic order' (e.g., private enterprise, public services, urban and rural development) and 'social order' (e.g., social security and social assistance, healthcare, education, sports, Indigenous peoples). The last part is Title XI, which contains miscellaneous provisions (e.g., rules to be followed by new states, notary publics).

8. The Federal Constitution is the supreme law of the land, and any inconsistency with it renders an act void, so that, as a rule, courts are required to set it aside. Any court is empowered to refuse enforceability to unconstitutional acts in regular adjudication, but the Federal Supreme Court can also decide on this matter *in abstracto*, on special suits which can be brought by institutional actors (e.g., the Prosecutor General of the Republic, the President of the Republic, state governors) or civil society entities (e.g., political parties, confederations of labour unions). In these cases, despite the principle of stare decisis not being adopted in Brazil, the Court's decision on the merits is binding on all other courts as well as for administrative officers.

9. Federal law includes the statutes approved by the Houses of Congress and signed by the President, as well as international treaties.[7] The Union's exclusive legislative powers include, e.g., civil, commercial, criminal, labour, and electoral law. It is also permitted to pass legislation, in concurrence with the states and the Federal District, regarding tax and financial law, education, culture, health, and protection of childhood and youth – although, when using its concurrent power, the Union can only enact 'general provisions' so that a reasonable expanse remains in which the states and the Federal District can approve their own laws.

10. The National Congress is the national legislative body. It is bicameral, consisting of the Chamber of Deputies and the Federal Senate. The number of seats in the Chamber that are assigned to each state and to the Federal District must be proportional to their respective populations, whist in the Senate, the states and the Federal District are each accorded three seats. There are currently 513 federal deputies and 81 senators. They serve four and eight-year terms, respectively, and the Senate seats are partially contested every four years so that people alternate between choosing one or two senators for their state (or the Federal District) at every general election. The federal executive consists of a President and a Vice President, directly elected for four-year terms, renewable for one immediate term, and of Ministers, who oversee the work of numerous departments and agencies. As for the Judiciary, the Union is responsible for maintaining the Federal Supreme Court (principally devoted to constitutional matters), the Superior Court of Justice (STJ) (devoted primarily to settling the interpretation of federal statutes and treaties), the Electoral Courts, the Labour Courts, the Federal Military Courts, and the courts of the Federal District and Territories.

7. For the legal status of treaties in Brazilian law, *see* Part IV, Ch. 1, §2 *infra*.

11. The states possess their own constitutions, and their organization broadly reflects the federal structure. Their executive branches are headed by directly elected governors and lieutenant governors, with four-year terms, renewable for one immediate term, and the secretaries they appoint. In each state, there is a unicameral Legislative Assembly, comprised of a number of state deputies calculated on the basis of each state's representation in the federal Chamber of Deputies. The states are also responsible for their court system, which is headed by a State Court of Appeals.

12. The Federal Constitution does not assign a comprehensive domain of legislation to states – since the most important powers are given to the Union, and the municipalities also have competencies of their own, the scope of the reserve state powers is not entirely relevant. Their main source of legislative powers is Article 24, but these are shared with the Union (concurrent powers). They include consumer protection, youth, education, and environmental protection, among others.

13. The municipalities' organization follow a similar pattern to that of the states: the Federal Constitution grants all municipalities the power to enact their individual charters, known as 'organic laws'; their executive is headed by directly elected mayors and deputy mayors, with four-year terms, renewable for one immediate term, who are assisted by their appointed secretaries; they have unicameral legislatures as well, known as Municipal Chamber or Chamber of Councillors. Municipal governments do not have a judicial branch.

14. Municipalities are empowered to legislate in all matters of predominant local matter, as well as to supplement federal and state laws when appropriate. They also regulate and collect their own taxes, and enact zoning, local transportation, education and healthcare initiatives.

15. The Federal District combines state and local features. It boasts self-organization powers, exercised by enacting and amending its organic law; its directly elected Governor and Lieutenant Governor, with a four-year term, renewable for an immediate one; and an elected legislature, called Legislative Chamber, with a number of deputies proportional to the District's representation in the federal Chamber of Deputies. The District Judiciary is part of the federal court system, being established and maintained by the Union. The Federal District cannot be subdivided into municipalities, so it merges almost all state and local legislative and administrative powers.

16. Brazilian law is part of the civil law tradition. As such, its primary sources are statutes approved under the proper legislative procedure. However, scholars have begun to observe some approximation with the common law tradition – and especially with American law.[8] The recently enacted Code of Civil Procedure of

8. *See*, e.g., Luís Roberto Barroso, *A Americanização do Direito Constitucional e Seus Paradoxos: Teoria e Jurisprudência Constitucional no Mundo Contemporâneo*, *in IV Temas de Direito Constitucional* 121 (2009).

2015 reinforced this trend by providing a new status to precedents, simplifying procedures when precedents are followed and requiring courts to adhere to them.[9]

17. As for comparative law, scholars and courts very frequently apply international and foreign materials – statutes and case law – in the interpretation of Brazilian domestic law. Opinions of the United States Supreme Court, of the Federal Constitutional Court of Germany, and of the Constitutional Courts of Portugal, Spain, Italy, Colombia, and South Africa, as well as judgments by the Inter-American and the European Courts of Human Rights and by the Court of Justice of the European Union, are commonly cited by academics, counsel briefs and judicial decisions.

§2. Social Facts about Religion

I. Official Census

18. When the last official survey was conducted in 2010,[10] Brazil recorded a population of 190,755,799 people,[11] notwithstanding, the census bureau (IBGE) estimates that in 2020, the number of inhabitants was approximately 212,755,700.[12]

II. Religious Demographics

19. The 2010 census included a question in relation to people's religious affiliation. The following table is based on the data obtained and published by the IBGE:[13]

9. *Código de Processo Civil (CPC)* [Code of Civil Procedure], Law No. 13105 of 16 Mar. 2015, e.g., Arts 311, III; 332, II and III; 489, para. 1, VI; 496, para. 4, II and III.
10. Another survey was supposed to be carried out in 2020, but it was postponed due to the COVID-19 pandemic.
11. Instituto Brasileiro de Geografia e Estatística, *Sinopse do Censo Demográfico: 2010*, 30 (2011), https://biblioteca.ibge.gov.br/visualizacao/livros/liv49230.pdf.
12. *Estimativas da População Residente no Brasil e em Unidades da Federação com Data de Referência em 1º de Julho de 2020*, *supra* note 4.
13. Instituto Brasileiro de Geografia e Estatística, *Censo demográfico: 2010 – Características Gerais da População, Religião e Pessoas com Deficiência*, 144, https://biblioteca.ibge.gov.br/visualizacao/periodicos/94/cd_2010_religiao_deficiencia.pdf (last visited 17 Jan. 2021). The census used the term Evangélicos (Evangelical) to refer to different Protestant denominations. I have opted to replace it with 'Protestant' just to avoid confusion with other, more restricted, meanings of 'Evangelical' in use in the world.

Major Religious Traditions in Brazil (2010)	*Percentage in the Population (%)*[14]
Christian	88.77
Roman Catholic	64.63
Protestant	22.16
Assembly of God	*6.46*
Baptist	*1.95*
Christian Congregation of Brazil	*1.20*
Universal Church of the Kingdom of God	*0.98*
The Foursquare Church	*0.95*
Seventh-day Adventist	*0.82*
Lutheran	*0.52*
Presbyterian	*0.48*
Other Protestant	*8.80*
Mormon	0.12
Jehovah's Witness	0.73
Brazilian Catholic	0.29
Orthodox	0.07
Other Christian	0.77
Other Religions	2.73
Spiritism	2.02
African-Brazilian	0.31
Umbanda	*0.21*
Candomblé	*0.09*
Other African-Brazilian	*0.01*
Buddhist	0.13
Jewish	0.06
World Messianity	0.05
Esoteric Traditions	0.04
Indigenous	0.03
Spiritualists	0.03
Muslim	0.02
Other	0.04

14. Children who were unable to inform their own religion were counted in their mothers' denomination. *Ibid.* at 27.

Major Religious Traditions in Brazil (2010)	*Percentage in the Population (%)*[14]
Unaffiliated	8.04
Atheist	0.32
Agnostic	0.07
Unreligious	7.65
Undetermined/Poorly Defined	0.33
Declaration of Multiple Religious Affiliation	0.01
Don't Know/Didn't Declare	0.13

III. Historic Patterns and Religious Trends

20. Catholicism is the prevalent denomination in Brazil. For centuries, it counted with formal support of the Portuguese Crown and, later, of Brazilian authorities not only for its maintenance but also to suppress or hinder the activities of some other religions. For many years, Judaism was repressed, as were Islam and African religions – both practised by enslaved people. The situation began to change in the nineteenth century when immigration led to the arrival of Protestant Christians, especially from Europe, and of Muslims and Jews, from Syria, Lebanon, and other territories. Missionaries from the United States also propagated a number of different Christian denominations in Brazil, such as the Church of Jesus Christ of Latter-day Saints (Mormon), Jehovah's Witness, and others.

21. Brazil has consistently morphed from the clear and undisputed hegemony of Catholicism to a more plural and diverse religious sphere. This movement has recently gained more and more headwind, with the number of Catholics decreasing rapidly whilst the groups of Protestants, members of 'other religions' (including African-Brazilian denominations), and unaffiliated (Atheist, Agnostic, and Unreligious) continue to surge.

22. Catholics constituted 99.7% of the population in 1872[15] and were still 91.8% in 1970. The decreasing numbers persisted in 1980 (89.0%) and 1991 (83.0%), but 2000 and 2010 recorded steeper falls, respectively to 73.6% and 64.6%. It was also the first time that the absolute number of Catholics reduced (from 125.5 million to

15. It should be noted, however, that 'the country had 8,419,672 free people and 1,510,806 slaves. Catholics amounted to 9,902,712 (including free people and slaves), and Non-catholics (registered only for free people) amounted to 27,766'. Enslaved people, being '[f]orbidden from practicing their own religion', were registered as Catholic, as explained by Maria Goreth Santos, Os Limites do Censo no Campo Religioso Brasileiro, *in Religiões em Conexão: Números, Direitos, Pessoas* 18, 19 (Christina Vital da Cunha & Renata de Castro Menezes eds., 2014).

123.3 million).[16] Protestants, who were 5.2% of the population in 1970, gained progressively higher traction over the years, growing to 6.6% in 1980, 9.0% in 1991, 15.4% in 2000, and finally 22.2% in 2010.[17] Whilst the Catholics surrendered 30% of their share, the group of Protestants has grown more than four times its size since 1970. And the group of the 'other religions' doubled its size, from 2.5% to 5% of inhabitants, within the same timeframe. Corresponding to a share of 40% of the remaining group, Spiritism attained a 70% growth.[18] As for the unaffiliated, their number was even greater: from 1970 to 2010, they surged from a mere 0.8% of the population to an impressive 8.1% – a tenfold increase.

23. It should be noted, however, that in a probable manifestation of structural racism and perhaps class prejudice, Indigenous and African-Brazilian religions were not even included as options in the surveys until at least 1980. Until then, whilst Indigenous religions were not listed, African-Brazilian denominations were simply fused with a larger group of Spiritism.[19] Scholars also stress that the number of followers of African-Brazilian religions is probably underestimated: due to persecution and prejudice, many of their adherents still declare to be Catholic. Also, their syncretic nature makes double or multiple religious affiliations more common.[20]

24. There is more religious affiliation among women, who also gravitate more between religions than do men. Religious migration is above average in the Southern parts of the country but is concentrated in the middle classes, especially among those with medium and lower degrees of education. Catholics appear to have conceded followers to most of the other segments, especially to Pentecostal Protestants and the unaffiliated.[21] In fact, a survey in 2016 identifies that little more than half (52%) of Pentecostal Evangelicals have migrated from other denominations, and 44% of them were once Catholic. Conversely, 90% of all Catholics had never been part of other denominations.[22] It seems clear, then, that the religious flow is from Catholics to other groups (especially Protestants), whereas few people convert to Catholicism.

---

16. Ricardo Mariano, *Mudanças no campo religioso brasileiro no Censo 2010*, 14 Debates do NER 119, 119 (2013).
17. Instituto Brasileiro de Geografia e Estatística, *supra* note 13 at 89–91.
18. Mariano, *supra* note 16 at 119–120.
19. Santos, *supra* note 15 at 21–22.
20. Reginaldo Prandi, *O Brasil com Axé: Candomblé e Umbanda no Mercado Religioso*, 18 Estudos Avançados 223, 224–226 (2004); Santos, *supra* note 15 at 25–26.
21. Ronaldo de Almeida & Paula Monteiro, *Trânsito religioso no Brasil*, 15 São Paulo em Perspectiva 92, 96–99 (2001). This study relies on a survey conducted in 1998 by the Brazilian Ministry of Health about sexual behaviour and perceptions about HIV/Aids.
22. *Perfil e opinião dos evangélicos no Brasil – total da amostra: PO913906 – 07 e 08/10/2016*, Datafolha (2016), http://media.folha.uol.com.br/datafolha/2016/12/28/da39a3ee5e6b4b0d3255bfef95601890afd80709.pdf.

25. Disestablishment and religious freedom have both resulted in the morphing of a dynamic religious sphere, in which, being it considerably easy to set up a religious organization, with competition expanding in ways that provide followers with an increasing number of options at their disposal.[23]

IV. Indigenous Peoples

26. From the arrival of the Portuguese in 1500 until the 1970s, the Indigenous population of Brazil dramatically decreased and many communities became extinct:[24] on average, one million individuals died every century in colonial Brazil.[25] It is estimated that 3,000,000 Indigenous people lived in the country in 1500, whilst only 70,000 remained in 1957. Since then, however, their share in the national population has swelled: from 0.10% in 1957 to 0.20% in 2000, which accounts for approximately 358,000 people.[26] In 2010, the Indigenous population comprised almost 325,000 people in urban areas and around 572,000 in rural areas, there in total 897,000 people (0.5% of the population). The majority (58%) lived in 'Indigenous Lands', especially demarcated for their use.[27] They were concentrated in the North (37.4%), but their presence was considerable in all other regions as well: Northeast (25.5%), Centre-West (16%), Southeast (12%), and South (9.2%). On average, Indigenous people corresponded to 0.4% of the states' populations; this being only surpassed in four Northern states – Roraima (11%), Amazonas (4.8%), Acre (2.2%), and Amapá (1.1%) – and in two states of the Centre-West – Mato Grosso do Sul (3%) and Mato Grosso (1.4%). Amazonas was the only state with more than 100,000 Indigenous individuals.[28]

27. Anthropologists have records of more than 387 Indigenous peoples in Brazil, each in possession of their own customs and languages, separated into four basic cultural branches: Tupi, Karib, Jê, and Aruak.[29] According to the 2010 Census, there were 305 ethnic groups in the country, with the Tikúna, the Guarani Kaiowá, and the Kaingang being the most populous. As for Indigenous languages, there were 274

23. Antônio Flávio Pierucci, *O Crescimento da Liberdade Religiosa e o Declínio da Religião Tradicional: A Propósito do Censo de 2010*, 1 Anuac 87, 91 (2012).
24. *Quem são*, Fundação Nacional do Índio, http://www.funai.gov.br/index.php/indios-no-brasil/quem-sao (last visited 25 Feb. 2021).
25. Laurentino Gomes, *Escravidão* vol. 1, 118 (Globo, 2019).
26. Marta Maria Azevedo, *Diagnóstico da População Indígena no Brasil*, 60 Ciência e Cultura 19, 13 (2008).
27. Instituto Brasileiro de Geografia e Estatística, *Censo Demográfico: 2010 – Características Gerais dos Indígenas: Resultados do Universo*, 54–55 (2010), https://biblioteca.ibge.gov.br/visualizacao/periodicos/95/cd_2010_indigenas_universo.pdf.
28. Instituto Brasileiro de Geografia e Estatística, *Os Indígenas no Censo Demográfico 2010: Primeiras Considerações com Base no Quesito Cor ou Raça*, 9–11 (2012), https://indigenas.ibge.gov.br/images/indigenas/estudos/indigena_censo2010.pdf.
29. Kaká Werá Jecupé, *A Terra dos Mil Povos: História Indígena do Brasil Contada por um Índio*, 2 (2020).

in Brazil. Among people of 5 years of age or older, 77% spoke Portuguese – the official language in Brazil – and 37% of those people also spoke an Indigenous language.[30]

28. In the early years of European settlement in Brazil, it was widely believed that the Indigenous peoples did not have a religion: since they did not display evidence of idols, temples, or priests, the Europeans could not comprehend any sense of their religiosity. They could only rationalize it a vague and rudimentary notion of deity, by transforming *Tupã*, a mythological being related to the sky and the thunder, as an equivalent of the Christian God. Although, as gentiles, Indigenous people were accorded as able – or even entitled – to convert to the 'true' religion, the prevailing notion, especially among Catholic priests and authorities, was that the devil, disguised or acting through the shamans (*pajés* or *caraíbas*) averted them from attaining the 'truth'.[31] Conversion and acculturation were driving forces throughout the country's history. To facilitate colonization and domination, the Jesuits 'articulated … a cunning strategy based on three vectors: indoctrinating children, demoralizing the *pajés*, and converting tribal leaders'.[32]

29. As a result, Christianity clearly predominates among Indigenous peoples. 77% of all individuals worship as either Roman Catholic (51%) or Protestant (26%). The non-religious group is relevant too, amounting to 14%. By comparison, only 5% adhered to Indigenous traditional religions, and more than 90% of them reside in rural areas. The greatest share of followers of traditional religions was in the Northern region, but even there they did not reach the 10% mark.[33]

30. The invasion of Indigenous lands subsequently led to the persecution and masking of religious tradition within many communities. It nevertheless survived, morphing Christian elements into the form of syncretic rituals.[34] Indigenous cultural and religious practices are also retained in the *caboclo* culture. The word *caboclo/cabocla* has been associated, by upper strata of society, to mean mixed-race people of Indigenous descent, and a not too subtle implication of poorer, rural, and supposedly 'uncultivated' people. The *caboclos*, however, are also seen as a heterogenous group that maintains and preserves Indigenous culture and practices, usually related to a manner of harnessing a respectful living from nature.[35] In the

---

30. Instituto Brasileiro de Geografia e Estatística, *supra* note 27 at 85, 89–90.
31. Cristina Pompa, *Profetas e Santidades Selvagens: Missionários e Caraíbas no Brasil Colonial*, 21 Revista Brasileira de História 177, 180–187 (2001).
32. Eduardo Bueno, *A Coroa, a Cruz e a Espada: Lei, Ordem e Corrupção no Brasil Colônia*, 136 (2006).
33. Claudio Santiago Dias Junior & Ana Paula Verona, *Perfil Religioso da População Indígena no Brasil: Considerações a Partir do Censo Demográfico de 2010*, 12 HORIZONTE – Revista de Estudos de Teologia e Ciências da Religião 1140, 1144–1145 (2015).
34. Mírian de Araújo Mafra Castro & Rubia Maria Farias Cavalcante, *Saberes de Cura e Práticas Corporais: Pajelança na Feira da Manaus Moderna*, 3 Marupiara: Revista Científica do Centro de Estudos Superiores de Parintins 153, 154 (2018).
35. For discussions about the *caboclo* identity – how the term was/is used, what it represents, and the tensions involved in it – *see* Carmen Izabel Rodrigues, *Caboclos na Amazônia: a Identidade na Diferença*, 9 Novos Cadernos NAEA 119 (2006); Fábio Fonseca Castro, *A Identidade Denegada.*

pajelança cabocla, the *pajé* is believed to incorporate invisible entities called *encantados* [enchanted] with the purpose of healing the sick. The healer also incorporates the knowledge of herbs and animal lard, as well as gestures and even Catholic prayers, in an obvious evidence of syncretism.[36] The traditional religions of the Indigenous peoples are fundamentally shamanistic:

> the shamanism of the native peoples [*povos da terra*] of Brazil, known as *pajelança*, is the foundation of their religion. Unlike the typical Latin-American shamanism, which promotes the use of hallucinogenic herbs, *pajelança* is closer to the original Asian shamanism. One can see, for example, that the Tupi-Guarani peoples … have *pajés* very much akin to the Siberian shamans. Their *pajés*, men or women, journey to the world of the spirits of nature by exercising ecstatic trance. They take possession of the spirits, perform healings, preside over prayers, counsel. Sometimes, believing that an infirmity was caused by the abandoning of the ill person's soul, they go forth in search to return the soul to the body of the sick individual so as to repair their health.[37]

V. African-Brazilian Religions

31. The colonization of Brazil was based on enslavement, especially of African people. Brazil was the country that received the greatest number of enslaved people in the Americas: approximately 4.8 million people or 40% of all African people who were brought from across the Atlantic to work in servitude, in ships where inhumane conditions guaranteed that near on 20% would not survive the ordeal.[38] It was only on 13 May 1888, that the so-called *Lei Áurea* (Golden Law), approved by the legislature, was signed into law by Princess Regent Isabel, abolishing slavery in Brazil.[39] The state, however, failed to provide any care or support for the emancipated people, and they remained marginalized in and by society. Eugenic ideas were

---

Discutindo as Representações e a Autorrepresentação dos Caboclos da Amazônia, 56 Revista de Antropologia 432 (2013). According to Leandro Mahalem de Lima, '[s]till in the middle of the twentieth century, the word "caboclo" referred to the category of the Indians, either pure or mixed, who inhabited riverside communities, far both from the centre of the villages, associated to the white people, and from the forest centres, associated to the so-called pure and tribal Indians. In populations of this kind, spoken Portuguese is deeply influenced by the grammar, phrases, and vocabulary systems of the Nheengatú [a Tupi-based Amazon General Language]. Their traditional mixed subsistence economy constitutes a clear update of Indigenous agricultural, fishing, and hunting techniques. So as the elementary forms of their religiosity – and the underlying socio-cosmological regime – are characterized by the existence of *encantados* and *pajés sacacas*, and the culture of festivities of saint'. *See* Leandro Mahalem de Lima, *Pajelança nas Adjacências do Rio Amazonas: Dimensões Sociopolíticas e Cosmológicas*, 3 Revista Ciências da Sociedade 61, 64 (2019).

36. Castro and Cavalcante, *supra* note 34 at 158–161.
37. Maria Cecilia Domezi, *Religiões na História do Brasil*, Chapter 1 (Paulinas 2016). Discussing the religion of the Tupi-Guarani peoples, *see* Roque de Barros Laraia, *As Religiões Indígenas: o Caso Tupi-Guarani*, 67 Revista USP 6, 8–9 (2005).
38. André Schröder, *A Era da Escravidão*, Super Interessante, 29 Mar. 2019, https://super.abril.com.br/especiais/a-era-da-escravidao/.
39. Law No. 3353 of 13 May 1888.

widely acknowledged as scientific facts, and 'the whitening of race' was a part of the government policies, which involved encouraging European immigration. African cultures were viewed as inferior and barbaric, and many of their manifestations – including *capoeira* – were subject to direct persecution by the state. The valuable contribution of African heritage to the Brazilian population and culture only began to be recognized in the 1930s.[40] Whilst much has changed since then, racism remains present in Brazil.

32. Enslaved African people and their descendants were generally divided into *nations*, a metaethical classification employed by the colonial powers, principally associated with their African ports of origin, but also related with their sharing of cultural distinction – especially language. The enslaved would quickly absorb this classification as they were deemed useful in the society of that time.[41] This differentiation of African nations could be clearly identified, in particular, in religious rituals and festivities, and even after waning political relevance, it remained, albeit with exclusively religious significance. With time, the nations began to identify those – being of African descent or not – who were part of a religious group in which a nation's rituals and theology predominated. These nations, however, are not exclusive, rigidly differentiated, groups. On the contrary, natural fluidity and continuous movement between groups amount to an abundance of eclecticism.[42] African-Brazilian religions are deeply syncretic. This resulted from:

> a peculiar amalgamation of distinct forms of religiosity of African nations forcibly obliged to live together by the power of slavery-based colonialism, which at the same time would also be transformed by contact with the white colonist world of Catholicism and with the religions of the Indigenous peoples native to America. Hence religious traditions, principally centred in the cult of ancestors, of the Bantu peoples … , who were incorporated earlier into the colonization process, as well as the rich Jeje universe of vodun worship, Fanti Ashanti religious forms or those of Islamized nations … , in many cases would end up fusing with, or be confused with, the Nago or Yoruba-originated pantheon of orixá worship.[43]

33. This is the origin of *Candomblé*, a family of religions deeply connected with its African origins, known under a variety of names in various places (*Batuque*, *Calundu*, *Xangô*, *Tambor-de-Mina*), which could be rightfully seen as an:

> institution of cultural resistance, first by Africans, and later by people of African descent, resistance to slavery and to the means of domination of the white

40. Maria Lucia Montes, *As Figuras do Sagrado: entre o Público e o Privado na Religiosidade Brasileira*, 40–41 (2012).
41. Luis Nicolau Parés, *The Formation of Candomblé: Vodun History and Ritual in Brazil*, 1–7 (2013).
42. *Ibid.* at 67–68.
43. Montes, *supra* note 40 at 36–38.

> Christian society who marginalized Black and mixed-race people even after the abolition of slavery. They were religions of preservation of the former slaves' descendants' ethnic heritage.[44]

34. The beliefs of Candomblé are 'incarnated in the symbols, myths, and rites', kept and passed on by religious leaders to the following generations. They involve a supreme creator of the universe (Olorum), who 'manifests through the forces of nature which are deified as *orixás*':

> Thunder and lightning are therefore associated to Xangô, storm and fire to Iansã or Oyá, rain and river to Oxum, fertility to Iemanjá, rainbow to Oxumaré, leaves to Ossaim, illnesses to Obaluaiyê, transformation to Omulu, the fauna to Oxossi, war to Ogum, the margins of rivers and streams to Logum-Edé, still waters and swamps to Nanã Burukê. The *orixás*, as deities connected to the cosmic order, regulate the social relations, ethics, [and] moral discipline of a group or a segment. …
>
> Nature, socialized, is viewed as a place of salvation because it is where the deities manifested for the first time. Salvation is repetition and invariable conservation of the mythical past, a model to social institutions and human behaviour. Tradition is essential. Innovations or changes must be very carefully examined so as to not introduce disorder.
>
> The final destiny of human life, salvation is obtained through the practice of rituals and propitiatory sacrifices that dynamize the life *axé*[45] of the deities. Exchanges bring benefits for life. The latter is the supreme good, and in this world it must be rich, long, prosperous, and harmonious, to be enjoyed in all its potential.
>
> …
>
> There is some flexibility in the concept of good and evil, which do not present themselves with striking dichotomic difference. The mythical identity legitimates the deeds and faults of the singular person. *The African gods are not ethical potencies who demand and reward good and chastise evil.*
>
> …
>
> In the Candomblé worldview, the individual person is a link between successive generations. They are inserted in a community that includes ancestors, sons, possible descendants. It binds the past, present, and future in a dynamic system of forces in continuous action. Within, there are threats and protection

---

44. Prandi, *supra* note 20 at 223.
45. Though it is central to Candomblé, the idea of *axé* it is very hard to define. Scholars point out that it has multiple meanings. *Axé* may designate 'a kind of impersonal power or force that permeates objects, plants, and human relations' or even 'sacred places and things, such as the foundations of the *terreiro* and the particular portions of sacrificial animals'. It may also be used to designate the Candomblé tradition, its customs, its nation, and its followers. 'Therefore, the notion of *axé* has a collective aspect to it which integrates things, people, and deities in the same plane, establishing property relationships that are not exclusive to an individual.' *See* Daniele Ferreira Evangelista, *Fundando um Axé: Reflexões Sobre o Processo de Construção de um Terreiro de Candomblé*, 35 Religião & Sociedade 63, 64 (2015).

coming from the forces of nature. All salvific practices are directed towards fulfilling, maintaining, and enlarging earthly life. In the beyond, life suffers the reductionism of shadows.
Among the worship rites, sacrifice, an overarching element, has a special place. It consists of an offering to a deity so to reinvigorate the system of exchanges between the *aiyê* (earth) and the *orun* (heaven) and to weaken the forces of evil. The life and blood of an animal – which is previously consecrated and sacralized – liberate the *axé*. It re-establishes and reinforces the mystical relationship between the one who makes the offering and the divine world of the *orixás*, especially after the sacrificial meal. The sacrifice builds upon the power of the *axé* that belongs to sacred things and is conceived as the internal dynamics of the whole universe, even being present even in inanimate objects. Through it lay the passage from the world of the profane to the sacred.[46]

35. Whilst the roots of Candomblé are traced to Bahia, *Umbanda* is said to have its origins in Rio de Janeiro. A 'synthesis' of traditional African religions and Kardecist Spiritism, and considered 'the "Brazilian religion" par excellence, Umbanda mixed white Catholicism, the tradition of the orixás of the Black strand, and symbols, spirits, and rituals of Indigenous reference, being thus inspired by the three basic sources of mixed-race Brazil'.[47] As explained by Maria Lucia Montes:

> By incorporating to the Kardecist belief in the possibility of communication with the dead, the tradition of ancestral worship inherited mainly from the Banto peoples, and morals claiming the heritage of Christian virtues, especially charity, to the assertion of scientificity of 'evolution' even in the spiritual plane, Umbanda shall seek to 'purge' African-Brazilian religions of some of their more 'barbaric' aspects, deemed appropriate to an 'inferior' form of religiosity. For example, animal sacrifices, seen as typical of 'lower Spiritism', of the *macumba* or the *quimbanda*, will be abandoned by the followers of Umbanda, who, in contrast, will try to devote themselves to more 'altruistic' objectives, of healing mental and physical illnesses and offering counsel about problems in the personal, family, or professional life of people ... Thus a new – white, civilized, and nationalist – respectability was secured to religions which, up until then, were undervalued as typical of uncultivated Black people, but paying the price of a transformation which would result in the 'white death of the Black sorcerer', as this process was adequately characterized by an analyst.[48]

36. In the 1960s, the process would start to flow in the opposite direction, as the age of the 'counterculture' brought with it a renewed interest in Candomblé. The

---

46. Sonia Apparecida de Siqueira, *Multiculturalismo e Religiões Afrobrasileiras: o Exemplo do Candomblé*, 9 Revista de Estudos da Religião – REVER 36, 43–45 (2009).
47. Prandi, *supra* note 20 at 223.
48. Montes, *supra* note 40 at 42.

adherents to Umbanda began transit from their more ascetic ways to what they viewed as being the 'purer' African-Brazilian religiosity of Candomblé:[49]

> An important part of the social legitimacy enjoyed by the Black culture of Candomblé today grew from a new aesthetics developed by the intellectualized middle class of Rio de Janeiro and São Paulo in the decades of 1960 and 1970, who increasingly adopted and appreciated Black aspects from the culture of Bahia, and its artists and intellectuals. Thus began what I called the process of Africanization of Candomblé …, in which the deliberated return to tradition means relearning the language, the rituals, and the myths that had been perverted and lost in the adversity of the Diaspora; returning to Africa not to be African or to be Black, but to re-establish a heritage whose presence in Brazil is now a cause of pride, wisdom, and public recognition, and as such, to be the holder of a culture which is concurrently Black and Brazilian, due to Brazil already recognizing itself in the orixá, a Brazil with axé.[50]

37. In rough simplification, both Candomblé and Umbanda are organized around the *terreiros* (or *tendas*), a word which designates both the communities of followers and their specific places of worship. The *terreiros* are small hierarchical groups under the leadership of a woman (*mãe-de-santo* or *iyalorixá*) or a man (*pai-de-santo* or *babalorixá*), regarded as the spiritual mother/father of the group, whose authority is to be respected by all their 'sons/daughters of saint' (*filhos/filhas-de-santo*).[51] The *terreiros* retain friendly relations, but they are self-sufficient entities, not being unified in a single institutional structure. Although there are some federations and associations of groups, there exist limitations as there is no higher authority than that of the *iyalorixá* or the *babalorixá*.[52]

38. Despite the regenerated interest in African-Brazilian religions, it remains starkly obvious that they and their followers continue to face prejudice and directed violence. Religious intolerance is not exclusively directed at them, but it is undeniable that as a manifestation of racism – i.e., as religious racism – intolerance towards African-Brazilian religions has a peculiar weight to it.[53] Initially, the Catholic Church and the public authorities usually did not interfere with the music and dance of enslaved people. They viewed it as means of amusement for the latter and therefore tolerated it for engendering tranquillity and facilitating submission. That was not the case of other manifestations, such as those involving spiritual possession, which were associated with demonic acts and condemned as the practice of witchcraft.[54]

---

49. *Ibid.* at 44–45.
50. Prandi, *supra* note 20 at 224.
51. Daniele Ferreira Evangelista, *'Emoção não é Coisa de Equede': Mudanças de Status e Relações de Poder no Candomblé*, 4 Intratextos 93, note 2 at 94 (2013).
52. Prandi, *supra* note 20 at 229.
53. Sidney Nogueira, *Intolerância Religiosa*, A Verdade Sobre a Intolerância Religiosa é Branca: Mais Um dos Tentáculos do Racismo (2020).
54. Paula Montero, *Religião, Pluralismo e Esfera Pública no Brasil*, 74 Novos Estudos CEBRAP 47, 55 (2006); Montes, *supra* note 40 at 39–40.

39. Seen as inferior and backwards by the white, Eurocentric, view that has always been hegemonical, African-Brazilian religions were under formal state siege even as late as the twentieth century. On the pretence of protecting the public health and scientific practices, Articles 156–158 of the Penal Code of 1890[55] criminalized a number of practices associated with Kardecist Spiritism and as African-Brazilian religions.[56] Later on, whereas the former came to be recognized and stopped being persecuted, the latter remained at risk, as they were supposedly linked to crime and drugs. It was only in the second half of the century that African-Brazilian denominations started to be respectfully recognized as legitimate religions.[57]

40. Even today, however, they are the focal point of intense hatred and intolerance, though not by the government. From 2012 through 2015, followers of African-Brazilian religions were the victims in more than 70% of the total of 1,014 cases of offences, abuses and violent acts of religious intolerance reported in the State of Rio de Janeiro.[58] In 2019, they were the offended parties in almost 60% of the cases of intolerance reported to the Federal District police precinct specialized in hate crimes – despite adherents of African-Brazilian religions representing only 0.2% of the District's population.[59] They are seen as enemies by numerous Evangelical Christians, who see African-Brazilian deities and spirits as manifestations of the devil, and their rituals and practices as being evil witchcraft. There are some Evangelical churches that do perform exorcism rites on supposedly possessed people. Instead of denying the tenets of African-Brazilian religiosity, they actually accommodate them in their belief systems, but as something to be fought.[60]

41. Conversely, racism, persecution, and intolerance have forged African-Brazilian religions a sense of pride and resistance for their followers and for Black Brazilians in general:

> [African-Brazilian religions] is a *quilombola* space which stores ancient knowledge of African origins that are part of the national identity. A space of existence, resistance, and (re-)existence. A political space. Territory of Black

---

55. *Código Penal* [Penal Code], Decree No. 847 of 11 Oct. 1890.
56. Emerson Giumbelli, *O 'Baixo Espiritismo' e a História dos Cultos Mediúnicos*, 9 Horizontes Antropológicos 247, 254 (2003).
57. Montero, *supra* note 54 at 53–56.
58. Jefferson Puff, *Por que as Religiões de Matriz Africana São o Principal Alvo de Intolerância no Brasil?*, BBC News Brasil, 21 Jan. 2016, https://www.bbc.com/portuguese/noticias/2016/01/160120_intolerancia_religioes_africanas_jp_rm.
59. Alan Rios, *Religiões de Matriz Africana são Alvos de 59% dos Crimes de Intolerância*, Correio Braziliense, 11 Nov. 2019, https://www.correiobraziliense.com.br/app/noticia/cidades/2019/11/11/interna_cidadesdf,805394/religioes-de-matriz-africana-alvos-de-59-dos-crimes-de-intolerancia.shtml.
60. Ari Pedro Oro, Intolerância Religiosa Iurdiana e Reações Afro no Rio Grande do Sul, *in Intolerância Religiosa: Impactos do Neopentecostalismo no Campo Religioso Afro-Brasileiro* 29, 46 (Vagner Gonçalves Silva ed., 2007).

gods and spiritual entities, through whom one seeks the practice of a religiosity, in tandem with the therapeutic and socio-historic-cultural, which turns to the African continent, crib of world in the New World.[61]

VI. Other Home-Grown Religious Denominations

42. Brazilian Catholic Apostolic Church – founded in June 1945 by Carlos Duarte Costa, a former Roman Catholic bishop who was excommunicated by the Pope. Even though the Church resembles the Roman Catholics, they do not operate under the supremacy of one bishop, being governed by an elective council of bishops; their priests and bishops are permitted to marry and often undertake other professions; children are baptized irrespective of their parents' marriage status; divorce is permitted and divorcees can marry again; and the priests do not hear confession, but only provide absolution.[62] In 1979, the Church's followers proclaimed its founder Saint Carlos of Brazil.

43. Santo Daime – Founded in 1920 in Acre, now a state in the Northern Region, by Raimundo Irineu Serra (master Irineu), the son of a formerly enslaved man. Master Irineu claimed to have received teachings by Our Lady of Conception the first time he drank the *ayahuasca* or *hoasca* tea, which he called *Santo Daime*. The Santo Daime movement lists its doctrine as one of 'Christian and eclectic nature, uniting Catholic, Spiritist, esoteric, *caboclo*, and Indigenous traditions'. The followers of Santo Daime believe that the tea creates conscience expansion, thus allowing them to contact the spiritual plane via one's 'True Self'.[63]

44. União do Vegetal – The *Centro Espírita Beneficente União do Vegetal* [Beneficent Spiritist Centre Union of the Vegetal] was founded in 1961 by José Gabriel da Costa (master Gabriel). It also interrelates the *ayahuasca* or *hoasca* tea, called *Vegetal*. According to the Centre, 'in their religious rituals, the disciples drink the Tea Hoasca to attain a state of mental focus known as *burracheira*. When the tea takes effect …, [followers] immerse into the spiritual teachings and the doctrine of master Gabriel, who, in his simple manner of teaching, explained that, with the Vegetal, he has discovered "a way of removing evil from the hearts of people"'.[64] The Centre is recognized in the United States legal scholarship due to an important Supreme Court opinion addressing freedom of religion.[65]

---

61. Nogueira, *supra* note 53 at Introdução.
62. *Quem somos nós?*, Igreja Católica Apostólica Brasileira, https://novo.igrejabrasileira.com.br/quem-somos-nos/ (last visited 18 Jan. 2021).
63. *O Que é o Santo Daime*, Santo Daime, http://www.santodaime.org/site/religiao-da-floresta/o-santo-daime/introducao (last visited 20 Feb. 2021). *See also* Ana Melo, *Conheça Tudo Sobre o Santo Daime: Ritual, Chá Ayahuasca e Orações*, Terra, 8 Dec. 2020, https://www.terra.com.br/vida-e-estilo/horoscopo/conheca-tudo-sobre-o-santo-daime-ritual-cha-ayahuasca-e-oracoes,f6df0ad2636c0fff35fa3cb9a9f5ff54h2g2bst5.html.
64. *Ritual*, Centro Espírita Beneficente União do Vegetal, https://udv.org.br/ritual-religioso-na-uniao-do-vegetal/ (last visited 21 Feb. 2021).
65. *Gonzales v. O Centro Espírita Beneficente União do Vegetal*, 546 U.S. 418 (2006).

45. Igreja Universal do Reino de Deus – Founded in Rio de Janeiro in 1977 by the current bishop Edir Macedo, the *Igreja Universal do Reino de Deus* (IURD) [Universal Church of the Kingdom of God] is an Evangelical church with an enormous relevance in the religious, cultural, and social environment. With impressive rates of growth – a 25.7% annual increase in the 1990s[66] – the IURD had more than 2.1 million followers in 2000. Despite recent signs of decrease (by 2010, it had lost around 10.8% of its followers),[67] the Church remains the focus of great attention. The purchase of a television network (Record), its 'heterodox means of collecting [money]', constant charges against African-Brazilian religions, alleged tax crimes and supposed involvement with drug trafficking led to police investigations, judicial proceedings, and even the arrest of bishop Macedo. More recently, the IURD appears at length to further distance itself from these allegations. It is known for its televised services, in which a banquet of miracles, healings, and exorcisms are performed.[68]

46. Suprema Ordem Universal da Santíssima Trindade (SOUST) [Supreme Order of the Holy Trinity] was founded in 1982 by Alvaro Theiss (INRI Cristo), who, since 1979, continues to claim ascent as the reincarnation of Jesus Christ.[69] Believing that the Roman Catholic Church had lost its way, INRI Cristo denounced the Church and, after interrupting a mass in Belém/PA in 1982, he then travelled to the Vatican in 1983 to sever the ties between God and the Roman Church. In 2000, the Judiciary granted him the right to change his name to Alvaro INRI Cristo Theiss.[70] Claiming to restore the 'essence of the early Christian church', SOUST declares to be a 'Mystical and Philosophical School, where the Perpetual Mentor Regent INRI CRISTO instructs human beings on how to live harmoniously in symbiosis with GOD, without the need to venture into temples constructed by men.' According to SOUST, being part of it does not mean belonging to a religion, because God is present in all people, and they therefore do not require anyone else to reconnect (*religare*, in Latin) to Him.[71]

---

66. Ricardo Mariano, *Expansão Pentecostal no Brasil: o Caso da Igreja Universal*, 18 Estudos Avançados 121, 125 (2004).
67. Hanrrikson de Andrade, *Censo 2010 Aponta Migração de Fiéis da Universal do Reino de Deus para Outras Igrejas Evangélicas*, UOL, 26 Jun. 2012, https://noticias.uol.com.br/cotidiano/ultimas-noticias/2012/06/29/censo-2010-aponta-migracao-de-fieis-da-universal-do-reino-de-deus-para-outras-igrejas.htm.
68. Mariano, *supra* note 66 at 125–126, 132–133.
69. Shaena Montanari, *INRI Cristo, o Homem que se Considera Jesus Reencarnado*, National Geographic Brasil, 8 Nov. 2017, https://www.nationalgeographicbrasil.com/fotografia/2017/08/inri-cristo-o-homem-que-se-considera-jesus-reencarnado.
70. Vera Irene Jurkevics, *INRI Cristo e a Escatologia Tupiniquim*, 1 Relegens Thréskeia: Estudos e Pesquisa em Religião 130, 137 (2012).
71. *SOUST, uma Escola Mística e Filosófica*, INRI Cristo: o Emissário do Pai, https://inricristo.org.br/soust-uma-escola-mistica-e-filosofica/ (last visited 21 Feb. 2021).

VII. Judaism

47. Jews suffered persecution in Portugal when the first Europeans settled in Brazil. In 1497 – three years before the Portuguese landed – King Manoel I had ordered all Jews to convert to Catholicism or be banished from Portugal, without their children and their property. A terrible massacre ensued, as well as forced conversions. The converted, known as *cristãos-novos* (New Christians), remained under suspicion of being *marranos*, or 'crypto-Jews', people who secretly retained their Jewish faith whilst publicly declaring to be Catholics. In 1547, the Portuguese Inquisition was installed, with one of its principal concerns being the punishment of *marranos*, many of whom, after being found guilty, were unceremoniously banished to Brazil.[72]

48. In the colony, life became easier for them, apparently no longer concerned in hiding or disguising Jewish practices (e.g., not working and wearing clean clothes on Saturdays).[73] They married with *cristãos-velhos* (Old Christians), owned sugar plantations, and had careers trading enslaved people, or as merchants or surgeons. Some of them even occupied important positions in colonial administration and the Church – all of this despite being formally prohibited to do so.[74] Since people were needed to settle and work in Brazil, and few *cristãos-velhos* were attracted to such a remote location, the authorities displayed considerable lenience to the *cristãos-novos*.[75]

49. Jews in the seventeenth century enjoyed the freedom to worship in the North-eastern region of Brazil when the Dutch conquered and occupied territory. This was also a time when a great number of Jews were migrating from Europe to Brazil, especially Pernambuco.[76] Some *cristãos-novos* at this time also chose to freely practice their Jewish faith.[77] A thriving community of more than 1,600 people – approximately the size of the Jewish community in Amsterdam – founded the first synagogues of the Americas.[78] When the Portuguese reconquered these lands from

72. Geraldo Pieroni, *'O Ar de Portugal faz os Judeus?' A Inquisição e os Cristãos Novos Degredados para o Brasil-Colônia*, 3 Locus: Revista de História 7, 7–14 (1997).
73. Nachman Falbel, *Dos Cristãos-Novos na Capitania de São Vicente e a Formação da Etnia Paulista*, 41 Revista da USP 112, 115–116 (1999).
74. *Cristãos-Novos no Brasil Colônia*, IBGE, https://brasil500anos.ibge.gov.br/territorio-brasileiro-e-povoamento/judeus/cristaos-novos-no-brasil-colonia.html (last visited 15 Feb. 2021).
75. Hélio Augusto de Moura, *Presença Judaico-Marrana Durante a Colonização do Brasil*, 18 Cadernos de Estudos Sociais 267, 276–277 (2002).
76. *Ibid.* at 278–279; João Henrique Santos, Existentes, mas Não Cidadãos: o Status Jurídico dos Judeus no Brasil Holandês (1630–1654), *in Judaísmo e Modernidade: Suas Múltiplas Inter-relações* 47, 63 (H. Lewin ed., 2009).
77. According to Robert M. Levine, '[b]y 1627, two synagogues, Zur Israel and Mogen Abraham, had been established' there. *See* Robert M. Levine, *Brazil's Jews During the Vargas Era and After*, 5 Luso-Brazilian Rev. 45, 46 (1968).
78. *Ibid.* at 46.

the Dutch, the Jews were persecuted, thus fleeing to what is now New York, where they established the first Jewish community in North America.[79]

50. Although the Inquisition was never installed in Brazil, its presence was felt by the occasional *visitações* (visits of officials) and the *familiares*, lay officers of the Inquisition – one of their principal targets being 'crypto-Jews'. In the eighteenth century, numerous royal decrees were issued to suppress the differentiation between old and new Christians and to adhere the Inquisition to the king, foreshadowing the entrance of a new age.

51. Post-independence, the Empire of Brazil remained Catholic whilst exhibiting a broad degree of tolerance to other religions. It was then that the first organized Jewish community was established in Brazil: the Guemilut Hassadim Israelite Association, in Rio de Janeiro. From then on, waves of Jewish immigration to Brazil were sparked by crises and persecutions, especially in Europe and the Middle East: the 1848 revolutions, Nazism, and the conflicts related to the creation of the State of Israel.[80] Brazil became a desired destination for Jews fleeing Europe in the 1920s, when other countries enforced limitations on immigrants from certain groups. It is estimated that from 1920 to the beginning of the Second World War, about 50,000 Jews migrated to Brazil.[81]

52. The spectre of Anti-Semitism remained ever-present, especially in the decades of 1930 and 1940, when the government of Getúlio Vargas – being at that point in time ideologically aligned to authoritarian regimes in Europe – conveyed a secret order to Brazilian diplomats, forbidding the issuance of visas to Jews.[82] Anti-Semitic ideology was also propagated by the *Ação Integralista Brasileira* [Brazilian Integralist Action], a right-wing movement which amassed some clout at the time. In general, though, Anti-Semitism did not result in actual violence, probably due to the fact that migrating primarily from Europe, Jews were considered 'white', and the principal 'concern' at the time was with 'whitening' the population.[83]

---

79. Raymond Colitt, *Oldest Synagogue in Americas Draws Tourists to Brazil* (Reuters, 12 Nov. 2001), https://www.reuters.com/article/us-brazil-synagogue/oldest-synagogue-in-americas-draws-tourists-to-brazil-idUSN2520146120071112.
80. Nachman Falbel, *Judeus no Brasil: Estudos e Notas*, 11 (Edusp 2008).
81. René Daniel Decol, *Judeus no Brasil: Explorando os Dados Censitários*, 16 Revista Brasileira de Ciências Sociais 147, 151 (2001).
82. Rachel Mizrahi, *Judeus: Do Descobrimento aos Dias Atuais*, 49 (Companhia Editora Nacional 2005). Many diplomats adhered to the order, but one notable exception was Luiz Martins de Souza Dantas, ambassador in France. He defied the regime's command, and was actually investigated for granting visas too liberally – it is said he even signed visas in restaurant menus and pre-dated his signature to days before the prohibition. His name is inscribed among the Righteous Among the Nations, by the Yad Vashem, in Israel, which honours those who took risks to save Jewish people during the Holocaust. *See* Luiz Antônio Araujo, *Quem Foi o Embaixador Brasileiro que Contrariou Hitler e Vargas para Ajudar Fugitivos do Nazismo*, BBC News Brasil, 4 Aug. 2018, https://www.bbc.com/portuguese/internacional-45065825.
83. Roney Cytrynowicz, *Além do Estado e da Ideologia: Imigração Judaica, Estado-Novo e Segunda Guerra Mundial*, 22 Revista Brasileira de História 393, 396, 399 (2002); Levine, *supra* note 77 at 48.

VIII. Islam

53. Until 1888, slavery was legal and widely practised in Brazil, and pockets of enslaved people who were shipped from Africa were Muslim. Being literate, they would sometimes occupy positions in commerce, even with salaries. Enslaved Muslims, known as *malês*, even plotted and executed an insurgency in Bahia, having captured the capital, Salvador, for hours before being eventually subdued. The authorities then began to disperse them throughout Brazil, but their religiosity was still present and noticeable. According to an imam from Baghdad who arrived in Brazil in 1866, there were communities of about 20,000 and 5,000 Muslims, respectively in Salvador and Rio de Janeiro. But they were not permitted to build mosques – only Catholic churches could have the external appearance of temples – and their practices were deeply influenced by other religions. In the end, they all but disappeared due to the constant repression and to lessened contact with the Islamic centres of Africa via merchants.[84]

54. A new wave of Muslim immigration began in 1880 and grew from 1918 onward, with people coming from Syria and Lebanon, following the decadence and collapse of the Ottoman Empire. After 1975, the conflicts in the Middle East also prompted immigration from Lebanon and Palestine. Almost all (99%) of the Muslims living in Brazil reside in urban areas, being concentrated especially in the Southeast and South, in the states of São Paulo, Paraná, Rio Grande do Sul and Rio de Janeiro.[85] As a result of the Syrian Civil War (2011–), many people fled to Brazil seeking refugee status: in 2018, of the 11,231 recognized refugees in Brazil, Syrians represented 36% (4,043).[86]

IX. Religious Composition of the Federal Branches

55. Presidents – Almost all Brazilian presidents were Catholic. The only exceptions were: (1) Getúlio Vargas (1930–1945 and 1951–1954), Agnostic; (2) Caffé Filho (1954–1955), Presbyterian; (3) Ernesto Geisel (1974–1979), Lutheran/Agnostic; and (4) Fernando Henrique Cardoso (1995–2003), Agnostic.

56. National Congress – In a 2018 survey, the Chamber of Deputies had a clear Christian majority of 72%, being 53% Catholic, 15% Protestant and 4% (unspecified) Christian. Since 5% of the federal deputies responded that they were not affiliated or preferred not to disclose their religion, and almost 20% of the Chamber did not respond at all, it is quite possible that the Christian majority could in fact be

84. Cristina Maria de Castro & Elaine Meire Vilela, *Muçulmanos no Brasil: Uma Análise Socioeconômica e Demográfica a Partir do Censo 2010*, 39 Religião & Sociedade 170, 171–173 (2019).
85. *Ibid.* at 173–180.
86. Pedro Peduzzi, *Brasil já Reconheceu Mais de 11 Mil Refugiados até 2018, Diz Conare*, Agência Brasil, 25 Jul. 2019, https://agenciabrasil.ebc.com.br/direitos-humanos/noticia/2019-07/brasil-ja-reconheceu-mais-de-11-mil-refugiados-ate-2018-diz-conare.

higher.[87] The survey did not factor in the Senate. In 2019, the Catholic Caucus included 207 deputies and 9 senators,[88] whilst the Protestant Caucus numbered 195 deputies and 8 senators,[89] however, some congresspeople participate in both caucus groups, and there are plans for a future joint caucus.[90] They already cooperate in promoting a common agenda, involving issues the likes of restricting abortion and LGBTQIA+ rights.[91]

57. Federal Supreme Court – Eleven Ministers sit on the Federal Supreme Court. The current composition includes seven Roman Catholics (Gilmar Mendes, Ricardo Lewandowski, Cármen Lúcia, Dias Toffoli, Edson Fachin, Alexandre de Moraes, and Nunes Marques), two Jewish individuals (Luiz Fux and Luís Roberto Barroso), and one Minister whose religious affiliation was not disclosed (Rosa Weber).[92] Minister Marco Aurélio Mello, who is Catholic, retired in July 2021. Fulfilling a promise to nominate a 'terribly Evangelical' person to the Court,[93] President Jair Bolsonaro chose André Mendonça, a former Union Attorney General,[94] who is also a Presbyterian minister.[95]

---

87. *Maioria na Câmara se declara católica; número de evangélicos cresce*, G1, 27 Nov. 2018, https://g1.globo.com/politica/noticia/2018/11/27/maioria-na-camara-se-declara-catolica-numero-de-evangelicos-cresce.ghtml.
88. *Frente Parlamentar Mista Católica Apostólica Romana*, Câmara dos Deputados, https://www.camara.leg.br/internet/deputado/frenteDetalhe.asp?id=54077 (last visited 19 Jan. 2021).
89. *Frente Parlamentar Evangélica do Congresso Nacional*, Câmara dos Deputados, https://www.camara.leg.br/internet/deputado/frenteDetalhe.asp?id=54010 (last visited 19 Jan. 2021).
90. *Parlamentares católicos planejam frente conjunta com Evangélicos*, Estado de Minas, 28 Jan. 2020, https://www.em.com.br/app/noticia/politica/2020/01/28/interna_politica,1117561/parlamentares-catolicos-planejam-frente-conjunta-com-evangelicos.shtml.
91. Luis Gustavo Teixeira da Silva, *Religião e Política no Brasil*, 64 Latinoamérica. Revista de Estudios Latinoamericanos 223, 249–251 (2017).
92. Rafael Moraes Moura, *STF não tem Ministros Evangélicos, Maioria é Católica*, O Estado de S. Paulo, 31 May 2019, https://politica.estadao.com.br/noticias/geral,stf-nao-tem-ministros-evangelicos-maioria-e-catolica,70002851820; *Discreto, Católico e Garantista, Saiba Quem é Kassio Nunes, Cotado para o STF*, O Tempo, 1 Oct. 2020, https://www.otempo.com.br/politica/discreto-catolico-e-garantista-saiba-quem-e-kassio-nunes-cotado-para-o-stf-1.2392992.
93. Fernanda Calgaro & Guilherme Mazui, *Bolsonaro Diz que Vai Indicar Ministro 'Terrivelmente Evangélico' para o STF*, G1, 10 Jul. 2019, https://g1.globo.com/politica/noticia/2019/07/10/bolsonaro-diz-que-vai-indicar-ministro-terrivelmente-evangelico-para-o-stf.ghtml.
94. The Union Attorneys' Office represent the Union in judicial and extra-judicial proceedings, and give legal advice to the federal Executive Branch. It is headed by the Union Attorney General, who is appointed and can be removed at the pleasure of the President of the Republic. *See* Const. (1988), Art. 131.
95. Mariana Schreiber, *Quem é André Mendonça, Advogado e Pastor que Será Indicado por Bolsonaro ao STF*, BBC News Brasil, 7 Jul. 2021, https://www.bbc.com/portuguese/brasil-57744271.

X. Political Alignment over Social Issues

58. In Brazil, people who identify with the left of the political spectrum are usually less religious, whilst those positioned on the right are more likely to be religious, especially Christian.[96] The voting behaviour of Brazilian electors, however, does not follow a sharp distinction between a morally progressive and economically more state-friendly left and a morally conservative and economically liberal right.[97]

59. Issues appear to be more important than labels. A 2002 survey[98] showed an intense alignment between religiosity and disqualifying opinions in relation to homosexuality: except for Kardecist Spiritists and Buddhists, most participants who declared themselves as being religious supported the idea that a TV programme defending marriage between same-sex couples should be banned. But, despite rallying around a presidential candidate who advocated for Christian values, those who believed it better to prohibit the show also included the majority of voters of all other main candidates. As for abortion, the majority of participants – in almost all religious groups – believed termination should be allowed, subject to the pregnancy resulting from rape. The exceptions were the groups including Mormons, Adventists, and Jehovah's Witnesses (the majority of whom would ban abortion in all cases), and Pentecostal Evangelicals (who split between a complete ban and allowing it in case of rape). When analysing the voters of the main presidential candidates, the greatest number, in each case, would agree to abortion should pregnancy result from sexual violence.[99]

60. All of this suggests that religious Brazilians, especially Christians, appear to lean toward moral conservatism. As for social and economic matters, however, one saw a 'supra-religious majority in favour of the presence of the state in activities of education, healthcare, and retirement [benefits] and social security', as well as infrastructure management: a strong majority of people in all groups supported the idea that the government should hold exclusive control over these portfolios. Approximately the same levels of support could be seen around state control of prices of goods and the government bailout of struggling businesses.[100]

61. Political parties, in Brazil, are required to register in the Superior Electoral Court. According to the Court, in March 2022, there were thirty registered parties in

96. Thiago Moreira Silva, *Para Além de Esquerda e Direita: A Multidimensionalidade das Crenças no Brasil Contemporâneo (1989–2014)*, Doctoral thesis, Institute of Politics, University of Brasília, Brasília (DF), 52–53 (2017).
97. Frederico Batista Pereira, *'Non Causa pro Causa': O Voto de Direita e Esquerda no Brasil*, 26 Opinião Pública 154 (2020). The author analyses votes in presidential elections.
98. *Estudo Eleitoral Brasileiro (ESEB) 2002*, CESOP/Unicamp-FGV, https://www.cesop.unicamp.br/vw/1IMHwTK0wNQ_MDA_ff413_/TF-01838.pdf (last visited 20 May 2021).
99. Katia Mika Nishimura, *Conservadorismo Social: Opiniões e Atitudes no Contexto da Eleição de 2002*, 10 Opinião Pública 339, 347, 352, 356–357 (2004).
100. Simone R. Bohn, *Evangélicos no Brasil. Perfil Socioeconômico, Afinidades Ideológicas e Determinantes do Comportamento Eleitoral*, 10 Opinião Pública 288, 319–323 (2004).

Brazil. Only three of those included Christian references in their names.[101] Together with two other parties, they comprise 'a sub-group aligned to the right in the ideological spectre', who pledge 'the defence of Christian values' as their purpose, or intend 'to directly represent this religious segment'.[102] Although ratios vary from one place to another, they indicate a relevant presence of Evangelicals and conservative Catholics.[103]

§3. Historical Background

I. Religion in Brazil in the Colonial Period (1500–1822)

62. The roots of Catholicism were immediately embedded when the first Europeans landed in Brazil in the sixteenth century. In 1500, a Portuguese fleet, sailing under the auspices of the Order of Christ, arrived in what is now the state of Bahia and claimed dominion of the land for the Portuguese Crown, under the name *Ilha de Vera Cruz* (Island of the True Cross) – which later oscillated between *Terra de Santa Cruz* (Land of the Holy Cross), *Brazil* (or *Brasil*, in Portuguese, a reference to the valuable brazilwood or redwood found in the territory), and different combinations thereof.[104] The presence of religion is obvious and intense, both in the first names given to the land and in the acts of the Portuguese: on their very third day, they conducted the first mass in the new land.

63. Portugal kept close ties with the Roman Church, and temporal authorities imposed some degree of authority over religious matters: the Church provided the monarchy with spiritual legitimacy and effectively acted as an arm of civil authority, whilst the king, in return, supported the temples and priests and defended the Church's religious monopoly – something that was especially relevant in the years after the Reformation.[105] In fact, Pope Callixtus III had granted the Order of Christ, and its head, the Portuguese king, extensive patronage rights in the lands it conquered. For example, he was granted the right to nominate people to be appointed as bishops by the pope, also the power to grant (or deny) the enforcement of papal decrees in these lands.[106] During the colonization, the Jesuits – members of the

101. They are: *Partido Trabalhista Cristão* [Christian Labour Party], *Partido Social Cristão* [Christian Social Party], and *Democracia Cristã* [Christian Democracy]. *See Partidos Políticos Registrados no TSE*, Tribunal Superior Eleitoral, https://www.tse.jus.br/partidos/partidos-registrados-no-tse (last visited 5 Mar. 2022).
102. Erico Tavares de Carvalho Junior & Ari Pedro Oro, *Eleições Municipais 2016: Religião e Política nas Capitais Brasileiras*, 18 Debates do NER 15, 20–21 (2017).
103. *Ibid.* at 21.
104. The defence of the 'mystical', Catholic, name, against the 'commercial' designation, related to the wood, reflected the mindset of the time. *See* Laura de Mello e Souza, *O Nome do Brasil*, 145 Revista de História 61 (2001).
105. Raymundo Faoro, *Os Donos do Poder: Formação do Patronato Político Brasileiro*, 229 (3rd ed., Globo 2001); Thiago Magalhães Pires, *Entre a Cruz e a Espada: Liberdade Religiosa e Laicidade do Estado no Brasil*, 19–20, 29–30 (Lumen Juris 2018).
106. Mons. Maurílio Cesar de Lima, *Breve História da Igreja no Brasil*, 21–24 (Loyola 2004).

Society of Jesus, a Catholic order – were very instrumental to the interests of Lisbon, being primarily devoted to the conversion of Indigenous people and to providing education to the colonists and their children.[107]

64. Indigenous and African cultures and religions were repressed, but survived, mostly due to the blending with Catholic symbols and references. Although Catholicism was the official religion in Brazil, there was a chasm between its official form, taught and enforced by the Portuguese religious elites, and the popular manifestations of beliefs that were widespread in the colony. Formal religious teaching was shallow, and ecclesiastical elites exercised little control. The substandard training of clerics also created a likelihood that they engaged in the prevailing customs, instead of imposing stricter regulation on the population. Syncretism was a powerful force, forging together elements of Indigenous and African culture and religion to Catholic rituals and festivities, thus moulding a new form of religiosity within a loose framework of Catholicism. Festivities and the veneration of saints – in almost magical terms – took the forefront of religious concern, whilst dogmatic and moral matters were relegated into the background.[108]

II. Religion in the Empire of Brazil (1822–1889)

65. Consequent to its Independence in 1822, Brazil became an empire, headed by Peter I, who was the heir to the Portuguese throne. The country's first constitution, imposed by the emperor in 1824, kept Roman Catholicism as the official religion and retained the rights of patronage which had been previously granted to the Order of Christ. The emperor, regents, and members of the General Assembly (the imperial parliament) and of the Council of State had to be of the Catholic faith. Although only Catholic churches were permitted to parade the external appearance of temples, the Constitution guaranteed religious freedom, and immigrant Protestants were broadly respected – despite the objections of the Church.[109]

66. Towards the end of the monarchical period, under Peter II, the regime began to assume secularizing trends. There had been twenty-three priests as deputies in the first General Assembly, but their number saw a consistent reduction throughout the ensuing years, and as such, in the last Assembly, only six deputies were priests. The clergy, who retained a special place in society due to their education, eventually

107. Paulo de Assunção, *Negócios Jesuíticos: O Cotidiano da Administração dos Bens Divinos*, 151 (Edusp 2004).

108. Montes, *supra* note 40 at 48–62; Emiliano Unzer Macedo, *Religiosidade Popular Brasileira Colonial: um Retrato Sincrético*, 7 Ágora 1 (2008). Only in the twentieth century would the Catholic Church – in a process of 'romanization' – move away from these forms of popular religiosity.

109. Emerson Giumbelli, *O Fim da Religião: Dilemas da Liberdade Religiosa no Brasil*, 245 (2002); Fábio Carvalho Leite, *Estado e Religião: A Liberdade Religiosa no Brasil*, 177–179 (2014). At the time, an American missionary wrote that 'in no other Catholic country in the world is there any more tolerance and a more liberal sentiment towards Protestantism' – translated from the citation by Montes, *supra* note 40 at 23.

ceded this ground to the new graduates of the first Law Schools created in Brazil.[110] Also, an electoral reform dissolved religious requirements for positions such as those of members of the General Assembly.[111]

67. The patronage provided the Roman Church with overarching control over morality and social values, especially in family life, but in truth, it was limited as an institution, subject to dependence on the state and somewhat distant from the Vatican. The Church had to operate under a shortage of priests and few available resources.[112]

68. The rise of *ultramontanism*[113] in the Roman Church and the overt liberal views of Emperor Peter II ultimately culminated in a clash between the clergy and the monarchy, which was one of the factors that led to the demise of the regime – alongside the discontent of the ruling class after the Abolition of Slavery in 1888 and of the military who, following the Paraguayan War,[114] sought more visibility and prestige.

III. Religion in the First Brazilian Republic (1889–1930)

69. On 15 November 1889, a military coup led to the Proclamation of the Republic. Emperor Pedro II and his family were banished from the country,[115] and the leader of the coup, Marshal Deodoro da Fonseca, became head of the Provisional Government. The republican movement included prominent adherents to Auguste Comte's positivism – also very pervasive in the Army at the time – which defended the separation between state and religion. Therefore, in its very first months, the new regime broke ties with Catholicism, extinguishing the patronage; forbade the establishment of religion at any level of government, as well as any discriminatory treatment based on religion; and proclaimed equal freedom of religion for all.[116] It also began to recognize solely civil marriages, secularized cemeteries and public teaching and eliminated religious holidays.[117] The first republican constitution, adopted in 1891, followed a similar path.

---

110. Gilson Ciarallo, *O Tema da Liberdade Religiosa na Política Brasileira do Século XIX: Uma Via para a Compreensão da Secularização da Esfera Política*, 19 Revista de Sociologia e Política 85, 86–87 (2011).
111. Decree No. 3029 of 9 Jan. 1881, known as *Lei Saraiva*, or Saraiva Act, after Antonio Saraiva, the President of the Council of Ministers (i.e., prime minister) at the time.
112. Paula Montero, *Religião, Laicidade e Secularismo. Um Debate Contemporâneo à Luz do Caso Brasileiro*, 7 Revista Cultura y Religi6n 13, 22–23 (2013); Ari Pedro Oro, *Religião e Política no Brasil*, 48–49 Cahiers des Amériques latines (2005), http://journals.openedition.org/cal/7951.
113. It was a movement, within the Catholic Church, in favour of more centralization under Rome. *See* Rudolf Zinnhobler, Idade Moderna, *in História da Igreja Católica* 205, 347 (Josef Lenzenweger et al. eds., Loyola 2006).
114. The Paraguayan War (or War of the Triple Alliance) was fought between Paraguay and the Triple Alliance (Brazil, Argentina, and Uruguay) from 1864 through 1870. The Alliance was victorious.
115. Decree No. 78-A of 21 Dec. 1889, Art. 1. This provision was repealed by Decree No. 4120 of 3 Sep. 1920, after the emperor and the empress died.
116. Decree No. 119-A of 7 Jan. 1890.
117. Giumbelli, *supra* note 109 at 243; Magalhães Pires, *supra* note 105 at 38–39.

70. In truth, nonetheless, the Catholic Church remained a religious reference, and even though it criticized the separation from the government, it also acknowledged the broader autonomy it would possess from then on. As Paula Montero explains, '[b]y withdrawing from the state, the Church could become an active force in building its counterpart: civil society'. It obtained an independent jurisdiction and could start working 'on its centralization and institutional strengthening'.[118]

71. Curiously, the prosecution of Protestants, absent under the (Catholic) monarchy, began to emerge in the secular republic. At the same time, religious authorities continued to oversee cemeteries, and Catholic symbols were still present in public buildings.[119] Also, in 1922, Christmas was restored as a public holiday.[120] Hence, the formal separation between the Church and the state was in essence accompanied by their silent – though clear – rapprochement.[121]

72. If the nineteenth century heralded the arrival of 'historical' Protestants – Lutherans, Anglicans, Baptists, Methodists, and others – the beginning of the twentieth century was the time when the first Pentecostal churches were established in Brazil: the Christian Congregation of Brazil (1910) and the Assembly of God (1911).[122] However, whilst small in number, their presence did not provoke an intense reaction by the Catholic Church, whose efforts were mainly directed against Spiritism and African-Brazilian religions.[123] Both also had their share of problems with the police: in a further demonstration that the separation of religion and state in Brazil were more apparent than real, the Articles 156–158 of the Penal Code of 1890[124] sanctioned a number of practices associated with Kardecist Spiritism and 'lower Spiritism', as African-Brazilian religions were frequently called:

> *Article 156.* To exercise medicine in any of its branches, dental artistry, or pharmacy; to practice homeopathy, dosimetry, hypnotism, or animal magnetism, without being licenced according to the laws and regulations:
>
> Punishments: cellular imprisonment for one to six months, and a fine of 100$ to 500$000.
>
> Sole paragraph. For the abuses committed in the illegal exercise of medicine in general, its perpetrators shall suffer, besides the established punishments, those related to the crimes which they caused.
>
> *Article 157.* To practice spiritism, magic and its spells, to use talismans and cartomancy to inspire sentiments of hatred or love, to inculcate cures for curable or uncurable diseases, in short, to fascinate and subjugate public credulity:

118. Montero, *supra* note 112 at 23.
119. Leite, *supra* note 109 at 2020; Magalhães Pires, *supra* note 105 at 41–42.
120. Decree No. 4497 of 19 Jan. 1922.
121. Jane Reis, *A Aplicação de Regras Religiosas de Acordo com a Lei do Estado: um Panorama do Caso Brasileiro*, XIII Revista da AGU 9, 13 (2014).
122. Montes, *supra* note 40 at 23.
123. *Ibid.* at 23–25.
124. *Código Penal* [Penal Code], Decree No. 847 of 11 Oct. 1890.

Punishments: cellular imprisonment for one to six months, and a fine of 100$ to 500$000.

Paragraph 1. If, under influence, or as a consequence of any of those means, the patient is deprived of their physical abilities, or has them either temporarily or permanently affected:

Punishments: cellular imprisonment for one to six years, and a fine of 200$ to 500$000.

Paragraph 2. In the same punishments, and also in the suspension of the exercise of the profession for the duration of the sentence, shall incur the physician who directly practices any of the aforementioned acts, or takes responsibility for them.

Article 158. To administer, or simply to prescribe, as a healing means, of internal or external use, and in any prepared form, a substance of any of the realms of nature, by performing, or thus exercising the profession the so-called healer [*curandeiro*]:

Punishments: cellular imprisonment for one to six months, and a fine of 100$ to 500$000.

Sole paragraph. If the use of any substance results in deprivation, or either temporary or permanent alteration, of the person's physical abilities or physiological functions, deformity, or failure of an organ or organic system, or, in sum, any illness:

Punishments: cellular imprisonment for one to six years, and a fine of 200$ to 500$000.

If it results in death:

Punishment: cellular imprisonment for six to twenty-four years.

73. Besides the prejudice against Spiritism and African-Brazilian religions, laws such as these advanced the interest of the medical profession, whose intention was to secure a monopoly over the 'art of healing'. The crimes mentioned above reflected the notion that 'spiritual cures' and 'magic' were fraudulent moves employed by charlatans to take advantage of the people. Repression of these practices was viewed as a matter of public health, and people were actually indicted and tried for these crimes.[125]

74. As summarized by Ricardo Mariano, despite the formal separation between state and religion, there was 'zero state neutrality in religious matters': the Roman Church retained its status as 'model of religion and religious worship and, simultaneously, as an antithesis of Spiritist and African-Brazilian "magical-religious" practices'.[126]

---

125. Giumbelli, *supra* note 56 at 254.
126. Ricardo Mariano, *Laicidade à Brasileira: Católicos, Pentecostais e Laicos em Disputa na Esfera Pública*, 11 Civitas – Revista de Ciências Sociais 238, 246 (2011).

IV. 'Neo-Christianity' and Military Regime (1930–1985)

75. In the last half of the First Republic, the Catholic Church pivoted towards a new pact with the state. Under popes Pius X, Benedict XV, and Pius XI, the Roman Church sought to reassert its place of dominance within society. This resulted in the movement of 'Catholic restoration', led by cardinal Leme.[127] Elaborating on the idea of a 'Catholic nation', the Church seized the troubled times of the 1930 Revolution – which put an end to the First Republic – to re-establish itself as a source of legitimacy, by offering support to the new regime, led by Getúlio Vargas.[128]

76. Since the idea was beneficial to both parties, the Catholic Church toiled effectively to harness the masses in support of Vargas. And so ushered in the period known as 'Neo-Christianity'[129] in the 1930s, when a new form of alliance – partly unofficial, partly legally embedded – was forged between the Catholic Church and the state, thus resulting in Catholicism being installed as the de facto religion of the state and of the elites of the country.[130] In 1930, the *Liga Eleitoral Católica* [Catholic Electoral League] was founded so as to influence Catholic voters and direct their votes to candidates aligned with the Church. Most of the candidates they supported were elected to the Constituent Assembly.[131]

77. The symbol of this new relationship between Church and state was the 1934 Constitution,[132] which reversed, in part, the separation of the First Republic, both symbolically and legally. In its Preamble, the members of the Constituent Assembly pledged their 'trust in God'. The Constitution conferred religious marriages the same legal status of civil ceremonies and allowed religious denominations to collaborate with the government 'in benefit of the collective interest' and to oversee the management of cemeteries. It also provided for ministers to offer spiritual support for the Armed Forces and for religious education in public schools.[133]

78. In 1937, Vargas – after being elected president by the Constituent Assembly – staged a coup, imposed a new constitution, and commenced his rule as a dictator,

---

127. Arthur Phillipe Pereira, *Uma Neocristandade no Brasil: A atuação do Cardeal Leme para tornar o Brasil um país Católico*, Doctoral thesis, Theology department, Pontifical Catholic University of Rio de Janeiro, Rio de Janeiro (RJ), Brazil, 15–16 (2018).
128. In 1931, the inauguration of the statue of Christ the Redeemer in Rio de Janeiro was used by the Cardinal Leme to show the strength of the Roman Catholic Church to the Provisional Government led by Getúlio Vargas. *See* Ralph Della Cava, *Igreja e estado no Brasil do século XX: sete monografias recentes sobre o catolicismo brasileiro, 1916/1964*, 12 Estudos CEBRAP 5, 14–15 (1975). The author reports that, in his speech, Cardinal Leme said: 'either the state … recognizes the God of the people, or the people will not recognize the state'. Vargas and his government watched as the Cardinal 'consecrated the nation "to the Most Holy Heart of Jesus, recognizing him forever as its King and Lord"', as cited in Boris Fausto, *História do Brasil*, 284 (14th ed., Edusp 2015).
129. The term is used by Giumbelli, *supra* note 109 at 239.
130. Della Cava, *supra* note 128 at 10.
131. Blasius Silvano Debald, *A relação da Igreja Católica com o Estado Brasileiro – 1889/1960*, 1 Pleiade 51, 56–57 (2007).
132. Oro, *supra* note 112.
133. Magalhães Pires, *supra* note 105 at 44.

with absolute powers. During the 'Vargas Age', the Church maintained a friendly relationship with the regime, having received its 'discreet support'.[134] Prompted by Catholic groups and others, the government so far as restricted the entry of Jewish people fleeing Nazism by means of secret letters sent to consular authorities abroad.[135]

79. After the Second World War, when Brazil aligned with the Allies, Vargas was ousted. After new elections, General Eurico Gaspar Dutra become the new president, with the public endorsement of Vargas, who was elected senator for the Rio Grande do Sul in the Constituent Congress.[136] In 1946, a new constitution was adopted, but as for religion it mainly followed the roadmap of the 1934 Constitution.

80. By this time, the religious environment was already somewhat different in Brazil. The end of the Second World War also marked the influx of 'a new kind of mass Protestantism, which [began] to grow in an astonishing manner, based in Pentecostal groups'. From then on, new denominations arrived, and others were founded, such as the *Igreja Pentecostal Deus é Amor* and *Brasil para Cristo*. This was the moment in which Protestantism began to ruffle the feathers of the Catholic Church, which eventually included it among its 'enemies'.[137]

81. Repression of Spiritism and African-Brazilian religions continued. In 1941, the police chief of the Federal District even suspended the operation of all 'Spiritism centres of this capital', requiring them to apply for a registration from the police.[138] Kardecists then commenced advocating for a religious status they had never really sought to obtain, in order to demonstrate that its practices did not involve deception or fraud, being actually rooted in a sincere belief system.[139] It further reorganized itself, both in doctrine and structure, and began negotiating and cooperating with the police, which culminated in the registration requirement being repealed in 1945.

82. African-Brazilian religions, however, did not actually benefit from this. The police chief had indeed revoked the ordinance in regard to the freedom of religion and the cooperation of the Spiritists, in general, but he emphasized that 'the practices of lower Spiritism and its typical exploitations' would still be under 'energetic repression'.[140] Although some Umbanda *terreiros* had begun to incorporate as religious associations – many of them chose to register as Spiritists so as to avoid police

134. Lima, *supra* note 106 at 162.
135. *See* General Introduction, §2, VII *supra*.
136. Fausto, *supra* note 128 at 340.
137. Montes, *supra* note 40 at 25.
138. Giumbelli, *supra* note 56 at 272–273.
139. Montero, *supra* note 54 at 52.
140. Giumbelli, *supra* note 56 at 274.

persecution – 'there seemed to be a silent consensus', distinguishing the African-Brazilian religions, associated with crime and drugs. Only in the ensuing decades from 1950 to 1970, they were properly recognized as legitimate religions.[141]

83. In 1964, a military coup removed President João Goulart from office and made way for a twenty-one-year-long military dictatorship. The regime had a new constitution approved by Congress in 1967, and even though it granted the president an excessive amount of power, the military rulers relied heavily on *Atos Institucionais* (Institutional Acts), extra-constitutional instruments manifesting the unlimited power claimed by the leaders of the coup. When exercising this power in 1969, the Ministers of the Navy, War, and the Airforce went as far as to impose a new text for the constitution – regarded by scholars as a new one – in the form of an amendment.

84. The Catholic Church did support the regime at first. The National Conference of the Bishops publicly thanked the military, who 'had risen in name of the supreme interests of the Nation' to prevent Brazil from becoming communist.[142] But the Church's endorsement waned by the end of the 1960s. After the Second Vatican Council (1962–1965), the Roman Catholic Church in Brazil began to focus on social and economic matters, and especially to integrate with the civil society and social movements. The National Conference portrayed a very important role in the defence of human rights and re-democratization.[143] Catholic authorities condemned the violence of the regime and the use of torture,[144] and the Church itself was targeted by the government as a public enemy:[145] priests and laypeople disappeared, were banished from the country, or were arrested, tortured, and killed. As an example, a foreign priest was expelled from Brazil for holding a mass dressed in black and reading the Universal Declaration of Human Rights during the sermon.[146]

85. Protestants were also targeted by the regime when thought to hold 'progressive' views. The headquarters of the Evangelical Confederation of Brazil were

141. Montero, *supra* note 54 at 53–56.
142. As cited in *CNBB Afirma que Golpe de 1964 Foi um 'Erro Histórico,'* Folha de S. Paulo, 3 Apr. 2014, https://m.folha.uol.com.br/poder/2014/04/1435249-cnbb-diz-que-golpe-de-1964-foi-erro-historico.shtml?origin=folha.
143. Dermi Azevedo, *A Igreja Católica e seu papel político no Brasil*, 18 Estudos Avançados 109, 112–113 (2004).
144. After realizing that torture was 'a policy of the state', part of the Catholic hierarchy started to denounce the violence of the regime: 'Priests informed their parishioners about the violence and arbitrariness. The National Conference of the Bishops of Brazil wrote countless formal or official complaints about imprisonments for political reasons in the country. Bishops frequently intervened with authorities on behalf of victims of the dictatorship. The Church used its own communication channels to circumvent censorship and bring to the international public opinion reports about the surge of torture in Brazil.' *See* Comissão Nacional da Verdade, *Relatório: Textos Temáticos*, 396–397 (2014).
145. *Ibid.* at 159.
146. *Ibid.* at 175.

invaded, their files seized, and many members of Protestant denominations were arrested, tortured, or had to flee the country.[147]

86. Indigenous communities and leaders were also seen as communists and enemies. According to the National Truth Commission, convened to address the regime violence, the state policy in relation to Indigenous peoples was to force or 'accelerate' their 'integration' into the 'national communion' and to 'colonize their lands whenever it was deemed strategic to the implementation of [the regime's] political and economic project'.[148]

87. In the 1970s, Neo-Pentecostal churches began to appear, with principal examples being the IURD, the *Igreja Internacional da Graça de Deus* [International Grace of God Church], and the *Igreja Renascer em Cristo* [Reborn in Christ Church]. They are known to rely heavily on media as a means of mass religious conversion. These denominations also stood out for being founded in Brazil, by Brazilian leaders.[149] These denominations would experience exponential growth in the following years, as the Catholic majority diminished.

88. During the presidency of General Ernesto Geisel (1974–1979), the regime transited towards opening up politically. In 1985, Tancredo Neves was elected president – the first civilian since João Goulart, deposed in 1964 – but Neves died before assuming office.

V. The New Republic (1985–)

89. The vice president-elect, José Sarney, was inaugurated as president in 1985 and submitted to Congress a bill to convene a constituent assembly. The proposition was approved as Constitutional Amendment No. 26 of 27 November 1985. The National Constituent Assembly convened in 1987, involved the enthusiastic participation of civil society groups, including religious denominations.[150] Within itself the Assembly was somewhat plural: it had thirty-two Evangelical members, whereas for example, in its 1946 counterpart, their membership amounted to one.[151] Evangelical and Catholic representatives worked in tandem to infuse the constitution with shared views in matters of morality (family, children).[152]

---

147. *Ibid.* at 176–195.
148. *Ibid.* at 251–252.
149. Montes, *supra* note 40 at 32–33, 35–36.
150. Cláudio Pereira Souza Neto & Daniel Sarmento, *Direito Constitucional: Teoria, História e Métodos de Trabalho*, 163–164 (Fórum 2012); Vinicius Parolin Wohnrath, *Duas Dinâmicas, Dois Resultados: A Igreja Católica na Assembleia Nacional Constituinte 1987–1988*, 28 Pro-posições 242, 263 (2017).
151. Leite, *supra* note 109 at 249.
152. Wohnrath, *supra* note 150 at 263.

90. On 5 October 1988, the Assembly adopted the Constitution of the Federative Republic of Brazil, currently in force, with six revision amendments[153] and 109 regular constitutional amendments.[154]

153. Revision amendments followed the procedure set forth in Art. 3 of the ADCT: in 1994, members of Congress gathered as one legislative chamber to revise the Constitution by majority vote.
154. Constitutional amendments are approved by a three-fifths majority, in two votes, in each of the Houses of Congress. *See* Const. (1988), Art. 60.

Part I. Legal Framework and Sources

Chapter 1. Constitutional Position of Religion

§1. Federal Constitution

91. The Preamble of the 1988 Federal Constitution includes an invocation to God:[155] the National Constituent Assembly declares that the enactment of the Constitution is made 'under God's protection'. It is a rather traditional formula in Brazil, rejuvenated by subtle variation in phrasing, in almost all the country's constitutions – the exceptions being the constitutions of 1891 and 1937. However, the Federal Supreme Court has stated that the invocation to God, in the Preamble, holds no legal effect.[156] The veritable constitutional position of religion in Brazil is thus defined by other provisions.

92. The Constitution lists many of the fundamental rights it enshrines in Article 5, including the *right of religious freedom*, to which it devotes three specific clauses:

> Article 5. All persons are equal before the law, without any distinction whatsoever, Brazilians and foreigners residing in the country being ensured of inviolability of the right to life, to liberty, to equality, to security and to property, on the following terms:
>
> ...
>
> VI– freedom of conscience and of belief is inviolable, the free exercise of religious cults being ensured and, under the terms of the law, the protection of places of worship and their rites being guaranteed;
>
> VII– under the terms of the law, the rendering of religious assistance in civil and military establishments of collective confinement is ensured;
>
> VIII– no one shall be deprived of any rights by reason of religious belief or philosophical or political conviction, unless he invokes it to exempt himself from a legal obligation required of all and refuses to perform an alternative obligation established by law.[157]

155. Only the Constitutions of 1891 and 1937 did not mention God in their preambles.
156. STF, Full Court, ADI 2076/AC, Rapp. Min. Carlos Velloso, *DJ* 8 Aug. 2003.
157. Throughout this monograph, transcripts of the English translation of the Federal Constitution were obtained at: *Constitution of the Federative Republic of Brazil* (Supremo Tribunal Federal, 2019), http://www.stf.jus.br/arquivo/cms/legislacaoConstituicao/anexo/brazil_federal_constitution.pdf.

93. The last clause deals with conscientious objections usually invoked with regard to military obligations. This matter is also addressed by Article 143, paragraph 1, of the Constitution, which provides for an 'alternative service' to be assigned by the Armed Forces, as prescribed by law, to those who object to perform military service because of their religious, philosophical, or political beliefs.[158]

94. In addition to these provisions, Article 19, I, explicitly prohibits all levels of government from hindering the activities of all 'religious sects or churches'. The Constitution also requires the non-mandatory religious teaching to be offered at public primary schools and attributes to religious marriages the same legal effects of civil ceremonies.[159]

95. In Title VIII, Chapter VIII, the Federal Constitution addresses the rights of the Indigenous peoples of Brazil. Article 231 demands that their 'customs' and 'creeds' be upheld. Given the special place that nature and the lands retain within their belief systems, the Constitution recognizes 'their original rights to the lands they traditionally occupy', which are 'those on which they live on a permanent basis', which are 'used for their productive activities', being 'indispensable to the preservation of the environmental resources necessary for their wellbeing and for their physical and cultural reproduction, according to their uses, customs and traditions'.[160] These rights eclipse any other titles of ownership or occupation of these lands, which are deemed void and extinct.[161] These lands are placed under the ownership of the Union, to be exclusively harnessed for the benefit of the peoples who reside there.[162] According to the Federal Supreme Court, the recognition of a traditionally occupied area as an 'Indigenous Land' does not render it a sovereign state or a political entity, but the government is required to hear their inhabitants and to duly consider their interests in regulating the land.[163] Specifically, in the matter of the presence of non-Indigenous religious missionaries and ministers, the Court concluded that it was up to the Indigenous communities to decide for themselves. In the words of Minister Luís Roberto Barroso:

> The purpose of the Constitution is to set aside, for the Indigenous peoples, an exclusive area in which they can preserve and live their traditions – which, in the majority of cases, does not require the complete prohibition of contact with people from outside the Indigenous land. … In principle, the same reasoning applies to the entry or the permanence of missionaries and the construction of temples of non-Indigenous denominations. Nonetheless, an important element should be considered, which justifies some additional caution: the presence of

158. Law No. 8239 of 4 Oct. 1991.
159. Const. (1988), Arts 210, para. 1, and 226, para. 2.
160. Const. (1988), Art. 231, *caput* and para. 1.
161. Const. (1988), Art. 231, para. 6.
162. Const. (1988), Art. 231, *caput* and paras 2–3. The exploitation of hydric resources and minerals require congressional authorization, after hearing the involved communities, who are also entitled to part of the revenue.
163. STF, Full Court, Pet 3388/RR, Rapp. Min. Carlos Ayres Britto, *DJ* 1 Jul. 2010; STF, Full Court, Pet 3388 ED/RR, Rapp. Min. Luís Roberto Barroso, *DJ* 4 Feb. 2014.

> individuals who intend to interfere with the Indigenous peoples' *religion*, an important aspect of their culture, is not legitimate. …
> However, it should not lead one to suppose – making the opposite mistake – that the Constitution works to protect the Indigenous peoples from their own choices, turning their right to preserve their culture in an unconstitutional duty of isolation. In this matter, the biggest mistake is to assume that it would be incumbent on anyone, but the Indigenous peoples themselves, to decide on their present and their future – which would happen either by imposing external values or by preventing them from having contact with other lifestyles. …
> … the Union's leadership role cannot involve some kind of *cultural dirigisme* by the government. There are two rights at stake, conferred exclusively upon the Indigenous peoples: (i) the protection of their cultures, as members of minority groups; and (ii) their individual freedom, as any other human beings. Being this the case, it must be incumbent on the Indigenous communities, on only to them, the right to *decide* whether, how, and in which circumstances the presence of the missionaries and their temples should be admissible.[164]

96. A similar, though not identical, situation is that of the *quilombolas*. Historically, *quilombos* were communities established by enslaved Black people who had escaped captivity to live and resist further oppression. These people were known as *quilombolas*. Throughout the centuries, even after the Abolition of Slavery in 1888, these communities cultivated identities, in various forms of relationship with other cultural groups of society, and were never far from the fight to protect their lands and culture.[165] In acknowledgement of their just claims, the debt society owes to the descendants of enslaved people, and the special connection between their lands and the survival of their culture, the Constitution confers to the 'remaining members' of *quilombo* communities the ownership of their lands.[166] This, however, is not an 'original' right, as is the one of Indigenous peoples. The government must expropriate these areas and compensate their owners. Ultimately, the lands do not fall under the ownership of the Union; the *quilombola* communities are designated a collective right of property over these lands.[167]

97. As for the relationship between government and religious organizations, Article 19, I, of the Constitution expressly forbids that the former, at all levels, 'establish religious sects or churches, subsidize them … , or maintain relationships of dependence or alliance with them or their representatives', but it does permits

---

164. STF, Full Court, Pet 3388 ED/RR, Rapp. Min. Luís Roberto Barroso, *DJ* 4 Feb. 2014 (opinion of Justice Barroso).
165. For interesting debates on the matter, *see*, e.g., Allyne Andrade e Silva, *Direito e Políticas Públicas Quilombolas* (2020); Ilka Boaventura Leite, *Os Quilombos no Brasil: Questões Conceituais e Normativas*, 4 Etnográfica 333 (2000); Alessandra Schmitt, Maria Cecília Manzoli Turatti & Maria Celina Pereira de Carvalho, *A Atualização do Conceito de Quilombo: Identidade e Território nas Definições Teóricas*, Ambiente & Sociedade 129 (2002).
166. ADCT, Art. 68.
167. Decree No. 4887 of 20 Nov. 2003; STF, Full Court, ADI 3239/DF, Rapp. Min. Rosa Weber, *DJ* 1 Feb. 2019.

'collaboration in the public interest in the manner set forth by law'. It provides the main textual basis for what is called *princípio da laicidade* (laicity principle, from the French *laïcité*). In short, this principle demands that government remains impartial in matters concerning religion so that it must not engage in disputes in relation to the validity of religious worldviews. This requirement reflects the deep respect that government owes not only to the individual's decisions on these issues but also to the equality of citizens under the law since privileges to one group over others would amount to unfair discrimination. Under the laicity principle, the Federal Supreme Court has struck down, e.g., a state constitutional provision requiring the assignment of an Evangelical minister to provide religious guidance to the members of the state military (policemen and firefighters)[168] and a state law that, without quoting scriptures sacred to any other religious groups, affirmed the Bible as the basis of 'principles, uses, and customs' of 'communities, churches, and groups'.[169]

98. However, as Article 19, I, clearly states, the Constitution does not require a strict separation between government and religion. On the contrary, the Constitution itself guarantees religious teaching in public schools[170] and permits public funding of non-profit religious schools.[171] It is also very common that religious organizations maintain hospitals and cater to those in need, situations where they may also be authorized to receive public funds.[172]

§2. Subnational Constitutional Law

99. Subnational constitutional law exists in Brazil at state and local levels, as well as in the Federal District. The states possess their own constitutions, whereas the Federal District and the municipalities retain organic laws. All must be consistent with the Federal Constitution and, in the case of municipalities, with the state constitution. It should be noted, however, that subnational constitutional space is very narrow due not only to the fact that the Federal Constitution deals with almost any conceivable matter – including the organization of subnational governments – but also to the STF's broad construction of the limitations placed on subnational constituent power.[173]

100. In matters of religion, subnational constitutional provisions in Brazil tend to circulate around five topics: (1) religious discrimination; (2) taxation; (3) religious teaching; (4) minority religions; and (5) laicity. In general, they simply mirror federal constitutional provisions in relation to religious freedom, tax immunity of temples, and prohibition on governmental support or hindrance of religions. But

168. STF, Full Court, ADI 3478/RJ, Rapp. Min. Edson Fachin, *DJ* 19 Feb. 2020.
169. STF, Full Court, ADI 5257/RO, Rapp. Min. Dias Toffoli, *DJ* 3 Dec. 2018.
170. Const. (1988), Art. 210, para. 1.
171. Const. (1988), Art. 213.
172. Const. (1988), Art. 199, para. 1, and Art. 204, I.
173. I have discussed this subject in more length in another monograph. *See* Thiago Magalhães Pires, *Sub-national Constitutional Law: Brazil*, IEL Constitutional Law (André Alen & David Haljan eds., 2021).

there does exist some innovative provisions, in the sense that they are not solely grounded on the text of the Federal Constitution.

101. As for religious discrimination, constitutional and organic law provisions mostly forbid it in broad terms,[174] but one also finds special prohibitions on discrimination of public servants[175] or school pupils.[176] In the State of Maranhão, public education must be oriented 'towards excluding any form of racist manifestation and religious discrimination ... '.[177] In the State of Acre (AC), public servants are entitled to have their weekly rest on Saturdays, instead of Sundays, if necessary according to their religious beliefs.[178]

102. Taxation provisions involving religion rarely go beyond mirroring the federal constitutional provision on the immunity of temples. In João Pessoa/PB, however, building licences for temples are free from local charges.[179]

103. There are select provisions in relation to religious teaching in public schools that elucidate openness to all creeds,[180] require it to be inter-denominational,[181] and forbid its funding by the government.[182] Some of them are constitutionally questionable in light of the Federal Constitution and the case law of the STF. That is the case of provisions requiring religious teaching in private schools in general,[183] or in secondary public schools.[184] In the State of Rondônia, the Constitution curiously requires that religious teaching be 'non-denominational with Biblical principles'.[185]

104. Another interesting topic is that of minority religions. The Organic Law of Manaus/AM requires local government to promote and encourage the protection and appreciation of Indigenous cultures and religions.[186] In São Luís/MA and São Paulo/SP, the government is responsible for the protection of popular, Indigenous, and African-Brazilian cultures and religions.[187] The State Constitution of Bahia

---

174. *See*, e.g., State Const. (BA), Art. 3, I; Const. (CE), Art. 14, III; State Const. (ES), Art. 12, *caput* and para. 1; State Const. (PE), Art. 5, XIV; State Const. (RJ), Art. 9, para. 1; Org. Law (DF), Art. 2, sole par.; Org. Law (Macapá/AM), Art. 7; Org. Law (Salvador/BA), Art. 1; Org. Law (Goiânia/GO), Art. 3, sole par.; Org. Law (Cuiabá/MT), Art. 5, XIII; Org. Law (Teresina/PI), Art. 9; Org. Law (São Paulo/SP), Art. 2, VIII.
175. *See*, e.g., State Const. (AL), Art. 55, VIII; State Const. (PA), Art. 31, XVII; Org. Law (Curitiba/PR), Art. 89, XVI.
176. Org. Law (Maceió/AL), Art. 133, III; Org. Law (Salvador/BA), Art. 183.
177. State Const. (MA), Art. 262.
178. State Const. (AC), Art. 27, XIII.
179. Org. Law (João Pessoa/PB), Art. 238.
180. State Const. (AM), Art. 199, I, *m*; *See* State Const. (PA), Art. 277, para. 1.
181. State Const. (ES), Art. 175; State Const. (PR), Art. 183, para. 1; Org. Law (Cuiabá/MT), Art. 136.
182. Org. Law (Porto Alegre/RS), Art. 178.
183. State Const. (MA), Art. 218, para. 3.
184. State Const. (MT), Art. 190, para. 5; State Const. (RN), Art. 137, para. 1; State Const. (RS), Art. 209, para. 1; *See* State Const. (TO), Art. 127, para. 1.
185. State Const. (RO), Art. 258, I.
186. Org. Law (Manaus/AM), Art. 370-A.
187. Org. Law (São Luís/MA), Art. 154; Org. Law (São Paulo/SP), Art. 193, II.

imposes on the government an obligation 'to preserve and secure the integrity, respectability, and permanence of the values of the African-Brazilian religion'.[188] In Manaus/AM and Belo Horizonte/MG, the organic laws provide that public officials are to be punished if they violate the freedom of expression and worship of African-Brazilian religions.[189]

105. Some states and municipalities forbid any database, owned or operated by the government, from storing information about people's religion, except when it involves statistical and non-individualized processing.[190] In Manaus/AM, the Organic Law requires public cemeteries to have an 'ecumenical chapel' and a 'designated area for popular religious acts'.[191]

188. State Const. (BA), Art. 275.
189. Org. Law (Manaus/AM), Art. 385-B, IV; Org. Law (Belo Horizonte/MG), Art. 182, sole par. IV.
190. State Const. (ES), Art. 8; State Const. (MT), Art. 10, XIII; State Const. (PI), Art. 6, sole par.; State Const. (RJ), Art. 21; State Const. (SE), Art. 3, para. 4; Org. Law (Rio de Janeiro/RJ), Art. 8, sole par.
191. Org. Law (Manaus/AM), Art. 225.

Chapter 2. Other Legislation with Regard to Religion

§1. Federal Legislation

106. In Brazil, the largest share of legislative power was assigned to the Union so that most matters can (or must) be governed by federal law. In this scenario, it should not be surprising that the foremost pieces of legislation related to religion are federal statutes.

I. Civil Law

107. The Civil Code[192] provides for almost all aspects of private life, including legal personality and capacity, contracts, torts, family and succession, and property law. It directly or indirectly affects religious matters in many aspects:

(1) *Religious organizations:* the Code regulates the acquisition of legal personality by corporations, and expressly includes *religious organizations* as a particular type of private legal person.[193] This is the form that denominations usually take when they are incorporated. The Civil Code does not impose any special requirement for their institution. On the contrary, Article 44, paragraph 1, declare to be free 'the creation, organization, internal structuring, and operation of religious organizations', prohibiting the government from denying recognition to them or registration of their constitutive and operational acts.
(2) *Other religious legal persons:* religious organizations aside, people may form other legal entities with religious purposes. They usually take the form of *associations* or *foundations*, both regulated by the Civil Code: whilst associations have members, who actively participate, foundations are created by setting assets aside for specific purposes.[194]
(3) *Marriage:* the Civil Code regulates family law in general, including marriages. As does the Constitution, the Code provides for free civil marriages and permits religious celebrations. The latter can be granted the effects of a civil ceremony if they respect the corresponding requirements and spouses duly register in the proper public offices up to ninety days after the wedding.[195]

108. Until very recently, Brazilian civil law was very much infused with Christian (especially Catholic) precepts. Marriages were deemed indissoluble until 1977 when a constitutional amendment and a statute modified the law to permit divorces. Even so, divorces were solely possible should the spouses be judicially separated

192. *Código Civil (CC)* [Civil Code], Law No. 10406 of 10 Jan. 2002.
193. CC, Law No. 10406 of 10 Jan. 2002, Art. 44, IV.
194. CC, Law No. 10406 of 10 Jan. 2002, Arts 53–61(associations), and Arts 62—69 (foundations).
195. CC, Law No. 10406 of 10 Jan. 2002, Arts 1512–1516.

for at least three years.[196] The required period before the parties could apply for divorce was reduced to one year by the Constitution of 1988, only to be totally removed in 2010.[197]

109. The influence of Christian precepts also created hurdles when recognizing legal effects to informal civil partnerships, common law marriages, which were pejoratively called *concubinato* (concubinage). The wording of the law also appears not to include same-sex unions, which were accepted in Brazil due to judicial construction. For more information, *see* Part X, Chapter 1, §3 and §4 *infra*.

II. Criminal Law

110. In order to protect the exercise of religion, the Penal Code,[198] Title V, establishes as 'crimes against the religious sentiment and against the respect for the dead': (1) 'To mock someone publicly because of their belief or religious function; to prevent or to disturb a ceremony or the act of religious worship; to publicly vilify an act or an object of religious worship'; (2) 'To prevent or to disturb burial or funeral ceremony'; (3) 'To violate or to profane a grave or funeral urn'; (4) 'To destroy, to steal, or to hide a corpse or part of it'; and (5) 'To vilify a corpse or its ashes'.[199]

111. Also, the crime of insulting someone by offending their dignity or decorum is considered much more serious should it consist in availing elements such as race or religion.[200] More recently, Law No. 9459 of 15 May 1997, established as crimes select actions involving discrimination of people – by government officials or private businesses and individuals – due to their religion.[201]

112. A significant part of the Penal Code has undergone reform and important amendments since was enacted in 1940. Such addition removed some of the original influx of the Catholic worldview. For example, adultery was a crime until the relevant provision was repealed in 2005.[202] Nevertheless, bigamy remains a crime.[203]

---

196. Const. (1969), Art. 175, para. 1, as amended by CA No. 9 of 28 Jun. 1977; Law No. 6515 of 26 Dec. 1977, Art. 25. Judicial separation is a legal proceeding that terminates the duties of cohabitation, reciprocal fidelity, and community property – 'as if the marriage had been dissolved', in the words of Art. 3 of Law No. 6515. Only after three years of said separation were the parties allowed to actually dissolve their marriage, so as to be able to marry someone else.
197. Const. (1988), Art. 226, para. 6, as amended by CA No. 66 of 13 Jul. 2010.
198. CP, Decree-Law No. 2848 of 7 Dec. 1940.
199. *Ibid.*, Arts 209–212.
200. *Ibid.*, Art. 140, para. 3.
201. Law No. 7716 of 5 Jan. 1989, Art. 1, as amended by Law No. 9459 of 15 May 1997.
202. CP, Decree-Law No. 2848 of 7 Dec. 1940, Art. 240, repealed by Law No. 11106 of 28 Mar. 2005, Art. 5.
203. CP, Decree-Law No. 2848 of 7 Dec. 1940, Art. 235.

III. Labour Law

113. Brazilian Labour Law can trace its roots in the Constitution: Article 7 enumerates the fundamental rights of workers, providing space for federal statutes as well as contractual provisions 'to improve … [the workers'] social conditions'. In sum, the Constitution establishes a minimum amount of protection, but other benefits to workers can be created via statutes, collective bargaining, or individual contracts. The only manifest connection between Article 7 and religion is the provision guaranteeing workers 'paid weekly leave, preferably on Sundays' (clause XV), as the preference for Sundays has obvious ties to Christianity.

114. The principal statutory source is the *Consolidação das Leis do Trabalho (CLT)* [Consolidation of Labour Laws],[204] enacted in 1943, and still in force today notwithstanding numerous amendments. It does not contain many references to religion, with exception of: (1) not considering working overtime hours those spent by employees in religious practices inside the employer's facilities;[205] (2) the preference for Sundays as the day of paid weekly leave;[206] (3) the prohibition of work on religious holidays (like national holidays), as defined by law;[207] (4) the requirement that worker representative committees, in each company, ensure that 'fair and impartial treatment' is provided to employees, 'preventing any form of discrimination on the grounds of … religion … '.[208]

115. According to the Federal Supreme Court, only the Union can establish holidays because of their impact on employer-employee relations.[209] Many of the national holidays are indelibly linked to Catholic holy days. There are those dates that are quite clear: Law No. 6802 of 30 June 1980 establishes 12 October as a national holiday 'for the public and official veneration of Our Lady of Aparecida, patron saint of Brazil'. But it can also be seen in the presence, in the list of holidays, of 2 November (All Souls' Day) and 25 December (Christmas). Also, the 1 January apparently boasts ties to Catholicism – it is the day of the Solemnity of Mary, Mother of God.[210] Federal law does not permit the states to create new holidays – except for one, on its *data magna* (great day) – but it empowers municipalities (and the Federal District)[211] to establish holidays, not only on the first and last

204. CLT, Decree-Law No. 5452 of 1 May 1943.
205. *Ibid.*, Art. 4, para. 2, I, included by Law No. 13467 of 13 Jul. 2017.
206. For services that require work on Sundays, the employer must set up a schedule of shifts of rotation, and, in any case, apply for a permit. *See* CLT, Decree-Law No. 5452 of 1 May 1943, Arts 67–68, and 385–386).
207. CLT, Decree-Law No. 5452 of 1 May 1943, Arts 70 and 385, sole par. However, it is possible to apply for a permit.
208. CLT, Decree-Law No. 5452 of 1 May 1943, Art. 510-B, V, included by Law No. 13467 of 13 Jul. 2017.
209. *See*, e.g., STF, Full Court, ADI 4820/AP, Rapp. Min. Dias Toffoli, *DJ* 3 Dec. 2018; STF, Full Court, ADI 6133/RJ, Rapp. Min. Ricardo Lewandowski, *DJ* 6 Jul. 2020.
210. Almost all national holidays are set forth by Law No. 662 of 6 Apr. 1949, Art. 1, as amended by Law No. 10607 of 19 Dec. 2002.
211. The District combines state and local legislative powers (*see* Const. (1988), Art. 32, para. 1).

day the municipality's centennial but also on up to four days of religious celebrations, 'according to local tradition', one of which being Good Friday.[212]

IV. Administrative Law: Federal Servants and Selection Procedure

116. Administrative Law in Brazil deals with many subjects, including the regulation of private businesses, the rights and duties of public servants, and contracts initiated with government entities and government-owned companies. In general, it is incumbent on each level of government to enact legislation in relation to these matters, but the Union has the power to pass some general provisions (e.g., regarding government contracts).

117. Federal servants are exempted from working on a designated holiday, even when established by state and local laws, and on days of *ponto facultativo* (optional day off). *Pontos facultativos* are most often immediately before or after a holiday, so to form a long weekend. It is also common to establish *pontos facultativos* on religious-related days, such as the Monday and Tuesday of Carnival and *Corpus Christi*. A list of the *pontos facultativos* of the following year is customarily published by the Federal Government in the last months of the current year.[213] Should a public servant observe a holy day not earmarked on the list of holidays and *pontos facultativos*, their superiors may authorize the time off, subject to compensation with extra hours of work on other days.[214]

118. A notable list of religious holidays, in addition to the ones above, applies to judges and civil servants of the Judiciary of the Union,[215] including the Superior Courts and the Federal Supreme Court. It comprises: (1) the Holy Week, from Wednesday through Easter Sunday; (2) the Monday and Tuesday before Ash Wednesday (Carnival); (3) 8 December (Justice Day – Immaculate Conception); and (4) 1 November (All Saints' Day).[216]

119. The law guarantees equal treatment to federal civil servants in general, who must not be deprived of rights or undergo any sort of discrimination within their workplace due to religious creed.[217] Despite the same provision also stating that religious beliefs do not exempt servants from duties, it must be read under Article 5, VIII, of the Constitution, which guarantees the right to conscientious objection.

---

212. Law No. 9093 of 12 Sep. 1995, Art. 2.
213. For 2021, *see Ministério da Economia* [Ministry of Economy], *Portaria* [Ordinance] No. 430 of 30 Dec. 2020, Art. 1.
214. *Ibid.*, Art. 3.
215. The *Justiça da União* (Judiciary of the Union) comprises: (1) Federal Courts; (2) Labour Courts; (3) Federal Military Courts; (4) Electoral Courts; and (5) Courts of the Federal District and Territories.
216. Law No. 5010 of 30 May 1966, Art. 62, II–IV.
217. Law No. 8112 of 11 Dec. 1990, Art. 239.

The Federal Supreme Court has ruled that public entities are permitted to set alternative rules for the work of servants and employees who claim that religious obligation prevents them from adhering to general directives, provided that certain requirements are met.[218]

V. Tax Law

120. All levels of government possess concurrent legislative jurisdiction regarding Tax Law, but the Union has the power to enact general provisions, applicable to all or to some of the taxes they levy.[219] The Constitution itself also includes considerable provisions in relation to taxation – including, e.g., the tax immunity of temples – which were discussed elsewhere (*see* Part VIII, Chapter 2, §1, *infra*).

121. The general provisions on Tax Law are, by and large, codified in the *Código Tributário Nacional (CTN)* [National Tax Code], which does not address religion, except to mirror the constitutional provision with regards to the immunity of temples.[220] Other federal statutes, however, provide religious groups with exemptions from certain taxes on received donations or contributions.[221]

VI. The Racial Equality Act

122. The *Estatuto da Igualdade Racional* (Racial Equality Act)[222] was enacted to ensure equal opportunity for Black people, as well as to protect their individual and collective rights, and to defend against discrimination and ethical intolerance.[223] When considering the historical persecution of African-Brazilian religions, the Act confirms an obligation of both government and society to defend their values,[224] and moreover, guarantees the remaining members of *quilombo* communities[225] the right to preserve their customs, traditions and religious manifests.[226]

123. In Chapter III, the Act deals extensively with freedom of conscience and the free exercise of religious practices. Article 23 reiterates the inviolability of the right to freedom of conscience and belief, as well as the protection guaranteed to places of worship, which is already mandated under the Constitution. Article 24 further qualifies this by stating that the religious freedom of the followers of African-Brazilian religions encompasses the rights: (1) to practice, organize gatherings, celebrate festivities and ceremonies; (2) to establish venues for these ends, as well

---

218. STF, Full Court, ARE 1099099/SP, Rapp. Min. Edson Fachin, *DJ* 12 Apr. 2021.
219. *See*, e.g., Const. (1988), Art. 24, I and pars 1–4; and Art. 146.
220. CTN, Law No. 5172 of 25 Oct. 1966, Art. 9, IV, *b*.
221. Provisional Measure No. 2158-35 of 24 Aug. 2001, Art. 14, X.
222. Law No. 12288 of 20 Jul. 2010.
223. *Ibid.*, Art. 1.
224. *Ibid.*, Art. 2.
225. For more on *quilombolas*, *see* Part I, Ch. 1, §1 *supra*.
226. Law No. 12288 of 20 Jul. 2010, Art. 18.

as charities related to their creed; (3) to make, sell, buy, and use religious items, except when a specific provision of law forbids certain conduct; (4) to produce and promote publications related to the practice and diffusion of their religions, including access to media and vehicles of communication; (5) to receive financial contributions from private sources to further their activities; (6) to inform the Public Prosecutors' Office of any case of religious intolerance so that it may initiate proper criminal proceedings.[227]

124. Article 25 specifies that those who practice African-Brazilian religions, like everyone else,[228] have access to religious assistance in hospitals or other 'institutions of collective confinement' (e.g., prisons). In express acknowledgement of the intolerance and discrimination faced by denominations of African heritage, Article 26 require that all levels of government adopt measures to grapple with this, especially by: (1) preventing the use of media to propagate ideas, images, or approaches 'which expose a person or a group to hate or despise' for reasons related to the religiosity of African heritage; (2) 'inventorying, repairing, and protecting documents, works, and other assets of artistic and cultural value, as well as monuments, springs, flora, and archaeological sites connected to the religions of African heritage'.

VII. The Rules of Procedure of the Houses of Congress

125. The federal legislature is bicameral: the National Congress is composed of the Federal Senate and the Chamber of Deputies. Each House and Congress itself apply their own rules of procedure to govern business. Both the rules of the Chamber and of the Senate require their respective Presidents to open each session invoking 'God's protection'.[229] In the Chamber of Deputies, it is also required that '[t]he Holy Bible ... remain, throughout the session, on the rostrum, available to anyone who wishes to consult it'.[230]

VIII. Agreement Between Brazil and the Holy See

126. A treaty was signed in the Vatican City in 2008, between Brazil and the Holy See, to regulate the legal status and situation of the Roman Catholic Church in the country.[231] The agreement attracted heated criticism from other denominations, civil society organizations, and even Catholic groups, for allegedly installing

227. Law No. 12288 of 20 Jul. 2010, Art. 24, I–VIII.
228. Under Art. 5, VII, of the Constitution.
229. Reg. Int. (SF), Resolution (SF) No. 93 of 1970, Art. 155, para. 1; Reg. Int. (CD), Resolution (CD) No. 17 of 1989, Art. 79, para. 2.
230. Reg. Int. (CD), Resolution (CD) No. 17 of 1989, Art. 79, para. 1.
231. *Acordo entre o Governo da República Federativa do Brasil e a Santa Sé relativo ao Estatuto Jurídico da Igreja Católica no Brasil* (Agreement Between the Government of the Federative Republic of Brazil and the Holy See Concerning the Legal Status of the Catholic Church in Brazil (13 Nov. 2008), approved by Congress by Leg. Dec. No. 698 of 7 Oct. 2009, and promulgated by the President by Dec. No. 7107 of 11 Feb. 2010 (hereinafter: 'Brazil-Holy See Agreement'). This

privileges to a particular denomination and as an undue entanglement of government with religion.[232] There was also some opposition to the text in Congress,[233] as many congresspersons – especially, but not exclusively, those from the Evangelical Caucus – viewed it as a token of favouritism to the Catholic Church. But resistance was limited to the Chamber of Deputies,[234] as the treaty passed the Senate with a unanimous vote.[235] As a reaction, the Chamber approved a bill, whose text mirrored that of the treaty, in the benefit of the other religious denominations. However, the bill of the so-called General Law of Religions did not pass the Senate and eventually 'died' in 2018.[236]

127. However, the text of the treaty does not appear to establish, and it certainly must not be construed so as to create, any kind of preferential treatment to the Catholic Church in comparison with other religious organizations. It does recognize the international legal personality of the Holy See, both implicitly – by the mere existence of the treaty – and expressly – by confirming the diplomatic ties between the Parties,[237] but far from innovating, the treaty simply reflects the peculiar status of the Holy See. Among other provisions, the Agreement recognizes the Church's right to keep conducting its 'apostolic mission', guaranteed by the religious freedom; confirms the legal personality of the Church and all 'Ecclesiastical Institutions' who have such personality under canon law, as long as they also conform to Brazilian law, as well as the Catholic Church's right to freely create, modify, or extinguish them; guarantees that no 'ecclesiastical circumscription' (e.g., dioceses) shall depend on a bishop seated in in foreign country; guarantees that, when devoted to social assistance and solidarity purposes, 'ecclesiastical legal persons' are entitled to the same rights and immunities of similar institutions, according to the law; recognize that the historical, artistic, and cultural estate of the Church, its libraries, and

---

was not the first agreement to be signed between Brazil and the Holy See: before it, the Parties signed an administrative agreement for the exchange of diplomatic mail (1935) and a treaty concerning military chaplains (1989). *See* Emerson Giumbelli & Jorge Scola, *Marcos Legislativos de Regulação do Religioso no Brasil: Estatuto da Igualdade Racial, Acordo Brasil-Vaticano e Lei Geral das Religiões*, 19 Numen: revista de estudos e pesquisa da religião 65, 69 (2016).

232. Ana Flor, *Igrejas Defendem a Rejeição de Acordo entre Brasil e Vaticano*, Folha de S. Paulo, 23 Mar. 2009, https://www1.folha.uol.com.br/fsp/brasil/fc2903200912.htm; Emerson Giumbelli, *O Acordo Brasil-Santa Sé e as relações entre Estado, sociedade e religião*, 13 Ciencias Sociales y Religión/Ciências Sociais e Religião 119, 120–121 (2011).

233. In Brazil, after being signed by the Executive, most international treaties require confirmation by both Houses of Congress. *See* Const. (1988), Art. 49, I.

234. Rodolfo Torres, *Evangélicos se opõem a acordo Brasil-Vaticano*, Congresso em Foco, 26 Aug. 2009, https://congressoemfoco.uol.com.br/especial/noticias/evangelicos-se-opoem-a-acordo-brasil-vaticano/.

235. Fábio Góis, *Senado confirma aprovação do acordo Brasil-Vaticano*, Congresso em Foco, 7 Oct. 2009, https://congressoemfoco.uol.com.br/especial/noticias/senado-confirma-aprovacao-do-acordo-brasil-vaticano/.

236. Under Art. 332 of the Senate Rules of Procedure, if a bill has not been approved or rejected by the end of the four-year legislative term, it is usually 'archived' (i.e., they 'die').

237. Brazil-Holy See Agreement, Art. 1.

documents are a 'a relevant part of the Brazilian cultural heritage' so that both Parties shall continue to cooperate to preserve those assets which are protected by Brazil as part of its artistic and cultural heritage.[238]

128. There appears to be a problem, though, when it comes to the recognition of ecclesiastical judgments in matrimonial matters. According to the Agreement, this recognition must follow the same rules applicable to foreign judgments in general.[239] Given that the Holy See is a subject of international law, its decisions apparently qualify as foreign judgments. For this reason, the STJ upheld the constitutional validity of this provision of the treaty.[240] However, since the courts of the Holy See usually decide on cases emanating from the Church's bodies in Brazil, the possibility of enforcing their decisions creates a particular system, applicable only to Catholics: in similar situations, decisions rendered by courts of other denominations seated in Brazil, not having been granted civil effects in foreign countries, cannot be recognized and enforced as foreign judgments in Brazil.[241] That does seem problematic, with people being treated differently solely on the basis of their religion.

§2. State, District, and Local Legislation

129. Although the Federal Union concentrates the most relevant share of legislative power, states, the Federal District, and municipalities also enact their own laws. Aside from the state constitutions, and the District and local organic laws, which outline their organization, they enact laws on subjects the likes of taxation, urban zoning and development, and business licences, commonly in domains where enactment of concurrent legislation by the Union is admissible. In these cases, federal law cannot entirely pre-empt state, District, and local laws, but only establish a framework which the subnational governments are required to respect.

130. In matters of religion, state, District, and local laws are more prevalent in domains such as taxation, especially to regulate the tax immunity of temples (*see* Part I, Chapter 1, §2 *supra*) and miscellaneous duties related to each government's

---

238. Brazil-Holy See Agreement, Arts 2–7.
239. Brazil-Holy See Agreement, Art. 12, para. 1.
240. STJ, *Corte Especial* [Special Panel], SEC 11962/EX, Rapp. Min. Felix Fischer, *DJ* 25 Nov. 2015.
241. The *leading case* was decided in 1969 by the Federal Supreme Court: it denied enforcement of a divorce decision passed by the Israelite Confessional Tribunal in São Paulo/SP, despite the fact that it had been confirmed by the Lebanese Ministry of Foreign Affairs because the religious court was seated in Brazil (*see* STF, Full Court, SE 2016/Lebanon, Rapp. Min. Luiz Gallotti, *DJ* 26 Sep. 1969). In 1971, the STF admitted the enforcement of a Catholic ecclesiastical judgment annulling a marriage, but only because it had been granted civil effects by an Italian court, thus making it a foreign decision (*see* STF, Full Court, SE 2004/Vatican, Rapp. Min. Thompson Flores, *DJ* 26 Nov. 1971). Ten years later, the Court denied enforcement to a divorce decision of an Orthodox court of Rio de Janeiro/RJ, even though it had been confirmed by the Embassy of Lebanon. Because the religious decision was passed in Brazilian territory, it could not be enforced like a foreign judgment (*see* STF, Full Court, SE 2838 AgR/Lebanon, Rapp. Min. Xavier de Albuquerque, *DJ* 18 Dec. 1981).

revenue service. But they also offer other tax exemptions and discounts to religious organizations. For example, long before the Constitution was amended to deal with this subject,[242] many municipalities exempted temples from the local property tax even when only leased by a religious organization.[243] In Salvador/BA, land ownership is also exempted from the property tax when contiguous to temples and utilized for social assistance.[244] Some municipalities also exempt religious temples from taxes which are not covered by the constitutional immunity, such as that levied to fund garbage collection services in Rio de Janeiro[245] and Recife.[246] In Porto Alegre, they enjoy a 50% break on such tax.[247]

131. States and the Federal District are not permitted to unilaterally create exemptions for their tax on the circulation of goods and certain services – such exemptions require previous agreements between governmental entities.[248] This prohibition notwithstanding, the Federal Supreme Court upheld a state law exempting temples from the tax levied on electricity, water, telephone and gas bills when the service is provided by the state or a private operator acting under state delegation. According to the Court, the prohibition of unilateral exemptions aims at avoiding a 'fiscal war' between subnational governments; since religious temples are not recognized as market players, it is lawful for a state to grant such an exemption.[249] A federal statute also permits that exemptions granted to temples (and other entities) despite the absence of the necessary agreement remain in force until 2032.[250]

132. It is also common that subnational laws involve religious tourism, religious assistance in hospitals, prisons, and military facilities,[251] and religious teaching in

242. Const. (1988), Art. 156, para. 1-A, included by CA No. 116 of 17 Feb. 2022.
243. *See*, e.g., Law (DF) No. 6466 of 27 Dec. 2019, Art. 4, II; *Código Tributário* [Tax Code] (Fortaleza/CE), Complementary Law (Fortaleza/CE) No. 159 of 23 Dec. 2013, Art. 281, I, *b*; Law (Goiânia/GO) No. 9986 of 27 Dec. 2016, Art. 1; *Código Tributário* [Tax Code] (Rio de Janeiro/RJ), Law (Rio de Janeiro/RJ) No. 691 of 24 Dec. 1984, Art. 61, XXII, included by Law (Rio de Janeiro/RJ) No. 1936 of 30 Dec. 1992, Art. 2; Law (São Paulo/SP) No. 13250 of 27 Dec. 2001, Art. 7, as amended by Law (São Paulo/SP) No. 17092 of 23 May 2019, Art. 4.
244. *Código Tributário e de Rendas* [Tax and Revenue Code] (Salvador/BA), Law (Salvador/BA) No. 7186 of 27 Dec. 2006, Art. 83, XII.
245. Law (Rio de Janeiro/RJ) No. 2687 of 27 Nov. 1998, Art. 5, V.
246. *Código Tributário* [Tax Code] (Recife/PE), Law (Recife/PE) No. 15563 of 27 Dec. 1991, Art. 63, VI, as amended by Law (Recife/PE) No. 18274 of 25 Nov. 2016, Art. 1.
247. Complementary Law (Porto Alegre/RS) No. 113 of 21 Dec. 1984, Art. 4, sole par.
248. Const. (1988), Art. 155, para. 2, XII, *g*; Complementary Law No. 24 of 7 Jan. 1975, Art. 2, para. 2.
249. STF, Full Court, ADI 3421/PR, Rapp. Min. Marco Aurélio, *DJ* 28 May 2010.
250. Complementary Law No. 160 of 7 Aug. 2017, Art. 3, para. 2, I, as amended by Complementary Law No. 170 of 19 Dec. 2019, Art. 1.
251. *See*, e.g., Law (AC) No. 1352 of 29 Dec. 2000; Law (GO) No. 19046 of 13 Jul. 2016; Law (PB) No. 11288 of 29 Dec. 2018; Law (PE) No. 14484 of 21 Nov. 2011; Law (RO) No. 834 of 21 Sep. 1999; Law (RR) No. 432 of 27 Apr. 2004; Law (RS) No. 14159 of 20 Dec. 2012; Law (SP) No. 10066 of 21 Jul. 1998.

public schools.[252] Other important topics are those of discrimination based on religion and religious intolerance, which are likewise subject to numerous state and District laws.[253] Some states also guarantee the observance of holy days and days of rest. In Mato Grosso do Sul, this is effected by means of providing alternative dates for public selection exams and school activities, and by conferring upon public servants the right to select a weekly day of rest other than Sunday.[254]

133. For its impressive breadth, it is worth mentioning the *Lei Estadual de Liberdade Religiosa* [State Law on Religious Freedom] of São Paulo.[255] Unlike most state statutes relating to religion or to religious organizations, it encompasses religious freedom in general – both on individual and collective bases – along with requirements deriving from the laicity principle.

252. *See*, e.g., Law (DF) No. 2230 of 31 Dec. 1998; Law (MA) No. 8197 of 6 Dec. 2004; Law (MG) No. 15434 of 5 Jan. 2005; Law (PI) No. 5356 of 11 Dec. 2003; Law (SE) No. 1396 of 14 Sep. 1966.
253. *See*, e.g., Law (AM) No. 4916 of 12 Sep. 2019; Law (BA) No. 13182 of 6 Jun. 2014; Law (DF) No. 3979 of 29 Mar. 2007; Law (MA) No. 10489 of 13 Jul. 2016; Law (MT) No. 11229 of 15 Oct. 2020; Law (RJ) No. 6483 of 4 Jul. 2013; Law (RJ) No. 8113 of 20 Sep. 2018; Law (RJ) No. 9210 of 11 Mar. 2021.
254. Law (MS) No. 5272 of 26 May 2000.
255. Law (SP) No. 17346 of 12 Mar. 2021.

Chapter 3. Typology of the System

134. In Brazilian law, the two dominant ideas in matters involving religion are *religious freedom* and the *laicity principle*. They may operate jointly to prevent state intervention in religious practices and organizations, but it is also possible that situations of conflict arise – for example, when it comes to deciding whether civil servants can wear religious attire. In these cases, since both are constitutional provisions, either express or implied, lawyers and courts are required to strike a balance between them. Most of the work here seems to have been progressed by scholars within academic journals and books because the Federal Supreme Court does not list a comprehensive set of opinions involving these issues. However, some landmark cases do provide indicators of the court's understanding of both provisions.

§1. Religious Freedom

135. Religious freedom finds an express constitutional basis in Article 5, VI–VIII, and Article 19, I. It involves the right to adopt a position in matters of religion – to identify with a denomination, to convert to another belief system, to create a new religion, to uphold atheist or agnostic opinion, etc. – as well as to live and act according to one's decision, individually and in the company of others, by means, e.g., of prayers, masses and services, rituals, specific forms of attire and dietary requirements, and the incorporation of religious entities. The scope of this right is extensive, as accentuated by constitutional scholars and human rights bodies. For more on this, *see* Part II *infra*.

§2. Laicity Principle

136. Article 19, I, of the Federal Constitution, also provides some textual basis for the laicity principle, which is also grounded in the state's duty to treat all citizens with equal respect. In short, it prohibits the state from taking sides in matters involving the truthfulness and legitimacy of religious views. The government is, thus, forbidden to adhere to religious doctrines and denominations, to foster them, or to show preference or dislike for them or their members. This, moreover, applies to agnosticism, atheism, and any other kind of position in relation to the validity of religions, specifically and as a whole. For more information, *see* Part V, Chapter 3.

Part II. Religious Freedom in General

Chapter 1. Individual Religious Freedom

§1. Constitutional Framework

137. Religious freedom in Brazil is rooted in the Constitution. The constitutional commitment to human dignity (Article 1, III) is reflected in a long list of fundamental rights, which includes: (1) the right to religious freedom – the Constitution provides that 'freedom of conscience and belief if inviolable' and guarantees the free exercise of religion as well as the 'protection of places of worship and their rites' (Article 5, VI); (2) the right to non-discrimination so that no-one can 'be deprived of any rights by reason of religious belief or philosophical or political conviction', unless when applied to refuse compliance with both general duty and an obligation, alternative to the said duty, established by law (Article 5, VIII).

138. Religious freedom is also guaranteed by the laicity principle (*see* Part V, Chapter III, *infra*). This demands that government remains impartial in matters concerning religion; it, therefore, must not take sides in disputes with regards to the validity of competing ideas on religion. It fosters religious freedom because it is based on the respect afforded to the individuals' capacity to decide these matters for themselves. Offence would naturally transpire should the state take a stance in matters of religion, thus conveying the message that certain groups are right whilst others are wrong.

139. Religious freedom is viewed frequently as a special manifestation of the *freedom of conscience*,[256] but it would not be proper to employ here a strict separation between the *forum internum*, of conscience and belief, and the *forum externum*, of exterior actions and practices. Belief and practice are deeply connected.[257] Actions are dictated or, at least, may be informed, by all manners of convictions and opinions, and as such, entitled in accordance to more or less protection. Also, one can usually only be seen as having adhered to certain beliefs because they act upon them or expose them to others. It is, hence, inappropriate to separate religion and

256. Reis, *supra* note 121 at 18; Gilmar Ferreira Mendes & Paulo Gustavo Gonet Branco, *Curso de Direito Constitucional*, 318–319 (14th ed., Saraiva 2019); Ingo Wolfgang Sarlet, Luiz Guilherme Marinoni & Daniel Mitidiero, *Curso de Direito Constitucional*, 530–531 (RT 2019).

257. Jayme Weingartner Neto, *Liberdade Religiosa na Constituição: Fundamentalismo, Pluralismo, Crenças, Cultos*, 115–116 (Livraria do Advogado 2007).

faith from other convictions and opinions. The same individual can hold different points of view, regarding all sorts of matters, involving balances and concessions. It is therefore more appropriate to view all 'freedoms of spirit' – i.e., the freedoms of conscience, thought, religion, speech, and opinion – as being connected under the same cluster-right to *self-determination*.[258] The Federal Supreme Court has decided that individual autonomy and each person's right to fully develop their personality derive directly from the recognition of human dignity.[259]

§2. Freedom of Belief

I. Scope of Protection

140. Freedom of belief protects the individual's right to define their singular orientation in matters of religion. It appropriately includes 'the *freedom to choose* one's religion, the *freedom to adhere* to any religious denomination, the *freedom* (or the *right*) to *change one's religion*' and also 'the *freedom to not adhere to any religion*, as well as the *freedom of disbelief*, the *freedom to be an atheist* and to express agnosticism'.[260] In sum, freedom of belief confers upon people the right to define what is true and valid for themselves in issues involving religion, so to freely join or exit any denomination, or even embrace a new religious path, or transform that which already exists. It protects, in equal standing:

> the affirmation of a specific creed, [as well as] atheism, agnosticism, apostasy, schism, conversion, heresy, and any other stance regarding religion (including the decision not to have an opinion). Protection is granted irrespective of the substance of the relevant belief, how old or deeply rooted [in society] it is, the number of its followers, its greater or lesser degree of institutionalization, or the existence or not of references to a Higher Being, another world, the supernatural, or sacred texts. What is protected, in sum, is personal self-determination – the capacity to decide for oneself – and not the product of said decision.[261]

---

258. Magalhães Pires, *supra* note 105 at 123–128.
259. STF, Full Court, RE 670422/RS, Rapp. Min. Dias Toffoli, *DJ* 10 Mar. 2020 (affirming transsexual people's right to modify their name and gender in their birth certificates on the grounds that individuals have the right to live according to their own views about who they are); STF, Full Court, ADI 5543/DF, Rapp. Min. Edson Fachin, *DJ* 26 Aug. 2020 (unconstitutionality of an ordinance that discriminated against homosexual and bisexual men by considering them a 'risk group' for purposes of donating blood, by stating that 'the principle of human dignity seeks to fully protect the individual as a person living in their own concrete existence', who must not be prevented from being who they are).
260. José Afonso da Silva, *Curso de Direito Constitucional Positivo*, 249 (35th ed., Malheiros 2012). But there are also those who see adherence to atheism as an exercise of freedom of conscience, not of freedom of belief. *See* Weingartner Neto, *supra* note 257 at 114–115.
261. Magalhães Pires, *supra* note 105 at 131–132. *See also* UNHRC General Comment No. 22 (48) (Art. 18), UN Doc. CCPR/C/21/Rev.1/Add.4 (27 Sep. 1993), at para. 2.

141. Since the freedom of belief confers upon individuals the right to freely decide on these matters, it respectively forbids attempts to interfere, coercively, in the person's sphere of autonomy. 'Brainwashing', indoctrination and 'de-programming' techniques, which would forcibly and intentionally try to shape an individual's convictions against their will are therefore inadmissible.[262] The same is true for attempts to coerce people into adhering to a certain religion (or denouncing it) by denying them rights or threatening them with penalties or sanctions.[263] The Constitution clearly provides that 'no one shall be deprived of any rights by reason of religious belief or philosophical or political conviction, unless he invokes it to exempt himself from a legal obligation required of all and refuses to perform an alternative obligation established by law' (Article 5, VIII). It would also be contrary to the laicity principle, as mentioned by Minister Alexandre de Moraes of the Federal Supreme Court:

> Coercion of human beings, so as to force them to renounce their faith or to make them profess a certain belief, amounts to disrespect to the democratic diversity of ideas, philosophies, and to spiritual diversity itself, because the constitutional proclamation of religious freedom is the true consecration of a maturity in the recognition of freedom of thought and the free manifestation of expression, ... guaranteeing the fundamental idea of religious tolerance and the prohibition of an official religion in violation of individual conscience [*foro íntimo*] ... .[264]

II. Limitations

142. It is generally contended that, as part of the *forum internum*, the freedom of belief must not – or even could not – be affected by any category of limitation. This right would be 'inviolable', or 'protected unconditionally', as respectively stated by the Constitution and the United Nations Human Rights Committee (UNRHC).[265] The very idea of indoctrination suggests, however, that it is feasible to interfere with one's belief against their will.

---

262. *Ibid.* at 133–135.
263. *See* International Covenant on Civil and Political Rights (ICCPR), Art. 18(2), and American Convention of Human Rights (ACHR), Art. 12(2). The English text of the ICCPR and the ACHR were obtained, respectively, at https://www.ohchr.org/en/professionalinterest/pages/ccpr.aspx (last visited 3 Jun. 2021) and https://www.cidh.oas.org/basicos/english/basic3.american%20convention.htm (last visited 3 Jun. 2021). *See also* UNHRC General Comment No. 22 (48) (Art. 18), *supra* note at para. 5. Examining a similar situation, the UNHRC decided that a governmental programme of 'ideological conversion' of people convicted on political charges violated Art. 18 of the ICCPR because it induced them to change their political opinions by offering preferential treatment to inmates. *See Yong-Joo Kang v. Republic of Korea*, CCPR/C/78/D/878/1999, UN Human Rights Committee (16 Jul. 2003).
264. STF, Full Court, ADI 4439/DF, Rapp. Min. Alexandre de Moraes, *DJ* 21 Jun. 2018 (opinion of the rapporteur).
265. UNHRC General Comment No. 22 (48) (Art. 18), *supra* note at para. 3.

143. In fact, if indoctrination is an issue, any attempt by the state or anyone else to educate somebody in matters involving, e.g., human rights or the promotion of pluralism, could be viewed as potentially problematic. The same would be true of beliefs that contradict core constitutional values, e.g., democracy and human rights: according to the Federal Constitution, political parties cannot be registered unless they commit to democracy and fundamental rights, for example.[266] At least, in theory, it means that should a party intend to advance the substitution of democracy for a theocracy, its registration could be denied. In this case, the right to organize political parties would be limited due to the beliefs of the pertinent group. It is, therefore, possible to interfere with the freedom of belief, even if not all of these cases of interference amount to the violation of a fundamental right.

144. According to the Federal Supreme Court, fundamental rights can be required to admit limitations to accommodate competing rights and, in some circumstances, public goals.[267] This is recognized by scholars too.[268] Limitations to fundamental rights cannot be rendered trivially, but they can and do occur, subject to conditions. To be constitutional, limitations must: (1) be imposed in accordance with the law; (2) serve to promote other fundamental rights or relevant public goals; and (3) promote other rights or public goals to such an extent that it justifies the degree of limitation imposed on the fundamental right.[269]

145. All of this applies to the freedom of belief. As it is a constitutional imperative to foster a plural political and social environment and to protect individuals from harm, one cannot say that the freedom of belief absolutely forbids the state, e.g., to promote tolerance (and decry intolerance) by imparting this view on people in general or even restricting, to a certain extent, the rights of those who do not adhere to these standards. Granted, no one could be sanctioned merely for holding

---

266. Const. (1988), Art. 17.

267. *See*, e.g., STF, *1ª Turma* [1st Panel], Pet 8824 AgR/DF, Rapp. Min. Luiz Fux, *DJ* 6 Jul. 2020; STF, *2ª Turma* [2nd Panel], HC 93250/MS, Rapp. Min. Ellen Gracie, *DJ* 27 Jun. 2008; STF, Full Court, M. Seg. 23452/RJ, Rapp. Min. Celso de Mello, *DJ* 12 May 2000; STF, Full Court, ADI 2566 MC/DF, Rapp. Min. Sydney Sanches, *DJ* 27 Feb. 2004. The idea that all rights may be limited is a controversial one, contested by legal scholars, who even point to opinions in which the STF itself declared some rights as absolute (*see*, e.g., Virgílio Afonso da Silva, *Direito Constitucional Brasileiro*, 116–118 (2021).

268. *See*, e.g., Ana Paula de Barcellos, *Curso de Direito Constitucional*, 193–195 (2018); Luís Roberto Barroso, *Curso de Direito Constitucional Contemporâneo: os Conceitos Fundamentais e a Construção do Novo Modelo*, 355–365 (4th ed., Saraiva 2013); Mendes and Branco, *supra* note 256 at 192–211; Jane Reis Gonçalves Pereira, *Interpretação Constitucional e Direitos Fundamentais*, 171–256 (2nd ed., Saraiva 2018); Sarlet, Marinoni and Mitidiero, *supra* note 256 at 390–397; Silva, *supra* note 267 at 118–122.

269. *See*, e.g., Humberto Ávila, *Teoria dos Princípios: da Definição à Aplicação dos Princípios Jurídicos*, 152 (5th ed., Malheiros 2006); Barroso, *supra* note 268 at 277; Clèmerson Merlin Clève & Alexandre Reis Siqueira Freire, Algumas Notas sobre Colisão de Direitos Fundamentais, *in Estudos de Direito Constitucional: em Homenagem a José Afonso da Silva* 231, 238 (Eros Roberto Grau & Sérgio Sérvulo da Cunha eds., Malheiros 2003); Mendes and Branco, *supra* note 256 at 197; Pereira, *supra* note 268 at 343; Virgílio Afonso da Silva, *O Proporcional e o Razoável*, 798 Revista dos Tribunais 23 (2006); Sarlet, Marinoni and Mitidiero, *supra* note 256 at 390.

said beliefs, but the very idea that the state may counter a set of principles is clear proof that freedom of belief is not an absolute right.

§3. Freedom of Worship

I. Scope of Protection

146. Article 5, VI, of the Constitution, guarantees freedom of worship. Also, Article 19, I, prohibits all levels of government from hindering the operation of religious groups and denominations.

147. Whilst the Constitution itself does not define 'worship', it is widely regarded as any expression, manifestation, or practice of a belief, either in private or in public.[270] Human rights treaties in force in Brazil clarify that this right encompasses people's 'freedom, either individually or in community with others and in public or private, to manifest his religion or belief in worship, observance, practice and teaching',[271] and also 'to profess or disseminate one's religion or beliefs, either individually or together with others, in public or in private'.[272] The protection is therefore not limited to actual ceremonies or rites; it includes the manifestation of one's beliefs however it may occur. In its substance, this is a 'freedom to live and act according to one's creed'.[273] As stated by the UNRHC:

> The concept of worship extends to ritual and ceremonial acts giving direct expression to belief, as well as various practices integral to such acts, including the building of places of worship, the use of ritual formulae and objects, the display of symbols, and the observance of holidays and days of rest. The observance and practice of religion or belief may include not only ceremonial acts but also such customs as the observance of dietary regulations, the wearing of distinctive clothing or headcoverings, participation in rituals associated with certain stages of life, and the use of a particular language customarily spoken by a group. In addition, the practice and teaching of religion or belief includes acts integral to the conduct by religious groups of their basic affairs, such as, *inter alia*, the freedom to choose their religious leaders, priests and teachers, the freedom to establish seminaries or religious schools and the freedom to prepare and distribute religious texts or publications.[274]

148. The 1981 Declaration on the Elimination of All Forms of Intolerance and of Discrimination Based on Religion or Belief also provides some clarifying remarks in its Article 6 by including 'inter alia, the following freedoms' in the 'right freedom of thought, conscience, religion or belief':

270. Silva, *supra* note 260 at 249; Sarlet, Marinoni and Mitidiero, *supra* note 256 at 533; Magalhães Pires, *supra* note 105 at 145.
271. ICCPR, Art. 18(1).
272. ACHR, Art. 12(1).
273. Magalhães Pires, *supra* note 105 at 145; Weingartner Neto, *supra* note 257 at 121–122.
274. UNHRC General Comment No. 22 (48) (Art. 18), *supra* note at para. 4.

a. To worship or assemble in connection with a religion or belief, and to establish and maintain places for these purposes;
b. To establish and maintain appropriate charitable or humanitarian institutions;
c. To make, acquire and use to an adequate extent the necessary articles and materials related to the rites or customs of a religion or belief;
d. To write, issue and disseminate relevant publications in these areas;
e. To teach a religion or belief in places suitable for these purposes;
f. To solicit and receive voluntary financial and other contributions from individuals and institutions;
g. To train, appoint, elect or designate by succession appropriate leaders called for by the requirements and standards of any religion or belief;
h. To observe days of rest and to celebrate holidays and ceremonies in accordance with the precepts of one's religion or belief;
i. To establish and maintain communications with individuals and communities in matters of religion or belief at the national and international levels.

149. The Federal Supreme Court has decided that freedom of worship includes, e.g., animal sacrifice[275] and proselytism.[276] The Court is also expected to decide on further relevant issues, such as: (1) whether the public healthcare system is required to pay for special, alternative, procedures for patients who refuse blood transfusions because of their religious beliefs;[277] and (2) if a person who wears religious attire can be required to remove it to take photographs for official identity documents.[278]

150. Religious freedom usually requires state abstentions – i.e., from interfering in personal decisions concerning religion – but it is not limited to that. The Constitution also imposes positive duties to the government, rendering it mandatory to act in a certain way to protect the exercise of religious freedom or to cooperate with those who exercise it.

151. The most important provision appears to be Article 5, VI, of the Constitution, which enshrines the freedom of worship and also demands that, under the law, the state protect the 'places of worship and their rites'. As to fulfil the government duty to protect 'places of worship and their rites', the Penal Code criminalizes a number of practices perpetrated against 'religious sentiment' or in disrespect for the dead, such as disruption of burials and violation of graves. For more on this, *see*

275. STF, Full Court, RE 494601/RS, Rapp. Min. Edson Fachin, *DJ* 19 Nov. 2019 (upholding a state law permitting animal sacrifices by African-Brazilian denominations).
276. STF, Full Court, RHC 134682/BA, Rapp. Min. Edson Fachin, *DJ* 29 Aug. 2017; STF, Full Court, ADI 2566/DF, Rapp. Min. Edson Fachin, *DJ* 23 Oct. 2018.
277. STF, Full Court, RE 979742 RG/AM, Rapp. Min. Luís Roberto Barroso, *DJ* 1 Aug. 2017.
278. STF, Full Court, RE 859376 RG/PR, Rapp. Min. Luís Roberto Barroso, *DJ* 1 Aug. 2017.

Part I, Chapter 2, §1, II *supra*. In practice, however, legal protection is clearly insufficient, as the actual destruction of *terreiros*, places of worship of African-Brazilian religions, for example, have swelled alarmingly.[279]

152. In 2003, the State of Rio Grande do Sul enacted a law that aims to protect animals, stipulating it as illegal to harm or improperly kill them. Some African-Brazilian religions, which incorporate animal sacrifice into their rites, began to endure persecution under the 2003 law. To circumvent this, and fully guarantee freedom of worship, the State passed a new statute, in 2004, excluding the rites of African-Brazilian religions from the prohibitions of the previous law. The State Prosecutor General challenged the validity of the 2004 statute before the State Court of Appeals, which, nonetheless, upheld it. The Prosecutors' Office appealed to the Federal Supreme Court, but it eventually affirmed the state court's decision, declaring that 'the practice and rituals related to animal sacrifice are [part of the] intangible cultural heritage', 'the communal dimension of religious freedom is worthy of constitutional protection' and, also, that offering particular guarantees to African-Brazilian religions was 'consistent with the principle of equality, because their stigmatization, resulting from structural prejudice, deserves special attention from the state'.[280]

153. There are, however, other positive actions mandated by the Constitution. The state is required to confer civil effects to religious marriages, subject to the proper legal conditions being met,[281] and to guarantee 'religious assistance in civil and military establishments of collective confinement'.[282] The latter does not imply that the government is supposed to appoint ministers for this, but only that it must permit denominations and ministers to access hospitals, prisons, juvenile detention centres,[283] and military facilities, in order to provide religious assistance to those who are confined within.[284] In the military, however, Law No. 6923 of 29 June 1981 establishes a corps of military chaplains in each of the three Armed Forces (Army,

279. Alba Valéria Mendonça, *Apesar de Criação de Delegacia, Templos de Religiões de Matriz Africana São Atacados até Durante a Pandemia no RJ*, G1, 22 Nov. 2020, https://g1.globo.com/rj/rio-de-janeiro/noticia/2020/11/22/apesar-de-criacao-de-delegacia-templos-de-religioes-de-matriz-africana-sao-atacados-ate-durante-a-pandemia-no-rj.ghtml; Fábio Marton, *Relatos Apontam Proliferação de Ataques às Religiões Afro-Brasileiras*, Folha de S. Paulo, 24 Sep. 2019, https://www1.folha.uol.com.br/ilustrissima/2019/09/relatos-apontam-proliferacao-de-ataques-as-religioes-afro-brasileiras.shtml.

280. STF, Full Court, RE 494601/RS, Rapp. Min. Edson Fachin, *DJ* 19 Nov. 2019.

281. Const. (1988), Art. 226, para. 2; CC, Law No. 10406 of 10 Jan. 2002, Arts 1515–1516.

282. Const. (1988), Art. 5, VII.

283. About the actual service of religious assistance in prisons and juvenile detention centres, especially in Rio de Janeiro, *see Religiões e Prisões* (Ana Maria Quiroga et al. eds., 2005); *Pescadores de Homens: O Perfil da Assistência Religiosa no Sistema Socioeducativo do Rio de Janeiro* (Pedro Simões ed., 2010).

284. Law No. 9982 of 14 Jul. 2000 (religious assistance in hospitals and prisons); Law No. 7210 of 11 Jul. 1984, Art. 24; *Estatuto da Criança e do Adolescente (ECA)* [Statute on the Child and Adolescent], Law No. 8069 of 13 Jul. 1990, Art. 124, XIV.

Navy, and Airforce) to offer religious assistance to their personnel. Whilst questionable that this system is consistent with the Constitution,[285] it does remain in force. According to the STF, military chaplains, being public servants, must be hired following approval in public selection proceedings.[286]

154. The Federal Constitution also prescribes that the 'teaching of religion', though 'optional', 'shall be offered during the regular school hours of public primary schools'.[287] In a somewhat contradictory fashion, the relevant statute recognizes that enrolment in religious teaching classes is optional, but even so, advocates it to be an element of 'the basic formation of the citizen'. The statute requires respect for the country's cultural diversity and, curiously, forbids 'any forms of proselytism'.[288] It is incumbent on the federal, state, and local school systems to decide on the content of religious education and how to accredit and hire teachers, after listening to a civil society entity formed by different religious denominations.[289]

155. Some of these provisions and those similar, being present in the Agreement Between Brazil and the Holy See,[290] were challenged before the Federal Supreme Court by the Prosecutor General of the Republic.[291] It was alleged that religious teaching in public schools could not impart specifically religious content or allow the government to employ representatives of denominations as teachers; it could only describe different doctrines and practices in an impartial manner. The Court, however, upheld the relevant provisions, stating that the constitutional requirement of religious teaching in public schools entitled the students who were willing to take part, to be instructed 'in accordance with the principles of their religious denomination and based in the dogmas of faith', which could not be 'confused with other branches of scientific knowledge, such as history, philosophy or science of religion'. According to the Court, nonetheless, the state must guarantee that enrolment is optional and afford 'absolute respect for agnostics and atheists', being also prohibited from establishing an official content to be taught and from offering preferential treatment to 'Biblical and religious interpretations of one or more groups in detriment of [those of] the others.'[292]

---

285. *See* Leite, *supra* note 109 at 325; Magalhães Pires, *supra* note 105 at 319–325. Upholding the law, at least for times of war or when the military personnel is in places where access to ministers is limited or impossible, *see* TRF – 1, *5ª Turma* [5th Panel], No. 0047405-03.2010.4.01.3400, Rapp. Federal Judge Maria Cecília de Marco Rocha, *DJ* 12 Feb. 2016.
286. STF, Full Court, ADI 6669/MA, Rapp. Min. Nunes Marques, DJ 25 Nov. 2021.
287. Const. (1988), Art. 210, para. 1.
288. Lei de Diretrizes e Bases da Educação Nacional (LDB) [Law on the Guidelines and Bases of National Education], Law No. 9394 of 20 Dec. 1996, Art. 33, *caput*.
289. LDB, Law No. 9394 of 20 Dec. 1996, Art. 33, pars 1 and 2.
290. Brazil-Holy See Agreement, Art. 11, para. 1.
291. The *Procurador-Geral da República*, in Portuguese, is the head of the Prosecutors' Office of the Union, an autonomous institution entrusted with defending the law, democracy, and human rights in general.
292. STF, Full Court, ADI 4439/DF, Rapp. Min. Alexandre de Moraes, *DJ* 21 Jun. 2018. Five of the eleven Justices dissented: Luís Roberto Barroso (original rapporteur), Rosa Weber, Luiz Fux, Marco Aurélio and Celso de Mello.

II. Limitations

156. In Brazil, it is widely recognized that fundamental rights in general can be limited by the state, as long as certain requirements are heeded. *See* Part II, Chapter 1, §2, II *supra*. The same is true for the freedom of worship. International human treaties also clarify that limitations to this right are – in the wording of the International Covenant on Civil and Political Rights (ICCPR) – admissible only when they are 'prescribed by law' and prove to be 'necessary to protect public safety, order, health, or morals', or 'rights and freedoms of others' – more specifically 'fundamental rights and freedoms of others'.[293] The American Convention on Human Rights (ACHR) also states that restrictions placed on any of its rights 'may not be applied except in accordance with laws enacted for reasons of general interest and in accordance with the purpose for which such restrictions have been established'.[294] The word 'laws' here is interpreted by the Inter-American Court of Human Rights as a reference to 'a general legal norm tied to the general welfare, passed by democratically elected legislative bodies established by the Constitution, and formulated according to the procedures set forth by the constitutions of the States Parties for that purpose'.[295] The Court has also decided that 'the general circumstances and conditions that authorize a restriction to the exercise of a specific human right must be clearly established by law', and the latter must be 'a law in the formal and substantial sense'.[296]

157. Additionally, the UN Human Rights Committee has stated that:

> According to article 20, no manifestation of religions or beliefs may amount to propaganda for war or advocacy of national, racial or religious hatred that constitutes incitement to discrimination, hostility or violence. … States parties are under the obligation to enact laws to prohibit such acts.
> … The Committee observes that paragraph 3 of article 18 is to be strictly interpreted: restrictions are not allowed on grounds not specified [in Article 18 (3) of the ICCPR], even if they would be allowed as restrictions to other rights protected in the Covenant, such as national security. Limitations may be applied only for those purposes for which they were prescribed and must be directly related and proportionate to the specific need on which they are predicated. Restrictions may not be imposed for discriminatory purposes or applied

293. ICCPR, Art. 18(3); ACHR, Art. 12(3).
294. ACHR, Art. 30.
295. *The Word 'Laws' in Article 30 of the American Convention on Human Rights*, Advisory Opinion OC-6/86, Inter-Am. Ct HR (ser. A) No. 6 (9 May 1986).
296. *Castañeda Gutman v. Mexico*, Preliminary Objections, Merits, Reparations and Costs, Judgment, Inter-Am. Ct HR (ser. C) No. 184, para. 176 (6 Aug. 2008).

in a discriminatory manner. The Committee observes that the concept of morals derives from many social, philosophical and religious traditions; consequently, limitations on the freedom to manifest a religion or belief for the purpose of protecting morals must be based on principles not deriving exclusively from a single tradition.[297]

158. International human rights treaties permit restrictions on freedom of religion when the rights of *others* are deemed at risk,[298] which serves to prevent paternalism. As such, one subject attracting notable controversy is that of restricting a person's religious freedom in order to promote or to protect other rights of that same individual. The textbook examples herein involve situations in which a person's life or health is at risk yet their belief system forbids a certain treatment that could save them. This is the case with Jehovah's Witnesses, who refuse blood transfusions due to creed. These are extreme situations because the respect for a person's religion and autonomy appears to hinder preventing their death.

159. The issue was confronted in Rio de Janeiro: a public hospital sought counselling from the State Attorneys' Office as to the proper course of action in situations such as this. The case divided opinions within the Office itself: state attorney Gustavo Binenbojm defended the patient's right to refuse treatment, but his opinion was rejected by the head of the section, Flávio de Araújo Willeman, who championed life above freedom of religion. The Attorney General then submitted the matter to then state attorney Luís Roberto Barroso – later appointed to the Federal Supreme Court – who opined that the patient had the right to decide whether or not to submit to the procedure.[299] His opinion was approved by the Attorney General. The courts, however, apparently remain divided on the matter but tend to set aside the patient's decision when their life is at stake.[300]

---

297. UNHRC General Comment No. 22 (48) (Art. 18), *supra* note at pars 7–8. The Committee cite Art. 20 of the ICCPR, which reads: '1. Any propaganda for war shall be prohibited by law. 2. Any advocacy of national, racial or religious hatred that constitutes incitement to discrimination, hostility or violence shall be prohibited by law.' The ACHR has a similar provision (Art. 13(5)): 'Any propaganda for war and any advocacy of national, racial, or religious hatred that constitute incitements to lawless violence or to any other similar action against any person or group of persons on any grounds including those of race, colour, religion, language, or national origin shall be considered as offenses punishable by law.'

298. ICCPR, Art. 18(3); ACHR, Art. 12(3).

299. Gustavo Binenbojm, *Autonomia Privada e Direito à Recusa de Tratamentos Médicos Invasivos: o Caso das Testemunhas de Jeová*, 5 Revista de Direito do Estado 475 (2010); Flávio de Araújo Willeman, *Recusa de Tratamento da Saúde com Fundamento em Crença Religiosa e o Dever do Estado de Proteger a Vida Humana. O Caso da Transfusão de Sangue em Testemunha de Jeová*, 5 Revista de Direito do Estado 483 (2010); Luís Roberto Barroso, *Legitimidade da Recusa de Transfusão de Sangue por Testemunhas de Jeová. Dignidade Humana, Liberdade Religiosa e Escolhas Existenciais*, 5 Revista de Direito do Estado 507 (2010).

300. *See* e.g., TJRS, *12ª Câmara Cível* [12th Civil Panel], AI 70032799041, Rapp. CAJ Cláudio Baldino Maciel, *DJ* 4 Aug. 2010 (reversing a lower court injunction which had allowed for a transfusion against the patient's will); TJMG, *7ª Câmara Cível* [7th Civil Panel], Ap. 5669883-73.2009.8.13.0024, Rapp. CAJ Wilson Benevides (denying reparation to an adult Jehova's Witness, who was submitted to a transfusion against her will because it was necessary to save her life); TJDFT, *6ª Turma Cível* [6th Civil Panel], Ap. 0712619-82.2019.8.07.0001, Rapp. CAJ Vera Andrighi, *DJ* 3 Jun. 2020 ('the right to life prevails over freedom of religion because the right to life

§4. Children and Freedom of Religion

160. Families are protected under the Federal Constitution. Departing from the previous model of male precedence,[301] it clearly states the rights and duties related to the family are to be exercised on an equal basis by both spouses (but a community formed by either parent and their offspring is also recognized as a family, and protected as such).[302] Constitutional protection is not dependent on a marriage – common-law marriages have a very similar status to that of formal marriages[303] – and this extends to same-sex couples.[304] The Constitution also demands that equal rights be granted to one's children, irrespective of whether they are biological or adopted, born in or out of wedlock.[305]

161. The family's role is one of prominence, but not of exclusive rights, in relation to progeny; children are not the property of their parents. They are under physical custody so the latter must always have the best interests of the child in mind when deciding on their behalf. In order to ensure that children's rights are guaranteed, the Federal Constitution relies not only on their families, but also on 'society and the State', requiring all of them to protect children 'from all forms of negligence, discrimination, exploitation, violence, cruelty, and oppression'.[306] It is also incumbent on the state to provide assistance to each family member, by 'creating mechanisms to suppress violence within the family'.[307] All of this is reinforced by provisions of the Civil Code regarding Family Law, as well as by the *Estatuto da Criança e do Adolescente (ECA)* [Child and Adolescent Act], Law No. 8069 of 13 July 1990 (ECA).

162. Family's duty may be conferred upon a 'substitute family', i.e., people other than a child's biological parents, who are entrusted with caring for the health,

---

is the greatest premise to the exercise of any other right … '); TJSP, *3ª Câmara de Direito Público* [3rd Public Law Panel], Ap. 1003243-34.2018.8.26.0347, Rapp. CAJ Marrey Uint, *DJ* 9 Mar. 2020 ('A religious conviction cannot prevail over life … ').

301. Until the current Civil Code came into force in 2003, the husband was the 'head of the conjugal society', a role he was expected to perform with 'the wife's cooperation, in the common interest of the couple and the children'. *See Código Civil* [Civil Code], Law No. 3071 of 1 Jan. 1916, Art. 233, as amended by Law No. 4121 of 27 Aug. 1962, Art. 1.
302. Const. (1988), Art. 226, *caput* and pars 4–5.
303. STF, Full Court, RE 878694/MG, Rapp. Min. Luís Roberto Barroso, *DJ* 6 Feb. 2018 (striking down a provision of the Civil Code which, for inheritance purposes, prescribed a different, worse, treatment for civil partners in comparison to that of spouses). The Court stated that this includes same-sex couples too (*see* STF, Full Court, RE 646721/RS, Rapp. Min. Luís Roberto Barroso, *DJ* 11 Sep. 2017).
304. The Federal Supreme Court recognized same-sex civil partnerships in 2011 (*see* STF, Full Court, ADI 4277/DF and ADPF 132/RJ, Rapp. Min. Carlos Ayres Britto, *DJ* 14 Oct. 2011). A few months later, the Superior Court of Justice followed suit, recognizing also marriages between same-sex couples (*see* STJ, *4ª Turma* [4th Panel], REsp 1183378/RS, Rapp. Min. Luis Felipe Salomão).
305. Const. (1988), Art. 227, para. 6.
306. Const. (1988), Art. 227, *caput*, as amended by CA No. 65 of 13 Jul. 2010, Art. 2.
307. Const. (1988), Art. 227, para. 8.

safety, education, and general upbringing of the child.[308] Brazilian case law has also recognized the effects of 'socio-affective parenthood', the situation in which a relationship between the parties nurtures from actual bonds of affection, irrespective of biological or formal circumstances.[309] According to the Federal Supreme Court, it is even plausible to recognize simultaneously socio-affective and biological parents.[310]

163. The Constitution does not specifically address the religious freedom of children, but Article 227 generally refers to their 'dignity' and 'liberty', which obviously include fundamental rights in general terms. Be that as it may, it is undeniable that, like any other people, children are entitled to the protection afforded by Article 5, VI, VII, and VIII. Also, the ECA clearly provides that respect accorded to children and adolescents' 'liberty' includes their freedoms of belief and religious worship,[311] and requires youth detention centres to provide them religious assistance.[312] It also stresses the parents' (or guardians') equal right to impart their beliefs and cultures within the family, as long as the rights of the child are respected.[313]

164. More specific provisions on this subject are set forth by the United Nations Convention on the Rights of the Child (CRC), which is supra-statutory law in Brazil (i.e., inferior to the Constitution but higher than statutory law).[314] In Article 14, the Convention provides:

1. States Parties shall respect the right of the child to freedom of thought, conscience and religion.
2. States Parties shall respect the rights and duties of the parents and, when applicable, legal guardians, to provide direction to the child in the exercise of his or her right in a manner consistent with the evolving capacities of the child.
3. Freedom to manifest one's religion or beliefs may be subject only to such limitations as are prescribed by law and are necessary to protect public safety, order, health or morals, or the fundamental rights and freedoms of others.

---

308. For the sake of simplicity, the terms 'guardian' and 'legal guardian' will be used here to refer to these individuals.
309. *See*, e.g., STJ, *3ª Turma* [3rd Panel], REsp 1500999/RJ, Rapp. Min. Ricardo Villas Bôas Cueva, *DJ* 19 Apr. 2016 ('Socio-affective parenthood materializes the very dignity of the human person by allowing an individual to have their life history and their social condition considered, recognizing, beyond formal aspects … the real factual truth'); STJ, *3ª Turma* [3rd Panel], REsp 1448969/SC, Rapp. Min. Moura Ribeiro, *DJ* 3 Nov. 2014 (setting aside a prohibition on the adoption of children by their grandparents in a case in which the child's mother had been adopted by the plaintiffs when she was pregnant, considering that her parents had always exercised socio-affective parenthood of her child).
310. STF, Full Court, RE 898060/SC, Rapp. Min. Luiz Fux, *DJ* 24 Aug. 2017.
311. ECA, Law No. 8069 of 13 Jul. 1990, Art. 16, III.
312. ECA, Law No. 8069 of 13 Jul. 1990, Art. 124, XIV.
313. ECA, Law No. 8069 of 13 Jul. 1990, Art. 22, sole par.
314. GA Res. 44/25, UN Doc. A/RES/44/25 (20 Nov. 1989); Leg. Dec. No. 28 of 14 Sep. 1990; Dec. No. 99710 of 21 Nov. 1990. All excerpts of the English text of the CRC were obtained at https://www.ohchr.org/en/professionalinterest/pages/crc.aspx (last visited 3 Jun. 2021).

165. The supreme concept is that of the 'best interest of the child', which, under the CRC, is supposed to be 'a primary consideration' for 'all actions concerning children, whether undertaken by public or private social welfare institutions, courts of law, administrative authorities or legislative bodies'.[315] The same requirement is derived from Article 227 of the Brazilian Constitution.[316] The notion of 'best interest of the child' underscores children's inherent human dignity, underlining that they are not (and cannot be seen as) the property of either their parents or guardians or of the state. Children are not under an absolute rule by either their family or the government. Whomever it falls upon to decide on issues involving a child's life must, as requisite, act solely in accordance with the best interests of the child. Of course, one must always place due regard to 'the evolving capacities of the child', as required by the Convention, so that older children and adolescents may partake in greater latitude when defining their personal goals and preferences.

166. In Brazilian case law, conflicts usually involve the protection of a child's well-being against possible risks resulting from religiously motivated acts of a parent. Courts in general do not defer to parental decision in matters involving, e.g., vaccination. A child's immunization is considered synonymous with their best interest, as well as providing an important step towards the eradication of diseases, as a benefit to society as a whole.[317] In Santa Catarina, the Court of Appeals stated that it did not reflect as 'constitutionally proper that parental religious doctrine can be invoked on behalf of a child who does not yet possess the capacity to exercise said freedom … . How can it be legitimate to impose this burden (that of a possible harm to [the child's] well-being) if it is still impossible for [the child] to express their religious choice?' According to the Court, allowing for their parents' refusal would amount to subordinating the child to the consequences of their parents' personal religious decisions.[318]

167. The matter is not confined to issues of vaccination. The State Court of Appeals of São Paulo upheld a fine imposed on a mother for having published an online video in which she and her child appeared inhaling snuff, this whilst the mother's partner instructed viewers as to how to partake. In her appeal, the mother alleged to be a victim of religious intolerance because the intake of the substance was in the context of a shamanic ceremony. According to the Court, despite its relevance, the mother's right to religious freedom did not permit her to impose risks to her child's well-being or to publicly broadcast this situation, which was deemed tantamount to parental negligence.[319]

---

315. CRC, Art. 3(1).
316. *See* e.g., STJ, *3ª Turma* [3rd Panel], AgInt no REsp 1808964/SP, Rapp. Min. Moura Ribeiro, *DJ* 11 Mar. 2020.
317. *See* e.g., TJMG, *4ª Câmara Cível* [4th Civil Panel], Ap. 1.0518.18.007692-0/01, Rapp. CAJ Dárcio Lopardi Mendes, *DJ* 17 Dec. 2019; TJRS, *7ª Câmara Cível* [7th Civil Panel], AI 70084496934, Rapp. CAJ Carlos Eduardo Zietlow Duro, *DJ* 30 Oct. 2020.
318. TJSC, *1ª Câmara de Direito Civil* [1st Civil Law Panel], Ap. 2011.089551-3, Rapp. CAJ Carlos Prudêncio, *DJ* 29 May 2020.
319. TJSP, *Câmara Especial* [Special Panel], Ap. 1016664-33.2018.8.26.0625, Rapp. CAJ Lidia Conceição, *DJ* 10 Dec. 2019.

168. A common scenario appears to be that of the refusal of medical procedures due to religious beliefs. Courts tend not to defer to parental decisions in these situations, stating that the well-being of a child – who cannot make their own choices – trumps their parents' religious beliefs. The Jehovah's Witness refusal to receive blood transfusions is frequently set aside when such refusal is expressed by parents or legal guardians on behalf of a child.[320] An interesting case involved a 17-year-old patient, who sided with his mother in refusing treatment. As the age of majority in Brazilian law is eighteen, his refusal could almost be considered that of an adult. The procedure, however, was authorized against his will, in an interim order which was upheld by a Judge in the State Court of Appeals of Santa Catarina. According to the Judge, notwithstanding the respect accorded to the family's religion and the patient's obvious maturity, he still lacked full civil capacity and, therefore, one should honour his best interest and the protection of life. Nevertheless, blood transfusion should only be employed as a last resort, in a situation where the patient's life is at risk.[321] Even when the life of the child is not at risk, courts tend to act so to protect their well-being. For example, a mother was mandated to administer medicine to treat her child's autism, as prescribed by a doctor, despite claiming to have had 'visions from God' in support of not doing so.[322]

169. There may be matters of a criminal nature, as illustrated by a case that went all the way to the STJ. It involved a 13-year-old girl, who had died in a hospital after her parents refused to consent to her receiving a blood transfusion, due to their religious beliefs. They were criminally charged for the alleged murder of their daughter, and the proceedings commenced in the state courts. The Superior Court, however, in a tied vote, granted a writ of habeas corpus to dismiss the charges against the parents. It underscored that the girl's right to life and her 'higher interests' outweighed the protection owed to parental religious belief. Nonetheless, having taken their child to the hospital, in a clear display of their concern for her health, the parents could not be accused of having committed their daughter's murder. The Court also noted that any penalty would be an excess, given that they had already suffered for their child's death and been submitted to a lengthy criminal proceeding. According to the Court, if anyone failed their duties it was the doctors and the hospital, who should have acted more forthright in attempting to save the girl's life, regardless of parental objection to the treatment.[323]

---

320. *See* e.g., Sorocaba/SP, *Vara da Infância e Juventude* [Children and Juvenile Court of First Instance], Proc. 1045451-44.2018.8.26.0602, *DJ* 1 Jul. 2019; Paulo Afonso/BA, *2ª Vara dos Feitos Cíveis* [2nd Civil Court of First Instance], Proc. 8002647-30.2017.8.05.0191, *DJ* 4 Feb. 2019; Americana/SP, *3ª Vara Cível* [3rd Civil Court of First Instance], Proc. 1012306-97.2018.8.26.0019, *DJ* 21 Nov. 2018.
321. TJSC, *Câmara Civil Especial* [Special Civil Panel], AI 4017005-65.2016.8.24.0000, Rapp. CAJ Luiz Zanelato, *DJ* 10 Dec. 2016 (in chambers). A few months later, the appeal was dismissed because the patient was discharged from the hospital, and blood transfusion was deemed unnecessary (*DJ* 4 Mar. 2017).
322. TJSP, *6ª Câmara de Direito Privado* [6th Private Law Panel], Ap. 0015879-15.2011.8.26.0664, Rapp. CAJ Claudia Grieco Tabosa Pessoa, *DJ* 25 Oct. 2012.
323. STJ, *6ª Turma* [6th Panel], HC 268459/SP, Rapp. Min. Maria Thereza de Assis Moura, *DJ* 28 Oct. 2014. Min. Sebastião Reis Júnior joined the rapporteur in granting the writ, whereas Min. Rogerio Schietti Cruz filed a dissenting opinion, in which he was joined by CAJ Marilza Maynard, who

170. Situations such as this, however, bear ramifications extending beyond actual procedure. A case was brought before the State Court of Appeals of São Paulo where the child of a Jehovah's Witness, having been submitted to a blood transfusion under a court order, against her mother's will, alleged that the religious organization had convinced their community to exclude both mother and daughter from associating with members of the church. The Court refused to interfere because the exclusion of member association would amount to a doctrinal matter, solely under the organization's right to freedom of religion.[324] Regardless of the Court decision, the case demonstrates that the previous judicial finding, inspired as it was to safeguard the rights of the child, culminated profoundly in the lives of both the girl and her mother, who were ostracized by their community.

171. Education presents another important topic. Many international treaties stress the parent's or guardian's right to ensure that their children or wards receive education in accordance with their personal convictions.[325] Notably, the International Covenant on Economic, Social and Cultural Rights (ICESCR) also highlights that said right includes choosing 'schools, other than those established by the public authorities' (Article 13(3)). In Brazil, the Constitution expressly guarantees both the existence of private schools (including denominational ones)[326] and the offer of non-mandatory religious classes in public schools,[327] allowing sufficient room for parents and guardians to decide. For further information, *see* Part IX *infra*.

§5. Conscientious Objection

172. The Constitution guarantees a right to conscientious objection by providing that 'no one shall be deprived of any rights by reason of religious belief or philosophical or political conviction unless he invokes it to exempt himself from a legal obligation required of all and refuses to perform an alternative obligation established by law'.[328] This refusal may lead to the suspension of political rights, since 'refusal to comply with an obligation imposed upon everyone or to render an alternative service, according to Article 5, item VIII', allows for the disfranchisement of the individual.[329] However, an objector can only be punished for non-compliance of

---

was summoned to sit temporarily in the Court. Since the Rules of the Court provide that tie votes in habeas corpus proceedings are decided in favour of the defendant (RISTJ, Art. 181, para. 4), the writ was issued.

324. TJSP, *10ª Câmara de Direito Privado* [10th Private Law Panel], Ap. 0000460-26.2012.8.26.0629, Rapp. CAJ Elcio Trujillo, *DJ* 19 Nov. 2014.
325. ICCPR, Art. 18(4); International Covenant on Economic, Social and Cultural Rights (ICESCR), Art. 13(3); ACHR, Art. 12(4); The English text of the ICESCR was obtained at https://www.ohchr.org/en/professionalinterest/pages/cescr.aspx (last visited 8 Jun. 2021).
326. Const. (1988), Arts 206, III, and 203.
327. Const. (1988), Art. 201, para. 1.
328. Const. (1988), Art. 5, VIII.
329. Const. (1988), Art. 15, IV.

duty if: (1) said duty is 'required of all' and established by law;[330] (2) the law provides for an alternative service; (3) the latter does not contravene the objector's conscience; and (4) the person fails to comply with the alternative obligation without reasonable justification.[331]

173. In an interesting opinion, the Federal Supreme Court decided that public servants could not be denied confirmation in their position just for a need to be absent on Fridays nights, in order to observe religious tenets. They could only bear consequences should an alternative service be offered which they subsequently declined to perform. Public entities are, as such, permitted to set alternative workplace requirements for servants and employees who claim that their religious obligations prevent them from undertaking the general directives, as long as: (1) the alternative rules are reasonable; (2) they do not deviate from the public servant's designated list of duties; (3) they do not create an unreasonable burden on the public entity, which must provide a reasoned decision on the matter.[332] The Court also ruled that the state can schedule examinations on different dates and times, in public selection proceedings, in order to accommodate candidates who, because of their beliefs, cannot participate on the scheduled date and time, if the modification: (1) is reasonable; (2) does not create unequal opportunities for some candidates; and (3) does not create an unreasonable burden on the public entity, which must provide a reasoned decision on the issue.[333] This was an important decision, since, prior to it, there were court rulings against claims such as this.[334]

174. Conscientious objection is particularly relevant regarding mandatory military service, since all men in Brazil – except religious ministers – are required to enlist in one of the Armed Forces at the age of 18.[335] The Constitution specifically provides, however, that the military, under the law, can assign 'an alternative service to those who, in times of peace, after being enlisted, claim imperative of conscience, which shall be understood as originating in religious creed and philosophical or political belief, for exemption from essentially military activities'.[336] According to the law, this alternative service shall consist of administrative,

330. Thiago Magalhães Pires, Notas Sobre a Objeção de Consciência, *in O Direito Público por Elas: Homenagem à Professora Jane Reis* 345, 349 (2018); Sarlet, Marinoni and Mitidiero, *supra* note 256 at 780; Silva, *supra* note 260 at 242.

331. Magalhães Pires, *supra* note 330 at 349; Mendes and Branco, *supra* note 256 at 826; Sarlet, Marinoni and Mitidiero, *supra* note 256 at 780; Silva, *supra* note 260 at 383–384; Silva, *supra* note 267 at 190.

332. STF, Full Court, ARE 1099099/SP, Rapp. Min. Edson Fachin, *DJ* 12 Apr. 2021.

333. STF, Full Court, RE 611874/DF, Rapp. Min. Edson Fachin, *DJ* 12 Apr. 2021. It should be noted that prior to this decision, the National Council of Justice had already upheld an act of the State Court of Appeals of Rio de Janeiro which recommended that judges should postpone hearings and trials scheduled to the Jewish holiday of Yom Kippur. *See* CNJ, PCA 0004536-35.2010.2.00.0000, Rapp. Councilmember Ives Gandra, *DJ* 25 Nov. 2010.

334. *See*, e.g., STJ, *2ª Turma* [2nd Panel], RMS 54042/CE, Rapp. Min. Herman Benjamin, *DJ* 13 Sep. 2017. In the case, however, the Court sided with the plaintiff, but only because a state statute required that public selection proceedings could only be held on Sundays or weekdays, from 8 a.m. to 6 p.m., so that it was illegal to have them on Saturdays.

335. Const. (1988), Art. 143, *caput* and para. 2.

336. Const. (1988), Art. 143, para. 1.

social, philanthropic, or productive activities – including training for acting in situations of disaster, emergency, or calamity – in military organizations or, if there is prior agreement, in civil governmental departments.[337]

175. Federal law requires schools and universities to offer students alternative exams and activities should they be unable to attend designated scheduled events due to their religion or conscience beliefs.[338]

176. Some states also have laws regarding conscientious objection. That is the case in Rio de Janeiro and São Paulo, for example.[339] Seeing that the State Court of São Paulo had not enforced the state law in a suit filed by a student, the STJ reversed its decision to order a tertiary education institution to provide alternative activities and examinations when mainstream events were scheduled on Friday nights.[340]

337. Law No. 8239 of 4 Oct. 1991, Art. 3.
338. LDB, Law No. 9394 of 20 Dec. 1996, Art. 7-A (included by Law No. 13796 of 3 Jan. 2019).
339. RJ, Law No. 6998 of 8 May 2015; SP, Law No. 17346 of 12 Mar. 2021, Arts 17–21. The law of Rio de Janeiro, however, was declared unconstitutional by the State Court of Appeals (*see* TJRJ, *Órgão Especial* [Special Panel], ADI 0057920-68.2016.8.19.0000, Rapp. CAJ Rogerio de Oliveira Souza, *DJ* 17 Sep. 2019).
340. STJ, *1ª Turma* [1st Panel], RMS 37070/SP, Rapp. Min. Benedito Gonçalves, *DJ* 10 Mar. 2014.

Chapter 2. Collective Religious Freedom

§1. Freedom of Worship and the Collective Dimension

177. The Federal Constitution protects religious freedom in a benevolent manner, and it is consensual that the collective exercise of the right to worship is a component.[341] Human rights treaties also recognize the collective dimension of freedom of religion.[342] It may or may not involve the actual incorporation of a legal entity for religious purposes – either way, their members are under constitutional protection – and it can even manifest in the transitory manner of parades, demonstrations, processions, and similar events. That is, the collective dimension of religious freedom can interconnect with both the freedom of association and the freedom of assembly, which are also protected under the Constitution.

§2. Freedom of Association

178. In Brazilian law, religious freedom comprises a collective dimension, known as *freedom of religious organization.* It results from 'a confluence between the freedom of religion and the associative freedoms in general' so that the prerogatives conferred by the right of association are attributed to the entities devoted to religious purposes, as well as to those who create the entity and its members.[343]

179. The Constitution details freedom of association in clauses XVII–XXI of Article 5. In sum, they safeguard the right of people to gather and organize voluntarily, in a stable group, so as to achieve common goals. This entails, e.g., the rights to create (and dissolve) a group (without paramilitary character); to enter into (or leave) existing associations; to admit (and expel) members; to freely organize and operate the group; and to incorporate as a legal entity, provided that reasonable conditions set forth by the law are met.[344] The joint interpretation of the relevant provisions of the Constitution segues to a right to religious organization which includes:

> (i) the right to freely incorporate entities with religious purposes, providing they do not have a paramilitary nature; (ii) the lack of previous authorization required for its creation, with a prohibition of State interference in its operation; (iii) the exclusive power of the judiciary to suspend the associations' activities or to dissolve the entity … (iv) the individual freedom to, at any

---

341. Magalhães Pires, *supra* note 105 at 160–161; Aloisio Cristovam Santos Junior, *A Liberdade de Organização Religiosa e o Estado Laico Brasileiro*, 84 (2007); Silva, *supra* note 260 at 248–250; Weingartner Neto, *supra* note 257 at 122–125.
342. *See* ICCPR, Art. 18(1); ACHR, Art. 12(1).
343. Magalhães Pires, *supra* note 105 at 162.
344. Mendes and Branco, *supra* note 256 at 310; Sarlet, Marinoni and Mitidiero, *supra* note 257 at 584; Silva, *supra* note 260 at 266–268.

moment, enter and remain in any organization, or depart from it; (v) the entities' right to represent their members before courts or extra-judicially, as long as authorized to do so.[345]

180. Freedom of association does not presuppose any particular legal form or even incorporation; 'it protects any kind of association that is stable and has a definite purpose', although the statutory regulation of specific forms of legal entities (e.g., civil associations and business companies) is a means of materializing the constitutional protection.[346] The same is then true of religious communities, which are not required to be incorporated or to possess any formal recognition to be protected under the Constitution. Denominations are commonly incorporated in the form of *religious organizations*, however, individuals can also establish *associations*, *foundations*, and even *business companies*, with a religious purpose or connection. For more on this, *see* Part III, Chapter 1, §1 *infra*.

181. Freedom of religious organization was historically under threat when minorities were involved. Spiritist and African-Brazilian groups struggled to maintain their rights under the state. In the 1940s, the police in Rio de Janeiro (which was then the Federal District) suspended the operation of their centres and required that they apply for a registration with the police department. The Kardecists were eventually successful in lifting these demands, but repression of African-Brazilian religions remained. It took decades for their proper recognition as legitimate religions.[347]

182. In 1949, the Federal Supreme Court examined a case involving dissidence from the Roman Catholic Church, which had led to the creation of the Brazilian Catholic Apostolic Church. Claiming that the latter had violated the freedom of worship of the former, a federal security department ordered the Brazilian Church to refrain from holding public outdoor services because it infringed on the Roman Catholic religious freedom by adhering to similar habits, symbols, and rites. The Brazilian Church and its founder challenged the order before the Federal Supreme Court, but it ruled against them. The Court majority ruled that the Brazilian Church had had its freedom of worship legitimately curtailed in order to protect the exercise of the same right by the Roman Church and to safeguard the public order against the confusion that the similar rites could create in the public. Minister Hahnemann Guimarães filed the only dissenting opinion, in which he declared that the issue was of a religious nature, and churches could not request the help of government authorities to settle schisms and dissidence.[348] Pontes de Miranda, a prestigious Brazilian scholar, qualified the majority opinion as 'medieval', claiming that

345. Magalhães Pires, *supra* note 105 at 162.
346. Silva, *supra* note 267 at 199. *See also* Mendes and Branco, *supra* note 256 at 311.
347. *See* General Introduction, §3, IV *supra*.
348. STF, Full Court, M. Seg. 1114/DF, Rapp. Min. Lafayette de Andrada, *DJ* 26 Jan. 1950. For commentary, *see* Leite, *supra* note 109 at 230–237; Weingartner Neto, *supra* note 257 at 123–124.

'Luther, had he resuscitated and requested a writ of mandamus, would not have had it granted. For the judges, Roger Williams did not exist'.[349]

183. In 1968, however, the Court ruled in favour of an Evangelical church which had been forbidden by the police to operate because two of its ministers had been accused of exploiting the people by offering religious healing. Despite declaring that the police was within its power to protect public order, the Court ruled that the religious activities of the church could not be hindered by the state. This outcome permitted the denomination's operation, 'as long as it did not infringe upon public order and *bons costumes* [morality]'.[350]

§3. Freedom of Assembly

184. Under Article 5, XVI, of the Constitution, everyone is entitled to join others in transient, peaceful, and unarmed, gatherings in public places, regardless of governmental authorization, as long as authorities are notified and meetings previously scheduled for the same location go unhindered. According to the Federal Supreme Court, the notification of the state is only required to guarantee that the assembly occurs in a peaceful manner and to prevent it from obstructing another gathering. Any effective notice to the government is sufficient and, hence, spontaneous gatherings cannot be rendered *ipso facto* illegal for the absence of notification.[351] The importance of freedom of assembly has been recognized in numerous other cases by the Court,[352] where it has stressed that it even protects the advocacy of legalizing activities currently defined as crimes.[353]

185. Streets and other public locations can be used for popular displays of religion, such as parades and processions,[354] and for advocating on behalf of religiously motivated values and policies. But all said, constitutional limitations must be respected. In 2013, the World Youth Day – a Roman Catholic event – was held in Rio de Janeiro, in the presence of Pope Francis and many public gatherings, which included a mass at Copacabana Beach. After a military officer, responsible for the security of the event, declared that they would not admit disruptive actors, a group of atheists, who intended to engage in peaceful protests, sought a writ of habeas corpus to prevent the military from hindering their assembly. The judge denied the order, among other reasons, because freedom of religion is as protected

349. Pontes de Miranda, *Comentários à Constituição de 1967: com a Emenda n. 1, de 1969* vol. 5, 125 (1967).
350. STF, *3ª Turma* [3rd Panel], RMS 16857/MG, Rapp. Min. Eloy da Rocha, *DJ* 24 Oct. 1969.
351. STF, Full Court, RE 806339/SE, Rapp. Min. Edson Fachin, *DJ* 19 Mar. 2021.
352. *See*, e.g., STF, Full Court, ADI 5852/MS, Rapp. Min. Luiz Fux, *DJ* 26 Nov. 2020; STF, *DJ* 1969/DF, Rapp. Min. Ricardo Lewandowski, *DJ* 31 Aug. 2007.
353. STF, Full Court, ADPF 187/DF, Rapp. Min. Celso de Mello, *DJ* 29 May 2014.
354. Mendes and Branco, *supra* note 256 at 323.

by the Constitution as freedom of assembly, and the Catholic event was a previously scheduled meeting and should not be subjected to disruption by a second assembly.[355]

§4. Impartiality of the State in Matters Involving Religion

186. The laicity principle requires that the state remain impartial in issues of religion. In sum, it means that: (1) government must remain 'organically differentiated' from religious denominations, so that the former and the latter cannot be a part of, control, or be controlled by, one another; (2) the state cannot identify with an orientation in matters of religion, a particular creed, or a group of religions; and (3) the government can neither favour nor disfavour any particular any denomination or set of denominations, atheism or agnosticism.[356] This arrangement protects the independence of the religious groups vis-à-vis the government and vice-versa.

187. The impartiality of the state does not demand a strict separation from religious organizations. Government cannot support, promote, or subsidize religious views and denominations, but the former and the latter can cooperate towards goals of public interest (e.g., education, healthcare, social assistance).[357] In any case, government regulation of matters relevant to religious groups must treat all equally, as a corollary to the equal treatment to which their members are entitled as citizens and human beings.[358]

§5. Autonomy of Religious Organizations

188. The autonomy of religious organizations is rooted in the Constitution: Article 5, VI, guarantees freedom of belief and worship, as well as the protection of rites and places of service, whilst Article 5, XXVII–XXI, provide for freedom of association in broad terms. Also, Article 19, I, expressly forbids all levels of government from hindering the operation of religious organizations. This results in autonomy regarding:[359]

(1) *Creation:* people are free to create religious groups, in the form and manner they prefer, as well as to incorporate (or not) a legal entity for this purpose.

355. Rio de Janeiro/RJ, *5ª Vara Federal Criminal* [5th Federal Criminal Court of First Instance], Proc. 0490290-70.2013.4.02.5101, 23 Jul. 2013.
356. Magalhães Pires, *supra* note 105 at 253–270.
357. Const. (1988), Art. 19, I.
358. Santos Junior, *supra* note 341 at 79–80.
359. This list is based, with a few adaptations, on *ibid.* at 89–159.

(2) *Self-Regulation:* religious organizations are free to adopt bylaws regulating: (a) member admission and expulsion procedures and conditions; (b) the powers and responsibilities of their internal bodies; (c) the form in which they are to be governed internally; (d) the manner, time, and amount of contributions owed by the members.[360]
(3) *Internal Structuring:* religious organizations are free to establish the bodies and departments which are entrusted with performing their activities and purposes.
(4) *Operation:* religious organizations are free to organize and hold events, acts of worship, teaching, services, marriages, as well as to acquire and dispose of property, enter into contracts, and perform generally all other acts a legal entity is required or permitted to undertake.

§6. Collective Dimension of Individual Freedoms

189. It is widely accepted in Brazil that legal entities are also entitled to multiple fundamental rights, such as the rights to property and due process of law. Some rights, however, presuppose capabilities which are inherently human and, therefore, cannot be associated with legal entities. One of these is freedom of belief since abstract entities cannot be said to possess an autonomous conscience, separate from that of their managers and members.[361] Legal entities, therefore, are entitled to rights which are compatible with their 'peculiar nature'.[362] Additionally, their entitlement to a fundamental right depends on its connection with the entity's purposes:[363] since the entity is created by people in pursuance of certain objectives, it can be applied as an instrument for people to exercise their own fundamental rights – and, to that extent, the entity itself can be entitled to protection.

190. It can be said, then, that legal entities, in general, cannot invoke the protection of religious freedom unless they are created to advance religious purposes and to the extent necessary to achieve said goals. Businesses in general, being different and separated from their owners and managers, usually exist to pursue commercial purposes, so that arguing for their entitlement to religious freedom would be rarely pertinent. Conversely, religious organizations – the formal status that denominations usually take – are obviously entitled to freedom of worship. They are created to enable or to support people in their religious endeavours, congregating them around similar worldviews, and providing services that make it possible for individuals to express their collective faith. This subject is discussed in more length in Part III *infra*.

360. Underscoring that 'interference with [religious] organizations must be minimal', just to ensure that no legal requirement is contravened, *see* TJRJ, *22ª Câmara Cível* [22nd Civil Panel], Ap. 0000560-80.2009.8.19.0208, Rapp. CAJ Odete Knaack de Souza, *DJ* 16 Jan. 2015.
361. Sarlet, Marinoni and Mitidiero, *supra* note 256 at 534; Weingartner Neto, *supra* note 257 at 132.
362. Mendes and Branco, *supra* note 256 at 172–173; Sarlet, Marinoni and Mitidiero, *supra* note 256 at 371–372; Silva, *supra* note 267 at 111–112.
363. Sarlet, Marinoni and Mitidiero, *supra* note 256 at 371.

191. Other legal entities may be created to promote and advance religious views, such as associations, foundations, and even business societies (e.g., publishers of religious books). Since they are also incorporated to promote religious ends, they may also be entitled to a certain degree of protection. But as one starts to morph religious and other general purposes – especially commercial purposes – the situation transits from that of the characteristically religious entity, and it becomes more arduous to advocate for protection under freedom of religion. This point draws on the distinction between expressive and non-expressive entities – i.e., those that are created for mobilizing protected speech and those that are not, respectively – entitling only the former to expressive rights, such as freedom of worship. Limiting member admission to people of a certain religion is conventionally irregular when instituted by leisure clubs, but it may be reasonable in the case of an association devoted to propagating that religion.[364]

192. Should the invocation of religious freedom by a legal entity result in the limitation of the rights of others – e.g., the right to non-discrimination – a balancing test must be undertaken to assess if the advancement of certain religious goals is indeed so relevant or necessary to warrant the limitation of the rights of others. The situation approximates that of the restriction of religious freedom itself, which was presented in Part II, Chapter, 1, §2, II, and §3, II *supra.*

364. Magalhães Pires, *supra* note 105 at 173; Mendes and Branco, *supra* note 256 at 314–316.

Chapter 3. Organizational Religious Freedom

§1. Autonomy of Religious Organizations

193. As mentioned above,[365] the autonomy of religious organizations is rooted in the Constitution, as a corollary of the freedoms of religion and association, requiring that the state refrains from interfering in their organization and operation.[366] The Civil Code also provides for this autonomy by guaranteeing the freedom to create, organize, and operate religious organizations.[367] This autonomy makes it unlawful for the state to intervene in the organizations' businesses and functioning, to unreasonably refuse them registration or to provide them too narrow a space to organize. Although religious organizations possess fundamental rights, it is out of concern for their members that this is so: they are the vehicle via which the individual exercises religious freedom and, as such, require protection.[368] Their autonomy reflects in a broad deference in relation to decision making, especially when they involve the interpretation of religious doctrines. In these cases, government interference would likely violate both the autonomy of the religious organization and the laicity principle.

194. A case worth mentioning opposed the Roman Catholic archbishop of Rio de Janeiro and a religious association, due to the former intervening in the management of the latter. The Federal Supreme Court ruled in favour of the archbishop, both in a panel and the full court. The rapporteur on the panel was Minister Hahnemann Guimarães, who wrote:

> The temporal authority cannot decide on a spiritual matter, arising between the ecclesiastical authority and a religious association. This impossibility results from the full spiritual freedom, principle of republican politics, which has led to the separation between church and state …
> It is exclusively incumbent on the ecclesiastical authority to decide about the rules of the religious denomination, which must be obeyed by an association devoted to worship. The latter is not exempted from the spiritual rules for being a legal entity of civil law, or for being, within the Catholic Church, an association *approbata*, rather than *erecta*.[369]

195. The association filed an appeal to the full court, but, by a split vote (4:3), the previous opinion was upheld. The dissenting opinions, led by Minister Henrique D'Ávila, emphasized the dual nature of the religious association, which placed it under the law for civil and management issues and under the church for spiritual

365. *See* Part II, Ch. 2 *supra*.
366. Mendes and Branco, *supra* note 256 at 323.
367. CC, Law No. 10406 of 10 Jan. 2002, Art. 44, para. 1.
368. Santos Junior, *supra* note 341 at 77–79; Magalhães Pires, *supra* note 105 at 163.
369. STF, *2ª Turma* [2nd Panel], RE 31179/DF, Rapp. Min. Hahnemann Guimarães, *DJ* 26 Jun. 1958 (opinion of the rapporteur).

matters. Since the controversy involved the administration of the association, it should then be decided by the judiciary according to state law. In the words of Minister D'Ávila:

> how could one deny the Judiciary the right to intervene in a legal controversy within its province, under the pretence that one of the parties, besides its temporal activities, also exercises responsibilities of a purely spiritual nature? This would be an unfair privilege that would indeed offend the equality of all under the law, the constitutional basis on which lies the discipline of human activities of all civilized peoples.[370]

196. In fact, state control has never been absent. According to Thesis No. 143, approved by the 3rd Civil Law Conference organized by the Council of the Federal Judiciary – a persuasive, non-binding, source – 'the freedom of operation of religious organization does not exclude the control of legality and legitimacy over their registration, nor the possibility of review, by the judiciary, of the consistency between their acts and the law and their bylaws'.[371] In fact, courts do review acts of religious organizations, including those involving the removal of ministers and other officials, thus assessing their compatibility with the law or the organization's bylaws, especially for formal and procedural characteristics, but the merits are reserved to the organizations' bodies.[372]

197. Judicial intervention does not always take the shape of a limitation to the autonomy of religious organizations; intervention can also prove relevant to protect said autonomy. In Bahia, the State Court of Appeals upheld injunctions issued, at the request of a church, prohibiting the appellants from participating in the services conducted by the appellee. The injunction was sought by the church as a means to secure the 'physical integrity of its members' against the appellants.[373] One of the parties filed a petition for habeas corpus in the STJ, but the latter confirmed the ruling from Bahia. It stated that the order proved necessary to protect the other churchgoers and did not restrict freedom of worship because it was limited to a specific place, so much so that the interested party maintained participation in religious services in another congregation of the same church.[374]

---

370. STF, Full Court, ERE 31179/DF, Rapp. Min. Hahnemann Guimarães, 10 *RTJ* 527, 533–534 (1959).
371. Enunciado 143, III Jornada de Direito Civil, Conselho da Justiça Federal, https://www.cjf.jus.br/enunciados/enunciado/233 (last visited 28 Mar. 2021).
372. *See*, e.g., TJAC, *Câmara Cível* [Civil Panel], AI 2007.003288-8, Rapp. CAJ Samoel Evangelista, *DJ* 9 Nov. 2011; TJBA, *3ª Câmara Cível* [3rd Civil Panel], AI 0162366-04.2016.8.05.0909, Rapp. CAJ Ivanilton Santos da Silva, *DJ* 13 Mar. 2018; TJDFT, *7ª Turma Cível* [7th Civil Panel], Ap. 20160610123855, Rapp. CAJ Getúlio de Moraes Oliveira, *DJ* 11 Jul. 2017; TJES, *4ª Câmara Cível* [4th Civil Panel], Ap. 0079970-96.2010.8.08.0035, CAJ Paulo Roberto Luppi, *DJ* 1 Jun. 2015; TJMG, *13ª Câmara Cível* [13th Civil Panel], Ap. 1.0271.11.005612-1/002, Rapp. CAJ Alberto Henrique; TJMS, *3ª Câmara Cível* [3rd Civil Panel], Ap. 0832933-58.2015.8.12.0001, Judge Vitor Luis de Oliveira Guibo, *DJ* 16 Dec. 2019.
373. TJBA, *1ª Câmara Cível* [1st Civil Panel], AI 8012718-14.2019.8.05.0000 and 8013525-34.2019.8.05.0000, Rapp. CAJ Mário Augusto Albiani Alves Júnior, *DJ* 11 Sep. 2019.
374. STJ, *3ª Turma* [3rd Panel], HC 632567/BA, Rapp. Min. Marco Aurélio Bellizze, *DJ* 29 Apr. 2021.

198. Judicial intervention may also be important to protect a religious organization against other groups. For instance, recognizing that organizations are required to observe and respect fundamental rights – including freedom of association – the Court of Appeals of the Federal District and Territories declared the validity of an act in which a church voluntarily departed its denomination's 'national convention', deeming therefore invalid its ensuing expulsion by the convention due to the latter no longer holding authority to expedite any such action.[375]

§2. Finances of Religious Organizations

199. Like any other human activity, religious gatherings and events require resources. To operate, religious organizations require venues, personnel, services, and funds to support their activities. As they cannot be subsidized by the state,[376] resources must be sought from individuals and private entities, by means of donations, tithes, and other voluntary contributions. Nonetheless, religious organizations and entities benefit from a variety of tax breaks. *See* Part VIII, Chapters 1–2 *infra.*

200. In 2009, a survey concluded that Evangelical churches collectively received donations of BRL 1,032,081,300 per month, whilst the Roman Catholic Church, despite its greater religious flock, mustered substantially less donation revenue: BRL 680,545,620. Among Evangelical churches, the Assembly of God and the IURD led the charge, with monthly revenues of almost BRL 600 million.[377]

§3. Right to Religious Schools

201. The Federal Constitution expressly demands the 'coexistence of public and private teaching institutions' and designates education services 'open to private enterprise', subject to government oversight, as long as general applicable rules are followed.[378] Also, under the ICESCR, the state is required to respect the right of parents or guardians 'to choose for their children schools, other than those established by the public authorities, which conform to such minimum educational standards as may be laid down or approved by the State and to ensure the religious and moral education of their children in conformity with their own convictions'.[379]

202. Therefore, in Brazil, there is a right to establish private schools, including those with a religious orientation. The Constitution even broaches religious schools in Article 213, so to allow them (and other non-profit institutions) to access public funds. For more on this, *see* Part IX, Chapter 2.

---

375. TJDFT, *4ª Turma Cível* [4th Civil Panel], Ap. 2007.01.1.100958-8, Rapp. CAJ Cruz Macedo, *DJ* 11 Oct. 2012.
376. Const. (1988), Art. 19, I.
377. Márcia Vieira, *Doações de Evangélicos Superam R$ 1 Bilhão por Mês*, O Estado de S. Paulo, 11 Oct. 2009, https://www.estadao.com.br/noticias/geral,doacoes-de-evangelicos-superam-r-1-bi-por-mes,449133.
378. Const. (1988), Arts 206, III, and 209.
379. ICESCR, Art. 13(3).

Part III. Legal Status of Religious Communities

Chapter 1. Formal Status of Religious Communities

§1. Registration and Incorporation

I. No Formal Registration Required

203. Religious communities do not require prior registration to exercise prerogatives involved in the right to religious freedom. This is a fundamental right, guaranteed by the Federal Constitution. Although its primary focus is on individuals and their autonomy to define their religious stance and live accordingly, since people usually congregate to learn, teach, and experience their religiosity, religious freedom protect both the individual and collective practices of religion. Religious communities are means by which people exercise their freedom of religion, and, as such, are entitled per se to constitutional protection, irrespective of any kind of formal registration. For more on this, *see* Part II, Chapters 2–3 *supra*.

204. Religious communities exist and are therefore entitled to protection before (or despite the absence of) registration. They cannot be deemed clandestine or their acts be disregarded simply for neither incorporating as a legal person nor being registered with the state. Nonetheless, the formal acquisition of legal personality is important, e.g., so that they can enter into contracts in their own name and for the purpose of proving their existence.[380] Religious communities have a right to incorporate, should they desire, this being a prerogative within the fundamental right to religious organization. *See* Part II, Chapter 2, §2 *supra*.

II. Incorporation as 'Religious Organizations'

205. Whilst religious freedom does not depend on prior registration, religious communities are permitted to become legal entities, under the form of *organizações religiosas* (religious organizations). Their incorporation is regulated by the Civil Code, which does not impose many requirements; quite the contrary, it merely states

380. Santos Junior, *supra* note 341 at 94–107.

that their 'creation, organization, internal structuring, and operation' are 'free', making it unlawful for the government 'to deny recognition or registration' of their acts of incorporation and those involved in their operation.[381] No quantitative requirements are demanded (e.g., number of members), and the law does not attempt to define what might be considered 'religious' for the purpose of establishing such an organization. One can assume therefore that, in the absence of a clear abuse, the state should not refuse to register a religious organization by denying its religiosity, at least when its members sincerely believe that to be the case.[382]

206. Nevertheless, because religious organizations are legally defined as private legal entities,[383] general provisions pertaining to the latter are also applicable to the former – and both the office of civil registration and the judiciary are required to assess if the relevant conditions are met.[384] It means that:[385]

– Religious organizations become legal entities when their acts of incorporation are registered by the office of civil registration of legal entities. Amendments of the acts of incorporation, and the decision to dissolve the organization, are also required to be registered.
– The registration act must declare: (1) the name of the organization, its purposes, duration, and assets, as well as the location of its headquarters; (2) identification (e.g., names, occupation) of its founding members and of those responsible for its management; (3) the form of its management and representation, in and outside courts; (4) if its acts of incorporation are subject to reform as to the organization's management and, if so, how it must be done; (5) if its members are subsidiarily responsible for the organization's obligations; (6) the conditions for dissolving the organization and, in this case, the destination to be given to its assets.[386]
– Interested parties have up to three years to file a suit to annul the incorporation of a religious organization due to defects of the pertinent act.
– Acts of the managers bind the organization when made within the powers granted to them by the acts of incorporation.
– If the organization lacks a person to manage its affairs, a judge must appoint a provisional manager, upon request of any interested party.

381. CC, Law No. 10406 of 10 Jan. 2002, Art. 44, para. 1.
382. Magalhães Pires, *supra* note 105 at 167–168.
383. CC, Law No. 10406 of 10 Jan. 2002, Art. 44, IV.
384. *See*, e.g., TJRS, *5ª Câmara Cível* [5th Civil Panel], Ap. 70027034164, Rapp. CAJ Jorge Luiz Lopes do Canto, 21 Jan. 2009 (ruling that a religious organization could not include the word *sociedade* in their name because it is reserved for business companies); TJRJ, *Conselho da Magistratura* [Judicial Council], Rem. Nec. 0311880-15.2017.8.19.0001, Rapp. CAJ Sérgio Ricardo de Arruda Fernandes, *DJ* 7 Oct. 2019 (the relevant office should cancel the registration of the acts of incorporation of a religious association for using terms which appeared to confer on it an official governmental capacity).
385. CC, Law No. 10406 of 10 Jan. 2002, Arts 45–52.
386. TJSP, *Conselho Superior de Magistratura* [Superior Judicial Council], Ap. 0018134-71.2014.8.26.0071, Rapp. CAJ Xavier de Aquino (upholding a lower court ruling against the registration of the acts of incorporation of a religious organization for not defining, e.g., the composition of its deliberative body and rules for amending the acts of incorporation).

- As a rule, the assets of religious organizations are separate and autonomous from those of its members, founders, and managers, but abuses of legal personality authorize courts to disregard it and seize private assets of its members or managers to pay for debts of the organization.
- After their dissolution, the organization remains in existence for the sole purpose of liquidation.
- Religious organizations are entitled to 'personality rights' – e.g., the protection of their name and reputation. They may even be awarded moral damages.[387]

207. In essence, it is surprisingly straightforward to incorporate a religious organization in Brazil. The whole process may be completed in less than a week, with a cost less than that of a monthly minimum wage.[388] It is far from surprising, then, that the number of religious entities has grown in impressive ratios: they represented 46.4%, 35.9%, 29.1%, and 43.5% of all non-profits incorporated, respectively, in the periods of 1971–1980, 1981–1990, 1991–2000, and 2011–2016.[389]

208. Religious 'temples' are constitutionally entitled to tax immunity encompassing all taxes classified as *impostos* (e.g., income tax, property tax). Said immunity does not depend on previous registration, but all legal persons – including religious organizations – are required to register at the *Secretaria da Receita Federal do Brasil (RFB)*, the department of federal revenue of the Ministry of Economy, and at this time they must declare their legal nature (i.e., religious organization).[390] The revenue departments of all three levels of government usually hold registration forms too, with which religious organizations can apply for the recognition of their immunity.

III. Incorporation as Other Types of Legal Entities

209. Aside from religious organizations, communities can also create legal entities of other genres for purposes such as publishing books, organizing groups, events and discussions, supporting religious practices, providing educational and healthcare services, and assisting people in need. People can form and adhere to *associações* (associations), or set aside assets for specific purposes (including religious purposes), which are incorporated as *fundações* (foundations).[391] For-profit businesses usually require the form of *sociedades empresárias* (business companies).[392]

387. STJ, *Súmula* [Thesis] No. 227.
388. André Ricardo Souza, *Determinados Contornos Jurídicos, Assistenciais e Econômicos de Organizações Cristãs*, 18 Civitas – Revista de Ciências Sociais 237, 247 (2018).
389. Instituto Brasileiro de Geografia e Estatística, *As Fundações Privadas e Associações sem Fins Lucrativos no Brasil: 2016*, 34–37 (2019).
390. Law No. 4503 of 30 Nov. 1964; *Instrução Normativa* [Normative Directive] (RFB) No. 1863 of 27 Dec. 2018.
391. CC, Law No. 10406 of 10 Jan. 2002, Arts 53–61 (associations), and 62–69.
392. CC, Law No. 10406 of 10 Jan. 2002, Arts 981–1195; *Lei das Sociedades Anônimas* [Law on Stock Corporations], Law No. 6404 of 15 Dec. 1976.

IV. Mechanics of Registration

210. Religious organizations become legal persons after the act of incorporation is registered with the *Registro Civil das Pessoas Jurídicas* (Civil Registry of Legal Entities). To do so, a person must file a form at the registry, and present the acts of incorporation, ensuring that it complies with all proper requirements, as explained in Chapter 1, II *supra*, and also that it is signed by a lawyer.[393] The creation of other types of legal entities follows a similar path, with the exception of business companies, which are registered at the *Junta Comercial* (Commercial Board) of their state, and may be required to provide separate documents and information.[394]

V. Oversight

211. There are no public offices specifically devoted to supervising religious entities. Oversight of religious organizations and other legal entities is shared between their own members or shareholders, and various public offices. Courts usually recognize that the former have the standing to sue for the annulment of deliberations, at least when they are voting members of the deliberating body,[395] or when they allege to have been harmed by an act of the organization.[396] The Public Prosecutors' Office is empowered to act on behalf of collective rights, bringing civil and criminal suits, and, in general terms, to supervise foundations.[397] Collective rights can be defended in court by other actors as well, including the Public Defenders' Office and private associations.[398] Religious entities are also under the general oversight of bodies such as the police, the tax department, and other authorities.

§2. Definition of Religion

212. Defining a belief system as a religion can present important legal consequences because religious beliefs, organizations, and temples are protected by the law. The influence of North-American and European case law and scholarship

393. Law No. 8906 of 4 Jul. 1994, Art. 1, para. 2.
394. CC, Law No. 10406 of 10 Jan. 2002, Arts 1150–1154; *Departamento Nacional de Registro Empresarial e Integração* [National Department of Business Registry and Integration], *Instrução Normativa* [Normative Directive] No. 81 of 10 Jun. 2020.
395. *See*, e.g., TJDFT, *5ª Turma Cível* [5th Civil Panel], Ap. 0035652-03.2014.8.07.0007, Rapp. CAJ Angelo Passareli, *DJ* 1 Sep. 2017 (standing of members of the church, with voting rights under its bylaws); TJSP, *6ª Câmara Cível* [6th Civil Panel], Ap. 1008228-48.2017.8.26.0196, Rapp. CAJ Rodolfo Pellizari, *DJ* 22 Apr. 2019 (standing of members of the church recognized after asserting that they had been unduly expelled from the church).
396. *See*, e.g., TJPR, *17ª Câmara Cível* [17th Civil Panel], Ap. 0035069-06.2018.8.16.0014, Rapp. Judge Antonio Carlos Ribeiro Martins, *DJ* 25 Aug. 2020 (former owners of a land, who had donated it to a church on the condition that the latter used it to build a temple of a certain denomination, had standing to challenge bylaw modifications that would distance the organization from the relevant denomination).
397. Const. (1988), Art. 129, I–III, and IV.
398. Law No. 7347 of 24 Jul. 1985, Art. 5.

within Brazil has directed authors to import the differentiation, frequently discussed abroad, between *essentialist* (or *substantive*), *functionalist*, and *typological* (or *analogical*) definitions of religion.[399]

I. Categories of Definitions

A. *Essentialist (or Substantive)*

213. Essentialist definitions seek to identify a feature or a set of features, present in all religions, and capable of setting them apart from other worldviews. That may involve the requirement that religions refer to gods or higher beings, to the supernatural realm, or that they include sacred books and special rites.

214. Essentialist views are criticized for unquestioning the inevitable subjective decision in relation to what characterizes religion. Since the selection of relevant features is based on a convention, the scope of constitutional protection of religions would depend entirely on a somewhat arbitrary decision. Besides, so to identify common elements to religions, one would have to start with a subset of them, that would then serve as a template against which all others would be measured. Traditional religions would, hence, not only be exempt from the test but, moreover, would provide the test for others. That might mean that minority and more recent denominations could be excluded from protection, simply for not conforming to the way religiosity is experienced by traditional religions. In a pluralistic society, however, 'there is no particular feature or plexus of features that all religions have in common' and a 'comprehensive definition [of religion] is particularly important so to maximize protection of religious manifestations'.[400]

215. That risk is not exclusively hypothetical. For example, in 2014, a judge in Rio de Janeiro decided that Umbanda and Candomblé, widely practised African-Brazilian religions, could not be considered religions because they lacked the 'necessary traits', which would be 'a basic text (Quran, Bible etc.)', a 'hierarchical structure', and 'a God to be worshipped'.[401] The decision was criticized by many religious denominations[402] and was later reversed by the same judge, who then stated that 'the strong support offered by the media and civil society demonstrates per se and undeniably the belief in the worship of said religions'.[403]

---

399. Leite, *supra* note 109 at 76–85; Magalhães Pires, *supra* note 105 at 327–336; Weingartner Neto, *supra* note 257 at 96–112.
400. Sarlet, Marinoni and Mitidiero, *supra* note 256 at 531.
401. Rio de Janeiro/RJ, *14ª Vara Federal* [14th Federal Court of First Instance], Proc. 0004747-33.2014.4.02.5101, 28 Apr. 2014.
402. Vinícius Lisboa, *Religiosos Criticam Decisão que não Considera Umbanda e Candomblé Religiões*, Agência Brasil, 19 May 2014, https://agenciabrasil.ebc.com.br/direitos-humanos/noticia/2014-05/religiosos-criticam-decisao-que-nao-considera-umbanda-e-candomble.
403. Rio de Janeiro/RJ, *14ª Vara Federal* [14th Federal Court of First Instance], Proc. 0004747-33.2014.4.02.5101, 20 May 2014.

216. Another example of essentialist definition was adopted in the Federal Supreme Court's refusal to consider Freemasonry as a religion. Acknowledging the fact that the group itself rejected its characterization as a religion, the STF confirmed a statement, by the lower court, describing Freemasonry as 'a life ideology' and not a religion, because '[i]t does not have dogmas. It is not a creed. It is only a big family', a 'fraternity that, first and foremost, preaches and professes a philosophy of life'.[404] This reasoning was also incorporated by the Court of Appeals of the Federal District and Territories to deny religious status to the Rosicrucian Order.[405]

B. Functionalist

217. Conversely, functionalist approaches do not attempt to identify what a religion *is*, but what actuates the *role* it serves in peoples' lives. They too would take a cluster of religions as a starting point but include under the constitutional protection any fashion of worldview that influence the believers' conduct in a similar way or have the same degree of importance.

218. The problem with functionalist definitions manifests in their breadth: since people may embrace many views – including philosophical and political doctrines – with the same passion, sincerity, and relevance others would ascribe to their religious beliefs, the functionalist approach seems to equate religion with conscience.

C. Typological (or Analogical)

219. Typological approaches do not work with *concepts* – based on the mandatory presence of certain elements – but rather with open *types*, which do not require that a number of characteristics be necessarily present. One should, in reality, place the relevant worldview side by side with different, widely acknowledged, religions to better comprehend what they share as common elements and where they differ. The result being a reasoned decision rendered as to whether that worldview deserves to be acknowledged as a religion. The idea is that one should look to traditional religions to find indications with which to build an open-ended template. By doing so, the typological approach purports to retain the connection with an informal, implicit, idea of religion, without limiting the protection afforded by the law to the most traditional, prominent, or common denominations.

220. An example of a typological approach was appropriated by Minister Marco Aurélio of the Federal Supreme Court in the case aforementioned involving Freemasonry. In his dissenting opinion, he recognized that, despite not being a 'genuine religion', there were similarities between Freemasonry and religions: 'elements of

---

404. STF, *1ª Turma* [1st Panel], RE 562351/RS, Rapp. Min. Ricardo Lewandowski, *DJ* 14 Dec. 2012.
405. TJDFT, *6ª Turma Cível* [6th Civil Panel], Ap. 0048970-86.2005.8.07.0001, Rapp. CAJ Ana Maria Amarante, *DJ* 31 Mar. 2016.

religiosity', especially 'rituals of spiritual elevation', which should place it under the constitutional provisions in relation to religion.[406]

II. The Limited Relevance of a Definition of Religion in Brazil

221. The effort to construct a definition of religion appears to be less relevant in Brazil than in others countries. The same constitutional provisions that protect religious beliefs and practices refer, more generally, to the freedom of conscience as well, and, regarding conscientious objections, include 'philosophical or political conviction' side by side with 'religious belief'.[407]

222. There is, however, one domain, in which this definition is viewed as important: tax law. As explained elsewhere (*see* Part VIII, Chapter 2, §1), the Constitution affords 'temples of any denomination' immunity to taxation regarding 'the property, income[,] and services related to [their] essential purposes'.[408] The reference to 'temples' suggests that only actual religious places are immune so that buildings and sites devoted to the discussion and propagation of other worldviews are outside the scope of the provision. That was the opinion of the Federal Supreme Court when it ruled against extending the immunity to Freemasonry.[409]

406. STF, *1ª Turma* [1st Panel], RE 562351/RS, Rapp. Min. Ricardo Lewandowski, *DJ* 14 Dec. 2012 (opinion of Min. Marco Aurélio).
407. Const. (1988), Art. 5, VI and VIII. *See also* Magalhães Pires, *supra* note 105 at 337–347.
408. Const. (1988), Art. 150, VI, and para. 4.
409. STF, *1ª Turma* [1st Panel], RE 562351/RS, Rapp. Min. Ricardo Lewandowski, *DJ* 14 Dec. 2012.

Chapter 2. Autonomy of Religious Communities

§1. General Principles

223. Religious organizations enjoy great autonomy in their structuring and operation. It derives from the collective dimension of religious freedom and the laicity principle. The premise is that the state must refrain from interfering in these organizations because their existence and activities are means for members to exercise freedom of religion and because an interference could result in the state taking a position in religious matters, which is unacceptable.

224. That does not mean that the autonomy of religious organizations is in totality immune to government oversight. Like fundamental rights in general, it can be limited in order to protect and promote the rights of others or to advance specifically relevant public goals. For example, following a criminal investigation, the acting president of a church was suspended temporarily and replaced by a court-appointed administrator.[410] During the COVID-19 pandemic, in-presence religious services were forbidden or restricted in many locations in order to prevent contagion and limit the transmission of the virus. The Federal Supreme Court upheld these measures, given the seriousness of the situation, in light of the scientific studies pointing to the necessity of limiting gatherings of people.[411]

§2. Intra-Organization Disputes

I. Organization Property Disputes

225. The mishandling of an organization's property and funds may trigger judicial review. Acts of fraud, dissimulation, or abuse of power, especially to circumvent bylaw provisions, are usually rendered void or set aside by courts.

226. In Acre, the State Court of Appeals declared the invalidity of acts resulting in the donation of assets owned by a church, which was later dissolved, for, among other reasons, the operation apparently sought to avoid compliance with a bylaw provision involving the destination of the assets in case of dissolution. Furthermore, the church in receipt of the donation was founded and run by individuals who also

---

410. Vila Velha/ES, *2ª Vara Criminal* [2nd Criminal Court of First Instance], Proc. 0042520-84.2012.8.08.0024, 22 Mar. 2013. However, since other officials were elected by the church after the investigated events, the State Court of Appeals put an end to the intervention, allowing newly elected church officials to exercise their functions, as long they were not defendants in the relevant criminal proceedings. *See* TJES, *2ª Câmara Criminal* [2nd Criminal Panel], M. Seg. 0011848-34.2013.8.08.0000, Rapp. CAJ Getúlio Marcos Pereira Neves, *DJ* 13 Nov. 2013.

411. STF, Full Court, ADPF 811/DF, Rapp. Min. Gilmar Mendes, *DJ* 25 Jun. 2021.

ran the church under dissolution.[412] Also, the State of Appeals of São Paulo recognized the right of an organization to demand that an affiliated church render management account: should the organization's bylaws require this to be adhered to, its managers cannot simply ignore their duties.[413]

II. Disputes over Membership and Leadership

227. The merits of decisions involving the removal of members or leaders tend not to be reviewed.[414] For example, the State Court of Appeals of São Paulo refused to revert the removal of a minister and to award him damages due to it being impossible to review the merits of the decision.[415] But the Court extensively reviewed the procedural aspects of the ex-communication of a priest, only to conclude that it could not discuss such a penalty when infliction was under the exclusive power of the church.[416] It also denied a plaintiff an order to obtain access to church records of a punishment procedure against him because the information could not be employed in courts to challenge his penalty.[417]

228. Courts, however, do assess compliance with procedures set forth by statutes and bylaws.[418] As stated by the State Court of Appeals of Rio de Janeiro, theological and canonical matters remain out of bounds for courts, being judicial intervention solely admissible to assess compliance with the organization's

412. TJAC, *1ª Câmara Cível* [1st Civil Panel], Ap. 0006505-83.2012.8.01.0001, Rapp. CAJ Luís Camolez, *DJ* 17 Feb. 2020.
413. TJSP, *6ª Câmara de Direito Privado* [6th Private Law Panel], Ap. 1002369-76.2017.8.26.0123, Rapp. CAJ Cristina Medina Mogioni, *DJ* 19 Nov. 2020.
414. *See*, e.g., TJBA, *3ª Câmara Cível* [3rd Civil Panel], AI 0162366-04.2016.8.05.0909, Rapp. CAJ Ivanilton Santos da Silva, *DJ* 13 Mar. 2018; TJMS, *3ª Câmara Cível* [3rd Civil Panel], Ap. 0832933-58.2015.8.12.0001, Rapp. Judge Vitor Luis de Oliveira Guibo, *DJ* 16 Dec. 2019; TJPR, *6ª Câmara Cível* [6th Civil Panel], Ap. 857.609-2, Rapp. Judge Joscelito Giovani Ce, *DJ* 10 Dec. 2013; TJPR, *8ª Câmara Cível* [8th Civil Panel], Ap. 1056289-1, Judge Osvaldo Nallim Duarte, *DJ* 26 Sep. 2013; TJRJ, *3ª Câmara Cível* [3th Civil Panel], Ap. 0153765-86.2011.8.19.0038, Rapp. CAJ Peterson Barroso Simão, *DJ* 31 Jan. 2018; TJRS, *9ª Câmara Cível* [9th Civil Panel], Ap. 70015766371, Rapp. CAJ Tasso Caubi Soares Delabary, *DJ* 13 Sep. 2006; TJSP, *10ª Câmara de Direito Privado* [10th Private Law Panel], Ap. 0000460-26.2012.8.26.0629, Rapp. CAJ Elcio Trujillo, *DJ* 19 Nov. 2014; TJTO, *2ª Câmara Cível* [2nd Civil Panel], AI 0024872-28.2018.8.27.0000, Rapp. CAJ Adolfo Amaro Mendes, 16 May 2019.
415. TJSP, *7ª Câmara de Direito Privado* [7th Private Law Panel], Ap. 1002466-71.2017.8.26.064, CAJ Luiz Antonio Costa, *DJ* 9 Jan. 2020.
416. TJSP, *7ª Câmara de Direito Privado* [7th Private Law Panel], Ap. 4003115-88.2013.8.26.0071, Rapp. CAJ Luiz Antonio Costa, *DJ* 23 Jul. 2015.
417. TJSP, *1ª Câmara de Direito Privado* [1st Private Law Panel], AI 0247672-06.2012.8.26.0000, Rapp. CAJ Paulo Eduardo Razuk, *DJ* 22 Feb. 2013.
418. *See*, e.g., TJES, *4ª Câmara Cível* [4th Civil Panel], Ap. 0079970-96.2010.8.08.0035, CAJ Paulo Roberto Luppi, *DJ* 1 Jun. 2015; TJPR, *6ª Câmara Cível* [6th Civil Panel], Ap. 857.609-2, Judge Joscelito Giovani Ce, *DJ* 10 Dec. 2013; TJPR, *8ª Câmara Cível* [8th Civil Panel], Ap. 1056289-1, Judge Osvaldo Nallim Duarte, *DJ* 26 Sep. 2013; TJRJ, *27ª Câmara Cível* [27th Civil Panel], Ap. 0009943-53.2016.8.19.0203, CAJ Marcos Alcino de Azevedo Torres, *DJ* 13 Feb. 2019.

bylaws.[419] As such, the Court annulled the vote to elect the board members of a religious organization for not complying with proper procedure.[420] In another case, a church official was found to have abused his power to remove and appoint members of the church's governing body, after previous members had refused to countersign his decision to sell the church's headquarters and to move it to another city.[421]

229. Military chaplains are in a peculiar situation since they are simultaneously part of the (public) military personnel and fall under the jurisdiction of religious organizations. In an interesting case, an Army chaplain, who was dismissed after losing his accreditation in the Roman Catholic Church, attempted to challenge his dismissal before the courts. The Federal Court of Appeals for the Fourth Region declined to hear the case for lack of jurisdiction, as the matter could only be decided by religious bodies.[422]

III. Organization Names

230. All legal entities possess their own names, which identify them and differentiate them from others. When a legal person – including a religious organization – is registered, its name must be declared and recorded.[423] Every person is entitled to the protection of their name, and this right is extended to legal entities,[424] so long as they are duly registered (i.e., possess legal personality).[425]

231. As such, it may be the case that a dispute can arise between two or more organizations over the use of certain names or designations. The STJ ruled on a case involving two organizations which referred in name to Mokiti Okada, a religious master. According to the Court, the law on trademarks was not applicable to the names of religious organizations because theirs was not a business activity, and nobody could claim an exclusive right to mention the name of a religious authority.

419. TJRJ, *3ª Câmara Cível* [3rd Civil Panel], Ap. 0030177-42.2011.8.19.0038, 0021171-11.2011.8.19.0038, and 0153765-86.2011.8.19.0038, Rapp. CAJ Peterson Barroso Simão, *DJ* 02 Feb. 2018; TJRJ, *2ª Câmara Cível* [2nd Civil Panel], Ap. 0512101-19.2014.8.19.0001, CAJ Antônio Iloízio Barros Bastos, *DJ* 10 May 2019.

420. TJRJ, *3ª Câmara Cível* [3rd Civil Panel], Ap. 0015421-45.2012.8.19.0021, Rapp. CAJ Cezar Augusto Rodrigues Costa, *DJ* 10 Sep. 2013.

421. TJDFT, *6ª Turma Cível* [6th Civil Panel], Ap. 20080110614755, Rapp. CAJ José Divino de Oliveira, *DJ* 15 May 2013.

422. TRF – 4, *4ª Turma* [4th Panel], Ap. 5004738-74.2013.4.04.7102, Rapp. FCAJ Vivian Josete Pantaleão Caminha, 7 Dec. 2016. The plaintiff filed an appeal to the Superior Court of Justice, but it was dismissed (STJ, *2ª Turma* [2nd Panel], REsp 1761486/RS, Rapp. Min. Herman Benjamin, *DJ* 22 Apr. 2019). Another appeal was directed to the Federal Supreme Court, but it ordered the lower court to decide it based on a precedent (STF, ARE 1211606/RS, Rapp. Min. Gilmar Mendes, *DJ* 5 Jun. 2019). The appeal was then dismissed (TRF – 4, Ap. 5004738-74.2013.4.04.7102, Vice President FCAJ Maria de Fátima Freitas Labarrère, 27 Jun. 2019).

423. CC, Law No. 10406 of 10 Jan. 2002, Art. 46, I.

424. CC, Law No. 10406 of 10 Jan. 2002, Arts 16–18, and 52.

425. STJ, *4ª Turma* [4th Panel], REsp 555086/RJ, Rapp. Min. Jorge Scartezzini, *DJ* 28 Feb. 2005.

Since there was no homonymy or risk that one entity could be mistaken for the other, they could both coexist and use a reference to Mikita Okada in their names.[426]

232. Years later, however, the Court did invoke trademark law in a dispute opposing Bible distributors and a religious organization over the use of the word 'Gideons'. The Court decided that the protection of legal entity names is usually geographically limited to the jurisdiction of the notary who registered them. It also noted that, although homonymy was not admitted, the mere use of 'Gideons' did not create such a problem, given that it is a common word among religious groups, and that the full names of the entities greatly differed. Furthermore, they were non-aligned in activity, which established that people would not mistake one party for the other.[427]

233. Lower courts, in more recent cases, have too referred to trademark law. The State Court of Appeals of São Paulo decided that the word 'lamb', in reference to the Christian phrase 'lamb of God', could not be exclusively appropriated by one denomination.[428] In the State of Espírito Santo, the Court of Appeals ruled in the same way against a church's claim to prevent another from using the phrase 'For Christ'.[429] On the other hand, in Minas Gerais, a court of first instance enjoined a church from referencing, in its name, the phrase 'God is Love' – which had been previously registered by another in the trademark office – as well as the image used in the plaintiff's logo.[430]

234. In a controversial case, the State Court of Appeals of São Paulo forbade a private association known as *Católicas pelo Direito de Decidir* [Catholic Women for the Right to Decide] from employing any reference to Catholicism in its name. According to the Court, by advocating for the legalization of abortion, the association contradicted the worldview of the Roman Catholic Church, which rendered it impossible to use the word 'Catholic'.[431] The association filed appeals to the STJ and to the Federal Supreme Court, which are currently pending.

426. STJ, *3ª Turma* [3rd Panel], REsp 66529/SP, Rapp. Min. Nilson Naves, *DJ* 19 Jun. 2000.
427. STJ, *4ª Turma* [4th Panel], REsp 555086/RJ, Rapp. Min. Jorge Scartezzini, *DJ* 28 Feb. 2005. The relevant facts occurred before the legislative enactment providing for 'religious organizations' as a particular type of legal entity, but it is nonetheless very interesting.
428. TJSP, *1ª Câmara Reservada de Direito Empresarial* [1st Separate Panel on Business Law], Ap. 1011716-29.2014.8.26.0224, Rapp. CAJ Enio Zuliani, *DJ* 23 Apr. 2015.
429. TJES, *2ª Câmara Cível* [2nd Civil Panel], Ap. 0015297-17.2012.8.08.0038, Rapp. CAJ José Paulo Calmon Nogueira da Gama, *DJ* 22 Mar. 2017.
430. Santa Luzia/MG, *1ª Vara Cível* [1st Civil Court of First Instance], Proc. 0209993-39.2013.8.13.0245, 23 Sep. 2020.
431. TJSP, *2ª Câmara de Direito Privado* [2nd Private Law Panel], Ap. 1071628-96.2018.8.26.0100, Rapp. CAJ José Carlos Ferreira Alves, *DJ* 26 Oct. 2020.

IV. Failure to Follow Internal Procedures

235. One particularly frequent instance of judicial review involves non-compliance with procedures set forth by the organizations' bylaws.[432] Sometimes it is even stated that, despite its undeniable importance, religious freedom is not absolute, and therefore does not preclude judicial review.[433] There are cases, nonetheless, in which decisions by a church assembly were reviewed with little or no consideration to the organization's autonomy,[434] or in fact to their peculiar status as religious denominations – even reading into the bylaws of a church a provision concerning private associations, assuming that, in the silence of the bylaws, said provisions should govern the business of religious organizations.[435]

432. TJAC, *1ª Câmara Cível* [1st Civil Panel], Ap. 0006505-83.2012.8.01.0001, Rapp. CAJ Luís Camolez, *DJ* 17 Feb. 2020; TJDFT, *2ª Turma Cível* [2nd Civil Panel], Ap. 20070710228035, Rapp. CAJ Silva Lemos, *DJ* 5 Feb. 2010; TJDFT, *3ª Turma Cível* [3rd Civil Panel], Ap. 20160710021514, Rapp. CAJ Alvaro Ciarlini, *DJ* 13 Sep. 2017; TJES, *1ª Câmara Cível* [1st Civil Panel], Ap. 0000630-08.2010.8.08.0002, Rapp. CAJ Janete Vargas Simões, *DJ* 12 Nov. 2014; TJES, *4ª Câmara Cível* [4th Civil Panel], Ap. 0079970-96.2010.8.08.0035, CAJ Paulo Roberto Luppi, *DJ* 1 Jun. 2015; TJMT, *2ª Câmara Cível* [2nd Civil Panel], Ap. 0116330-59.2007.8.11.0000, Rapp. Judge Clarice Claudino da Silva, 25 Jun. 2008; TJPR, *17ª Câmara Cível* [17th Civil Panel], Ap. 0035069-06.2018.8.16.0014, Rapp. Judge Antonio Carlos Ribeiro Martins, *DJ* 25 Aug. 2020.

433. TJAC, *1ª Câmara Cível* [1st Civil Panel], Ap. 0006505-83.2012.8.01.0001, Rapp. CAJ Luís Camolez, *DJ* 17 Feb. 2020; TJDFT, *6ª Turma Cível* [6th Civil Panel], Ap. 20080110614755, Rapp. CAJ José Divino de Oliveira, *DJ* 14 May 2013.

434. TJAM, *1ª Câmara Cível* [1st Civil Panel], Ap. 0608236-47.2013.8.04.0001, Rapp. CAJ Sabino da Silva Marques, *DJ* 24 Nov. 2015.

435. TJDFT, *6ª Turma Cível* [6th Civil Panel], Ap. 0712997-83.2020.8.07.0007, Rapp. CAJ Esdras Neves, *DJ* 19 Feb. 2021.

Chapter 3. Fundamental Rights and Religious Communities

§1. Fundamental Rights of Religious Communities

236. As previously mentioned (*see* Part II, Chapter 2, §4), legal entities are entitled to fundamental rights, but only to the extent that they are compatible with their peculiar nature. Therefore, the freedoms of conscience and belief cannot, for example, be invoked by a legal person. But the law does offer it numerous rights, including, e.g., the protection of their property, and the rights of access to justice and to due process of law.

§2. Fundamental Rights of Members of Religious Communities

237. Members of religious communities retain all rights as human beings and citizens, irrespective of their partaking (and to the degree of their participation) in a religious group. Notably, they are free to leave the community whenever they please and are entitled to the protection of life and integrity.

238. In an interesting case, the State Court of Appeals of Rio Grande do Sul denied damages to a woman who allegedly suffered 'coercion' by a church so she could marry a minister. According to her, the organization possessed a 'veto' power over her marriage and employed it to coerce her into undertaking chores without salary and to forbid her, who was also a singer, from performing at a music concert. Despite underscoring the ambiguity of the evidence presented, the Court concluded that there was no proof of coercion. In the words of the rapporteur, 'internal rules of cults are unenforceable', so 'no-one is forced to adhere, unless they agree with them'. Being able to make her own decisions, the plaintiff could have submitted or not to the church's rules. In choosing to adhere, she could not hold the church liable for her personal decision.[436]

239. In Espírito Santo, the State Court of Appeals awarded damages to a person who was humiliated and injured during a religious service: claiming that the 'devil was escaping', members of the church took him to the altar against his will, bruising him, so that the minister could invoke a prayer. In the words of the Court, even in the exercise of its freedom of worship, the church cannot offend other rights and values which are equally important, such as human dignity and the physical and moral integrity of those present.[437]

436. TJRS, *10ª Câmara Cível* [10th Civil Panel], Ap. 0157805-84.2015.8.21.7000, Rapp. Min. Túlio de Oliveira Martins, *DJ* 17 Sep. 2015.

437. TJES, *3ª Câmara Cível* [3rd Civil Panel], Ap. 0017944-27.2016.8.08.0011, Rapp. Min. Telemaco Antunes de Abreu Filho.

§3. Religious Communities and the Fundamental Rights of Third Parties

240. In Brazil, fundamental rights are directed not only at the government but also at private individuals and entities, who should refrain from violating the rights of others, and, to a certain extent, may have the duty to promote such rights. In these cases, however, since both parties are entitled to fundamental rights, one must balance the conflicting rights to establish the proper outcome of the case.[438]

241. For example, it is undeniable that religious denominations can harbour critical views of certain family types, such as those involving same-sex unions, whilst also believing in their own entitlement to propagate these views as an expression of their religion. However, the protection of the physical and moral integrity of homosexual people, including their equality as citizens, are also relevant constitutional imperatives. Consequently, if a religious group engage in hate speech or incite violence against homosexual people, they can have their freedom of (religious) speech limited by the state.[439]

438. For discussions on this subject, *see*, e.g., Mendes and Branco, *supra* note 256 at 176–183; Jane Reis Gonçalves Pereira, Apontamentos sobre a Aplicação das Normas de Direito Fundamental nas Relações Jurídicas entre Particulares, *in A Nova Interpretação Constitucional: Ponderação, Direitos Fundamentais e Relações Privadas* 119 (Luís Roberto Barroso ed., 2008); Sarlet, Marinoni and Mitidiero, *supra* note 256 at 386–389; Daniel Sarmento, *Direitos Fundamentais e Relações Privadas* (2006); Silva, *supra* note 267 at 113–116.

439. Ribeirão Preto/SP, *6ª Vara Cível* [6th Civil Court of First Instance], Proc. 0045315-08.2011.8.26.0506, *DJ* 15 Sep. 2014, confirmed by TJSP, *4ª Câmara de Direito Privado* [4th Private Law Panel], Ap. 0045315-08.2011.8.26.0506, Rapp. CAJ Natan Zelinschi de Arruda, *DJ* 17 Dec. 2015.

Chapter 4. Contractual Religious Freedom

§1. Contractual Freedom in General

242. Contractual freedom in Brazil is rooted in the freedom of enterprise and in the private autonomy guaranteed by the Constitution to individuals and legal entities.[440] This freedom is confirmed and developed by statutory law, especially the Civil Code. It means that, in principle, parties are free to choose what, with whom, when, and how to negotiate, thus defining obligations, including prices to be paid. This freedom, however, is placed under various limitations, in relation to, e.g., the capacity of the parties. In certain cases, the law affords special protection to some parties who presumably possess less bargaining power (e.g., consumers and workers). Contracts with state and government-owned entities also differ in rules and limitations.

243. Under their freedom of operation (*see* Part II, Chapter 2, §3, *supra*), religious organizations are entitled, as any other legal entity, to enter into contracts whenever they please, in order to advance their needs and preferences and to support their activities.

244. A particularly controversial issue involves the legal nature of contributions gifted to religious organizations by their members. Arguing that the law allows for donations to be revoked when the donee seriously offends the donor,[441] an individual claimed from his former church all amounts previously gifted as tithes because a minister had allegedly offended him. The judiciary sided with the church: the STJ decided that tithes, as contributions based on duties of conscience, could not be treated as proper donations – contracts under Civil Law, based on sheer generosity – and therefore could not be revoked on the grounds of ingratitude.[442]

245. This reasoning, however, appears to be dependent upon the nature of the act – if it was enacted (or not) by an actual duty. Also, some courts appear to view tithes and other contributions to religious organizations as donations.[443] For example, they review the circumstances surrounding donations so to ascertain any defect of consent. A donation, made by a church member in difficult financial troubles, was rendered void by the State Court of Appeals of Mato Grosso do Sul because the member was induced by the church to believe that donating would

---

440. Const. (1988), Art. 1, IV; Art. 5, *caput* and II; Art. 170. Invoking contractual freedom as a constitutional right, *see*, e.g., STF, Full Court, RE 958252/MG, Rapp. Min. Luiz Fux, *DJ* 13 Sep. 2019 (declaring the validity of outsourcing).
441. CC, Law No. 10406 of 10 Jan. 2002, Art. 557.
442. STJ, *3ª Turma* [3rd Panel], REsp 1371842/SP, Rapp. Min. Sidnei Beneti, *DJ* 17 Dec. 2013.
443. TJDFT, *7ª Turma Cível* [7th Civil Panel], Ap. 0703534-58.2018.8.07.0017, Rapp. CAJ Romeu Gonzaga Neiva, *DJ* 6 Jul. 2020 (declaring void the contribution of a large sum of money to a church because it was not made under a public deed, contrary to what is legally required for donations of higher values).

resolve his problems.[444] In São Paulo, the State Court of Appeals upheld the validity of donations made to a church, despite their amount, because the plaintiffs were sufficiently learned, had adequate assets, and had donated for such a long period of time that one could not view them as ingenious people who had been coerced into gifting money to the church.[445] The State Court of Appeals of Minas Gerais also denied relief to a donor, given that she failed to prove any defect of consent.[446]

§2. Employment in Religious Entities

246. Employment in religious entities is regulated by general Labour Law. The only exception involves ministers, who are not considered employees of the organizations to which they belong. This matter is further developed below – *see* Part VI *infra.*

§3. Arbitration Clauses Incorporating Religious Law

247. Arbitration procedures in Brazil can be settled by law or equity,[447] the latter understood as a reference to the arbiters' sense of fairness.[448] Also, parties are free to choose the law to be enforced, so long as they do not violate *bons costumes* [common decency] or *ordem pública* [public order].[449] Therefore, at least in theory, it is possible to conceive that controversies be settled in accordance with religious norms. Since arbitration, in Brazil, can only be applied to decide issues involving purely negotiable rights, it is unlikely that the choice of religious law would intrude upon common decency or the public order.

444. TJMS, *5ª Câmara Cível* [5th Civil Panel], Ap. 0024340-49.2010.8.12.0001, Rapp. CAJ Sideni Soncini Pimentel, *DJ* 3 Oct. 2018.
445. TJSP, *10ª Câmara de Direito Privado* [10th Private Law Panel], Ap. 1006628-78.2019.8.26.0565, Rapp. CAJ Jair de Souza, *DJ* 5 Feb. 2021.
446. TJMG, *14ª Câmara Cível* [14th Civil Panel], Ap. 3742436-31.2004.8.13.0024, Rapp. CAJ Valdez Leite Machado, *DJ* 11 May 2010.
447. Law No. 9307 of 23 Sep. 1996, Art. 2, *caput.*
448. Luiz Antonio Scavone Junior, *Manual de Arbitragem: Mediação e Conciliação*, 12 (2016).
449. Law No. 9307 of 23 Sep. 1996, Art. 2, para. 1.

Part IV. International, Transnational, Regional Effects on Religious Communities

Chapter 1. International Law Effects on Religious Communities

§1. Basic Principles of International Law in Brazil

248. In Brazil, international instruments are signed by the President of the Republic[450] and brought before both Houses of the National Congress for approval under a legislative decree.[451] Afterwards, the President ratifies the treaty and promulgates it with a decree – at this point, it becomes binding law in Brazil. The Constitution does not expressly require this promulgation, but it is widely recognized as necessary.[452] Congressional approval is not required for international acts that do not intend to modify domestic law or to create rights and obligations to the Republic, such as memoranda of understanding or protocols of intentions. The states, the Federal District, and the municipalities are not subjects of international law and therefore cannot be parties to international treaties. They are permitted, however, to sign contracts with foreign entities, e.g., to obtain loans and acquire goods and services.

§2. Effects of International Agreements

249. Enduringly, the Federal Supreme Court stated that international treaties held the same rank as ordinary statutes so that inconsistencies between them were resolved by the traditional criteria applied in statutory law in general.[453] When the

450. Const. (1988), Art. 84, VIII.
451. Const. (1988), Art. 49, I.
452. STF, Full Court, ADI 1480 MC/DF, Rapp. Min. Celso de Mello, *DJ* 18 May 2001. According to the rapporteur, the President's power of promulgation derives from their status as Head of State.
453. STF, Full Court, RE 80004/SE, Rapp. Min. Xavier de Albuquerque, *DJ* 29 Dec. 1977.

1988 Constitution came into force, it did not deal with the legal status of international documents.[454] However, its Article 5, paragraph 2, provided that 'the rights and guarantees' prescribed by the Constitution did not 'exclude others deriving … from the international treaties in which the Federative Republic of Brazil is a party', prompting scholars to defend that human rights treaties had the status of constitutional law in Brazil. The STF, however, disagreed, and for an enduring period, all treaties remained equated with ordinary statutes.[455]

250. In 2004, Constitutional Amendment (CA) No. 45 inserted a paragraph 3 in Article 5 of the Constitution, making it possible for human rights treaties to obtain the status of constitutional amendments, provided that both Houses of Congress approved them in two voting rounds with a three-fifths majority. The Federal Supreme Court also changed its opinion in relation to paragraph 2, construing it to confer supra-statutory status to human rights treaties.[456] Currently, then, international treaties on human rights are either superior to statutory law and inferior to the Constitution (under Article 5, paragraph 2), or have the rank of constitutional amendments (if they are approved pursuant to Article 5, paragraph 3).[457]

251. As for international declarations in general, they are seldom recognized in Brazil as legally binding sources of rights and obligations. However, some appear to have been incorporated into mainstream discourse. Holding considerable weight in opinions of supra- and international human rights courts and of domestic courts, they are progressively becoming binding, at least to some extent, either as parts of 'international custom' or as 'general principles of law'. This, for example, is arguably the case of the Universal Declaration of Human Rights (UDHR).[458]

---

454. In the domain of international transportation, however, Art. 178, para. 1, demanded domestic regulation to respect the agreements signed by the Republic, as long as reciprocity was assured. CA No. 7 of 15 Aug. 1995 amended this article, but a similar idea remains in force in what is now Art. 178, *caput*.
455. *See* e.g., STF, Full Court, Ext 662/Peru, Rapp. Min. Celso de Mello, *DJ* 30 May 1997; STF, Full Court, ADI 1480 MC/DF, Rapp. Min. Celso de Mello, *DJ* 18 May 2001; STF, Full Court, Ext 795/USA, Rapp. Min. Sepúlveda Pertence, *DJ* 6 Apr. 2001.
456. *See* STF, Full Court, RE 349703/RS, Rapp. Min. Gilmar Mendes, *DJ* 5 Jun. 2009; STF, Full Court, HC 97256/RS, Rapp. Min. Carlos Ayres Britto, *DJ* 16 Dec. 2010; STF, Full Court, ADI 5240/SP, Rapp. Min. Luiz Fux, *DJ* 1 Feb. 2016.
457. As of today, the status of constitutional amendments has been granted to four human documents: the Convention on the Rights of Persons with Disabilities and its Optional Protocol, GA Res. 61/106, UN Doc. A/RES/61/106 (13 Dec. 2006) (Leg. Dec. No. 186 of 9 Jul. 2008; Dec. No. 6949 of 25 Aug. 2009); the Marrakesh Treaty to Facilitate Access to Published Works for Persons Who Are Blind, Visually Impaired or Otherwise Print Disabled, WIPO Lex TRT/MARRAKESH/001 (27 Jun. 2013) (Leg. Dec. No. 261 of 25 Nov. 2015; Dec. No. 9522 of 8 Oct. 2018); and the Inter-American Convention against all Forms of Discrimination and Intolerance, AG/RES. 2804 (XLIII-O/13) (6 Jun. 2013) (Leg. Dec. No. 1/2021; Dec. No. 10932 of 10 Jan. 2022).
458. Celso D. de Albuquerque Mello, *Curso de Direito Internacional Público* vol. 1, 869–871 (2004); Flávia Piovesan, *Direitos Humanos e o Direito Constitucional Internacional*, 233–236 (2017); Ian Brownlie, *Principles of Public International Law*, 534–535 (2003); Malcolm Shaw, *International Law*, 207 (1997).

§3. International Instruments Addressing Religious Issues to Which Brazil Is a Party

252. The international human rights system comprises documents adopted, and bodies operating, under the auspices of the UN. The so-called *International Bill of Rights*[459] includes the Universal Declaration of Human Rights (UDHR), adopted in 1948,[460] as well as two treaties which intended to enforce the Declaration's provisions: the ICCPR and the ICESCR, both adopted in 1966.[461]

253. The UDHR enshrines religious freedom in Article 18, which reads: 'Everyone has the right to freedom of thought, conscience and religion; this right includes freedom to change his religion or belief, and freedom, either alone or in community with others and in public or private, to manifest his religion or belief in teaching, practice, worship and observance.' Limitations are nonetheless admissible so long as some conditions are met: the exercise of religious freedom, like that of any other right set forth by the Declaration, 'shall be subject only to such limitations as are determined by law solely for the purpose of securing due recognition and respect for the rights and freedoms of others and of meeting the just requirements of morality, public order and the general welfare in a democratic society', as stated by Article 29(2).

254. The ICCPR has supra-legal status in Brazilian law. It provides for religious freedom in Article 18, which reads:

1. Everyone shall have the right to freedom of thought, conscience and religion. This right shall include freedom to have or to adopt a religion or belief of his choice, and freedom, either individually or in community with others and in public or private, to manifest his religion or belief in worship, observance, practice and teaching.
2. No one shall be subject to coercion which would impair his freedom to have or to adopt a religion or belief of his choice.
3. Freedom to manifest one's religion or beliefs may be subject only to such limitations as are prescribed by law and are necessary to protect public safety, order, health, or morals or the fundamental rights and freedoms of others.
4. The States Parties to the present Covenant undertake to have respect for the liberty of parents and, when applicable, legal guardians to ensure the religious and moral education of their children in conformity with their own convictions.

255. The right of parents and legal guardians set forth in Article 18(4) is enshrined, in a more detailed manner, in Article 13(3) of the ICESCR, which reads:

---

459. Piovesan, *supra* note 458 at 247–249.
460. GA Res. 217 (III) A, UN Doc. A/RES/217(III)A (10 Dec. 1948).
461. GA Res. 2200 (XXI) A, UN Doc. A/RES/2200(XXI)A (6 Dec. 1966). In Brazil, *see* Leg. Dec. No. 226 of 12 Dec. 1991; and Dec. No. 591 and 592 of 6 Jul. 1992.

The States Parties to the present Covenant undertake to have respect for the liberty of parents and, when applicable, legal guardians to choose for their children schools, other than those established by the public authorities, which conform to such minimum educational standards as may be laid down or approved by the State and to ensure the religious and moral education of their children in conformity with their own convictions.

256. There are numerous other treaties and declarations that address various aspects of religious freedom. For example, in matters involving children, the main source is the Convention on the Rights of the Child (CRC).[462] In times of war, the Geneva Conventions provide for issues such as the rights of religious personnel (chaplains) and the freedom of religion of prisoners, the proper respect for the religion of the deceased when tending to their bodies.[463] The prohibition of discrimination based on religion, which is ubiquitous in international documents,[464] is the subject of the United Nations Educational, Scientific and Cultural Organization Convention against Discrimination in Education of 1960.[465] For more on this, *see* Part VII, Chapter 7, §1, *infra.*

257. The most important bodies in the international human rights systems are the United Nations Human Rights Committee (UNHRC) and the United Nations Committee on Economic, Social and Cultural Rights (CESCR). These entities are empowered to monitor the implementation of the ICCPR and the ICESCR, respectively, by the State Parties, and to issue general comments to guide the interpretation and application of covenant provisions.[466] Their views are to be seen – at least – as persuasive authorities by Brazilian courts and officers, who are expected to seriously acknowledge them.[467]

258. There are also other important documents, such as the Declaration on the Elimination of All Forms of Intolerance and of Discrimination Based on Religion or Belief,[468] and the Declaration on the Rights of Persons Belonging to National or Ethnic, Religious and Linguistic Minorities.[469]

462. GA Res. 44/25, UN Doc. A/RES/44/25 (20 Nov. 1989).
463. The four Geneva Conventions were signed in 1949. They were approved by Leg. Dec. No. 35 of 12 Sep. 1956 and promulgated by Dec. No. 42121 of 21 Aug. 1957. *See* 1st Geneva Convention, Arts 6, 7, and 17; 2nd Geneva Convention, Arts 6, 7, 36, and 37; 3rd Geneva Convention, Arts 34–37, and 120; and 4th Geneva Convention, Art. 130.
464. *See*, e.g., UDHR, Art. 2; ICCPR, Arts 2 and 24(1); ICESCR, Art. 2(2).
465. The Convention was approved by Leg. Dec. No. 40 of 15 Nov. 1967, and promulgated by Dec. No. 63223 of 6 Sep. 1968.
466. *See*, especially, UNHRC General Comment No. 22 (48) (Art. 18), *supra* note, and CESCR General Comment No. 13 (21), pars 28–29, UN Doc. E/C.12/1999/10 (8 Dec. 1999).
467. Virgílio Afonso da Silva, Colisões de direitos fundamentais entre ordem nacional e ordem transnacional, *in Transnacionalidade do direito: novas perspectivas dos conflitos entre ordens jurídicas* 101, 109 (Marcelo Neves ed., 2010).
468. GA Res. 36/55, UN Doc. A/RES/36/55 (25 Nov. 1981).
469. GA Res. 47/135, UN Doc. A/RES/47/135 (3 Feb. 1992).

§4. References to International Law in Brazilian Cases

259. International law is part of Brazilian law and, as such, it is applicable by any public officer, including courts, in any case or procedure. There are numerous opinions of the Federal Supreme Court, especially over more recent years, enforcing international treaties and discussing their relation with domestic law, in matters such as consumer protection in international air transportation,[470] rights in criminal proceedings,[471] and the invalidity of laws prohibiting schools from discussing issues of gender and sexual orientation.[472]

260. The same is true in cases involving religion. When the Court debated the alternative service requirements for public servants who invoked conscientious objection to refuse participation in regular activities, Minister Edson Fachin stressed the integration between the Constitution, the ACHR and the ICCPR, and made reference to a general comment of the UNHRC – described as being 'of fundamental importance to the normative concretization of the human rights provided for in the text of the [ICCPR]', despite not being formally binding.[473] In the case involving religious teaching in public schools, Minister Fachin referred to the UNESCO Convention against Discrimination in Education, the CRC, and the 1981 Declaration on the Elimination of All Forms of Intolerance and of Discrimination Based on Religion or Belief.[474] The UDHR, the ICESCR, and the CRC were also discussed in the case involving the constitutionality of homeschooling.[475]

261. The ICCPR, the ACHR, and an opinion of the Inter-American Court of Human Rights were cited by the Court to declare the invalidity of a law forbidding proselytizing speech in community broadcasting.[476] The ICCPR and the ACHR were also invoked as in a case referencing religious service within the military police in the State of Rio de Janeiro.[477]

262. In the decision that submitted homophobia and transphobia to the same criminal provisions regarding racism, Minister Celso de Mello relied heavily on the

---

470. STF, Full Court, ARE 766168/SP, Rapp. Min. Luís Roberto Barroso, *DJ* 13 Nov. 2017; STF, Full Court, RE 636331/RJ, Rapp. Min. Gilmar Mendes, *DJ* 13 Nov. 2017 ('Under Art. 178 of the Constitution of the Republic, international provisions and treaties limiting the liability of passenger air carriers, especially the Warsaw and Montreal Conventions, prevail over the Consumer Defence Code').
471. STF, Full Court, HC 17118/SP, Rapp. Min. Gilmar Mendes, *DJ* 17 Aug. 2020 (ruling that, under the ICCPR and the ACHR, Brazilian authorities cannot criminally prosecute someone who has been already tried for the same facts in another country).
472. *See*, e.g., STF, Full Court, ADPF 526/PR, Rapp. Min. Cármen Lúcia, *DJ* 3 Jun. 2020; STF, Full Court, ADPF 460/PR, Rapp. Min. Luiz Fux, *DJ* 13 Aug. 2020.
473. STF, Full Court, ARE 1099099/SP, Rapp. Min. Edson Fachin, *DJ* 12 Apr. 2021 (excerpt from the opinion of the rapporteur).
474. STF, Full Court, ADI 4439/DF, Rapp. Min. Alexandre de Moraes, *DJ* 21 Jun. 2018.
475. STF, Full Court, RE 888815/RS, Rapp. Min. Alexandre de Moraes, *DJ* 21 Mar. 2019.
476. STF, Full Court, ADI 2566/DF, Rapp. Min. Edson Fachin, *DJ* 23 Oct. 2018.
477. STF, Full Court, ADI 3478/RJ, Rapp. Min. Edson Fachin, *DJ* 19 Feb. 2020.

ACHR, the ICCPR, and on decisions and documents of bodies of the Inter-American and international systems of human rights. This material was employed both for supporting a prohibition on discrimination and intolerance and for underscoring that freedom of speech – including religious speech – should be limited so as to prevent hate speech. Other Ministers as well have referred to international documents.[478]

263. Curiously, however, in the decision relating to animal sacrifice in African-Brazilian religious services, the Court made only passing references to international documents. Minister Fachin referred to the 2003 UNESCO Convention for the Safeguarding of the Intangible Cultural Heritage[479] to support his statement that sacrificial practices are part and parcel of the intangible cultural heritage.[480]

478. STF, Full Court, ADO 26/DF, Rapp. Min. Celso de Mello, *DJ* 6 Oct. 2020.
479. Leg. Dec. No. 22 of 1 Feb. 2006; Dec. No. 5753 of 12 Apr. 2006.
480. STF, Full Court, RE 494601/RS, Rapp. Min. Edson Fachin, *DJ* 19 Nov. 2019.

Chapter 2. Transnational Law Effects on Religious Communities

§1. Brazilian Law with International Effects

264. The main bodies of Brazilian law associated with international effect appear to be those of data protection and anti-corruption. Concerning the former, Brazilian law seemingly purports to apply to almost any processing of data, irrespective of the country where the processing entity is headquartered,[481] thus rendering it as somewhat comprehensive. It also regulates international transfer of data, making it only lawful in certain cases, such as those where countries or international organizations who receive such data duly comply with similar standards to those it establishes.[482] In the fight waged against corruption, Law No. 12846 of 1 August 2013 provides for strict civil and administrative liability for actions perpetrated against Brazilian or foreign governmental entities. Even events that occur abroad are governed by this law, should they ascribe to a Brazilian legal entity.[483]

265. Whilst these matters do not directly concern religion, religious organizations are also required to adhere to these statutes.

§2. Foreign Laws with Effects in Brazil

266. Data protection laws – particularly the General Data Protection Regulation (GDPR), passed by the European Union[484] – tend to present implications in Brazil as consequence to numerous companies and organizations that operate in the country undertaking activities or being headquartered in foreign states. This results in many Brazilian entities being required to comply, to a certain extent, with these laws and regulations. The same applies to anti-corruption laws, like the US Foreign Corrupt Practices Act and the UK Bribery Act 2010.

267. Foreign law can also prove relevant for granting asylum (refugee status) in Brazil. The status of refugee is granted by a collegiate body – the *Comitê Nacional para os Refugiados (CONARE)* [National Committee for Refugees] – under the Minister of Justice, who also decides on appeals against decisions denying an individual the condition of refugee.[485] Under Brazilian law, the status of refugee is to be granted to those who cannot, or are not willing to, rely on the protection of their country of nationality due to a well-founded fear of, among others, being persecuted for religious reasons.[486] However, the vast majority of CONARE decisions granting refugee status are grounded in serious and widespread violations of human

---

481. *Lei Geral de Proteção de Dados (LGPD)* [General Data Protection Law], Law No. 13709 of 14 Aug. 2018, Art. 3.
482. LGPD, Law No. 13709 of 14 Aug. 2018, Art. 33, I and II.
483. Law No. 12846 of 1 Aug. 2013, Art. 28.
484. Regulation (EU) 2016/679 of the European Parliament and of the Council of 27 Apr. 2016 (General Data Protection Regulation).
485. Law No. 9474 of 22 Jun. 1997, Arts 12, I, 26, 28, and 29.
486. Law No. 9474 of 22 Jun. 1997, Art. 1, I.

rights (93%), and less than 6% of the remaining decisions relate to fear of religious persecution. In this group, most cases involve people from Pakistan (38.92%), Morocco (8.37%) and Egypt (7.88%).[487]

487. Data about decisions rendered from January 2016–April 2021, obtained at Projeto de Cooperação para Análise das Decisões de Refúgio no Brasil, https://app.powerbi.com/view?r=eyJrIjoiNTQ4MTU0NGItYzNkMi00M2MwLWFhZWMtMDBiM2I1NWVjMTY5IiwidCI6ImU1YzM3OTgxLTY2NjQtNDEzNC04YTBjLTY1NDNkMmFmODBiZSIsImMiOjh9 (last visited 25 May 2021).

Chapter 3. Regional Law Effects on Religious Communities

§1. The Inter-American Human Rights System

268. Brazil is part of the Inter-American human rights system, which comprises documents and bodies within the scope of the Organization of American States (OAS). The most important references of note are the American Declaration of the Rights and Duties of Man (ADRDM), adopted a few months before the UDHR, in 1948,[488] and the ACHR, also known as the Pact of San José, adopted in 1969.[489]

269. Despite being a declaration, the ADRDM is recognized as legally binding on all State Parties to the Charter of the OAS, at least to the extent necessary for the interpretation of duties imposed on them by the Charter itself or other treaties.[490] The Declaration addresses religious freedom in its Article 3, which states: 'Every person has the right freely to profess a religious faith, and to manifest and practice it both in public and in private.' Also, in Article 22, the ADRDM guarantees the freedom of association in order 'to promote, exercise and protect … legitimate interests of a … religious, … or other nature'.

270. The ACHR is an international treaty, being therefore unquestionably binding on all of the State Parties – including Brazil. Its Article 12 enshrines the right to freedom of conscience and religion in the following terms:

1. Everyone has the right to freedom of conscience and of religion. This right includes freedom to maintain or to change one's religion or beliefs, and freedom to profess or disseminate one's religion or beliefs, either individually or together with others, in public or in private.
2. No one shall be subject to restrictions that might impair his freedom to maintain or to change his religion or beliefs.
3. Freedom to manifest one's religion and beliefs may be subject only to the limitations prescribed by law that are necessary to protect public safety, order, health, or morals, or the rights or freedoms of others.
4. Parents or guardians, as the case may be, have the right to provide for the religious and moral education of their children or wards that is in accord with their own convictions.

271. According to Article 27(1) of the ACHR, the right to religious freedom cannot be suspended by a State Party even in 'time of war, public danger, or other emergency that threatens [its] independence or security'.

---

488. Adopted by the 9th International Conference of American States, Bogotá, Colombia, 2 May 1948.
489. Adopted at the Inter-American Specialized Conference on Human Rights, San José, Costa Rica, 22 Nov. 1969. *See* Leg. Dec. No. 27 of 26 May 1992; Dec. No. 678 of 6 Nov. 1992.
490. *Interpretation of the American Declaration of the Rights and Duties of Man Within the Framework of Article 64 of the American Convention on Human Rights*, Advisory Opinion OC-10/89, Inter-Am. Ct HR (ser. A) No. 10 (14 Jul. 1989).

272. The Convention also protects the freedom of association 'for … religious … or other purposes', in its Article 16(1).

273. Another important source is the Inter-American Convention Against All Forms of Discrimination and Intolerance, adopted at La Antigua (Guatemala) in 2013. The Convention entered into force on 20 February 2020, following the deposit of instruments of ratification forwarded by Mexico and Uruguay. Brazil signed the Convention in 2013, and Congress approved it in 2021 with the status of a constitutional amendment.[491]

274. The Inter-American system accommodates two main bodies: the Inter-American Commission on Human Rights, established by the Charter of the OAS, and the Inter-American Court of Human Rights, created under the ACHR. Not all members of the OAS have ratified the ACHR[492] and recognize the jurisdiction of the Court, but all remain under the oversight of the Commission, regarding their obligations under the ACHR (for the State Parties thereof) and/or under the ADRDM (all members of the OAS).[493] Whereas opinions of the Court – both in its contentious and advisory jurisdiction – are expected to be adhered to by the States, even they are not parties to the proceedings,[494] the Commission can only issue recommendations and, after that, submit the matter to the Court if it deems necessary.[495] The Commission's recommendations, however, are worthy of serious consideration and should be acknowledged as incorporating persuasive authority.[496]

491. Under Leg. Dec. No. 1 of 18 Feb. 2021. The Convention was promulgated by Dec. No. 10932 of 10 Jan. 2022.

492. Two notable examples are the United States and Canada: the latter did not sign the Convention, whereas the former, having signed it, did not ratify it.

493. Piovesan, *supra* note 458 at 356.

494. *See Rights and Guarantees of Children in the Context of Migration and/or in Need of International Protection*, Advisory Opinion OC-21/14, Inter-Am. Ct HR (ser. A) No. 21, para. 31 (19 Aug. 2014); *Almonacid-Arellano et al. v. Chile*, Preliminary Objections, Merits, Reparations and Costs, Judgment, Inter-Am. Ct HR (ser. C) No. 154, para. 124 (26 Sep. 2006). Parties in contentious cases are bound by res judicata under the ACHR (Art. 68); all other States Parties to the Convention, though not formally bound, are expected to observe its interpretation by the Court. *See Gelman v. Uruguay*, Monitoring Compliance with Judgment, Order of the Court, Inter-Am. Ct HR, paras 67–69 (20 Mar. 2013). In this last situation, the decision has persuasive authority. *See* Luís Roberto Barroso, *Responsabilidade Internacional de Estado-Membro da Federação. Eficácia Jurídica das Recomendações da Comissão Interamericana de Direitos Humanos da OEA. Possibilidade e Meios de Seu Cumprimento pelo Estado do Rio de Janeiro (Parecer nº 01/2008 – LRB)*, 65 Revista de Direito da Procuradoria-Geral do Estado do Rio de Janeiro 269, 276–277 (2010).

495. ACHR, Arts 48–51.

496. Barroso, *supra* note 494 at 277–279.

275. Thus far, the Court has not examined many cases involving religious freedom,[497] but the Commission reports have dealt with some interesting matters, such as the right to conscientious objection to military service.[498]

497. In general, the relevant opinions of the Court discuss freedom of religion in connection with Indigenous rights. *See* Fernando Arlettaz, *La Libertad Religiosa en el Sistema Interamericano de Derechos Humanos*, 1 Revista Internacional de Derechos Humanos 39, 53 (2011). The only specific case involving religious freedom was related to a film depicting Jesus Christ which had allegedly been censored in Chile. The Court did not find any violation to the ACHR. *See Case of 'The Last Temptation of Christ' (Olmedo-Bustos et al.) v. Chile*, Merits, Reparations and Costs, Judgment, Inter-Am. Ct HR (ser. C) No. 73, para. 79 (5 Feb. 2001).

498. *See Cristián Daniel Sahli et al. v. Chile*, Case 12.129, Inter-Am. Comm'n HR, Report No. 43/05, OEA/Ser.L/V/II.124 doc. 5 (2005). For a thorough analysis, *see* Xiomara Lorena Romero Pérez, *La Libertad Religiosa en el Sistema Interamericano de Protección de los Derechos Humanos (Análisis Comparativo con el Ordenamiento Jurídico Colombiano)*, 29 Revista Derecho del Estado 215 (2012).

Part V. Religion and Politics

Chapter 1. Religious Influence in Politics

§1. Constitutional Principles

276. The Federal Constitution embraces democracy and, therefore, the equal standing of all citizens to participate in public affairs. The principle of 'one person, one vote' is expressly enshrined in the Constitution, which also establishes most of the rules in relation to suffrage.[499] The rights to vote and to run for elective office are conferred upon all citizens older than 16 years, but special conditions do apply to certain positions (e.g., only people who are 35 years old or older can run for Senator and President of the Republic). Voting is mandatory for citizens once they turn 18 years of age, with the exception of illiterate people and those over 70 years of age. Political rights may be suspended in certain situations (e.g., criminal conviction) or removed, should a person forfeit their Brazilian nationality.[500] Portuguese nationals may enjoy the rights of naturalized Brazilians, including the rights to vote and to run for elective offices, if they require so, whilst residing permanently in Brazil, provided that Portugal offers the same rights to Brazilian nationals.[501]

277. Being citizens, ministers and members of religious organizations are entitled to all these rights. But that was not always the case in Brazil. The 1824 Constitution reserved elective positions to Catholics and excluded religious ministers and those living in convents from the right to vote and run for office.[502] A provision akin to the latter was included in the 1891 Constitution: it stated that members of religious orders who, by virtue of their vows, had renounced their individual liberty, could not vote or seek elective positions.[503] Since the 1934 Constitution, however, this restriction has been non-existent.

278. Political parties are an essential part of the political process – individuals are required to register with a party to run for office.[504] The creation, merger, and

499. Const. (1988), Art. 14.
500. Const. (1988), Art. 15.
501. Const. (1988), Art. 12, para. 1.
502. Const. (1824), Arts 92, IV, 94, and 95, III.
503. Const. (1891), Art. 70, para. 1, no. 4.
504. There is one exception: military personnel, who are forbidden to register in political parties, may run, nonetheless. *See* Const. (1988), Art. 14, pars 3, V, and 8; and Art. 142, V.

dissolution of political parties are free, provided they respect national sovereignty, democracy, the multi-party system, and the fundamental rights of people. They must be national in scope (i.e., regional or state parties are not permitted), cannot receive funds, or be subordinated to, foreign entities and governments, and are also forbidden from soliciting paramilitary organizations.[505] Parties enjoy considerable autonomy, but after incorporation, they are required to register with the Superior Electoral Court and submit to the supervision of electoral courts.[506]

279. Freedom of speech is an integral part of the democratic regime, as the Federal Supreme Court has reiterated over the years. Specifically when it comes to elections, the free flow of ideas, opinions, and criticism – even by comedy and satire – must be protected.[507] As for campaign donations, the Court deemed unconstitutional a statutory provision regulating contributions by legal entities. According to the Court, 'donations from legal entities to election campaigns, instead of reflecting some political preference, display a strategic course of action by these big donors, so to strengthen their relations with the state' and are usually made in pursuit of private ends. As the relevant provision failed to provide sufficient safeguard against this problem, it was declared invalid. Individuals, on the other hand, are permitted to donate to campaigns.[508]

§2. Restrictions Imposed under Electoral Law

I. Campaigns and Advertising

280. The law forbids religious entities, and non-profits in general, from donating to political parties or candidates, 'including by means of advertising of any nature'.[509] Campaign advertising in religious temples is also prohibited,[510] and the Electoral Courts have frequently enforced this provision.[511] According to the Superior Electoral Court, religious speech is free under the Constitution, especially when uttered during religious services, but the use of churches to endorse candidates places it under the limits set forth by Electoral Law.[512]

505. Const. (1988), Art. 17, *caput*, I and II, and para. 4.
506. Const. (1988), Art. 17, III and para. 2.
507. *See*, e.g., STF, Full Court, ADI 4451/DF, Rapp. Min. Alexandre de Moraes, *DJ* 6 Mar. 2019.
508. STF, Full Court, ADI 4650/DF, Rapp. Min. Luiz Fux, *DJ* 24 Feb. 2016.
509. Law No. 9504 of 30 Sep. 1997, Art. 24, VIII.
510. Law No. 9504 of 30 Sep. 1997, Art. 37, *caput* and para. 4.
511. *See*, e.g., TSE, AgRg em AI 23930 – Rio de Janeiro/RJ, Rapp. Min. Admar Gonzaga, *DJ* 3 Aug. 2018; TSE, AgRg em AI 781963 – Volta Redonda/RJ, Rapp. Min. Gilmar Mendes, *DJ* 3 Feb. 2017, TSE, AgRg em AI 15028 – Campos dos Goytacazes/RJ, Rapp. Min. Dias Toffoli, *DJ* 7 Nov. 2013.
512. TSE, RO 265308 – Porto Velho/RO, Rapp. Min. Henrique Neves da Silva, *DJ* 5 Apr. 2017.

II. Abuse of Religious Power

281. The law provides for the annulment of elections when there is 'interference of economic power' or a 'misuse or abuse of power by an authority, in detriment of the freedom to vote'.[513] Religious entities may be involved in these acts: the illegal use of financial resources in campaign advertising may characterize an abuse of economic power.[514] Nonetheless, according to the Superior Electoral Court, this kind of abuse is only relevant when the facts are so serious that they can be said to have affected the legitimacy of the election and equality between the candidates.[515] For example, the Court confirmed that a religious event amounted to an abuse of economic power because it was held less than a day before the election, with a cost of approximately BRL 930,000, and during the event, a religious minister asked for votes for certain candidates.[516]

282. In this opinion, Minister Rosa Weber, in *dicta*, mentioned that the courts would have to deal with the impact that religious organizations and leaders could have on the electoral process – in an actual abuse of religious power. In the case at hand, it was unnecessary, given that the facts characterized an abuse of economic power, but it would soon be required to confront situations of outright religious abuse. According to Minister Weber, 'it is undeniable that public statements of endorsement of, or preference towards, a certain candidacy are protected by the constitutionally guaranteed freedom of expression'. But the 'use of religious discourse as a propellant of candidacies, infusing the political orientation of religious leaders so to unduly influence the political choice of their followers does not seem compatible with the very laicity that imbues the Brazilian state'. The power exerted by religious leaders could induce voting based 'not only on public conscience, but primarily on reverential awe'.

283. The matter came to be discussed in another case. Minister Edson Fachin stressed that 'the imperative of state neutrality does not entail … the complete elimination of the religious aspect from the political experience and, as consequence, from the context of electoral competition'. But religious groups could not annul their members' autonomy and unduly imbalance the elections in favour of a candidate. And that, according to Minister Fachin, led to the recognition of the abuse of religious power as an autonomous instance of illicit behaviour, so that, in future cases, the electoral courts could enforce its prohibition. This conclusion, however, was not supported by the majority of the Court. The risk of undue limitation of religious speech, the absence of an express statutory provision regarding this issue, and the existence of other limitations to religious entities when it came to

513. *Código Eleitoral* [Electoral Code], Law No. 4737 of 15 Jul. 1965, Arts 222 and 237.
514. TSE, RO 265308 – Porto Velho/RO, Rapp. Min. Henrique Neves da Silva, *DJ* 5 Apr. 2017.
515. *See*, e.g., TSE, REspE 61867 – Diadema/SP, Rapp. Min. Sergio Silveira Banhos, *DJ* 13 May 2021; TSE, AgInt no RO 060187690 – Porto Velho/RO, Rapp. Min. Luis Felipe Salomão, *DJ* 4 May 2021.
516. TSE, RO 537003 – Belo Horizonte/MG, Rapp. Min. Rosa Weber, *DJ* 27 Sep. 2018.

elections (e.g., prohibition on donations) led the Court to decide that the law did not include the abuse of religious power per se as an instance of forbidden behaviour.[517]

§3. Role of Religion in Political and Social Movements

284. In a deeply religious country such as Brazil, one could hardly expect religion to play a minor role in political and social movements. In fact, the position of the clergy – especially the Catholic Church – in relation to the most pressing and relevant issues was far from irrelevant: they abetted to undermine and to legitimize the enslavement of Indigenous and African people, respectively, and there was rarely a crisis in the country which did not involve the Church or a priest. The following topics discuss a few examples of movements and crises in which religion played a significant role in Brazil.

I. Slavery

285. The Catholic Church supported and legitimized the enslavement of people regarded as 'enemies of Christ' or when it was associated as a penalty for sins or the allegedly natural inferiority of certain 'races'. Sectors of the clergy, however – especially the Society of Jesus – opposed the enslavement of Indigenous peoples, as they were viewed as being born free and apt to being 'educated'.[518] Eventually, in 1537, pope Paul III forbade the enslavement of Indigenous people, and those who perpetrated it were to be excommunicated. Nonetheless, the colonists strongly resisted these ideas because they relied on Indigenous forced labour. Conflicts between colonists and the clergy were common and violent.[519] But enslavement remained intact, at times with the support of the government: a number of laws were passed by the Crown on the enslavement of Indigenous individuals, so as to prohibit, limit, or allow it until it was definitively forbidden in 1831.[520] Hence, 'due to the influence of the Catholic Church, whose participation in the colonial enterprise was very important, the Portuguese Absolutist State in general favoured the defence of the legal freedom of the Indians, whenever such freedom did not conflict with the interests of those detaining power'.[521]

517. TSE, REspE 8285 – Luziânia/GO, Rapp. Min. Edson Fachin, *DJ* 6 Oct. 2020.
518. J. Capistrano de Abreu, *Capítulos de História Colonial (1500–1800)*, 94–95 (1988). However, there was quite some ambiguity here, since the Jesuits themselves owned Indigenous slaves and also referred to the curse of Cam – used to legitimize the enslavement of African people – so as to admit the forced labour of Indigenous individuals. *See* Bueno, *supra* note 32 at 131–132.
519. Gomes, *supra* note 25 at 133.
520. Anderson José Machado de Oliveira, *Igreja e Escravidão Africana no Brasil Colonial*, 10 Cadernos de Ciências Humanas – Especiaria 355, 358–360 (2007); Manuel Martin Pino Estrada, *Panorama Jurídico da Escravidão Indígena no Brasil*, 18 Argumenta 207, 212–214 (2013).
521. Manoel Maurício de Albuquerque, *Pequena História da Formação Social Brasileira*, 31 (1981).

286. Conversely, the enslavement of African people and their descendants was more naturally avowed by the Church,[522] which also 'owned' enslaved people. They were regarded as having been 'marked' as the supposed descendants of Cam, Noah's son, who, according to the Bible, was declared, by his father, as 'servant to the servants' of his other children. Also, many of them had been imprisoned in Africa to be 'sold' to Europeans as slaves, so they were not recognized as being 'free' when 'bought' by the Portuguese.[523] Colonial canon law dealt extensively with enslaved people, and although it required that slave owners did not excessively punish, provide the enslaved a minimum of sustenance and clothing, and permit the undertaking of Christian obligations, it did not put into question slavery itself. 'On the contrary, [it] consider[ed] it a legitimate institution already in existence for 200 years in Portuguese colonies, legally permitted by the government, and accepted by most of the moralists of the time.'[524] Joaquim Nabuco, one of the leaders of the abolitionist movement, explained why, in Brazil, abolition was not fought under religious doctrines, like, for example, in the United States:

> In other countries, the defence of emancipation was a religious movement, preached from the pulpit, supported with devotion by the various churches and religious communions. Amidst us, the abolitionist movement, unfortunately, owes nothing to the Church of the State [i.e., Roman Catholic]; on the contrary, the possession of men and women by convents and all the secular clergy completely demoralized the religious sentiment of slave owners and slaves. In the priest the latter saw nothing more than a man who could buy them, whereas the former saw him as the last person who would remember to accuse them. The desertion, by our clergy, of the position that the Gospel had assigned them, was as shameful as it could possibly be … The Catholic Church, despite its immense power in a country that, for its most part, is still fanaticized by it, *never* elevated [its] voice in Brazil in favour of emancipation.[525]

287. It was only at the very end of the nineteenth century and of the monarchy that the Church began to support the abolition of slavery. Until then, its position on the matter had been, at best, ambiguous, due to the subordination of the Church to the state (patronage) and to the interest in avoiding a rupture within the social and economic establishment. In the end, however, even pope Leo XIII issued an encyclical on the matter, and local bishops finally spoke out against slavery, much due to the insistence of Joaquim Nabuco.[526]

---

522. Gomes, *supra* note 25 at 130–131.
523. Inácio Strieder, *A Igreja e a Escravidão no Brasil*, 28 Ciência & Trópico 219, 220 (2000); Oliveira, *supra* note 520 at 360–361.
524. Strieder, *supra* note 523 at 223.
525. Joaquim Nabuco, *O Abolicionismo*, 21–22 (2012).
526. Camila Mendonça Pereira, *Abolição e Catolicismo: A Participação da Igreja Católica na Extinção da Escravidão no Brasil*, 30–47 (2011).

II. Political Insurrections in the Colony and the Empire

288. In Brazilian colonial society, the clergy was part of the intellectual elite and many priests journeyed to Europe to complete their studies. Liberalism was on the rise in the eighteenth century, even in Portugal, and Catholic ministers brought these ideas to the colony, inspired by both the French and American Revolutions.[527] The Seminary of Olinda, in Pernambuco, for example, became a centre of study and diffusion of these new ideas.[528]

289. It is hardly surprising, then, that many insurrections involved priests, especially in North-eastern Brazil. Notably, one of the most famous was friar 'Caneca', who was involved in the 1817 Pernambucan Revolution and, after Brazilian Independence (1822), led the 1824 Confederation of the Equator, a separatist movement against the centralization of powers in the hands of Emperor Peter I, who had just dissolved the 1823 Constituent Assembly and unilaterally decreed the 1824 Constitution.[529]

III. Crises in the Empire

290. The demise of the Brazilian monarchy, in the second half of the nineteenth century, saw the rise of *ultramontanism* in the Roman Catholic Church, which was a movement of ecclesiastic centralization which sought to edge the Church towards closer control by Rome and, especially, the pope.[530] The Church, in Brazil, was under the system of patronage, being a part of, and subject to control by, the state. Rules and decisions of the Holy See could only be enforced if they were confirmed by the imperial authorities.[531] Imbued with the spirit of ultramontanism, two Brazilian bishops immediately enforced restrictions imposed by the Vatican on Catholic individuals who were freemasons. The government ordered them to recant, but they refused and were marched off to jail. The situation of unrest remained even after they were amnestied, bringing about a religious crisis that, alongside crises of other natures, helped to bring about the end of the monarchy and usher in the Proclamation of the Republic.[532]

IV. Proclamation of the Republic

291. Interestingly, one of the most relevant groups among those who proclaimed the Republic, in 1889, was the Positivists, especially Benjamin Constant.

---

527. Riolando Azzi, *A Influência do Pensamento Liberal no Clero Brasileiro (1789–1824)*, 11 Síntese 27 (1984).
528. Albuquerque, *supra* note 521 at 222.
529. *Ibid.* at 221–225, 345–349.
530. Zinnhobler and Moderna, *supra* note 113 at 347.
531. Const. (1824), Art. 102, XIV.
532. Magalhães Pires, *supra* note 105 at 36–37.

There was even some dispute as to whether he was the actual 'father' of the Republic, rather than of Marshal Deodoro da Fonseca, who led the coup that deposed the monarchy. Inspired by the ideas of Auguste Comte, the Brazilian Positivists defended the separation of church and state, a strong executive branch, and scientific and technological progress. Some prominent Brazilian Positivists even followed Comte's transformation of his philosophy into a theology – a religion of humanity – thus establishing, in Rio de Janeiro, the Positivist Church.[533]

V. Liberation Theology and Social Concerns

292. For the most part of Brazilian history, the Roman Catholic Church was aligned with the interests of the elites, being itself a part of them, as a source of moral and religious legitimacy. However, in the mid-twentieth century, a significant portion of the Church became more attuned to social matters, such as inequality and the living conditions of the poor. Archbishop Hélder Câmara is generally acknowledged as the most renowned cleric who championed these concerns. It was also during this period that, in Brazil – and in Latin America in general – important priests began to uphold the 'liberation theology', a more progressive interpretation of the Bible, that sought to transform reality itself.[534] The prominent advocates of this theology were Leonardo Boff and Cardinal Paulo Evaristo Arns – who, as archbishop of São Paulo, conducted an ecumenical service, in the cathedral, after journalist Vladimir Herzog was killed by the military regime, and who sold the episcopal palace to raise money to build houses for the poor.[535] By this time, the Church leadership had started to run counter to the military government – which it had initially supported.

VI. Anti-Abortionist Movement and LGBTQIA+ Rights

293. Focal points of unity for Christian groups in matters of fundamental rights and public policy are those involving reproductive and LGBTQIA+ rights. The legalization of abortion, as well as marriage and adoption by same-sex couples, are agendas that unify Catholic and Evangelical groups in Congress and in the streets. A survey, interviewing 106 prominent Christian individuals, confirmed that both charismatic Catholics and Evangelicals are aligned in principle on matters of 'sexual morality' and 'family'.[536]

---

533. José Murilo de Carvalho, *A Formação das Almas: O Imaginário da República no Brasil*, 29–30, 36–51 (2017).

534. Paulo Vitor de Souza Pinto, *As Alterações Políticas da Igreja Católica entre 1967 e 1971*, 9 Social Review 217, 218–221 (2020).

535. Marcelo Musa Cavallari, *Dom Paulo Evaristo Arns (1921 – 2016): Um Bispo de seu Tempo*, Época, 16 Dec. 2016, https://epoca.oglobo.globo.com/sociedade/noticia/2016/12/dom-paulo-evaristo-arns-1921-2016-um-bispo-de-seu-tempo.html.

536. Maria das Dores Campos Machado, *Religião e Política no Brasil Contemporâneo: Uma Análise dos Pentecostais e Carismáticos Católicos*, 35 Religião & Sociedade 45, 62–65 (2015).

Chapter 2. Political Influence in Religion

§1. Constitutional Framework

294. Religious freedom – especially in its collective form (freedom of religious organization) – prevents the state from interfering in the structure and operation of religious groups and communities. The laicity principle also forbids that the government establish, subsidize, enter into alliances or relationships of dependence with, or hinder the operation of religious denominations. *See* Part II, Chapters 2 and 3, *supra*, and Part V, Chapter 3, *infra*. Therefore, political influence on religion, if any, can only be informal and voluntary.

§2. Political Pressure on Religious Groups

295. In the past, only Catholicism was permitted in Brazil and, even when religious freedom was guaranteed, other denominations could not congregate in public services or gather in buildings with the external appearance of temples. This situation changed in 1890, with the implementation of the separation of government and church.

296. However, minority religions – especially of Indigenous and African-Brazilian communities – continued to be repressed by the state. The official discourse did not refer to religious prosecution, instead preferring other, more 'modern', pretexts, such as the protection of public health and morality. Indigenous and African-Brazilian religions were frequently persecuted for allegedly involving fraudulent practices in the administration of religious cures and treatments. More recently, nonetheless, this formal persecution has become rare, even though informal social discrimination and prejudice remain commonplace. Yet whilst not being ubiquitous, it still exists: there are cases involving the alleged prohibition of the use of African-Brazilian religious attire under the uniform by a student in a public school,[537] and of a local child protections service committee who filed an action to remove a 12-year old from her mother's custody for participating in a Candomblé ritual in which the juvenile's hair was shaved.[538] A judge initially placed her in the custody of her grandmother, but later reversed the decision to return the child to her mother.[539] In another case, the Prosecutors' Office charged a mother with battery for taking her 10-year-old daughter to a Candomblé ritual in which she was submitted

537. Mariucha Machado, *Aluno é Barrado em Escola Municipal do Rio por Usar Guias do Candomblé*, G1, 2 Sep. 2014, http://g1.globo.com/rio-de-janeiro/noticia/2014/09/aluno-e-barrado-em-escola-municipal-do-rio-por-usar-guias-do-candomble.html.

538. Rayane Moura, *Mãe Perde Guarda da Filha após Jovem Participar de Ritual do Candomblé*, UOL, 7 Aug. 2020, https://noticias.uol.com.br/cotidiano/ultimas-noticias/2020/08/07/mae-perde-guarda-da-filha-apos-jovem-participar-de-ritual-do-candomble.htm.

539. Márcio Zeni & Adrieli Fiorani, *Justiça Devolve Guarda de Adolescente para Mãe Denunciada por Maus-Tratos em Ritual de Candomblé*, G1, 14 Aug. 2020, https://g1.globo.com/sp/sao-jose-do-rio-preto-aracatuba/noticia/2020/08/14/justica-revoga-guarda-provisoria-concedida-a-avo-de-menina-que-passou-por-um-ritual-de-candomble.ghtml.

to scarification. The judge, however, dismissed the charges because the action, resulting in very small scars, was deemed protected under religious freedom.[540]

540. Campinas/SP, *Vara de Violência Doméstica e Familiar contra a Mulher* [Court of First Instance for Cases of Domestic and Family Violence Against Women], Proc. 1507648-71.2021.8.26.0114, 15 Jul. 2021.

Chapter 3. Interaction Between Religion and State on a Political and Legal Level

§1. The Laicity Principle

297. The laicity principle forbids the government from endorsing a position in debates in relation to the truth or validity of religious belief. It must remain impartial in discussions involving matters of religion. The laicity principle requires the state to abstain from endorsing or adhering to, specific perspectives about religion, from entangling with religious organizations (so as to be part of them or to make them a part of itself), and from endorsing preferential or detrimental treatment to certain religious convictions.

298. That is why statutes permitting or requiring the acquisition of the Bible by state institutions the likes of public libraries and schools, are declared unconstitutional.[541] Despite not invoking the laicity principle, the State Court of Appeals of Mato Grosso deemed that the misuse of public funds, which had been directed to a church for social assistance purposes but were employed to support its religious ends, amounted to a gross violation of public law (administrative improbity).[542] Some religious ministers have, nonetheless, been granted diplomatic passports, and courts do not find this illegal, refusing to hinder the Executive's discretion in issuing such passports.[543]

299. It is usually stressed that laicity does not presuppose any kind of animosity towards religion or distrust in religious views and practices; it does not expel religious people and worldviews from the public sphere, nor does it require the state to act as if religion did not exist or was irrelevant.[544] On the contrary, it simply means that the government should show equal respect for all reasonable doctrines whilst refraining from promoting or from illegitimately obstructing any such religion. According to the Federal Supreme Court, laicity cannot be misconstrued for 'the imposition of a secular perspective'; it rather 'materializes the respect and equal consideration that the state must guarantee to all people within a multicultural reality'.[545] Therefore, 'it purports to exclude the invocation of religious motivation in the public space as a justification for imposing obligations'.[546]

---

541. *See*, e.g., STF, Full Court, ADI 5258/AM, Rapp. Min. Cármen Lúcia, *DJ* 27 Apr. 2021; TJRJ, *Órgão Especial* [Special Panel], ADI 0018946-93.2015.8.19.0000, Rapp. CAJ Carlos Santos de Oliveira, *DJ* 4 Mar. 2016; TJRJ, *Órgão Especial* [Special Panel], ADI 0066288-37.2014.8.19.0000, Rapp. CAJ Carlos Eduardo da Rosa da Fonseca Passos, *DJ* 15 Oct. 2015; TJSP, *Órgão Especial* [Special Panel], ADI 2219902-57.2019.8.26.0000, Rapp. CAJ Cristina Zucchi, *DJ* 15 Jun. 2020.
542. TJMT, *2ª Câmara de Direito Público e Coletivo* [2nd Public and Collective Law Panel], Ap. 0003179-33.2005.8.11.0050, Rapp. CAJ José Zuquim Nogueira, *DJ* 20 Dec. 2016.
543. *See*, e.g., TRF – 3, *6ª Turma* [6th Panel], Ap. 5007691-61.2018.4.03.6100, Rapp. FCAJ Fábio Prieto, *DJ* 10 Sep. 2020.
544. Mendes and Branco, *supra* note 256 at 325; Sarlet, Marinoni and Mitidiero, *supra* note 256 at 532.
545. STF, Full Court, ADI 3478/RJ, Rapp. Min. Edson Fachin, *DJ* 19 Feb. 2020.
546. STF, Full Court, RE 494601/RS, Rapp. Min. Edson Fachin, *DJ* 19 Nov. 2019.

300. The Federal Constitution, however, permits cooperation between the state and religious denominations on issues of public interest, such as in education, healthcare, and assisting the destitute.[547] It then seems clear that the Brazilian laicity principle is closer to the United States' Establishment Clause than it is to the French *principe de laïcité.*

§2. Legislative Prayer

301. The laicity principle notwithstanding, the Houses of Congress are required, by rules of procedure, to open sessions invoking 'God's protection'.[548] The same occurs in state Legislative Assemblies,[549] and in Municipal Chambers.[550]

§3. Religious Symbols on Public Property

302. The laicity principle makes it unlawful for the government to display adherence to any religious denomination, or even atheism or agnosticism. The presence of religious symbols in public property is therefore a clear violation of this requirement,[551] and monuments to the Bible or content with religious symbols or citations in public property are forbidden.[552]

303. Nevertheless, the presence of Christian (especially Catholic) symbols is commonplace in government buildings. When the Chamber of Deputies – one of the two Houses of Congress – is in session, a copy of the Bible must be made available for all those who desire counsel.[553] It is also common that courthouses display crucifixes. Although the State Courts of Appeals of Rio de Janeiro and Rio Grande do

547. Const. (1988), Art. 19, I.
548. Reg. Int. (SF), Resolution (SF) No. 93 of 1970, Art. 155, para. 1; Reg. Int. (CD), Resolution (CD) No. 17 of 1989, Art. 79, para. 2.
549. *See*, e.g., Reg. Int. (ALEAM), Legislative Resolution (ALEAM) No. 469 of 2010, Art. 68, I; Reg. Int. (ALECE), Resolution (ALECE) No. 389 of 1996, Art. 169; Reg. Int. (ALERJ), Resolution (ALERJ), No. 810 of 1997, Art. 71, para. 1; Reg. Int. (ALERGS), Resolution (ALERGS) No. 2288 of 1991, Art. 94, para. 3, as amended by Resolution (ALERGS) No. 2978 of 2006.
550. *See*, e.g., Reg. Int. (CM) (Campo Grande/MS), Resolution (CM) (Campo Grande/MS) No. 1109 of 2009, Art. 7; Reg. Int. (CM) (Goiânia/GO), Resolution (CM) (Goiânia/GO) No. 26 of 1991, Art. 55; Reg. Int. (CM) (Rio de Janeiro/RJ), Resolution (CM) (Rio de Janeiro/RJ) No. 679 of 1992, Art. 29, sole par.; Reg. Int. (CM) (São Paulo/SP), Resolution (CM) (São Paulo/SP) No. 2 of 1991, Art. 137.
551. Historic landmarks are exceptions to this, due to their cultural value (*see* Part XI, Ch. 1, §4, *infra*).
552. *See,* e.g., TJCE, *2ª Câmara de Direito Público* [2nd Public Law Panel], Ap./Rem. Nec. 0023200-29.2010.8.06.0071, Rapp. CAJ Luiz Evaldo Gonçalves Leite, *DJ* 21 Jun. 2017; TJSP, *10ª Câmara de Direito Público* [10th Public Law Panel], Ap. 1004126-47.2016.8.26.0477, Rapp. CAJ Marcelo Semer, *DJ* 10 Sep. 2018. Reaching the opposite conclusion, *see* TJSP, *9ª Câmara de Direito Público* [9th Public Law Panel], Ap. 1006914-54.2016.8.26.0438, Rapp. CAJ Rebouças de Carvalho, *DJ* 17 Oct. 2017.
553. Reg. Int. (CD), Resolution (CD) No. 17 of 1989, Art. 79, para. 1.

Sul have ordered their removal,[554] the National Council of Justice admits their presence, as an alleged testament to customs in society.[555] In the Federal Supreme Court, the courtroom displays a crucifix in a prominent position, on the wall behind the President, placed higher than the Brazilian coat of arms. This is evidence of the strong influence that Christian ideas have forged in Brazil.

§4. Civil Religion

304. References to God are common in politics, as the legislative examples confirm (*see* Part V, Chapter 3, §2, *supra*). The President's oath of office does not include a reference to any deity or religion,[556] but, to date, at least seventeen presidential inauguration speeches have referenced God: Rodrigues Alves (1902), Affonso Penna (1906), Eurico Gaspar Dutra (1946), Getúlio Vargas (1951), Juscelino Kubitschek (1956), João Goulart (1961), Castello Branco (1964), Costa e Silva (1967), Emílio G. Médici (1969), Ernesto Geisel (1974), João B. Figueiredo (1979), Luís Inácio Lula da Silva (2003[557] and 2007[558]), Dilma Rousseff (2011 and 2015),[559] Michel Temer (2016),[560] and Jair Bolsonaro (2019).[561] The latter actually campaigned under the slogan *Brasil Acima de Tudo. Deus Acima de Todos* [Brazil Above Everything. God Above Everyone].

---

554. TJRS, *Conselho da Magistratura* [Judicial Council], Proc. 0139-11/000348-0, Rapp. CAJ Cláudio Baldino Maciel, *DJ* 9 Mar. 2012; Marina Ito, *Zveiter Assume TJ do Rio e Manda Retirar Crucifixos*, Consultor Jurídico, 3 Feb. 2009, https://www.conjur.com.br/2009-fev-03/luiz-zveiter-toma-posse-tj-rio-manda-retirar-crucifixos-corte. The former decision, however, was reversed by the National Council of Justice. *See*, e.g., CNJ, PCA 0001418-80.2012.2.00.0000, Rapp. Councilmember Emmanoel Campelo, *DJ* 5 May 2016). According to the Councilmember, the presence of religious symbols did not violate the laicity principle, whereas the State Court's decision amounted to discrimination.
555. CNJ, PP 1344, 1345, 1346, and 1362, Rapp. Councilmember Oscar Argollo, 6 Jun. 2007.
556. Under Art. 78 of the Constitution, the president and the vice president pledge 'to maintain, defend and carry out the Constitution, obey the laws, promote the general wellbeing of the Brazilian people, sustain the union, the integrity and the independence of Brazil'.
557. *Palavra de Presidente: Os Discursos Presidenciais de Posse, de Deodoro a Lula*, 82, 92, 231, 238, 248, 263, 272, 279, 282, 292, 303, 307 and 311 (João Bosco Bezerra Bonfim ed., 2008).
558. *Discurso de Posse – 2º Mandato (Lula)*, Presidência da República, http://www.biblioteca.presidencia.gov.br/presidencia/ex-presidentes/luiz-inacio-lula-da-silva/discursos/discursos-de-posse/discurso-de-posse-2o-mandato/@@download/file/posse%20lula%202007.pdf (last visited 13 May 2021).
559. *Íntegra do Discurso da Presidente Dilma Rousseff na Cerimônia de Posse*, Agência Senado, https://www12.senado.leg.br/noticias/materias/2011/01/01/integra-do-discurso-da-presidente-dilma-rousseff-na-cerimonia-de-posse (last visited 13 May 2021); Íntegra do Discurso de Posse da Presidente Dilma Rousseff no Congresso, Câmara dos Deputados, https://www.camara.leg.br/noticias/448217-integra-do-discurso-de-posse-da-presidente-dilma-rousseff-no-congresso/ (last visited 13 May 2021).
560. *Leia Íntegra do Discurso de Posse do Presidente Interino Michel Temer*, Folha de S. Paulo, 12 May 2016, https://www1.folha.uol.com.br/poder/2016/05/1770780-leia-integra-do-discurso-de-posse-do-presidente-interino-michel-temer.shtml.
561. *Leia Íntegra do Discurso de Bolsonaro na Cerimônia de Posse no Congresso*, Folha de S. Paulo, 1 Jan. 2019, https://www1.folha.uol.com.br/poder/2019/01/leia-a-integra-do-discurso-de-bolsonaro-na-cerimonia-de-posse-no-congresso.shtml.

305. Brazil has adopted numerous currencies throughout its history. Since the Cruzado (1986), at the request of President Sarney, bills display the inscription *Deus Seja Louvado* [God Be Praised]. In 1994, Real, the currency still in circulation, was introduced without the phrase, but it was readopted shortly after, never to be removed again. The Federal Prosecutors' Office filed a suit to have it expunged from the bills, but the courts denied it (there are appeals pending).[562]

§5. Religion and Politics

306. The 1824 Constitution required that the emperor, the imperial princess/prince (presumptive heir to the throne), regents, and members of the Council of State[563] took an oath of office that swore 'to keep the Roman Catholic Apostolic Religion'.[564] The same was demanded of Senators in the 1826 House Internal Rules.[565] Also, only Catholics were allowed to serve in the Chamber of Deputies (one of the two Houses of the General Assembly, the national legislature).[566] The percentage of clerics in the legislature was proportionally higher at first (ca. 30%), but over time their presence gradually diminished.[567] As a further symptom of the growing distance between state and religion, the refusal of a Deputy to take the religious oath did not prevent him from assuming office and, in 1881, a law removed all religious restrictions to elective offices. It also dispensed with the religious ceremonies that preceded the electoral work and forbade the use of temples as voting centres, unless in the case of an 'absolute lack of other buildings' for this purpose.[568]

307. After the Proclamation of the Republic (1889), the Provisional Government, in 1890, separated the state from the Roman Catholic Church and religion in general terms. From then on, no religious oath or affiliation was required from any office holder in Brazil. However, the number of Christians – especially Roman

562. TRF – 3, *6ª Turma* [6th Panel], Ap./Rem. Nec. 0019890-16.2012.4.03.6100, Rapp. FACJ Johonsom di Salvo, *DJ* 21 Dec. 2017. According to the Court, the reference to God in the bills did not offend atheists, who 'must tolerate and respect the belief of others and public exposure to religious expressions and symbolisms'. References to God 'are rooted in Brazilian History and in the customs of our people; it is not an offense to any cult or religion in particular' or to those who declare to be atheists. 'This practice to refer or to direct oneself to a deity – generically treated as God – reached 73.6% of Brazilians in 2016. And it is far from bringing offence to the circa 8.00% who claim to have no religion'. The Prosecutors' Office filed appeals to the STJ and the STF. The first was dismissed (*see* STJ, AREsp 1748279/SP, Rapp. Min. Francisco Falcão, *DJ* 9 Apr. 2021; in chambers). The second still lies before the Federal Supreme Court (ARE 1330911/SP).
563. The Council of State was composed of up to ten (later twelve) people, appointed for life by the emperor. It was supposed to act as a source of guidance and advice to the monarch and the ministers. The Council was suppressed by a constitutional reform in 1834, but was reinstated under ordinary statute in 1841, with a few modifications. *See* José Antônio Pimenta Bueno, *Direito Público Brasileiro e Análise da Constituição do Império*, 283–285 (1978).
564. *See* Const. (1824), Arts 103, 106, 127, and 141.
565. 1826 Reg. Int. (Imperial Senate), Art. 18.
566. Const. (1824), Arts 95, III.
567. Ciarallo, *supra* note 110 at 86–87.
568. '*Lei Saraiva*', Law No. 3029 of 9 Jan. 1881, Arts 10 and 15, pars 2 and 6.

Catholics – who occupy the most important positions in the Republic is still very high. *See* General Introduction, §2, XI *supra*.

Part VI. Labour Law Within Religious Communities

Chapter 1. Scope of Application of Labour Law

§1. General Background

308. The fundamental rights of workers are guaranteed in Brazil via the Constitution,[569] which authorizes more benefits and greater protection to be afforded by other means, such as individual contracts and collective bargaining. Labour law is a subject of exclusive federal legislative jurisdiction,[570] the most important statute on the matter being the *CLT* [Consolidation of Labour Laws] of 1943.[571] This applies to all relationships involving an employer and an employee, regardless of a formal contract, and adopts broad definitions of both terms: the former includes, for example, private businesses and non-profits[572] – including religious organizations and other religious-oriented entities – whilst the latter encompasses any natural person providing services in a continuous basis to an employer, to whom they are subordinated, in exchange for a salary.[573]

309. Workers and employers are free to organize unions, who are then entitled to represent the whole industry sector (e.g., teachers, schools, healthcare workers, hospitals) in a given place, both in negotiations with individual employers or their unions and before the courts. There are specialized labour courts in the federal judiciary, structured within a three-tiered system, with the *Tribunal Superior do Trabalho (TST)* [Superior Labour Court] at its apex. Appeals against decisions of the TST can only be filed before the Federal Supreme Court.

569. Const. (1988), Arts. 7–10.
570. Const. (1988), Art. 22, I.
571. CLT, Decree-Law No. 5452 of 1 May 1943.
572. It should be noted, however, that labour law does not apply to civil servants and military personnel, whose relationships with the state are governed by Administrative Law.
573. CLT, Decree-Law No. 5452 of 1 May 1943, Arts 2, *caput* and paras 1 and 3.

§2. Non-discrimination in Labour Law

310. Employers are required to treat their employees equally,[574] and it is actually a crime to discriminate against an employee because of their religion.[575] An employer can also be punished with an administrative fine and be excluded from obtaining loans from official financial institutions.[576] In the case of wrongful (discriminatory) termination, a former employee can claim compensation for moral damages, as well as reinstatement with pay for the duration after their dismissal, or not to return to their list of duties, thus receiving double of this amount.[577] Employers can also pay damages for not mending a hostile work environment, in which employees are subjected to religious-based insults from colleagues.[578]

311. Statutory law does not expressly require an employer to respect the employee's days of religious observance, although this obligation can be inferred from a duty to treat all staff members equally, which provides a grounding basis for a duty of reasonable accommodation of religious claims.[579] However, the Superior Labour Court appears not to hold a clear opinion on this matter. In two cases involving claims of Adventist employee exemption from work duties on Saturdays, the Court decided in opposite ways: in the first, it required reasonable accommodation and granted the employee's claim,[580] whilst, in the second, the Court upheld employee termination on grounds that to permit absence from work on Saturdays would be tantamount to a privilege vis-à-vis the other employees.[581]

§3. Social Security

312. The social security system is funded by budgetary appropriations and, especially, by *contribuições sociais* (contributions to social welfare), levied, e.g., on both employers and employees. When devoted to operations in the domains of education, healthcare, and social assistance, non-profit entities – including those with religious purposes – can apply for a certification as *entidades beneficentes de assistência social* (charitable social assistance entities). This certification renders

574. The landmark case here did not involve religion, but the Federal Supreme Court did state that it is unconstitutional for employers to discriminate against their employees on the grounds of 'sex, race, nationality, religious belief etc.'
575. Law No. 7716 of 5 Jan. 1989, Arts 4 and 20.
576. Law No. 9029 of 13 Apr. 1995, Art. 3.
577. Law No. 9029 of 13 Apr. 1995, Art. 4. *See also* TST, *8ª Turma* [8th Panel], AIRR 1786-76.2013.5.10.0016, Rapp. Min. Jane Granzoto Torres da Silva, *DJ* 8 May 2015.
578. TST, *6ª Turma* [6th Panel], RR 37200-77.2006.5.02.0025, Rapp. Min. Aloysio Correa da Veiga, *DJ* 13 Sep. 2013; TST, *6ª Turma* [6th Panel], ARR 725-66.2012.5.04.0281, Rapp. Min. Katia Magalhães Arruda, *DJ* 15 May 2015.
579. Magalhães Pires, *supra* note 105 at 228–233.
580. TST, *1ª Turma* [1st Panel], RR 51400-80.2009.5.21.0017, Rapp. Min. Hugo Carlos Scheuermann, *DJ* 30 jun. 2015.
581. TST, *7ª Turma* [7th Panel], RR 548-89.2010.5.09.0069, Rapp. Min. Ubirajara Carlos Mendes, *DJ* 7 Dec. 2018.

them 'immune' to paying contributions to social welfare.[582] Also, amounts paid to religious ministers and similar individuals (e.g., friars) are not considered salaries for the purposes of calculating the contributions to social welfare owed by the organization.[583]

582. Const. (1988), Art. 195, para. 7; Law No. 12101 of 27 Nov. 2009.
583. Law No. 8212 of 24 Jul. 1991, Art. 22, pars 13–14.

Chapter 2. Religious Ministers and Labour Law

313. For the purposes of Labour Law, as a rule, ministers are not considered employees of the religious organizations to which they belong. According to the Superior Labour Court, their work being 'a gift and a calling in the service of the faith', it is not possible to categorize them as employees, even when they do receive some compensation.[584] However, this is not a rule; there is rather a presumption of voluntary work, which depends on the relationship between minister and organization remaining directed to religious ends, and not to other, more commercial profit-seeking objectives.[585]

314. Religious ministers are required to pay income tax and contributions to social welfare because the immunities and exemptions of the organizations do not extend to the amounts received by their ministers and employees.[586]

584. TST, *6ª Turma* [6th Panel], AIRR 1259-32.2016.5.12.0027, Rapp. RCJ Cilene Ferreira Amaro Santos, *DJ* 23 Nov. 2018.
585. TST, *2ª Turma* [2nd Panel], Ag-AIRR 664-33.2017.5.12.0048, Rapp. Min. Maria Helena Mallmann, *DJ* 14 Aug. 2020; TST, *8ª Turma* [8th Panel], AIRR 748-66.2014.5.03.0023, Rapp. Min. Maria Cristina Irigoyen Peduzzi.
586. Law No. 7713 of 22 Dec. 1988, Art. 7, II; RFB, *Solução de Consulta* [Advisory Opinion] No. 254-Cosit of 26 May 2017.

Chapter 3. Other Church Employees and Labour Law

315. Aside from ministers, church employees adhere to the same rules that apply to employees of businesses and non-profit organizations. Despite their nature or purposes, religious organizations and religious-oriented entities are also required to respect the freedom of religion of their employees. Consequently, employees must not be harassed by religious entities into participating in services or other religious practices.[587]

587. *See*, e.g., TRT – 6, *2ª Turma* [2nd Panel], RO 0001547-97.2010.5.06.0013, Rapp. RCJ Eneida Melo Correia de Araújo, *DJ* 2 Aug. 2011.

Part VII. Religious Communities and Protections of the Individual

Chapter 1. Protection of Privacy

§1. Constitutional Protection of Privacy

316. The Federal Constitution provides for a fundamental right to privacy in Article 5, X, which reads: 'the privacy, private life, honour and image of persons are inviolable, and the right to compensation for property or moral damages resulting from their violation is ensured'. The Constitution, therefore, not only protects privacy but also ensures compensation in cases of its violation by anyone.

317. Privacy is usually described as encompassing a right to decide who can access information concerning one's personal life, tastes, beliefs and opinions, as well as their inner circle of friends and family.[588] Protection is greater the more intimate and personal the information is, but it is commonly said to include sensitive data involving, e.g., the religious or political affiliation of a person, diaries, financial and tax records, personal files, mail, telephone and online conversations or messages, as well as access to one's house and work environment. The Federal Supreme Court has also affirmed an unwritten right to the protection of personal data (informational self-determination), so to empower the individual to control the flow of any relative personal data.[589]

318. In some instances, the Constitution and the case law of the Federal Supreme Court reserve special regimes. One can only enter another person's house with their consent, 'except in the event of *flagrante delicto* or disaster, or to provide assistance, or, during the day, by court order'.[590] Also, the secrecy of telephone and data communications can only be set aside – so as to record conversations – by order of a court, when proven necessary in a criminal procedure or investigation, and other legal requirements are met.[591] Letters, telegrams, and packages cannot be

588. Weingartner Neto, *supra* note 257 at 129.
589. STF, Full Court, ADI 6390 MC-Ref/DF, Rapp. Min. Rosa Weber, *DJ* 12 Nov. 2020.
590. Const. (1988), Art. 5, XI.
591. *Ibid. See also* Law No. 9296 of 24 Jul. 1996. The Federal Supreme Court has decided that telephone records (lists of calls made and received by a number) and data stored in electronic devices are not as protected as actual communications, whose recording/interception is limited to the situations prescribed by the Constitution. *See*, e.g., STF, *1ª Turma* [1st Panel], RHC 169682 AgR/RS,

opened, except under the law or a court ruling.[592] The protection of financial and tax records is less stringent so that they can be produced without a court order, at the direct request of administrative and investigative bodies (e.g., revenue service departments, parliamentary committees of inquiry).[593] It is even possible to publish the wages of public servants online,[594] and the state cannot restrict access to information regarding refunds paid to congresspersons[595] – all because citizens possess the right to know how public funds are spent.

319. The right to privacy is usually seen as guaranteeing the individual the sole power to decide whether or not to share their personal information and with whom. It is primarily concerned, then, with the disclosure of data about a person. As for self-determination in general, other fundamental rights and provisions máy apply, making it unnecessary to resort to privacy. Nonetheless, it has been invoked by the Federal Supreme Court in cases involving, e.g., termination of pregnancy with anencephalous foetuses,[596] recognition of same-sex unions,[597] transgender people's right to change their name and gender in the public records.[598]

§2. Privacy in International Documents Signed by Brazil

320. The right to privacy is also enshrined by international declarations and treaties signed by the Federative Republic of Brazil. A few worthy of note are the UDHR, the ICCPR, the ADRDM, and the ACHR, which read, respectively:

> No one shall be subjected to arbitrary interference with his privacy, family, home or correspondence, nor to attacks upon his honour and reputation. Everyone has the right to the protection of the law against such interference or attacks.[599]
>
> 1. No one shall be subjected to arbitrary or unlawful interference with his privacy, family, home or correspondence, nor to unlawful attacks on his honour and reputation.

Rapp. Min. Luiz Fux, *DJ* 12 May 2020; STF, *2ª Turma* [2nd Panel], HC 91867/PA, Rapp. Min. Gilmar Mendes, *DJ* 20 Sep. 2012. More recently, however, there appears to have been a slight change in the understanding of the STF so as to require a court warrant to grant access to data stored in cellphones. *See* STF, *2ª Turma* [2nd Panel], HC 168052/SP, Rapp. Min. Gilmar Mendes.

592. STF, Full Court, RE 1116949/PR, Rapp. Min. Edson Fachin, *DJ* 2 Oct. 2020.
593. *See*, e.g., STF, Full Court, RE 601314/SP, Rapp. Min. Edson Fachin, *DJ* 16 Sep. 2016; STF, Full Court, RE 1055941/SP, Rapp. Min. Dias Toffoli, *DJ* 18 Mar. 2021; STF, Full Court, M. Seg. 23452/RJ, Rapp. Min. Celso de Mello, *DJ* 12 May 2000.
594. STF, Full Court, ARE 652777/SP, Rapp. Min. Teori Zavascki, *DJ* 1 Jul. 2015.
595. STF, Full Court, M. Seg. 28178/DF, Rapp. Min. Luís Roberto Barroso, *DJ* 8 May 2015.
596. STF, Full Court, ADPF 54/DF, Rapp. Min. Marco Aurélio, *DJ* 30 Apr. 2013.
597. STF, Full Court, ADI 4277/DF and ADPF 132/RJ, Rapp. Min. Carlos Ayres Britto, *DJ* 14 Oct. 2011.
598. STF, Full Court, RE 670422/RS, Rapp. Min. Dias Toffoli, *DJ* 10 Mar. 2020.
599. UDHR, Art. 12.

2. Everyone has the right to the protection of the law against such interference or attacks.[600]

Every person has the right to the protection of the law against abusive attacks upon his honour, his reputation, and his private and family life.[601]

1. Everyone has the right to have his honour respected and his dignity recognized.
2. No one may be the object of arbitrary or abusive interference with his private life, his family, his home, or his correspondence, or of unlawful attacks on his honour or reputation.
3. Everyone has the right to the protection of the law against such interference or attacks.[602]

321. According to the Inter-American Court of Human Rights, the protection of private and family life enshrined in the ACHR includes the right of transgender people to change their names and to rectify public records and identity documents to conform to their self-perceived identities, and the right of same-sex couples to have their unions and marriages recognized by the state without any form of discrimination. That is because 'the right to private life' extends beyond mere privacy, encompassing 'the capacity [of an individual] to develop their own personality and aspirations, determine their identity, and define their personal relationships', including 'the capacity to develop their own personality and aspirations, determine their identity, and define their personal relationships'.[603]

§3. Federal Laws Concerning Privacy

I. Civil Code

322. The Civil Code refers to 'the private life of the natural person' as 'inviolable', empowering judges, 'at the request of the interested party' to 'adopt the necessary measures to prevent or to stop an act in contradiction with this provision'.[604] In a controversial article, the Code also seemed to allow individuals to forbid (and to claim damages for) the disclosure of writings, the transmission of words, or the exposure or use of one's image if they affect their honour or are made for profit.[605]

---

600. ICCPR, Art. 17.
601. ADRDM, Art. 5.
602. ACHR, Art. 11.
603. *See Gender Identity, and Equality and Non-discrimination of Same-Sex Couples. State Obligations Concerning Change of Name, Gender Identity, and Rights Derived from a Relationship Between Same-Sex Couples (Interpretation and Scope of Articles 1(1), 3, 7, 11(2), 13, 17, 18 and 24, in Relation to Article 1, of the American Convention on Human Rights)*, Advisory Opinion OC-24/17, Inter-Am. Ct HR (ser. A) No. 24, para. 87 (24 Nov. 2017).
604. CC, Law No. 10406 of 10 Jan. 2002, Art. 21.
605. CC, Law No. 10406 of 10 Jan. 2002, Art. 20.

That reference apparently meant that biographies, for example, could only be published with the consent of the depicted persons, but the Federal Supreme Court ruled that such an interpretation would violate the freedoms of thought and speech.[606]

II. Data Protection Laws

323. As mentioned before, the Federal Supreme Court has affirmed a fundamental right to the protection of personal data (*see* Part VIII, Chapter 1, §1, *supra*).[607] Also, like many other countries, Brazil has recently enacted laws to regulate the use of personal data, especially in the context of the Internet. In 2014, Congress passed the *Marco Civil da Internet (MCI)* [Civil Framework Law for the Internet], which forbids their disclosure without consent or in the absence of one of the situations prescribed by the law (e.g., when it is necessary for civil or criminal proceedings). It also guarantees the data subject's right to request the erasure of their data (when their storage is not required by law).[608]

324. The most comprehensive statute on this issue is the *Lei Geral de Proteção de Dados (LGPD)* [General Data Protection Law], enacted in 2018. It is particularly broad in its scope, so as to apply to almost any use of personal data.[609] In a nutshell, the LGPD safeguards the privacy of data subjects and confers upon them a number of rights (e.g., to confirm that a processing is taking, or has taken, place; to have access to their data; to correct data stored; to know with whom their data have been shared).[610] In particular, the LGPD considers it unlawful to process personal data unless (at least) one of the legal bases for such use applies (e.g., when the subject has consented to the processing of their data when it is necessary to comply with legal or regulatory duties of the controller,[611] to protect someone's life or

606. STF, Full Court, ADI 4815/DF, Rapp. Min. Cármen Lúcia, *DJ* 1 Feb. 2016.

607. In the interest of transparency, I should inform readers that, as an attorney-at-law, I currently represent an application service provider before courts. Also, the law firm I work with provides services to companies and organizations who wish to adapt their operations so to ensure compliance with Brazilian data protection laws. Although I strongly believe that this situation does not amount to any form of conflict of interest, and despite being committed to reporting Brazilian law in the fairest possible way, one can never rule out the possibility that my professional relationship with the subject-matter may result in an unconsciously biased view. I hope that it does not, and I encourage readers to inform me if they feel that a different point of view should be incorporated to any part of this monograph.

608. *Marco Civil da Internet* [Civil Framework Law for the Internet], Law No. 12965 of 23 Apr. 2014, Arts 3, III; 7, VII, VIII, and X; 10–17; and 22.

609. The law regulates *treatment* of *personal data*. It defines the latter as 'information related to an identified or identifiable natural personal', and the former as 'any operation carried out with personal data, such as those related to [their] collection, production, receiving, classification, use, access, reproduction, transmission, distribution, processing, filing, storage, erasure, evaluation or control of the information, modification, communication, transfer, diffusion, or extraction'. *See* LGPD, Law No. 13709 of 14 Aug. 2018, Art. 5, I and X. The word 'processing' shall be used in this monograph, in lieu of 'treatment' because it is more frequently used in this context.

610. LGPD, Law No. 13709 of 14 Aug. 2018, Art. 18, I, II, III, and VII.

611. The controller is the person or entity who decides about the processing of data. *See* LGPD, Law No. 13709 of 14 Aug. 2018, Art. 5, VI.

health, or to serve purposes of legitimate interests sought by the controller or a third party).[612] The law provides special protection for *sensitive data*, i.e., those in relation to an individual's 'racial and ethnic origin, religious conviction, political opinion, membership to trade unions or organizations with a religious, philosophical, or political character' or to one's 'health or sex life, genetic or biometric data'.[613] Processing sensitive data requires more caution, and only certain legal bases authorize their use without the subject's consent – invoking legitimate interests of the controller, for example, does not warrant the processing of sensitive data.[614]

325. To comply with the LGPD, persons and entities are required to adopt proper measures to ensure the protection and secrecy of the personal data that they process.[615] Controllers must also appoint a data protection officer to serve as a liaison between them, the data subjects, and the *Autoridade Nacional de Proteção de Dados (ANPD)* – the data protection authority.[616]

326. Like any other private entities, religious organizations process personal data – of their ministers, employees, members, third parties – and are thus required to comply with the LGPD. Since data referring to religious convictions of people and their affiliation to religious-oriented entities are considered sensitive data, a relevant part of all information processed by religious organizations can require special caution under the law. The same goes for employers who offer special regimes to their employees due to their religions (e.g., paid leaves on days of worship) and, for that reason, maintain a record of their religious affiliation.

327. As for the MCI, it is fundamentally directed at Internet providers of connection or applications; in some cases, however, it has been invoked by public institutions and private entities – including religious organizations – not to protect, but to restrict the secrecy of personal data of users when they allegedly offended a religious creed or denomination or engaged in acts of religious intolerance. As evidence of illegality is required by the law to warrant the disclosure of a user's connection or access records,[617] only when the freedoms of speech or religion do not afford sufficient protection to an act can a court enjoin a provider to disclose user connection/access records to the requesting party.[618]

---

612. LGPD, Law No. 13709 of 14 Aug. 2018, Art. 7, I, II, and VII.
613. LGPD, Law No. 13709 of 14 Aug. 2018, Art. 5, II.
614. For the legal bases applicable to the processing of sensitive data, *see* LGPD, Law No. 13709 of 14 Aug. 2018, Art. 11.
615. LGPD, Law No. 13709 of 14 Aug. 2018, Arts 46–49.
616. LGPD, Law No. 13709 of 14 Aug. 2018, Arts 5, VIII, and 41.
617. *Marco Civil da Internet* [Civil Framework Law for the Internet], Law No. 12965 of 23 Apr. 2014, Art. 22, sole par., I.
618. *See*, e.g., TJDFT, *6ª Turma Cível* [6th Civil Panel], Ap. 0701352-70.2020.8.07.0004, Rapp. CAJ Vera Andrighi, *DJ* 10 Mar. 2021 (denying disclosure because the user's criticism of a church and its leaders were protected by freedom of speech); TJSP, *6ª Câmara de Direito Privado* [6th Private Law Panel], AI 2067268-47.2017.8.26.0000, Rapp. CAJ Rodolfo Pellizari, *DJ* 15 Aug. 2017 (denying disclosure because the user's posts about a church were protected by freedom of speech); TJSP,

III. Non-disclosure of Finances of Religious Organizations

328. Religious organizations, like any other private legal entities, are entitled to the protection of fundamental rights which are compatible with their nature (*see* Part II, Chapter 1, §5, *supra*). That includes the right to privacy – especially in relation to the secrecy of their financial and tax records, which may only be disclosed in the situations prescribed by law.[619] These involve, e.g., the investigation of crimes.

IV. Privacy in Judicial, Administrative, and Legislative Proceedings

329. The Constitution requires that all judicial proceedings be conducted publicly so that everyone can have access to the files, trials, and judgments unless the protection of the privacy or public interest demand otherwise.[620] These situations include, e.g., suits involving marriages and divorces, intimate information, and those related to arbitration (should the latter be confidential, according to the parties' stipulation).[621] In criminal cases, the interest in protecting the victim from undue exposure authorizes the judge to seal certain data and files.[622] Jurors' votes are also confidential,[623] and two years after a conviction time is served, the records are then sealed.[624] An investigation can also be conducted in secrecy, should it prove necessary not to frustrate its purpose, but the attorneys of the parties involved have to right to access any documents attached to the files, except those regarding ongoing diligence.[625]

330. The Administration is also required to operate in a transparent manner, under the 'publicity principle'.[626] The Constitution confers a fundamental right of access to information, which includes the right to receive all information of individual concern or of collective interest, except for classified documents and data, when secrecy is necessary to protect the security of society and the state. The Federal Constitution even establishes the *habeas data*, a special procedure in which the plaintiff can request access to information about them, stored in records or data banks with a public character, correction of erroneous information, or justification of true data under litigation.[627]

6ª Câmara de Direito Privado [6th Private Law Panel], AI 20677526-57.2017.8.26.0000, Rapp. CAJ Rodolfo Pellizari, *DJ* 26 Sep. 2017 (confirming a lower court order which had granted disclosure of data requested by a church).

619. CTN, Law No. 5172 of 25 Oct. 1966, Art. 198; Complementary Law No. 105 of 10 Jan. 2001.
620. Const. (1988), Arts 5, LX, and 93, XI.
621. CPC, Law No. 13105 of 16 Mar. 2015, Art. 189, II, III, and IV.
622. *Código de Processo Penal (CPP)* [Code of Penal Procedure], Decree-Law No. 3689 of 3 Oct. 1941, Art. 201, para. 6, included by Law No. 11690 of 9 Jun. 2008, Art. 1.
623. Const. (1988), Art. 5, XXXVIII, *d.*
624. CP, Decree-Law No. 2848 of 7 Dec. 1940, Arts 93–95.
625. *See* CPP, Art. 20; STF, *Súmula Vinculante* [Binding Thesis] No. 14; STF, *2ª Turma* [2nd Panel], HC 93767/DF, Rapp. Min. Celso de Mello, *DJ* 1 Apr. 2014.
626. Const. (1988), Art. 37, *caput.*
627. Const. (1988), Art. 5, XIV, XXXIII, and LXXII; Law No. 12527 of 18 Nov. 2011; Law No. 9507 of 12 Nov. 1997.

331. According to the Federal Supreme Court, publicity is a rule also in legislative proceedings – votes can be only cast secretly when the Federal Constitution demands so.[628] Secrecy is required, e.g., in the Senate confirmation of officials appointed by the President.[629]

332. Another important topic in privacy matters is that of priest-penitent privilege. It is dealt with in a specific chapter of this monograph (*see* Part VII, Chapter 5, *infra*).

§4. Disclosure of Religious Affiliation

333. Although neither the Federal Constitution nor the ICCPR expressly guarantees a right not to disclose one's belief or opinion in matters of religion, the presence of both the rights to privacy and to freedom of belief provides such protection to individuals. They can therefore refuse to reveal their views on these matters and cannot be compelled to do so.[630] In Brazil, the legislation awards greater protection to personal data involving one's religion (*see* §3, II, *supra*).

---

628. STF, Full Court, ADPF 378 MC/DF, Rapp. Min. Luís Roberto Barroso, *DJ* 8 Mar. 2016; STF, Full Court, ADI 1057 MC/BA, Rapp. Min. Celso de Mello, *DJ* 6 Apr. 2001.
629. Const. (1988), Art. 52, III and IV.
630. UNHRC General Comment No. 22 (48) (Art. 18), *supra* note at para. 3; Weingartner Neto, *supra* note 257 at 116–117 and 128–131; Magalhães Pires, *supra* note 105 at 144.

Chapter 2. Freedom to Marry

§1. Introduction

334. As mentioned above (*see* Part I, Chapter 2, §1, I), Christian precepts – especially those of the Roman Catholic Church – have always exerted enormous influence on Brazilian law. Marriage was initially the sole basis of families, divorce was not permitted, and informal civil partnerships – pejoratively called *concubinatos* [concubinages] – were not recognized by the state. The situation has dramatically transformed over the years, as the law was compelled to deal with reality, and Catholicism concede ground in Brazil. Instead of this single-modelled family, one now speaks of a 'pluralism of family relationships', in which the traditional, matrimonial, kind is but one species in a larger genus.[631] This development has been incremental, but the 1988 Constitution was an unquestionable milestone in this path.

335. The actual existence of common-law marriages led to the progressive recognition of rights to their participants[632] until the 1988 Constitution recognized them in explicit terms: under the name of *uniões estáveis* [stable unions], they are currently a legitimate form of family, and the state is required to facilitate their conversion into marriages.[633] Nowadays, the difference between stable unions and marriages seem to be mainly symbolic because the Federal Supreme Court has recently equated their legal effects.[634] A stable union is deemed to exist when the parties create a life together, in a public, continuous, and lasting way, with the purpose of constituting a family. People who are forbidden to marry cannot engage in a stable union recognized by the state[635] – except for those who, despite not having yet divorced, have separated from a previous spouse. It is also possible for parties to declare their union before a notary so that it can be verified by a publicly registered contract.[636] The percentage of unions between unmarried couples has progressively increased over the years: extending from 11.7% of all unions in 1980, 18.5% in 1991, 28.6% in 2000, and 36.4% in 2010.[637]

336. The Federal Constitution also recognizes as a family 'the community formed by either parent and their descendants' (single-parent families).[638] Whilst the percentage of couples with children has decreased from 65.6% in 1991 to 54.9% in 2010, single-parent families appear to be steadily common: graduating from 16.7% of families in 1991 to 18.5% in 2010. Most compose of a woman, her children, and

631. Maria Berenice Dias, *Manual de Direito das Famílias*, 131 (2015).
632. *Ibid.* at 238–239.
633. Const. (1988), Art. 226, para. 3.
634. STF, Full Court, RE 646721/RS, Rapp. Min. Luís Roberto Barroso, *DJ* 11 Sep. 2017. It is worth noting that the case involved a same-sex partnership.
635. These are the situations which are now considered *concubinatos*.
636. CC, Law No. 10406 of 10 Jan. 2002, Arts 1723–1727.
637. Instituto Brasileiro de Geografia e Estatística, *Censo Demográfico: 2000 – Nupcialidade e Fecundidade: Resultados da Amostra*, 39 (2000); Instituto Brasileiro de Geografia e Estatística, *Censo Demográfico: 2010 – Nupcialidade, Fecundidade e Migração: Resultados da Amostra*, 59 (2010).
638. Const. (1988), Art. 226, para. 4.

sometimes other extended relatives: in 2010, this scenario represented 87.4% of all single-parent households and, impressively, 16.2% of all families, whereas male, single-parent households constitute a mere 2.3% of the total amount.[639]

I. Right to Marry

337. The Constitution does not explicitly mention a right to marry, but it clearly derives from the fundamental rights to freedom, equality, and privacy (Article 5, *caput*, I and X), as well as from the principle of human dignity (Article 1, III). The imposing of marriage against someone's will or forbidding them unreasonably or capriciously would constitute a clear contravention to those provisions.

338. International human rights treaties also provide a basis for a right to marry in Brazil, where they have (at least) a supra-statutory status (*see* Part IV, Chapter 1, II, *supra*). The ICCPR expressly provides that 'the right of men and women of marriageable age to marry and to found a family shall be recognized', and that 'no marriage shall be entered into without the free and full consent of the intending spouses' (Article 23(2) and (3)). It should be noted that some apparent restrictions of this right may well prove to enforce it: as stated by the UNHRC, the law should prescribe minimum age requirements so as to ensure that the spouses give their 'free and full consent' to marry.[640]

339. The freedom to choose one's partner and to create a family underlies the opinions in which the STF and the STJ recognized the validity of same-sex unions and marriages (*see* Part VII, Chapter 2, §1, II, *infra*). It is also abundantly clear in the Civil Code provisions regarding the parties' declaration of will and capacity to marry. Fraud, coercion, misrepresentation, and incapacity are grounds for invalidity (*see* Part X, Chapter 1, §4, *infra*).

II. Civil Effect of Religious Marriages

340. The UNHRC notes that the freedom of thought, conscience, and religion requires states to admit both religious and civil marriages, but it is possible to require that the former 'be conducted, affirmed or registered also under civil law'.[641] Religious marriages in Brazil possess civil effects, as long as the legal requirements for marriages in general are met (e.g., capacity), a licence is granted, and the marriage is registered within the public record (*see* Part X, Chapter 1, §3, *infra*).

---

639. Instituto Brasileiro de Geografia e Estatística, *Censo Demográfico: 2000 – Famílias e Domicílios: Resultados da Amostra*, 49 (2000); Instituto Brasileiro de Geografia e Estatística, *Censo Demográfico: 2010 – Famílias e Domicílios: Resultados da Amostra*, 70–71 (2010).
640. UNHRC General Comment No. 19 (Art. 23), HRI/GEN/1/Rev.1 (29 Jun. 1994), at para. 4.
641. *Ibid.* at para. 4.

III. Polyamorous and Simultaneous Relationships

341. A controversial issue involves polyamorous unions, i.e., families formed by more than two partners or spouses, and of simultaneous relationships, in which one person is a spouse or a partner in more than one family at the same time. Both exist and the latter are not rare. Nonetheless, adherence to monogamy as the sole model of a relationship[642] still fabricates these unions as invisible and remove any legal protection from the parties – especially women, as it is usually the man who has more than one partner. Moreover, children are equally protected, whether they are conceived in or out of wedlock. In fact, although adultery ceased to be a criminal offence in 2005,[643] bigamy remains a crime in Brazil.[644]

342. In 2018, the National Council of Justice forbade notaries from formalizing deeds of polyamorous unions. According to the Council, the 'new' reality of this kind of family deemed necessary that they were previously recognized and regulated by statutory law. The Council also mentioned that 'monogamy [is acknowledged by Brazilian society] as a structural element' of a family, and the fact that the parties themselves declared their commitment to each other before a notary did not create a 'new type of family', neither did the possession of the contract provide them with any rights and obligations under Family Law.[645]

343. More recently, the recognition of polyamorous families was denied by the Federal Supreme Court in a split decision (6:5). The opinion states that 'notwithstanding the developments in the dynamics and form of treatment conferred upon the most variegated family nuclei … in our legal system monogamic ideals remain [in force] for the recognition of marriages and stable unions … '.[646]

§2. Marriage and Race

344. Marriages between Indigenous people and those with European origins were not uncommon in colonial Brazil – they were even officially encouraged in the

642. The so-called *mononormativity*. *See* Duina Porto, *Mononormatividade, Intimidade e Cidadania*, 14 Direito GV 654 (2018). According to the author, monogamy is not a constitutional principle, but its status as a central legal principle of Family Law is 'defended by most scholars and contested by few' (at 665). One of the exceptions is Dias, *supra* note 631 at 137–139.
643. CP, Decree-Law No. 2848 of 7 Dec. 1940, Art. 240, repealed by Law No. 11106 of 28 Mar. 2005, Art. 5.
644. CP, Decree-Law No. 2848 of 7 Dec. 1940, Art. 235. However, there is at least one case in which a court refused to convict a person for bigamy because 'penal law, as *ultima ratio*, should be concerned exclusively with conducts which are the most harmful to social coexistence and should act only when the other parts of the law reveal unable to provide proper protection to relevant values … '. Since the defendant's behaviour did not prove to cause great offence to values protected by the crime of bigamy, the civil annulment of the second marriage was a sufficiently proportional response to his act. *See* TJMG, *1ª Câmara Criminal* [1st Criminal Panel], Ap. 1.0525.10.012754-3/001, Rapp. CAJ Flávio Leite, *DJ* 7 Aug. 2017.
645. CNJ, PP 0001459-08.2016.2.00.0000, Rapp. Min. João Otávio de Noronha, 26 Jun. 2018.
646. STF, Full Court, RE 1045273/SE, Rapp. Min. Alexandre de Moraes, *DJ* 9 Apr. 2021.

eighteenth century, as a means of assimilation of the Indigenous communities.[647] It should be noted, however, that nowadays Indigenous individuals and their descendants still suffer discrimination. The law also did not forbid interracial marriages involving people of African descent, even when enslaved, but it is abundantly clear that society frowned upon it, which was seen as a 'stain' on the other spouse.[648]

345. Despite the absence of legal impediments to interracial marriages – it is an actual crime to prevent a marriage based on race[649] – the spouse's race is still a very relevant factor in unions: according to the 2010 Census, in 70% of all marriages, the spouses were of the same race, with endogamy being higher among white people (74.5%). The census bureau estimated that, if racial questions were to prove irrelevant, unions between people of the same group would be around 42%.[650]

§3. SAME-SEX MARRIAGE

I. Constitutional Status of Same-Sex Marriage

346. Christian influence in Brazilian Civil Law has also meant that same-sex couples could not marry or even have their stable unions (*see* §1 *supra*) recognized. There was a long-standing tradition in Civil Law according to which the diversity of genders between the spouses was a condition for the *existence* of a marriage – more than merely invalid, same-sex marriages were deemed non-existent – and the Civil Code, enacted in 2002, still requires or assumes, in many provisions, that marriages involve a man and a woman.[651] Even the progressive Constitution of 1988, provides that 'the rights and the duties of marital society shall be exercised equally by the man and the woman', and as for common-law marriages, recognizes as a family entity 'the stable union between a man and a woman'.[652]

347. Nevertheless, in 2011, the Federal Supreme Court decided that the constitutional recognition of stable unions included same-sex partnerships.[653] A few months later, the STJ decided that the Civil Code, as read in accordance with the Constitution, did not forbid formal marriages between same-sex couples.[654] In 2013, the National Council of Justice – which exercises administrative and financial oversight over the Judicial Branch – issued a resolution declaring it forbidden for any

647. Vânia Maria Losada Moreira, *Casamentos Indígenas, Casamentos Mistos e Política na América Portuguesa: Amizade, Negociação, Capitulação e Assimilação Social*, 19 Topoi 29 (2018).
648. Eni de Mesquita Samara, *A Família Negra no Brasil*, 120 Revista de História 27, 40–42 (1989).
649. Law No. 7716 of 5 Jan. 1989, Art. 14.
650. Instituto Brasileiro de Geografia e Estatística, *supra* note 637 at 63–64.
651. *See* e.g., CC, Law No. 10406 of 10 Jan. 2002, Arts 1514; 1517; 1535; 1541, III; 1565; 1567.
652. Const. (1988), Art. 226, pars 3 and 5.
653. STF, Full Court, ADI 4277/DF and ADPF 132/RJ, Rapp. Min. Carlos Ayres Britto, *DJ* 14 Oct. 2011.
654. STJ, *4ª Turma* [4th Panel], REsp 1183378/RS, Rapp. Min. Luis Felipe Salomão, *DJ* 1 Feb. 2012.

official or officer to refuse to license or to perform civil marriage ceremonies for people of the same sex, as well as to deny conversion of same-sex stable unions into marriages.[655]

348. Some prosecutors have insisted on opposing the issuance of licenses to same-sex marriages, and judges have refused to admit divorces or to convert stable unions into marriages on the grounds that the law did not admit the marriage of same-sex couples. Nonetheless, the courts of appeal do seem to be relatively consistent in reaffirming the rights to enter into a stable union and to marry.[656]

349. Whilst the number of marriages has recorded an average yearly decrease of 1.6% since 2014, same-sex marriages have increased by an impressive rate of 15.6% on average – and in 2018, the number was 61.7% higher than that of 2017.[657] This spike was probably due, in a large part, to the election of President Jair Bolsonaro in 2018. As a long-standing vocal opponent of same-sex unions, whose campaigned platform included the 'defence' of the so-called traditional family (i.e., with heterosexual couples), many people believed his election could herald the demise of the recognition of same-sex marriages. In fact, these unions recorded a 360% increase in December 2018 alone, right after Mr Bolsonaro's electoral win.[658]

II. Conscientious Objection to Performing Same-Sex Marriages and Providing Wedding-Related Services

A. *State Officials*

350. It would seem unlikely that state officials, such as justices of the peace, could rightfully object to perform same-sex marriage ceremonies on conscientious grounds. Acting on behalf of the state, they are required to exercise their powers and

655. CNJ, Resolution No. 175 of 14 May 2013.

656. Reversing lower court rulings against same-sex marriages, *see*, e.g., TJRJ, *21ª Câmara Cível* [21st Civil Panel], Ap. 0098969-25.2012.8.19.0002, Rapp. CAJ Regina Lucia Passos, *DJ* 9 Nov. 2018; TJRJ, *18ª Câmara Cível* [18th Civil Panel], Ap. 0000197-57.2014.8.19.0810, Rapp. CAJ Margaret de Olivaes Valle dos Santos, *DJ* 10 Apr. 2014. Denying appeals of the Public Prosecutors' Office against decisions allowing marriage licenses to be issued to same-sex couples, *see*, e.g., TJSC, *5ª Câmara de Direito Civil* [5th Civil Law Panel], Ap. 5000432-45.2019.8.24.0091, Rapp. CAJ Cláudia Lambert de Faria, 9 Dec. 2020; TJSC, *6ª Câmara de Direito Civil* [6th Civil Law Panel], Ap. 0001964-76.2018.8.24.0091, Rapp. CAJ André Carvalho; TJSP, *Conselho Superior de Magistratura* [Superior Judicial Council], Ap. 9000012-51.2011.8.26.0590, Rapp. CAJ José Renato Nalini, 21 Mar. 2013; TJSP, *Conselho Superior de Magistratura* [Superior Judicial Council], Ap. 9000002-32.2012.8.26.0344, Rapp. CAJ José Renato Nalini, *DJ* 27 Jun. 2013.

657. Raw data obtained at Instituto Brasileiro de Geografia e Estatística, https://biblioteca.ibge.gov.br/index.php/biblioteca-catalogo?view=detalhes&id=7135 (last visited 20 Apr. 2021).

658. Diego Garcia, *Casamentos entre Pessoas do Mesmo Sexo Saltam 360% Após Eleição de Bolsonaro, diz IBGE*, Folha de S. Paulo, 4 Dec. 2019, https://www1.folha.uol.com.br/cotidiano/2019/12/casamentos-entre-pessoas-do-mesmo-sexo-saltam-360-apos-eleicao-de-bolsonaro-diz-ibge.shtml.

responsibilities in an impartial manner, under the laicity principle.[659] In fact, it is a crime to prevent people from getting married on the grounds of their gender or sexual orientation.[660]

B. Religious Organizations and Officials

351. Religious marriage ceremonies are conducted according to the beliefs and practices of the relevant denomination, and their freedom of worship prevents the state from enjoining them to perform a religious ceremony, especially when doing so would violate the tenets of their religion. It would then be unlawful to require a religious organization or official to perform a marriage in disaccord with their beliefs.[661] Civil marriages are always a possibility for those who do not wish to comply with religious requirements.

C. Other Religious Entities

352. Denominations usually take the form of religious organizations, although people can incorporate other legal entities to pursue religious purposes or other objectives, somehow related to religion (*see* Part III, Chapter 1, §1, II and III, *supra*). Obvious examples are schools, hospitals, and nursing homes managed by religious groups. As mentioned before, legal entities generally cannot invoke the protection of the freedom of religion, unless they are specifically devoted to religious objectives, and only insofar as it is necessary to achieve such goals (*see* Part II, Chapter 1, §5, *supra*). So, expressive entities of a religious character (e.g., music bands) may exercise the right not to perform in same-sex marriages, but they could not refuse to hire a secretary just for being married to a person of the same gender.

D. Other Private Entities

353. As a rule, non-expressive legal entities cannot refuse to provide wedding-related goods or services to same-sex couples. Consumer law guarantees equality in the provision of goods and services and forbids businesses from refusing to sell to customers who are willing to pay directly unless the goods are no longer available

---

659. Magalhães Pires, *supra* note 105 at 315–316.

660. Law No. 7716 of 5 Jan. 1989, Art. 14, extended to homophobia and transphobia by the Federal Supreme Court. *See* STF, Full Court, MI 4733/DF, Rapp. Min. Edson Fachin, *DJ* 29 Sep. 2020; STF, Full Court, ADO 26/DF, Rapp. Min. Celso de Mello, *DJ* 6 Oct. 2020.

661. *See* Leite, *supra* note 109 at 318. *See also* TJGO, *5ª Câmara Cível* [5th Civil Panel], Ap. 58752-10.2005.8.09.0051, Rapp. Judge Delintro Belo de Almeida Filho, *DJ* 26 Aug. 2016 (awarding a church compensation for moral damages for having been compelled to perform a religious marriage contrary to their tenets by a court injunction).

in stock.[662] It is also a crime to deny access or service to consumers based on their sexual orientation.[663] Some states have also passed laws providing for administrative penalties for such conduct.[664]

354. An interesting case occurred in the State of Paraná. A photographer signed a contract to work at a wedding, but shortly before the ceremony, having learnt that it involved a union of two women, refused to provide the service. The courts awarded damages to the couple, due not only to the time of the cancellation but also to their having been victims of discrimination. According to the Appeals Panel, the defendant was hired to work as a photographer, and not to perform the marriage, so she could not invoke her religious freedom to avoid paying damages.[665] Setting aside the issue of short notice, it is questionable whether an expressive and artistic work, such as that of a photographer, when performed by an individual, should be equated to the mere provision of goods or other, non-expressive, services (e.g., painting a house), by a business company.[666] Individuals are entitled to the full protection of the freedom of religion, especially when it comes to artistic or otherwise expressive performances, whereas legal entities, on the contrary, could hardly invoke the same kind of protection.

---

662. *Código de Defesa do Consumidor* [Consumer Defense Code], Law No. 8078 of 11 Sep. 1990, Art. 6, II, and Art. 39, II and IX, as amended by Law No. 8884 of 11 Jun. 1994.
663. Law No. 7716 of 5 Jan. 1989, Arts 5–10, extended to homophobia and transphobia by the Federal Supreme Court. *See* STF, Full Court, MI 4733/DF, Rapp. Min. Edson Fachin, *DJ* 29 Sep. 2020; STF, Full Court, ADO 26/DF, Rapp. Min. Celso de Mello, *DJ* 6 Oct. 2020.
664. *See*, e.g., Law (RJ) No. 7041 of 15 Jul. 2015; Law (RS) No. 11872 of 19 Dec. 2002; Law (SP) No. 10948 of 5 Nov. 2001 (upheld by TJSP, *Órgão Especial* [Special Panel], Arg. Inconst. 0056828-94.2015.8.26.0000, Rapp. CAJ Tristão Ribeiro, *DJ* 18 Jun. 2016).
665. PR, *1ª Turma Recursal dos Juizados Especiais* [1st Appellate Panel of the Special Courts], RI 0009125-87.2018.8.16.0018, Rapp. Judge Maria Fernanda Scheidemantel Nogara Ferreira da Costa, *DJ* 17 Dec. 2019.
666. Magalhães Pires, *supra* note 105 at 174.

Chapter 3. Freedom of Expression

§1. Right to Profess

355. The right to possess (and to profess) religious beliefs is guaranteed in the Federal Constitution and in many human rights treaties in force in Brazil. Everyone is entitled to decide their own orientation in matters of religion. Even though it is commonly asserted that the right to profess religious beliefs is absolute, it is incorrect to separate thought and conviction from action, especially because one's beliefs are only visible to others through their actions. For more on this, *see* Part II, Chapter 1 (especially §2), *supra*.

§2. Right to Propagate

356. The right to propagate religion – i.e., to engage in proselytism and religious indoctrination or teaching – is protected under the freedoms of religion and expression, enshrined in the Federal Constitution and in the relevant human rights treaties (*see* Part II, Chapter 1, §3). According to the Federal Supreme Court, 'religious freedom is exercisable not only in private, but also in the public space, and it includes the right to try to convince others, by means of teaching, to change their religion. Proselytist speech is, therefore, inherent to the freedom of religious expression'.[667]

357. In the State of Rio de Janeiro, a man claimed to have been prevented by local officers from preaching in public without a licence – which he had requested but was denied. The municipality argued that said licence was required to guarantee public tranquillity and order, but the courts recognized the plaintiff's right to preach in public places, without requiring prior licences, so long as he did not employ sound equipment, the likes of voice amplifiers, or affect the circulation of people.[668]

§3. Admissible Limitations to the Freedom of Expression

358. Despite the preeminent/preferential status of freedom of expression in the legal order,[669] Brazilian constitutional scholarship and case law recognize that freedom of speech – as almost any other fundamental right – can be abridged when it proves necessary to protect or to promote the rights of others or, in certain cases, to

667. STF, Full Court, ADI 2566/DF, Rapp. Min. Edson Fachin, *DJ* 23 Oct. 2018.

668. TJRJ, *17ª Câmara Cível* [17th Civil Panel], Ap. 0007712-43.2008.8.19.0006, Rapp. CAJ Elton Martinez Carvalho Leme, *DJ* 18 Dec. 2009.

669. Underscoring the preferential status of freedom of speech in Brazilian law, *see*, e.g., STF, Full Court, RE 685493/SP, Rapp. Min. Marco Aurélio, *DJ* 17 Aug. 2020; STF, Full Court, ADI 4451/DF, Rapp. Min. Alexandre de Moraes, *DJ* 6 Mar. 2019; STF, Full Court, ADI 2566/DF, Rapp. Min. Edson Fachin, *DJ* 23 Oct. 2018; STF, Full Court, ADI 2404/DF, Rapp. Min. Dias Toffoli, *DJ* 1 Aug. 2018; STF, *1ª Turma* [1st Panel], Rcl 22328/RJ, Rapp. Min. Luís Roberto Barroso, *DJ* 10 May 2018; STF, Full Court, ADI 4815/DF, Rapp. Min. Cármen Lúcia, *DJ* 1 Feb. 2016.

pursue relevant public goals.[670] Human rights treaties also authorize that freedom of expression be limited to guarantee the respect owed to the rights and reputations of others, as well as to protect national security, public order, public health, and morals.[671] The term 'morals', however, cannot be construed as a reference to a 'single tradition' of thought or belief, keeping in mind the inevitable pluralism of democratic societies.[672] Treaties also prohibit propaganda for war and the advocacy of hatred (including religious hatred) that incites violence or discrimination (hate speech).[673]

359. Not all situations are equally sensitive, but due consideration must always be given to the relevant fundamental rights – including the freedom of religious expression. It cannot be simply disregarded or set aside, but its limitation is possible. It all applies to religious speech. For example, a couple who owned an apartment was ordered to refrain from using it to regularly hold religious services because the units could only be used for residential purposes, so as to not disturb the peace of other residents in the building.[674] Another situation involved preaching in public trains: the Public Prosecutors' Office was victorious in a suit it brought to enjoin the company operating the service to provide orientation to the commuters and inspect the trains to avoid unwanted preaching that disturbed the tranquillity of other passengers.[675]

360. As a rule, however, even when religious speech is conveyed loudly or in a manner that disturbs public peace, it violates the Constitution to order its suppression – especially because it is possible to solve the problem by requiring that the organization or the people involved comply with the noise levels set forth by the law.[676]

---

670. *See*, e.g., Ingo Wolfgang Sarlet & Jayme Weingartner Neto, *Liberdade de Expressão: Algumas Ponderações em Matéria Penal à Luz da Constituição Federal do Brasil*, 18 Espaço Jurídico: Journal of Law 637, 652 (2017); Luís Roberto Barroso, *Liberdade de Expressão versus Direitos da Personalidade. Colisão de Direitos Fundamentais e Critérios de Ponderação, in 3 Temas de Direito Constitucional* 79, 105–110 (2008). *See also* STF, Full Court, ADI 4613/DF, Rapp. Min. Dias Toffoli, *DJ* 3 Dec. 2018 (upholding a statute requiring advertising pieces for automobiles to convey educational messages about traffic safety).
671. ICCPR, Art. 19(3); ACHR, Art. 13(2).
672. UNHRC General Comment No. 34 (Art. 19), para. 32, UN Doc. CCPR/C/CG/34 (12 Sep. 2011), with reference to UNHRC General Comment No. 22 (48) (Art. 18), *supra* note
673. ICCPR, Art. 20; ACHR, Art. 13(5).
674. TJRJ, *19ª Câmara Cível* [19th Civil Panel], Ap. 0010402-89.2010.8.19.0001, Rapp. CAJ Lúcio Durante, *DJ* 5 Sep. 2014.
675. TJRJ, *12ª Câmara Cível* [12th Civil Panel], AgInt na Ap. 0221325-98.2007.8.19.0001, Rapp. CAJ Cherubin Schwartz, *DJ* 26 Sep. 2014. This ruling was confirmed by the Federal Supreme Court. *See* STF, *1ª Turma* [1st Panel], ARE 1315221 AgR/RJ, Rapp. Min. Alexandre de Moraes, *DJ* 20 Aug. 2021.
676. TJRJ, *10ª Câmara Cível* [10th Civil Panel], AI 0028834-77.2001.8.19.0000, Rapp. CAJ João Nicolau Spyrides, *DJ* 7 Apr. 2003; TJSC, *1ª Câmara Cível* [1st Civil Panel], AI 0137975-36.2014.8.24.0000, Rapp. CAJ Carlos Adilson Silva, *DJ* 13 Dec. 2016. It is not rare to find court decisions enjoining churches to respect loudness limits. *See*, e.g., TJSP, *36ª Câmara de Direito Privado* [36th Private Law Panel], Ap. 1015041-20.2016.8.26.0037, Rapp. CAJ Maria Cláudia Bedotti, *DJ* 4 Jun. 2018.

§4. Protecting Religious Sensitivities

I. Blasphemy

361. In colonial Brazil, blasphemy and recanting God or the Catholic Saints were punishable by fines, whipping, forced exile to Africa, or even galley sentence.[677] During the Empire, to mock religions publicly or to deny the 'fundamental truths of the existence of God and the immortality of the soul' were crimes punishable by incarceration and fines.[678] In the first republican Penal Code, it was a crime to insult a religion by vilifying acts or objects of worship, or by publicly disrespecting or profaning their symbols.[679] The current Code still criminalizes the action of publicly vilifying an act or object of religious worship.[680] Another statute includes a similar provision regarding Indigenous ceremonies and traditions.[681]

362. Blasphemy, however, is not (and cannot be) a crime. As stated by Minister Celso de Mello of the Federal Supreme Court, 'nobody can be punished, under our positive law, for blasphemy or apostasy, because … a lay state does not hold any interest of a religious character, being it indifferent to it the personal choice of any citizen in religious matters … '.[682] A prohibition of blasphemy would require the state to position itself as an arbiter of the religious truth, which would contradict the laicity principle and the right to religious freedom.

363. As for the latter, the UNHRC has specifically declared that '[p]rohibitions of displays of lack of respect for a religion or other belief system, including blasphemy laws, are incompatible with the [ICCPR]', except when they are enacted to prevent the 'advocacy of national, racial or religious hatred that constitutes incitement to discrimination, hostility or violence', under Article 20(2) of the ICCPR. Even in this case, however, 'it would be impermissible for any such laws to discriminate in favour of or against one or certain religions or belief systems, or their adherents over another, or religious believers over non-believers'. It would also be unlawful 'for such prohibitions to be used to prevent or punish criticism of religious leaders or commentary on religious doctrine and tenets of faith'.[683]

---

677. 5 *Codigo Philippino, ou, Ordenações e Leis do Reino de Portugal: Recopiladas por Mandado d'el-Rey D. Filipe I*, 1149–1150 (Cândido Mendes de Almeida ed., 1870). The 1603 *Ordenações Filipinas* was a legal codification enacted by King Phillip I of Portugal (Phillip II of Spain). With some modifications, it remained in force in Brazil for a long time, having been confirmed, after the Independence, by the Law of 20 Oct. 1823. Some of its parts were only repealed by the 1916 Civil Code.
678. *Código Criminal* [Criminal Code], Law of 16 Dec. 1830, Arts 277–278.
679. CP, Dec. No. 847 of 11 Oct. 1890, Art. 185.
680. CP, Decree-Law No. 2848 of 7 Dec. 1940, Art. 208.
681. Law No. 6001 of 19 Dec. 1973, Art. 58.
682. STF, Full Court, ADO 26/DF, Rapp. Min. Celso de Mello, *DJ* 6 Oct. 2020 (opinion of the rapporteur).
683. UNHRC General Comment No. 34 (Art. 19), *supra* note at para. 48.

II. Defamation

364. As mentioned above (*see* §3), freedom of speech can be limited to protect the rights of other people – and that includes their reputation. The Constitution recognizes a person's honour to be 'inviolable' (Article 5, X). Human rights treaties also allow for limitations on the freedom of expression, when they are necessary to ensure respect for the reputation of others.[684] Furthermore, the protection of the equal dignity of all human beings and of their freedom of religion may justify that offensive statements be repressed by the law when they are based on people's religious orientation.

365. In Brazil, it is a crime to practice, induce, or incite discrimination or prejudice based on religion,[685] or to offend someone because of their religion.[686] Offences to a person or a group's honour or reputation can also be grounds for paying damages in civil suits. Some of the registered cases involve the propagation of untrue statements associating the Halal certification of food to the financing of terrorist groups,[687] and vociferous shouting, from a church, thus associating a nearby Candomblé *terreiro* to Satan.[688]

366. The situation becomes more complicated when the defamatory speech itself is grounded on or refers to, religious beliefs. The Federal Supreme Court has recognized that 'the freedom[s] of religion and speech constitute founding elements of the constitutional order and must be exercised with due regard to the other fundamental rights and guarantees, not encompassing … practices revealing discrimination'. According to the Court, however, the mere comparison of religions, or even the display of 'some hierarchization or animosity' for other creeds, is not unlawful per se. For that, the speech has to contain a defence of: (1) an 'inequality between the groups and/or individuals'; (2) the 'supposed relation of superiority between them'; and (3) 'the domination, exploitation, enslavement, elimination, suppression or reduction of fundamental rights' of the supposedly 'inferior' people or groups.[689] In another opinion, the Court has suggested that freedom of religion does not protect 'a speech about someone else's belief, especially when it is manifested with the intent to offend it, to debase it, or to belittle it (or its followers)', but the case involved 'incitement to hatred', according to the rapporteur.[690]

---

684. ICCPR, Art. 19(3)(a); ACHR, Art. 13(2)(a).
685. Law No. 7716 of 5 Jan. 1989, Art. 20.
686. CP, Decree-Law No. 2848 of 7 Dec. 1940, Art. 140, para. 3.
687. TJSP, *7ª Câmara de Direito Privado* [7th Private Law Panel], AI 2251173-50.2020.8.26.0000, Rapp. CAJ Rômulo Russo, *DJ* 27 Jan. 2021.
688. *See* TJBA, *1ª Câmara Criminal* [1st Criminal Panel], Ap. 0502347-89.2015.8.05.0039, Rapp. CAJ Nilson Soares Castelo Branco, *DJ* 3 Mar. 2021.
689. STF, *1ª Turma* [1st Panel], RHC 134682/BA, Rapp. Min. Edson Fachin, *DJ* 29 Aug. 2017 (holding that the incitement to the Catholic community, in a book, to 'save' adherents to Spiritism, without suggesting violence or domination – though 'intolerant, pedantic and arrogant' – was protected by the Constitution).
690. STF, *2ª Turma* [2nd Panel], RHC 146303/RJ, Rapp. Min. Dias Toffoli, *DJ* 7 Aug. 2018.

III. Hate Speech

367. As previously mentioned (*see* §3, *supra*), not only can hate speech justify limitations to the freedom of expression but the States Parties to the ICCPR and the ACHR – like Brazil – are under an obligation to prevent it.[691]

368. The Constitution requires the law to punish 'any act of discrimination offensive to fundamental rights and freedoms' (Article 5, XLI), but, for some time, only acts of racism or racial prejudice were crimes.[692] In an important ruling, the Federal Supreme Court stated that anti-Semitism was to be considered racism – and as such punishable under the law – making specific references to the horrors perpetrated by Nazism.[693]

369. Years later, the Court had to adjudicate on speech that could amount to homophobia or transphobia. In the previous case, a religion (Judaism) was the target, but it could also be construed as a racial group and, therefore, placed under the protection of the existing law. That was not the situation regarding gender identification and sexual orientation. Also, in this case, religion and the victim were not aligned; on the contrary, religion was frequently invoked in an attempt to support or justify homophobic or transphobic speech. As the case involving anti-Semitism, the relevant statute had since been amended to include discrimination or prejudice based not only on race or skin colour but also on ethnicity, religion, and national origin.[694] But homophobia and transphobia were not mentioned.

370. The Court declared, then, that Congress had not yet complied with Article 5, XLI, of the Federal Constitution in this regard, and that amounted to an unconstitutional legislative omission. In a notorious ruling, it decided that, until a law was passed on this matter, the law that criminalizes racism would extend to all practices involving 'heinous aversion to a person's sexual orientation or gender identity'. As for religiously motivated speech, the Court made it clear that they were not impaired, insofar as they did not involve hate speech:

> The criminal repression to the practice of homo-transphobia does not encompass nor limit the exercise of the freedom of religion, whatever the religious denomination professed, whose members and ministers … have guaranteed the right to freely preach and propagate, through word, image, or any other means, their thought and to externalize their convictions in accord with that which is contained in their sacred books and codes, as well as to teach according to their doctrinal and/or theological orientation, being it possible to seek and to attract proselytes and to practice acts of worship and the pertinent liturgy, regardless of the venue, public or private, of their individual or collective

691. ICCPR, Art. 20(2); ACHR, Art. 13(5). On the former, *see* UNHRC General Comment No. 11 (Art. 20), HRI/GEN/1/Rev.1 (29 Jun. 1994).
692. Law No. 7716 of 5 Jan. 1989.
693. STF, Full Court, HC 82424/RS, Rapp. Min. Maurício Corrêa, *DJ* 19 Mar. 2004.
694. Law No. 7716 of 5 Jan. 1989, Art. 1, as amended by Law No. 9459 of 15 May 1997.

activity, as long as such manifestations do not characterize hate speech, thus understood those exteriorizations inciting discrimination, hostility, or violence towards people due to their sexual orientation or their gender identification.[695]

371. In civil cases, religiously motivated homophobic acts had been deemed illegal even before the Federal Supreme Court's ruling. The Court of Appeals of São Paulo, in a suit filed by the Public Defenders' Office, confirmed a lower court decision enjoining a religious entity not to place billboards against homosexual people. The case began after the defendant placed a billboard with excerpts from the Bible, describing homosexual acts as 'abominable' and worthy of 'punishment', and exhorting homosexuals to repent and 'turn to God'. According to the lower court, the 'compilation conveys an intolerant, degrading and discriminatory message, besides really fomenting hatred and violence against human beings who are, solely, not heterosexual'. Also, the billboard was placed only four days prior to an LGBT-QIA+ pride parade, denoting that 'the defendant sought to communicate directly to homosexual individuals, and convey … a message of true repulse'.[696] In another case, a member of a child protection board was stripped of her position for imposing religious tenets on children and adolescents, and for also displaying discriminatory behaviour, suggesting to a transgender person that, if she were her mother, she would ban her from the home because, in her view, God had only created men and women.[697]

§5. Religious Newspapers and Broadcast Companies

372. The Constitution guarantees the freedoms of press and broadcast, forbidding any form of censorship.[698] Print media outlets do not require prior licensing,[699] whilst broadcast services operate under concessions, permissions, or authorizations issued by the Union, which assigns them a part of the radio frequency spectrum.[700] Cable channels and similar services fall under a different regime, being non-dependent on public airwaves.[701] The Constitution requires that broadcast companies adhere to various principles, including 'respect for the ethical and social values of the person and family',[702] but, in light of the pluralism inherent in a democratic society, that does not entail the submission of these companies to a particular worldview.

695. STF, Full Court, ADO 26/DF, Rapp. Min. Celso de Mello, *DJ* 6 Oct. 2020.
696. Ribeirão Preto/SP, *6ª Vara Cível* [6th Civil Court of First Instance], Proc. 0045315-08.2011.8.26.0506, *DJ* 15 Sep. 2014, confirmed by TJSP, *4ª Câmara de Direito Privado* [4th Private Law Panel], Ap. 0045315-08.2011.8.26.0506, Rapp. CAJ Natan Zelinschi de Arruda, *DJ* 17 Dec. 2015.
697. TJRS, *4ª Câmara Cível* [4th Civil Panel], Ap. 0060472-93.2019.8.21.7000, Rapp. CAJ Antonio Vinicius Amaro da Silveira, *DJ* 21 Nov. 2019.
698. Const. (1988), Arts 5, IX, and 22, *caput* and pars 1–2.
699. Const. (1988), Art. 220, para. 6.
700. Const. (1988), Art. 223; Law No. 4117 of 27 Aug. 1962.
701. They are primarily regulated by Law No. 12485 of 12 Sep. 2011.
702. Const. (1988), Art. 221, IV.

373. The law guarantees the freedom of broadcasting, including 'criticism and unfavourable concepts, even when vehement, as well as the reporting of true facts, under the limitations prescribed by law, including of acts of any branches of the state'.[703] Freedom of expression is also guaranteed for cable networks and related services.[704] Journalism is specially protected by the Constitution, according to a number of important opinions of the Federal Supreme Court: for example, it declared that the 1967 Press Act, passed by the 1964–1985 Military Regime, was inconsistent with the democratic values and commitment to freedom of the 1988 Constitution.[705] The Court also ruled that it was unconstitutional to require a tertiary degree in journalism for someone to work in this field.[706]

374. Religious people and organizations are permitted to own and manage newspaper, radio and television companies and are therefore entitled to operate these entities freely. However, in the broadcasting area, since companies are occupying public airwave slots, there is some questioning as to the possibility of their offering purely religious programmes. This criticism is rooted in the laicity principle: the spectrum, being public and limited, could not be employed to advance a specific worldview. Nevertheless, the connection between some broadcast outlets and churches is widely known: from 2006 to 2016, the number of television stations linked to religious groups surged from 1,687 to 2,841, in a 69% increase. The lion share is owned by Catholic entities, but the greatest growth trend involved Evangelical groups – with the ubiquitous IURD prominent with 63% of all Evangelical networks.[707] Also, a court has ruled that time slots in broadcast channels can be sold to religious organizations without the need to respect the 25% limit set forth by the law for advertisers because religious content cannot be considered 'commercial advertising'.[708]

375. A survey conducted in 2017 highlighted that nine out of the fifty media outlets with the highest ratings, including print, online, and broadcasting, were controlled by religious groups, all from Christian denominations. Among the eleven most popular television networks, three were owned by Evangelical institutions, and one was the property of a Catholic group. As for radio networks, one was Catholic and two were Evangelical.[709] The survey also included websites:

---

703. Law No. 4117 of 27 Aug. 1962, Arts 52 and 54.
704. Law No. 12485 of 12 Sep. 2011, Art. 3, I.
705. STF, Full Court, ADPF 130/DF, Rapp. Min. Carlos Ayres Britto, *DJ* 6 Nov. 2009.
706. STF, Full Court, RE 511961/SP, Rapp. Min. Gilmar Mendes, *DJ* 13 Nov. 2009.
707. Janaine Sibelle Freires Aires et al., *Quando Religião, Política e Mídia se Confundem: As Estratégias Políticas e Midiáticas do PRB, da Record e da Igreja Universal do Reino de Deus*, 19 Revista Eptic 88, 90–91 (2017).
708. TRF – 3, *3ª Turma* [3rd Panel], Rem. Nec. 0022869-77.2014.4.03.6100, Rapp. FCAJ Cecília Marcondes, *DJ* 3 Mar. 2020. An appeal is still pending.
709. Olívia Bandeira, *Igrejas Cristãs no Topo da Audiência*, Le Monde Diplomatique Brasil, 16 Apr. 2018, https://diplomatique.org.br/igrejas-cristas-no-topo-da-audiencia/.

among the ten websites with the highest ratings and the seventeen paid print outlets with higher circulation, two appear which are owned by religious leaderships: the portal *R7* and the daily paper *Correio do Povo*, both owned by Evangelical bishop Edir Macedo, leader of the Universal Church of the Kingdom of God (Iurd). This number would be greater if we factored in print papers which are distributed for free, and are not built into the survey: Iurd's *Folha Universal*, for example, has print run of 1.8 million copies, substantially higher than major circulated daily newspapers, the likes of *Folha de S. Paulo* (about 300 thousand copies/day) and weekly magazines, such as *Veja* (about 1.1 million copies).[710]

376. A study from a Brazilian regulatory agency with data from 2016 concluded that the 'dominant genre' in TV broadcasting is religious: 21.2% of the programming time of open access channels was dedicated to religious content. Religion, in fact, has been absorbing a larger share of the programming year after year: religious content accounted for less than 14% of the programming of these networks in 2012, 16% in 2013, 19.7% in 2014, and 21.1% in 2015.[711] This content is almost exclusively Christian, Catholic and Protestant, including that of *TV Brasil*, a state-run network, though it also has the only inter-religious programme identified in the study.[712]

§6. Public Officers and Public Servants: Religious Symbols and Speech

377. Public officials and servants are entitled to the protection of freedom of religion like any other person. Societal pluralism is expected to reflect in the corps of public servants, and it is not a problem should they choose to display religious symbols and garments at work. The laicity principle requires the state not to affirm any opinion in matters of religion, but it does not extend to the individual public servants and employees. It should be noted, however, that this freedom does not authorize people to avail their public service positions to forward any specific view or orientation regarding religion, as that would then violate the laicity principle. A public officer/servant decides and acts on behalf of the state, so they are not permitted to anchor their decisions and actions on values and beliefs which the state, as a moral entity, cannot sustain or defend.[713]

---

710. *Id.*

711. Agência Nacional do Cinema, *TV Aberta – Informe Anual 2016 (01/01/2016 a 31/12/2016)*, 59 (2017), https://oca.ancine.gov.br/sites/default/files/repositorio/pdf/informe_tvaberta_2016.pdf.

712. Bandeira, *supra* note 709.

713. Magalhães Pires, *supra* note 105 at 312–316.

Chapter 4. Due Process Norms and Religious Groups

§1. Due Process under the Constitution

378. The Federal Constitution guarantees due process of the law for anyone whose freedom or property is at risk (Article 5, LIV). In other provisions, it enunciates rights that are directly connected to this fundamental idea of fair process, such as one's right to know, and to respond to, allegations made against them, in administrative and judicial proceedings (Article 5, LV).

§2. Application of Due Process to Religious Groups and Other Private Actors

379. In Brazil, fundamental rights can apply as well to private parties. Some are specifically tailored for such an application (e.g., the workers' rights in Article 7 of the Constitution), but private actors may also be subject to other rights. However, since they too are entitled to fundamental rights (e.g., private autonomy or freedom of enterprise), statutes (or, in its absence, the courts) are required to strike a balance between the competing rights as to determine the proper outcome for the case.[714]

380. The Federal Supreme Court has long stated that the due process clause applies to private actors, e.g., when an association excludes one of its members.[715] It is not infrequent to unearth cases involving due process within religious organizations: unless the matter is clearly based in a theological or doctrinal perspective, the courts usually do not refrain from enforcing the organization's bylaws to review its decisions, invoking the right to due process of law. For more information, *see* Part III, Chapter 2, §2, IV, *supra*.

§3. Due Process under Statutory Law

381. For private associations, the Civil Code provides that a member's expulsion can only be effected if there is a good cause, recognized in a procedure which guarantees the right to defend oneself and to file an appeal.[716] Religious organizations, however, possess more leeway to regulate their proceedings and operations. Yet, they are bound by the Federal Constitution – so some degree of due process is more than likely mandatory – and further to this, by way of their bylaws, which are frequently enforced by courts (*see* Part III, Chapter 2, §2, IV, *supra*).

---

714. *See* note 436 *supra*.

715. *See* STF, Full Court, RE 201819/RJ, Rapp. Min. Gilmar Mendes, *DJ* 27 Oct. 2006; STF, Full Court, RE 158215/RS, Rapp. Min. Marco Aurélio, *DJ* 7 Jun. 1996.

716. CC, Law No. 10406 of 10 Jan. 2002, Art. 57.

Chapter 5. Professional Secrecy

382. Professional secrecy is protected in Brazil. The Penal Code makes it a crime for one to reveal, without due cause, a secret that they have come to know because of their work, or ministerial position, when its disclosure may cause damage to others.[717] It is a means of protecting the privacy of the person who confided with others in order to gain benefit from their services, therefore making said services viable when receiving privileged information proves a necessary component of them. Due to their positions, religious ministers may be placed under this duty, so to refrain from disclosing information of which they become aware in relation to the members of their denomination, by means, e.g., of confession.[718] For that reason, ministers – and other people in similar situations – cannot be heard as a witness, unless the person who confided in them consents to their deposition.[719]

383. In Catholicism, the sacramental seal is inviolable, so that a person's confession must remain secret.[720] Being heavily influenced by this denomination – the official religion of the state until 1889 – Brazilian law respects the priest-penitent privilege in civil and criminal proceedings: in addition to lawyers (attorney-client privilege), anyone whose profession requires secrecy is exempt from testifying about facts related to its exercise.

717. CP, Decree-Law No. 2848 of 7 Dec. 1940, Art. 154.
718. Luiz Regis Prado, *Tratado de Direito Penal Brasileiro* vol. 4, Art. 154 (2014).
719. *See* CPC, Law No. 13105 of 16 Mar. 2015, Art. 448, II; CPP, Decree-Law No. 3689 of 3 Oct. 1941, Art. 207. *See also* Guilherme Madeira Dezem, *Curso de Processo Penal*, 11.18.8 (2021); 2 Humberto Dalla Bernardina de Pinho, *Direito Processual Civil Contemporâneo*, 233–234 (2018).
720. 1983 Code of Canon Law c. 983–984.

Chapter 6. Medical Deontology

§1. General Introduction

384. In Brazil, norms of medical deontology are established by the *Conselho Federal de Medicina (CFM)* [Federal Council of Medicine] and administered by a *Conselho Regional de Medicina (CRM)* [Regional Council of Medicine] in each State and the Federal District.[721] Almost all of the members of these councils are elected by the physicians registered in each state and in the Federal District, with the exception of one member of each council, who represents the *Associação Médica Brasileira* [Brazilian Medical Association] (in the CFM), and the pertinent state medical associations (in the CRMs).

§2. Medical Ethics

385. The current *Código de Ética Médica (CEM)* [Code of Medical Ethics] was approved in 2018 by the CFM. It safeguards and demands the autonomy of physicians, who must not be 'compelled to offer services which contravene the tenets of their conscience ..., except for situations of absence of other physicians, in case of urgency or emergency, or when their refusal may cause damages to the patient's health'.[722] Physicians are also allowed to refrain from performing 'medical acts which, despite being permitted by law, are contrary to the tenets of their conscience'.[723]

386. Physicians' rights and those of patients may clash in certain situations. The Civil Code provides that no one can be forced to submit to medical treatment or surgical intervention when their life is at risk.[724] But patients' autonomy seems to extend far beyond these situations, as a result of a paradigm change in Bioethics: the beneficence principle, based on medical paternalism, gave way to the autonomy principle, under which the patient has the right to grant or deny consent for general procedures, in a free and informed decision.[725] According to the CEM, physicians must respect the right of patients or their parents/guardians to decide in relation to contraceptive means,[726] and about diagnostic and therapeutic practices – except in

721. Law No. 3268 of 30 Sep. 1957, Arts 1–4; 5, *d*; 12–13; 15, *c* and *d*. The CFM hears appeals against CRM decisions (Art. 5, *i*).
722. CEM, Resolution (CFM) No. 2217 of 27 Sep. 2018, Ch. I – Fundamental Principles, VII.
723. CEM, Resolution (CFM) No. 2217 of 27 Sep. 2018, Ch. II – Physicians' Rights, IX.
724. CC, Law No. 10406 of 10 Jan. 2002, Art. 15.
725. Barroso, *supra* note 299 at 509–512; Adriana Campos & Daniela Rezende de Oliveira, *A Relação entre o Princípio da Autonomia e o Princípio da Beneficência (e Não-Maleficência) na Bioética Médica*, 115 Revista Brasileira de Estudos Políticos 13 (2017). For more on these (and other) principles which inform Bioethics, *see* Sergio Rego, Marisa Palácios & Rodrigo Siqueira-Baptista, *Bioética para Profissionais da Saúde*, 44–49 (2009).
726. CEM, Resolution (CFM) No. 2217 of 27 Sep. 2018, Ch. V – Relation with Patients and Family Members, Art. 42.

cases of 'imminent risk of death'.[727] It is actually a crime to submit patients to procedures against their will unless their life is in imminent peril.[728]

387. Conflicts between the rights of physicians and patients led the CFM to pass a specific resolution, recognizing not only the right of the latter to refuse treatment but also the rights of the former not to continue to attend to that patient, thus ushering them on to the care of another professional. It also allows the physician to ignore the patient's decision, e.g., when there is no other doctor available, in situations of urgency or emergency, and when the refusal can bring about foreseeable damages to the patient's health.[729] This appears to contradict the respect afforded to the patient's autonomy. That is why, in a suit involving childbirth, a federal court has ruled that only when there is risk of death for the woman or for the foetus is the physician then permitted to overrule the woman's decision regarding the birth.[730]

§3. Conscientious Objection of Physicians

388. Physicians usually invoke conscientious objection in procedures of abortion, assisted reproduction and therapies with stem cells.

I. Abortion

389. The Penal Code classifies abortion as a crime – whether it is performed with or without the consent of the woman – except when it is necessary to save the mother's life or when the pregnancy results from a rape.[731] Also, the Federal Supreme Court has decided that the prohibition of abortion does not encompass the interruption of pregnancy in cases of anencephalous foetuses.[732] And, in one case, a panel of the Court also stated that the criminalization of an abortion performed with the consent of the woman in the first trimester of pregnancy is incompatible with the Constitution.[733]

390. The CFM has not issued specific regulations about conscientious objections in these cases, but that simply appears to signal that the Council believes the CEM provisions to be sufficient to safeguard the physician's right.[734] Some scholars, however, dispute the almost absolute character that this right apparently has: since physicians who strongly oppose abortions should not (and likely do not) take

727. CEM, Resolution (CFM) No. 2217 of 27 Sep. 2018, Ch. IV – Human Rights, Art. 24; Chapter V – Relation with Patients and Family Members, Art. 31.
728. CP, Decree-Law No. 2848 of 7 Dec. 1940, Art. 146, para. 3, I.
729. Resolution (CFM) No. 2232 of 17 Jul. 2019.
730. São Paulo/SP, *8ª Vara Cível Federal* [8th Federal Civil Court of First Instance], Proc. 5021263-50.2019.4.03.6100, 17 Dec. 2019.
731. CP, Decree-Law No. 2848 of 7 Dec. 1940, Arts 124, 125, and 128.
732. STF, Full Court, ADPF 54/DF, Rapp. Min. Marco Aurélio, *DJ* 30 Apr. 2013.
733. STF, *1ª Turma* [1st Panel], HC 124306/RJ, Rapp. Min. Luís Roberto Barroso, *DJ* 17 Mar. 2017.
734. *See*, e.g., Resolution (CFM) No. 1989 of 14 May 2012, Explanatory Statement.

part in teams devoted to this procedure, they should justify their refusal to participate in specific cases, by explaining how and why this would seriously violate their freedom of conscience.[735]

II. Assisted Reproduction

391. Assisted reproduction is but merely acknowledged by statutory law,[736] although the CFM has issued a resolution to regulate these techniques, including various entailed ethical issues.[737] The resolution permits said techniques to be used by heterosexual, homosexual, and transgender individuals, whether they are single or not. Following in the steps of a previous modification in 2020,[738] the resolution does not mention that physicians are entitled to conscientiously object to participating in these procedures. That, however, does not necessarily mean that the Council refuses to recognize it: even though the 2021 resolution does not incorporate similar reasoning, the one approved in 2020 stated that it was unnecessary to refer to the right of conscientious objection because the CEM already had guaranteed it.[739]

III. Embryonic Stem-Cell Therapies

392. Research and therapy with embryonic stem cells are authorized in Brazil under the *Lei de Biossegurança* [Bio-security Law],[740] whose constitutionality was declared by the Federal Supreme Court.[741] All this debate involved intense participation and criticism from religious groups, especially Christian denominations, so it is expected that it could prove as fertile grounds for invoking an objection of conscience.

---

735. For some discussions, *see* Debora Diniz, *Objeção de Consciência e Aborto: Direitos e Deveres dos Médicos na Saúde Pública*, 45 Revista de Saúde Pública 981 (2011); Adilon Passinho Koury, *A Objeção da Consciência do Médico em sua Relação com o Paciente*, 153–160 (2015), https://www.cesupa.br/MestradoDireito/dissertacoes/ObjecaoConscienciaMedico_A_Koury.pdf.
736. CC, Law No. 10406 of 10 Jan. 2002, Art. 1597, III–V (presumption of paternity in cases of assisted reproduction).
737. Resolution (CFM) No. 2294 of 27 May 2021.
738. Resolution (CFM) No. 2168 of 21 Sep. 2017, Schedule II, No. 2, as amended by Resolution (CFM) No. 2283 of 1 Oct. 2020, Art. 1.
739. At least, that is what the CFM declared in Resolution (CFM) No. 2283 of 1 Oct. 2020, Explanatory Statement.
740. Law No. 11105 of 24 Mar. 2005, Art. 5.
741. *See* STF, Full Court, ADI 3510/DF, Rapp. Min. Carlos Ayres Britto, *DJ* 28 May 2010.

Chapter 7. Non-discrimination

§1. Non-discrimination in the Constitution and Human Rights Treaties

393. The Constitution is strongly committed to combating all forms of discrimination. It declares that '[a]ll persons are equal before the law, without any distinction whatsoever' (Article 5, *caput*) and guarantees that 'no one shall be deprived of any rights by reason of religious belief or philosophical or political conviction, unless he invokes it to exempt himself from a legal obligation required of all and refuses to perform an alternative obligation established by law' (Article 5, VIII). It is very clear, then, that the state must refrain from unduly discriminating against individuals or groups of people. But the Constitution goes further: the 'fundamental objectives of the Federative Republic of Brazil', include the duties 'to reduce social and regional inequalities' and 'to promote the well-being of all, without prejudice as to the origin, race, sex, colour, age and any other forms of discrimination' (Article 3, III and IV). It also provides that 'the law shall punish any discrimination which may attempt against fundamental rights and liberties' (Article 5, XLI), elucidating that the state's role includes fighting discrimination in all spheres, including in private relationships.

394. This is also of great concern under international law, in which a 'fundamental principle of equality and non-discrimination' has been recognized.[742] In effect, many documents offer support to this principle, including the UDHR,[743] the ICCPR,[744] the ADRDM[745] and the ACHR.[746]

395. In matters of religion, there is also the 1981 Declaration on the Elimination of All Forms of Intolerance and of Discrimination Based on Religion or Belief, which defines discrimination as 'any distinction, exclusion, restriction or preference based on religion or belief and having as its purpose or as its effect nullification or impairment of the recognition, enjoyment or exercise of human rights and fundamental freedoms on an equal basis' (Article 2(2)). The Declaration recognizes such discrimination as 'an affront to human dignity and a disavowal of the principles of the Charter of the United Nations' so that it 'shall be condemned as a violation of the human rights and fundamental freedoms proclaimed in the Universal Declaration of Human Rights and enunciated in detail in the International Covenants on Human Rights, and as an obstacle to friendly and peaceful relations between nations' (Article 3). It also requires states to 'take effective measures to prevent and eliminate discrimination on the grounds of religion or belief in the recognition, exercise and enjoyment of human rights and fundamental freedoms in all fields of civil, economic, political, social and cultural life', as well as to 'make all efforts to enact

742. *Accordance with International Law of Kosovo's Declaration of Independence*, Advisory Opinion, 2010 ICJ Rep. 403, at 598 (22 July) (separate opinion of Judge Cançado Trindade).
743. UDHR, Art. 1.
744. ICCPR, Art. 26.
745. ADRDM, Preamble and Art. 2.
746. ACHR, Art. 24.

or rescind legislation where necessary to prohibit any such discrimination, and to take all appropriate measures to combat intolerance on the grounds of religion or belief in this matter' (Article 4(1) and (2)). Regarding labour relations, another important source is the ILO Discrimination (Employment and Occupation) Convention 158 (No. 111).[747]

396. In 2022, by presidential decree, the 2013 Inter-American Convention Against all Forms of Discrimination and Intolerance became binding law in Brazil. It bans discrimination, including when it is based on religion, in broad terms, so that it encompasses relationships between private parties and indirect discrimination. The Convention also requires the adoption of affirmative action policies.[748]

§2. Non-discrimination in Statutory Law

397. As noted above (*see* Part II, Chapter 1, §2, I), freedom of belief prevents the state from punishing, threatening, or denying rights to an individual due to religious affiliation. This would also amount to a discrimination based on belief. Indirect discrimination – i.e., situations in which an apparently neutral act disproportionately affects a certain group in a negative way[749] – is also prohibited. It should be noted, however, that not all differences in legal treatment are unlawful, but only those that are deemed unreasonable (e.g., for not serving legitimate, legal, purposes, or for being inapt to advance them).[750]

398. In Brazil, acts of religious discrimination – such as denying customers access or service in private establishments the likes of shops, bars, restaurants, sports venues, and hotels, or refusing enrolment of students in schools because of the customer/pupil's religion – can be punished as crimes under Law No. 7716 of 5 January 1989. Some states also provide for administrative penalties (reprimands,

747. Leg. Dec. No. 104 of 24 Nov. 1964; Dec. 62150 of 19 Jan. 1968; Dec. 10088 of 5 Nov. 2019, Art. 2, XXVIII.

748. Inter-American Convention Against All Forms of Discrimination and Intolerance, Arts 1(1) and (2), 2, 8, and 5.

749. For a comprehensive analysis of the matter in Brazil, *see* Wallace Corbo, *Discriminação Indireta: Conceito, Fundamentos e uma Proposta de Enfrentamento à Luz da Constituição de 1988*, 184 (2017).

750. *See*, e.g., Luís Roberto Barroso, *Razoabilidade e Isonomia no Direito Brasileiro*, *in 1 Temas de Direito Constitucional* 153 (2006); Celso Antônio Bandeira de Mello, *Conteúdo Jurídico do Princípio da Igualdade*, 11, 21–43 (2005); Carlos Roberto de Siqueira Castro, *O Princípio da Isonomia e as Classificações Legislativas*, 16 Revista de Informação Legislativa 89, 91 (1979). In the Federal Supreme Court caselaw, *see* e.g., STF, Full Court, ADI 5577/DF, Rapp. Min. Rosa Weber, *DJ* 19 Dec. 2017; STF, Full Court, ADI 4276/MT, Rapp. Min. Luiz Fux, *DJ* 18 Sep. 2014; STF, Full Court, ADI 1076 MC/DF, Rapp. Min. Sepúlveda Pertence, *DJ* 7 Dec. 2000.

fines, punishment of public servants) for cases like these. This is the case in São Paulo[751] and Rio de Janeiro.[752] Some municipalities appear to follow a similar path, with the city of Rio de Janeiro/RJ being one example.[753]

751. Law (SP) No. 17157 of 18 Sep. 2019.
752. Law (RJ) No. 1814 of 24 Apr. 1991.
753. Org. Law (Rio de Janeiro/RJ), Art. 5, para. 3.

Chapter 8. Penal Law and Religion

§1. General Background

399. Penal law in Brazil is under federal legislative jurisdiction.[754] Only the Union can create and abolish criminal offences and set forth their penalties. Prisons, however, are under concurrent federal and state/District jurisdiction, so that the Union can set general provisions, whilst the states and the Federal District are allowed to pass their own legislation, so long as they respect the federal law.[755]

I. Penal Laws Criminalizing Manifestations of Religion

400. The Federal Constitution guarantees 'the freedom of conscience and belief', as well as the freedom to practice religions, making it forbidden to deprive people of their rights due to religious belief.[756] A provision criminalizing a religious practice would therefore likely be unconstitutional unless there existed very compelling reasons. For a discussion about limitations imposed on religious freedom, *see* Part I, Chapter 1, §2, II, and §3, II *supra*.

401. Nevertheless, the Penal Code still echoes some prejudice to minority religions and practices. One example can be found in Article 248, which criminalizes healers, who act by 'ordinarily prescribing, administering, or applying any substance', by 'using gestures, words, or any other means', or by 'making diagnoses'.[757] This appears to stem from an approach to traditional medicine that regards it as pure superstition.[758] It is hardly surprising, then, that these actions are only punishable when the victim is deemed 'unlearned', 'ignorant' or 'rude'.[759] Many religions offer some manner of spiritual healing as part of their practices, and the latter are prima facie protected by the right to religious freedom, but the actual targets of the persecution seem to be minorities, whose practices do not adhere to

754. Const. (1988), Art. 22, I.
755. Const. (1988), Art. 24, I.
756. Const. (1988), Art. 5, VI and VIII.
757. CP, Decree-Law No. 2848 of 7 Dec. 1940, Art. 284.
758. *See* General Introduction, §3, III and IV, *supra*.
759. STF, *2ª Turma* [2nd Panel], HC 85718/DF, Rapp. Min. Cezar Peluso, *DJ* 5 Dec. 2008.

mainstream standards.[760] To the extent that this criminal provision may unduly intrude upon religious freedom, it is unconstitutional.[761]

402. The use of forbidden narcotics may also prove to be a problem for the relation between Criminal Law and the freedom of religion. Some denominations, for example, consume controlled substances in rituals. That is the case of the *ayahuasca* or *hoasca* tea, drank as part of religious practices by groups such as the Santo Daime and União do Vegetal. In 1985, the *ayahuasca* was listed as a controlled substance and banned, only to see government suspend the measure one year later, so to study the religious use of the tea. In subsequent years, the legitimacy of religious consumption of *ayahuasca* was recognized in multiple instances and, hence, it is not a crime to consume it in religious rituals.[762]

II. Other Penal Laws Dealing with Religion

403. The Constitution imposes on the government the duty to guarantee 'the protection of places of worship and their rites' (Article 5, VI). Federal law indeed makes it a crime to publicly vilify an act or object of worship,[763] including Indigenous ceremonies and traditions.[764]

404. The Penal Code also criminalizes the actions of practising, inducing, or inciting discrimination or prejudice on the grounds of religion,[765] and of offending someone because of their religion.[766] Religious discrimination – e.g., by denying goods and services, as well as access to job vacancies – is also a crime, under Law No. 7716 of 5 January 1989.

§2. Religious Freedom of Incarcerated Persons

405. An incarcerated person retains their religious freedom, even though it can be limited – like with any other person – in light of sufficiently compelling reasons,

760. *See* Mariana Lins de Carli Silva, *Curandeirismo: O Bem Jurídico Saúde Pública a Serviço de uma Política Criminal Racista*, 152 Revista Brasileira de Ciências Criminais 145 (2019). According to Hoshino and Chueiri, Art. 248 echoes an 'archaic' prohibition against witchcraft and, in practice, it is applied unequally among religions: courts typically exempt practices of European religions from any penalty, employing them as templates of legitimate (and constitutionally protected) belief systems. *See* Thiago de Azevedo Pinheiro Hoshino & Vera Karam de Chueiri, *As Cores das/os Cortes: Uma Leitura do RE 494601 a Partir do Racismo Religioso*, 10 Direito e Práxis 2212, 2230, note 24 (2019).
761. Magalhães Pires, *supra* note 105 at 155–156. The Superior Court of Justice has hinted as to the unconstitutionality of this provision. *See* STJ, *6ª Turma* [6th Panel], HC 1498/RJ, Rapp. Min. Luiz Vicente Cernicchiaro, *DJ* 16 Aug. 1993.
762. Andréa Depieri de Albuquerque Reginato, *Regulamentação de Uso de Substância Psicoativa para Uso Religioso: o Caso da Ayahuasca*, 17 Tomo 57, 63–66 (2010).
763. CP, Decree-Law No. 2848 of 7 Dec. 1940, Art. 208.
764. Law No. 6001 of 19 Dec. 1973, Art. 58.
765. Law No. 7716 of 5 Jan. 1989, Art. 20.
766. CP, Decree-Law No. 2848 of 7 Dec. 1940, Art. 140, para. 3.

in order to protect and promote the rights of others or relevant public goals. The Constitution also guarantees that 'religious assistance' be on hand to those people in prisons and detention centres (Article 5, VII). That does not mean that the government is required to hire people to provide this assistance, but simply that it must offer the necessary conditions so that ministers and denominations can properly access inmates.

406. Statutory law demands that incarcerated people be allowed to participate in religious services conducted at the prisons or detention centres, if they choose to do so, as well as to keep, in their possession, books associated with religious teaching. It also requires that these facilities provide a proper place for religious services.[767] A minister or any other person who offers religious assistance in correctional facilities must comply with all legal provisions and internal bylaws so as to preserve the security of the prison or detention centre.[768] They can employ religious items, as long as they do not pose a threat to security, but the places where services are conducted cannot showcase features referring to particular denominations.[769] As for diets, attire, and grooming, the government must seek to adapt the routine of the facilities, thus demonstrating regard to 'religious imperatives'.[770]

767. Law No. 7210 of 11 Jul. 1984, Art. 24.
768. Law No. 9982 of 14 Jul. 2000, Art. 2.
769. Resolution (CNPCP) No. 8 of 9 Nov. 2011, Art. 2.
770. Resolution (CNPCP) No. 8 of 9 Nov. 2011, Art. 11. Indigenous people who are detained or sentenced to imprisonment must also have said rights guaranteed, with the necessary adaptations demanded by their traditions e customs. See Resolution (CNPCP) No. 13 of 4 Feb. 2021). Although the resolution treats this as a recommendation, it is actually a clear obligation under the Constitution (Art. 231).

Part VIII. Church Financing

Chapter 1. Direct Financing of Religious Communities

§1. Historical Background

407. For most of Brazilian history since the first European settlements, the Roman Catholic Church and the state were deeply connected through the right of patronage. The Portuguese king and, later, the emperor of Brazil possessed special rights, granted by the pope: in exchange for advancing Catholicism and maintaining the Church, they received the power to appoint bishops and to collect religious revenues and tithes.[771] The Roman Church was, therefore, a quasi-department of the state, which had the obligation to support it.

408. The situation began to change in 1890, when the newly established Republic extinguished the patronage, despite guaranteeing that the government would continue paying the salaries of the Catholic clergy.[772] The first republican Constitution (1891), however, forbade the state from subsidizing religious denominations,[773] and all other Constitutions thereafter have repeated this prohibition.[774]

§2. Laicity: The State Cannot Support Religious Organizations

409. The Federal Constitution explicitly prohibits all tiers of government from subsidizing or maintaining 'relationships of dependence or alliance with [religious denominations] or their representatives'.[775] Cooperation between the state and religious entities is permitted, as long it involves the advancement of public interests

771. Lima, *supra* note 106 at 23.
772. Decree No. 119-A of 7 Jan. 1890, Arts 4 and 6.
773. Const. (1891), Art. 11, No. 2.
774. Const. (1934), Art. 17, II; Const. (1937), Art. 32, *b*; Const. (1946), Art. 31, II; Const. (1967), Art. 9, II; Const. (1969), Art. 9, II; Const. (1988), Art. 19, I.
775. Const. (1988), Art. 19, I.

(e.g., social assistance, education, healthcare). It is therefore inadmissible that public funds be employed to support religious activities and institutions. For this reason, state courts of appeals usually deem invalid acts of donations of public lands or conferring rights of use over them for religious organizations to construct churches.[776]

§3. Government Funding of Religious Schools

410. Cooperation between the state and religious entities in matters of education is explicitly permitted by the Constitution: religious schools and other private educational institutions may receive public funds should they meet the required conditions.[777] For more information on this, *see* Part IX, Chapter 2, §2 *infra*.

776. *See*, e.g., TJGO, *4ª Câmara Cível* [4th Civil Panel], Ap. 5370617-70.2017.8.09.0043, Rapp. CAJ Carlos Escher, *DJ* 22 Feb. 2021; TJPR, *4ª Câmara Cível* [4th Civil Panel], Ap. 937721-9, Rapp. CAJ Maria Alice Aparecida Blanco de Lima, *DJ* 19 Jun. 2015; TJSP, *Órgão Especial* [Special Panel], Arg. Inconst. 0020774-56.2020.8.26.0000, Rapp. CAJ James Siano, *DJ* 3 Sep. 2020; TJSP, *Órgão Especial* [Special Panel], ADI 2120132-62.2017.8.26.0000, Rapp. CAJ Alvaro Passos, *DJ* 9 Nov. 2017. However, in a specific case, the State Court of Appeals of Santa Catarina upheld the donation because it benefited several religious entities (TJSC, *4ª Câmara de Direito Público* [4th Public Law Panel], Rem. Nec. 0001153-65.2009.8.24.0113, Rapp. CAJ Rodolfo Cezar Ribeiro Da Silva Tridapalli, 5 Sep. 2019).

777. Const. (1988), Art. 213.

Chapter 2. Indirect Financing of Religious Communities

§1. Indirect Financing Through Federal and State Tax Laws

411. The Federal Constitution grants immunity to 'temples of any denomination', regarding *impostos*[778] levied on property, revenues, and services related to their 'essential purposes'.[779] According to the Federal Supreme Court, the immunity is not limited to the temples per se; it rather includes any place employed for religious purposes (e.g., religious cemeteries),[780] property leased by religious organizations,[781] and even vacant lots.[782] The immunity, however, does not encompass taxes other than *impostos*, nor does it affect indirect taxes, which are included in prices that the organizations pay as consumers.[783] The tax immunity also does not exempt the entity from other duties, such as filing the necessary forms and withholding taxes owed by their ministers and employees.[784]

412. Religious organizations and entities can also benefit from various other tax benefits, established by federal and state law. These were discussed in more length in Part I, Chapter 2, §2, and Part VI, Chapter 1, §3 *supra*.

§2. Funding of Religiously Affiliated Social Services

413. The Federal Constitution admits cooperation between religious denominations and the state in matters of public interest.[785] Charities, whether religious or not, can collaborate with the state in areas such as healthcare initiatives, education, and social assistance. Under conditions established by law, they may even be entitled to receive public funds. That is the case, for example, of private schools,[786] hospitals,[787] and social assistance entities[788] administered by religious groups.

---

778. *Impostos* are but one species of tax in the complex taxation system adopted in Brazil. A few examples of *impostos* are the (federal) income tax, the (state) tax on the circulation of goods and some services, the (local) tax on services in general, and the (federal) tax on financial operations.
779. Const. (1988), Art. 150, VI, *b*, and para. 4.
780. STF, Full Court, RE 578562/BA, Rapp. Min. Eros Grau, *DJ* 12 Sep. 2008.
781. *See*, e.g., STF, Full Court, RE 325.822/SP, Rapp. Min. Gilmar Mendes, *DJ* 14 May 2004.
782. STF, *1ª Turma* [1st Panel], ARE 800395 AgR/ES, Rapp. Min. Luís Roberto Barroso, *DJ* 14 Nov. 2014.
783. *See*, e.g., STF, Full Court, ADI 5816/RO, Rapp. Min. Alexandre de Moraes, *DJ* 26 Nov. 2019. Indirect taxes are those that are levied on suppliers of goods and services, who then pass them on to their customers, within the price of their merchandise or service.
784. CTN, Law No. 5172 of 25 Oct. 1966, Art. 9, para. 1.
785. *See* Const. (1988), Art. 19, I.
786. For government funding of religious schools, *see* Part IX, Ch. 2, §2 *infra*.
787. According to the Constitution, healthcare services can be provided by private parties, who may opt to integrate them to the public healthcare system. However, only non-profit private entities qualify to receive public funds. *See* Const. (1988), Art. 199, pars 1 and 2; Law No. 8080 of 19 Sep. 1990, Art. 38.
788. Law No. 8742 of 7 Dec. 1993, Art. 3; Decree No. 7788 of 15 Aug. 2012, Arts 4, I, and 10.

414. As for indirect financing, the Constitution grants a tax immunity regarding 'the property, income or services … of nonprofit education and social assistance institutions, observing the requirements of the law'.[789] As with temples, this immunity 'encompasses only the property, income and services related to the essential purposes' of these entities.[790] According to the Federal Supreme Court, the immunity includes property leased by charities, if the income is employed in maintaining the latter's relevant services,[791] and also property which is temporarily vacant.[792]

415. The Constitution provides that 'benevolent entities of social assistance which meet the requirements established in law shall be exempt from contribution to social welfare'.[793] These benefits may be claimed irrespective of the entity's status, whether religious or not, so long as they meet the requirements set forth by the law to determine their standing as 'benevolent entities of social assistance'.

789. Const. (1988), Art. 150, VI, *c*.
790. Const. (1988), Art. 150, para. 4.
791. STF, *Súmula Vinculante* [Binding Thesis] No. 52.
792. *See*, e.g., STF, Full Court, RE 767332 RG/MG, Rapp. Min. Gilmar Mendes, *DJ* 22 Nov. 2013.
793. Const. (1988), Art. 195, para. 7.

Part IX. Education

Chapter 1. Religious Education in Public and Private Schools

§1. Historical Background

416. Education in colonial Brazil was a religious endeavour, with the Society of Jesus in the forefront. They focused on the Indigenous peoples – with the purpose of conversion and acculturation – and, later, graduated their focus onto the children of the elite. Higher education in Brazil remained limited to Catholic seminaries; those who wanted to enrol in other courses had to venture to Europe, notably the University of Coimbra. In the late eighteenth century, under the government of the Marquis of Pombal, Portugal expelled the Jesuits, supplanting them with a public system of education in Brazil. However, the situation endured as the model of teaching was similar and most of the teachers remained fixed in office.[794]

417. Changes occurred after the arrival of the Portuguese royal family, who settled in Rio de Janeiro in 1808. Prince Regent John – later King John VI – created the first non-theological higher degrees in Brazil: Engineering, Surgery, Anatomy, Medicine, Economy, Agriculture, Chemistry, and Technical Design.[795] The first Law Schools were established, after the Independence (1822), by Emperor Peter I, in São Paulo and Olinda (1827).[796]

418. During the monarchy, emphasis was placed on higher education, with primary and secondary tiers receiving little attention and being placed under the control of private entities. Many reforms were attempted and passed, garnering unimpressive results. In 1834, the provinces assumed responsibility for primary and secondary education, but they sadly lacked financial resources, culminating in the complete 'abandonment' of these tiers, which remained under the care of private parties.[797]

---

794. Ailton Camargos, *Educação no Brasil: Da Colônia ao Início da República*, 17 Revista Brasileira de Educação e Cultura 129, 130–133 (2018); Paulo Rennes Marçal Ribeiro, *História da Educação Escolar no Brasil: Notas para uma Reflexão*, 4 Paidéia 15, 15–16 (1993); Gleidson Silva & Simone Silveira Amorim, *Apontamentos sobre a Educação no Brasil Colonial (1549–1759)*, 18 Interações 185, 186–188 (2017).
795. Dermeval Saviani, *A Expansão do Ensino Superior no Brasil: Mudanças e Continuidades*, 8 Poíesis Pedagógica 4, 5 (2010).
796. *Ibid.* at 5.
797. Ribeiro, *supra* note 794 at 17; Camargos, *supra* note 794 at 136–137.

419. At first, the Proclamation of the Republic (1889) did not effectuate significant change to the scenario.[798] In 1872, illiteracy was widespread, encompassing 82.3% of individuals of 5 years of age or older; in 1920, the ratio had somewhat reduced to 71.2% but was still very high.[799] At the beginning of the new century, the former provinces, now states, were the protagonists in primary education, whereas the Union concerned itself with secondary and higher tiers.[800]

420. Until the first half of the twentieth century, education was a privilege, from which the majority of the population was excluded.[801] The focus only shifted to primary and secondary schools during the dictatorship of Getúlio Vargas (1937–1945), but throughout the first decades of the second half of the twentieth century, there was continuous tension between those advocates of private schools (including the Catholic Church) and those of public schools.[802] From 1931 through 1961, the Union became protagonist, passing reforms and investing in education.[803] As a result, from 1920 to 1960, illiteracy rates began to drop steeply, with a 24.5% reduction, to include 46.7% of the population.[804] In 1967, enrolment in schools became mandatory, and disfavoured groups gained actual access to education.[805] Nevertheless, the illiteracy rate slowed its pace of reduction from 1970 to 2000, when impacting upon 16.7% of the population.[806]

421. The 1988 Constitution extensively addressed this issue. Access to education is a fundamental right – and a duty, as enrolment remains mandatory for those between the ages of four and seventeen. To guarantee the enjoyment of this right, the Constitution calls upon state, society, and families. It also expressly permits private schools (including religious ones) to be established.[807] All levels of government are involved in education, albeit with differing priorities: municipalities must focus on pre-school and primary education, whereas the states must prioritize primary and secondary education, and the Union must focus on tertiary education.[808] The Constitution also demands that, at each level of government, a certain amount of revenue be allocated to education.[809]

798. Ribeiro, *supra* note 794 at 18–19.
799. Alceu Ravanello Ferraro & Daniel Kreidlow, *Analfabetismo no Brasil: Configuração e Gênese das Desigualdades Regionais*, 29 Educação & Sociedade 179, 182, 185 (2004).
800. Dermeval Saviani, *A Política Educacional no Brasil*, *in III Histórias e Memórias da Educação no Brasil* 29, 29–31 (Maria Stephanou & Maria Helena Camara Bastos eds., 2005).
801. Jurandir de Almeida Araújo, *Educação e Desigualdade: A Conjuntura Atual do Ensino Público no Brasil*, 2 Revista Direitos Humanos e Democracia 125, 127 (2014).
802. Ribeiro, *supra* note 794 at 22–25.
803. Saviani, *supra* note 800 at 29, 31–34.
804. Ferraro and Kreidlow, *supra* note 799 at 186.
805. Araújo, *supra* note 801 at 127.
806. Alceu Ravanello Ferraro, *Analfabetismo e Níveis de Letramento no Brasil: O Que Dizem os Censos?*, 23 Educação & Sociedade 21, 33 (2002).
807. Const. (1988), Arts 206, 208, I, and 209.
808. Const. (1988), Art. 211, pars 1–3.
809. Const. (1988), Arts 212 and 212-A, the latter having been included by CA 108 of 26 Aug. 2020.

422. Around 1990, primary schools attained the capability to accommodate all children in the relevant age groups,[810] and in 2011 the illiteracy rate fell to 9.83%.[811] A 2020 survey found that the country had almost 180,000 primary and secondary schools, 60% of which are owned by municipalities. Private schools represent 23% of the total.[812]

423. Inequality, nonetheless, remains an important problem: illiteracy rates – which were geographically uniform in 1872 – reduced more intensely in the South and Southeast regions of the country, comprising the richest states, and in the Federal District, leaving the North, Northeast, and Centre-West to languish behind. In 2000, the highest and lowest rates were found, respectively, in the State of Alagoas (36.5%) and the Federal District (8.8%), so that the proportion of illiterate people in the former was more than four times that of the latter.[813] Illiteracy rates are also considerably higher among Black people (14.4%) than that of white individuals (5.6%).[814]

§2. Religious Teaching in Public Schools

424. The Constitution expressly requires that the state offer religious teaching in the regular schedule of public fundamental schools.[815] The LDB further states that religious teaching is 'an integral part of the basic formation of the citizen', requires 'respect for the religious cultural diversity of Brazil', and forbids 'any form of proselytism'.[816] Each level of government must set forth provisions for the selection of teachers and procedures to define the content of these classes (after hearing a private entity formed by 'different denominations').[817]

425. There is a chasm, however, between the law and reality in relation to this subject. According to Minister Luís Roberto Barroso of the Federal Supreme Court:

> Throughout Brazil, [religious] teaching models with very different contours were established, which may be classified as (i) *denominational teaching*; (ii) *inter-denominational teaching*; and (iii) *teaching about religions*. Besides the variation in the models, there are also differences in the way that content is

810. Romualdo Portela de Oliveira, *Da Universalização do Ensino Fundamental ao Desafio da Qualidade: Uma Análise Histórica*, 28 Educação & Sociedade 661, 667 (2007).
811. Séries Histórias e Estatísticas, IBGE, https://seriesestatisticas.ibge.gov.br/default.aspx (last visited 26 May 2021).
812. Instituto Nacional de Estudos e Pesquisas Educacionais Anísio Teixeira, *Censo da Educação Básica 2020: Resumo Técnico (Versão Preliminar)*, 49 (2021).
813. Ferraro and Kreidlow, *supra* note 799 at 188.
814. Araújo, *supra* note 801 at 137.
815. Const. (1988), Art. 210, para. 1. In Brazil, the *basic* levels are: (1) *pre-school* (nursery and kindergarten); (2) *fundamental*, with nine years, roughly corresponding to elementary and middle schools in the United States, and (3) *middle level* (three years), which roughly corresponds to high school in the United States.
816. LDB, Law No. 9394 of 20 Dec. 1996, Art. 33.
817. *Ibid.*, pars 1 and 2.

imparted so that there are cases in which religious teaching is not offered in the form of a class, but rather in a transversal way by the teacher of the grade. There are also systems[818] in which enrolment is automatic, so that the student must request their exclusion, if they wish; and others in which student enrolment requires an express declaration. Besides that, religious teaching hours may or may not be considered in the minimum amount required by the LDB; and class results are or not considered for student promotion purposes. Only a few systems offer alternative activities for those who do not opt to take part in the [religious teaching] class. Finally, there is also great variation as to teacher admission requirements, among which it is worth highlighting the demand (i) of a certificate in Sciences of Religion, accreditation and/or specialization in religious teaching; (ii) of a bachelor's degree in the areas of Education, History, Philosophy, Sociology, Social Sciences, Psychology; or the hiring (iii) of people appointed or accredited by religious authorities; (iv) [of] people certified as having graduated from training courses offered by religious institutions; or even (v) volunteers in the community.
Since there are no national standards for this class, there is no mechanism to support that the content of religious teaching is offered without proselytism and with respect to the religious freedom of students in all fundamental-level schools in Brazil. As a result, reports of religious discrimination are not uncommon, are frequently severe and even involve physical violence, especially related to religions of African heritage.[819]

426. In 2017, a survey was conducted with 70,000 public school principals.[820] Of them, 34% responded that their schools did not offer religious classes, whilst 36% answered that they did offer religious teaching, which was mandatory, the Constitution and the LDB notwithstanding. According to 56% of principals, their schools did not offer alternative activities for students who did not wish to enrol in religious classes. Also, a study of public schools in the State of Rio de Janeiro showed that the optional character of these classes was unclear for students and parents, and many had to actively ask the school not to enrol them or their children in religious classes. In the schools that were analysed by the paper, the number of Catholic teachers usually predominated, followed by Protestant teachers, and only one had a Spiritist teacher.[821] Therefore, 'religious teaching in [public] schools in Rio [de Janeiro] has been totally contained within the sphere of the Protestant and Catholic religions'; there is an 'implicit consensus' in which 'when one speaks of religion, everyone refers exclusively to Christian religions', with an awkward silence permeating any meaningful acknowledgement of African-Brazilian religiosity.[822]

---

818. Every level of government consists of a school system. *See* LDB, Law No. 9394 of 20 Dec. 1996, Arts 8 and 16–18.
819. STF, Full Court, ADI 4439/DF, Rapp. Min. Alexandre de Moraes, *DJ* 21 Jun. 2018 (dissenting opinion of Min. Luís Roberto Barroso).
820. *Diretores*, QEdu, https://www.qedu.org.br/brasil/pessoas/diretor (last visited 11 Apr. 2021).
821. Ana Maria Cavaliere, *O Mal-Estar no Ensino Religioso nas Escolas Públicas*, 37 Cadernos de Pesquisa 303, 315–316, 322 (2007).
822. *Ibid.* at 325.

427. In light of the laicity principle, these problems raise important issues. They have led the Prosecutor General of the Republic to file a direct action of unconstitutionality before the Federal Supreme Court, seeking a declaration that religious teaching in public schools could not be denominational and that the state was forbidden to hire representatives of denominations as teachers. The Court, however, ruled against the plaintiff, in a split decision (6:5). According to the STF, the Constitution guarantees students 'who expressly and voluntarily enrol' in these classes, a right to religious teaching 'in accord with the principles of their religious beliefs and based in the dogmas of the faith'. The opinion stated that the laicity principle was observed by ensuring the voluntary nature of enrolment, including respect for agnostics and atheists; by implicitly prohibiting the state from creating its own, 'artificial', content for said classes; and by forbidding that some groups' religious interpretations prevailed over those of others.[823]

§3. Other Manifestations of Religion in Public Schools

428. It seems clear that the laicity principle and freedom of religion forbid official or mandatory religious practices in public schools. Pupils, teachers, and other employees cannot be compelled to participate in religious services, and public authorities cannot convey or suggest an official endorsement of a religious worldview. However, mandated or encouraged moments of prayer are not uncommon, creating discomfort and even reported discrimination against those who refuse to participate. In the State of Piauí, the students of a local school begin their day reciting the Lord's Prayer and singing a religious song about the presence of God and the Holy Spirit; children also learn the Hail Mary, which is opposed by non-Catholic parents. In Minas Gerais, after refusing to recite the Lord's Prayer, an atheist pupil was targeted by Catholic students, who replaced the last words for 'deliver us from [the student's name], being his name. He then sought help from an association of atheists and agnostics, who intervened in his favour and successfully had the State Department of Education request the teacher to refrain from organizing prayers.[824]

429. Some municipalities have even enacted laws or bylaws requiring prayers in public schools, but courts have consistently declared them unconstitutional.[825] In

823. STF, Full Court, ADI 4439/DF, Rapp. Min. Alexandre de Moraes, *DJ* 21 Jun. 2018. I have made some remarks about this issue in Magalhães Pires, *supra* note 105 at 297–312.

824. Efrém Ribeiro, *Orações Obrigatórias Afetam Ateus e Minorias Religiosas na Rede Pública*, O Globo, 23 Mar. 2013, https://oglobo.globo.com/sociedade/educacao/oracoes-obrigatorias-afetam-ateus-minorias-religiosas-na-rede-publica-7928328.

825. *See*, e.g., TJBA, Full Court, ADI 0021850-08.2017.8.05.0000, Rapp. CAJ Abelardo Paulo da Matta Neto, *DJ* 25 Oct. 2018; TJGO, *Corte Especial* [Special Panel], ADI 5236450-85.2016.8.09.0000, Rapp. CAJ Itaney Francisco Campos; Barra Mansa/RJ, *4ª Vara Cível* [4th Civil Court of First Instance], Proc. 0013080-15.2017.8.19.0007, 14 Jan. 2020. In this last case, an injunction issued by the Court was confirmed by a Judge of the State Court of Appeals (TJRJ, *19ª Câmara Cível* [19th Civil Panel], AI 0068944-59.2017.8.19.0000, Rapp. CAJ Ferdinaldo Nascimento, 27 Feb. 2018).

the State of Rio de Janeiro, the Court of Appeals confirmed a ruling prohibiting public prayers, the reading of religious texts, and worship services in state-run public schools.[826] There are even cases in which damages were awarded to students who were forced to participate in religious acts in public schools.[827]

§4. Religious Freedom of Students

430. As with any other individual, students retain their religious freedom whilst at school. They are entitled, for example, to wear religious symbols and garments in classes. If religious days of rest require the absence of a student, the law demands that schools and universities provide the same activity on a different date and time or replace it with a written assignment.[828] Although the law exempts military schools from these demands, it appears to be an unconstitutional provision, since no reason justifies this different treatment.[829]

826. TJRJ, *14ª Câmara Cível* [14th Civil Panel], Rem. Nec. 0323579-81.2009.8.19.0001, Rapp. CAJ Plínio Pinto Coelho Filho, *DJ* 8 May 2014.
827. TJSP, *5ª Câmara de Direito Público* [5th Public Law Panel], Ap. 1005816-02.2017.8.26.0114, Rapp. CAJ Maria Laura Tavares, *DJ* 22 Mar. 2019.
828. LDB, Law No. 9394 of 20 Dec. 1996, Art. 7-A (included by Law No. 13796 of 3 Jan. 2019).
829. For a brief discussion on this, *see* Thiago Magalhães Pires, *Lei 13.796/2019 é Avanço no Tratamento da Liberdade Religiosa nas Escolas*, Consultor Jurídico, 31 Jan. 2019, https://www.conjur.com.br/2019-jan-31/thiago-magalhaes-avanco-liberdade-religiosa-escolas.

Chapter 2. Religious Schools

§1. Right to Private Education

431. Parents and guardians are not obligated to enrol children in public schools. On the contrary, the Constitution demands respect for the 'freedom to learn, teach, research and express thought, art and knowledge' and for 'pluralism of pedagogic ideas and conceptions and coexistence of public and private teaching institutions' (Article 206, II and III). It also states that '[t]eaching is open to private enterprise, provided that' private schools comply 'with the general rules of national education' and that they submit to governmental supervision (Article 209).

432. Accordingly, the LDB classifies schools into three categories: (1) public schools, operated by the government; (2) private schools, operated by private parties; and (3) community schools, to be defined by law. The second and third categories may or may not be philanthropies, being characterized as 'religious schools' should they adhere to specific religious persuasions or to specific ideologies.[830] These provisions are aligned with Article 13(3) of the ICESCR, which entitles parents and legal guardians to 'choose for their children schools, other than those established by the public authorities, which conform to such minimum educational standards as may be laid down or approved by the State and to ensure the religious and moral education of their children in conformity with their own convictions'.

433. Therefore, anyone – including religious organizations and groups – can establish religious schools, as an exercise of their freedoms of worship and enterprise.[831] Private pre-schools are supervised by municipalities, whilst elementary and high schools and higher institutions are under state and federal supervision, respectively.[832]

434. In 2019, on average, 2.2% of all elementary and high school students in each state and the Federal District were enrolled in religious, community, and philanthropic schools. Eleven states recorded higher rates, the highest include: Rio de Janeiro (2.8%), Minas Gerais (2.9%), Paraná (3.1%), Santa Catarina (4.2%), and Rio Grande do Sul (6.4%).[833]

435. With regards to tertiary education, religious institutions are among the most prominent in the country, leading research efforts within the private sector. They

830. LDB, Law No. 9394 of 20 Dec. 1996, Art. 19, II and III, and pars 1 and 2.
831. The Constitution guarantees the freedom of enterprise in Arts 1, IV, and 170. It also provides that '[f]ree exercise of any economic activity is ensured to everyone, regardless of authorization from government agencies, except in the cases set forth by law' (Art. 170, sole par.).
832. LDB, Law No. 9394 of 20 Dec. 1996, Arts 16, II, 17, III, and 18, II.
833. Iuri Pitta, *Sul tem Maior Proporção de Alunos em Escolas Filantrópicas e Confessionais*, CNN Brasil, 15 Dec. 2020, https://www.cnnbrasil.com.br/nacional/2020/12/15/sul-tem-maior-proporcao-de-alunos-em-escolas-filantropicas-e-confessionais.

only rank below public universities.[834] Some of the most prestigious religious universities are the Pontifical Catholic Universities of Rio de Janeiro, São Paulo, Rio Grande do Sul, Minas Gerais, and Paraná. There are also renowned Protestant institutions, such as Mackenzie Presbyterian University. However, the number of community and religious tertiary institutions and student enrolment at them has been decreasing, whereas for-profit private institutions have registered significant growth.[835]

436. The members of the *Associação Nacional de Educação Católica do Brasil* [National Association of Catholic Education of Brazil] are present in 900 municipalities, with 89 higher education institutions, 1,100 schools, and 1,500,000 students.[836] Evangelical institutions boast impressive numbers too: comprising nine denominational associations, the larger *Associação Brasileira de Instituições Educacionais Evangélicas* [Brazilian Association of Evangelical Educational Institutions] represents 909 members, of which Adventists constitute the largest share (ca. 53%).[837]

437. Homeschooling is a controversial topic. Under the Constitution, education is compulsory for children (4–7 years old),[838] and ECA requires parents and guardians to enrol their children or wards in the regular school systems,[839] which led courts to rule against homeschooling.[840] The matter reached the Federal Supreme Court, where it was decided that although the Constitution did not forbid homeschooling, only a law, passed by Congress, could make it legal so as to preserve all interests involved. According to the Court, the fundamental right to education is essential to the individual and society because it dignifies the person and enlightens the community, being incumbent on both the family and the State to guarantee its fruition by children, adolescents, and youngsters.[841] Parents and guardians are not the focus and cannot exercise total control as to the education of their children and wards. Therefore, should Congress decide to regulate homeschooling, it must guarantee, e.g., that the period of compulsory education is observed (4–7 years old), as

834. Danae Stephan, *Entre Universidades Particulares, Religiosas Lideram Ranking de Pesquisas*, Folha de S. Paulo, 7 Oct. 2019, https://ruf.folha.uol.com.br/2019/noticias/entre-universidades-particulares-religiosas-lideram-ranking-de-pesquisas.shtml.

835. Valdemar Sguissardi, *O Que Será das Instituições de Educação Superior Comunitárias e Confessionais?*, 25 Comunicações 27, 34–35 (2018).

836. *Associadas*, Associação Nacional de Educação Católica do Brasil, https://anec.org.br/associadas/ (last visited 15 Feb. 2021).

837. *Associadas*, Associação Brasileira de Instituições Educacionais Evangélicas, https://www.abiee.org.br/associadas-abiee (last visited 29 Jun. 2021).

838. Const. (1988), Art. 208, I.

839. ECA, Law No. 8069 of 13 Jul. 1990, Art. 55.

840. *See*, e.g., TJRS, *7ª Câmara Cível* [7th Civil Panel], Ap. 70069284933, Rapp. CAJ Liselena Schifino Robles Ribeiro, *DJ* 8 Jul. 2016.

841. Under Brazilian law, children [*crianças*] are individuals below the age of 12 years, whereas adolescents [*adolescents*] are those with 12 to 18 years of age. Youngsters [*jovens*], being 15 to 29 years old, are primarily under ECA until they reach 18 years of age and different provisions become applicable. *See* ECA, Law No. 8069 of 13 Jul. 1990, Art. 2; Law No. 12852 of 5 Aug. 2013, Art. 1, para. 1.

well as the government's duty to set the basic curriculum and to supervise and assess the standards of education provided to these children.[842]

§2. Financing of Private Schools

438. Private schools rely on tuition fees and donations to function. Public funds must be primarily directed to the public schools, but the Constitution and the law allow for its use in private schools, especially in the form of scholarships to those in need, when the public system proves insufficient to accommodate all students. However, only community, religious, or philanthropic private schools can receive public funds, and, even so, as long as they: (1) are non-profit and not-for-profit institutions; (2) direct their financial surplus to educational services; (3) guarantee that their assets be assigned to another community, religious, or philanthropic school – or to the state – should they cease their operational activities; (4) render accounts to the government regarding the revenue they receive.[843]

842. STF, Full Court, RE 888815/RS, Rapp. Min. Alexandre de Moraes, *DJ* 21 Mar. 2019.
843. Const. (1988), Art. 213; LDB, Law No. 9394 of 20 Dec. 1996, Art. 77, I–IV.

Part X. Matrimonial and Family Law

Chapter 1. Legal Position of Religious Marriage

§1. Introduction

439. In Brazil, marriages are regulated by federal statutes on Civil Law. Marriages can be performed by a state official or a religious representative. Civil and religious marriages possess the same legal effects, provided that the latter comply with the conditions set forth by the law and be registered in the public records. A state-issued marriage licence is required in all cases; for religious marriages, the licence can be issued after the ceremony, being it a condition for its registration (and for granting it civil effects). The law does not differentiate between religions for these purposes, as well as for defining the parties' rights and duties. Whatever may be the status of unions under religious precepts, their situation is the same under the law.

§2. Federal Law

440. Family Law is a traditional component of Civil Law. Marriages are therefore regulated solely by federal law,[844] especially the Civil Code. People older than 18 years are free to marry, but 16 and 17-year-olds are also permitted to be married, provided that their parents allow it.[845] Before 2019, individuals who were younger than 16 could marry, in exceptional circumstances, if it was necessary to avoid criminal penalties or in case of pregnancy, but that is no longer the case – nowadays, no underage person can marry.[846]

441. Other subsets of people who are forbidden to marry include: (1) descendants with their ascendants; (2) anyone with a former spouse's ascendants or descendants; (3) a parent with their adopted child's former spouse; (4) a person with their adopted parent's former spouse; (5) siblings; (6) aunts/uncles with their nieces/nephews; (7) adopted and biological children of the same person; (8) people who

844. Const. (1988), Art. 22, I.
845. CC, Law No. 10406 of 10 Jan. 2002, Art. 1517.
846. CC, Law No. 10406 of 10 Jan. 2002, Art. 1520 (as amended by Law No. 13811 of 12 Mar. 2019).

are already married; (9) anyone with a person who has been sentenced for the murder (or attempted murder) of the former's spouse.[847]

442. Before marrying, people must obtain a licence from a notary. The latter issues a public notice, so that anyone can oppose the licensing and, after a fifteen-day period, should all necessary conditions be met, the licence is then issued. Should the notary, the Public Prosecutors' Office, or a third party oppose the issuing of the licence, the matter is to be taken before a judge.[848] In requesting a licence, the parties also will choose the matrimonial regime they are going to adopt post marriage.[849]

443. The ceremony itself is usually presided by a justice of the peace[850] or a religious minister (*see* Part X, Chapter 1, §3 *infra*), but some states also confer this power on other officials. In the State of Rio de Janeiro, for example, some judges are also authorized to perform marriage ceremonies.[851] Before the presiding official and the witnesses, after the parties (or a designee) confirm their willingness to marry, the official declares them to be married.[852] After the ceremony, the notary registers the marriage in the public records.[853] Any spouse may change their name to include the surname of the other.[854]

444. Spouses are to be companions, bearing equal authority and responsibilities within their family. They owe each other fidelity, cohabitation, assistance, respect, and consideration, and they are both also required to collaborate in sustaining, protecting, and educating their children, and in supporting the household.[855]

445. Valid marriages can only be dissolved by the death of a spouse or by divorce,[856] but it is also possible to have a marriage voided or declared to be void (*see* §4 *infra*).

§3. Status of Religious Marriage

446. At first, only Catholic marriages were allowed in Brazil. They were recognized by law as a sacrament, so their validity depended on conduction by a Catholic priest, involving a woman and a man of the same denomination, according to the

847. CC, Law No. 10406 of 10 Jan. 2002, Art. 1522.
848. CC, Law No. 10406 of 10 Jan. 2002, Arts 1525–1532. *See also* Law No. 6015 of 31 Dec. 1973, Arts 67–69.
849. CC, Law No. 10406 of 10 Jan. 2002, Art. 1640, sole par.
850. Const. (1988), Art. 98, II.
851. RJ, Law No. 6956 of 13 Jan. 2015, Art. 49, I.
852. CC, Law No. 10406 of 10 Jan. 2002, Art. 1535.
853. CC, Law No. 10406 of 10 Jan. 2002, Art. 1536.
854. CC, Law No. 10406 of 10 Jan. 2002, Art. 1565, para. 1.
855. Const. (1988), Art. 226, para. 5; CC, Law No. 10406 of 10 Jan. 2002, Arts 1565–1570.
856. CC, Law No. 10406 of 10 Jan. 2002, Art. 1571, para. 1.

1707 First Constitutions of the Archbishopric of Bahia and the Council of Trent.[857] In the nineteenth century, however, the growing number of Protestant immigrants made it more common to find 'mixed marriages' – i.e., (illegal) marriages between Catholics and non-Catholics[858] – and some cases drew a lot of popular attention,[859] bringing about a political discussion about adopting civil marriage. The Holy See issued directives allowing the clergy to grant dispensations from matrimonial impediments, including that of spouses' religions, but they required frequent negotiations between the Vatican and Brazilian officials. All this led to numerous bills being proposed, one of which eventually passed in 1861. It did not regulate civil marriages, but it did extend the civil effects of marriages to those between non-Catholics, performed in accordance to their own religious rites, so long as they were registered as prescribed by law.[860] The law, however, was never enforced, and a few other bills were discussed.[861] Its only effect was to prevent other measures from being enacted, under the pretence that the matter had already been settled.[862]

447. Catholicism ceded its status as the official state religion in 1890. When the monarchy was abolished, the Provisional Government of Marshal Deodoro da Fonseca issued a decree instituting civil marriage in Brazil. Religious ceremonies could be conducted, but only 'before or after civil marriage', making it clear that only the latter was legally valid.[863] Under the first republican Constitution (1891), the state 'only recognize[d] the civil marriage'.[864]

---

857. The Council of Trent (1545–1563) required that provincial councils and diocesan synods be held to enforce its decrees. *See* Zinnhobler and Moderna, *supra* note 113 at 240–243. In 1707, the synod convened by D. Sebastião Monteiro da Vide, the fourth archbishop of Salvador, approved the Constitutions, which became one of the most important sources of Canon Law in Brazil for a long time. *See* Lima, *supra* note 106 at 81–82.
858. According to Title LXVII, para. 285(6), of the First Constitutions of the Archbishopric of Bahia (1707), 'disparity of religion' was an impediment to marriage. *See* Sebastião Monteiro da Vide, *Constituições Primeiras do Arcebispado da Bahia*, 117 (1853), https://www2.senado.leg.br/bdsf/handle/id/222291.
859. Two of these cases are mentioned by scholars. One involved Catharina Scheid, a Protestant woman, who married Francisco Fagundes, a Catholic man. After a year, he abandoned her, and she asked for a dissolution of their marriage, but the authorities denied her any rights, since her relationship was not deemed an actual marriage. The other case was that of Margarida Kerth and João Schop, both Protestant. She left her husband, converted to Catholicism, and sought a licence to marry a Catholic man (Franklin Brasileiro Jansen Lima). The licence was granted by the bishop of Rio de Janeiro, who declared void her previous marriage due to not obeying the rules of the Council of Trent. *See* Ítalo Domingos Santirocchi, *O Matrimônio no Império do Brasil: uma Questão de Estado*, 4 Revista Brasileira de História das Religiões 81, 88–90 (2012).
860. Decree No. 1144 of 11 Sep. 1861.
861. For a detailed description of these events, the debates within Government and Parliament, and the influence of papal delegates in the process, *see* Ivo Pereira Silva, *Do Casamento Misto ao Casamento Civil no Brasil: Debates Parlamentares em Torno do Matrimônio na Segunda Metade do Século XIX*, 46 Revista Portuguesa de História 391, 398–408 (2015); Santirocchi, *supra* note 859 at 114–120.
862. Silva, *supra* note 861 at 408.
863. Law No. 181 of 24 Jan. 1890, especially Art. 108, sole par.
864. Const. (1891), Art. 72, para. 4.

448. In the period of Neo-Christianity (*see* General Introduction, §3, IV, *supra*), the state and the Roman Catholic Church again edged towards a closer relationship. The 1934 Constitution extended the effects of civil marriages to religious ceremonies, so long as the legal requirements were met and the marriages were registered in the public records.[865] The 1937 Constitution did not provide for the matter, but previously, that same year, a statute was passed regulating this issue.[866] Provisions resembling the 1934 text were inserted in the Constitutions of 1946,[867] 1967,[868] and 1969.[869]

449. The current Constitution, adopted in 1988, follows in the footsteps of the others. It simply provides that 'religious marriage has civil effects, in accordance with the law'.[870] The matter is governed by the Articles 1515 and 1516 of the Civil Code, according to which: (1) religious and civil marriages are equated, if the former meet the requirements of the latter and are registered in the public records;[871] (2) if the parties obtain a licence prior to the ceremony, they must request the registration of their marriage within ninety days after the wedding (if the deadline is not met, a new licence must be obtained); (3) civil effects may be granted to religious marriages at any time, but the spouses must request a licence and have their marriage registered within ninety days of its issuance; (4) the civil registration of a religious marriage shall be declared void if one of the spouses is already in a civil marriage with someone else. After a religious marriage is properly registered, its civil effects operate retroactively from the date of the ceremony. Unregistered religious marriages are not equated to civil ones, but the proof of the former can be presented, at least, to demonstrate the existence of a stable union (common-law marriage).[872]

450. The percentage of religious marriages is seemingly decreasing: in 1980, 8.1% of the couples declared to be in solely religious marriages whilst 63.9% of the unions were religious marriages with civil effects (or couples having married before a judge and a minister, in different ceremonies); these numbers reduced to 5.2% and 58.3% in 1991, 4.4% and 49.4% in 2000, and eventually 3.4% and 42.9% in 2010.

865. Const. (1934), Art. 146.
866. Law No. 379 of 16 Jan. 1937. It was later amended by Decree-Law No. 3200 of 19 Apr. 1941, Arts 4 and 5.
867. Const. (1946), Art. 163, pars 1 and 2. Under this Constitution, Congress passed Law No. 1110 of 23 May 1950, which repealed Law No. 379 of 16 Jan. 1937, as well as Arts 4 and 5 of Decree-Law No. 3200 of 19 Apr. 1941.
868. Const. (1967), Art. 167, pars 2 and 3.
869. Const. (1969), Art. 175, pars 2 and 3.
870. Const. (1988), Art. 226, para. 2.
871. The registration procedure is governed by Law No. 6015 of 31 Dec. 1973, Arts 71–75.
872. *See*, e.g., TJSP, *2ª Câmara de Direito Privado* [2nd Private Law Panel], Ap. 1001772-69.2017.8.26.0362, Rapp. CAJ Rosangela Telles, *DJ* 23 Oct. 2019; TRF – 3, *7ª Turma* [7th Panel], Ap. 6105867-64.2019.4.03.9999, Rapp. FCAJ Toru Yamamoto, *DJ* 27 May 2020.

Conversely, purely civil marriages have remained roughly at the same levels throughout the years: from 16.3% in 1980 to 18.4% in 1991, 17.5% in 2000, and 17.2% in 2010.[873]

§4. Illegal Marriages

451. Illegal marriages are either void or voidable. A marriage is *void* when it involves people who are forbidden to marry. It is *voidable* when: (1) those involved have not attained the proper age; (2) the parents' authorization, being required, is absent; (3) a person is coerced into marrying; (4) after the ceremony, a spouse becomes aware of facts that make it unbearable to live with the other (e.g., a crime which they have committed); (5) one of the spouses was, in fact, unable to provide free consent at the time; (6) the party's designee and spouse were unaware that the other spouse had revoked the former's powers to represent them (providing that the spouses do not start living together anyway); (7) the presiding official lacked the necessary authority to perform the ceremony.[874]

452. Void marriages are declared as such by a judge, in a lawsuit brought, at any time, by any interested party or by the Public Prosecutors' Office. Voidable marriages, on the other hand, can only be invalidated within certain time frames, in suits filed by the spouses themselves or their ascendants, guardians or heirs, depending on the situation.[875] In any case, the judicial decision operates retrospectively, so as to deprive the marriage of all legal effects, except those involving the couple's children and the spouse that entered into the marriage in good faith.[876]

§5. Divorce

453. One of the most overt demonstrations of Catholic influence in Brazilian law relates to divorce. In accordance with the dogmas of the Roman Church, marriages were indissoluble. As a testament to the importance of the issue, indissolubility was established in the country's Constitutions.[877]

454. The situation remained as such until almost the last quarter of the twentieth century, when Constitutional Amendment No. 9 of 28 June 1977 allowed for the dissolution of marriages under circumstances prescribed by law, if the parties remained judicially separated, after a court ruling, for more than three years. The Divorce Act was passed later that year.[878] It provided for: (1) *judicial separation* – after a court

873. Instituto Brasileiro de Geografia e Estatística, *supra* note 637 at 39; Instituto Brasileiro de Geografia e Estatística, *supra* note 637 at 59.
874. CC, Law No. 10406 of 10 Jan. 2002, Arts 1548, 1550, and 1556–1558.
875. CC, Law No. 10406 of 10 Jan. 2002, Arts 1549, 1552, 1555, and 1559–1560.
876. CC, Law No. 10406 of 10 Jan. 2002, Arts 1561 and 1563.
877. Const. (1934), Art. 144; Const. 1937, Art. 124; Const. (1946), Art. 163; Const. (1967), para. 1; Const. (1969), Art. 175, para. 1.
878. Law No. 6515 of 26 Dec. 1977.

ruling, the mutual duties of the spouses ended, 'as if the marriage were dissolved';[879] and (2) *divorce* – the actual dissolution of the marriage.[880] Judicial separation could be freely requested by both spouses if they had been married for at least two years; or, by either party, if the other had displayed dishonourable behaviour; seriously violated their duties, making living together unbearable; if conjugal life had actually ceased beyond reconciliation for more than five years; or if, after the wedding, the other displayed signs of a serious mental illness.[881]

455. These conditions were eased in the 1988 Constitution, which allowed for divorces after more than one year of judicial separation or two years of de facto separation, and Law No. 8408 of 13 February 1992. Later, the matter became regulated by the 2002 Civil Code.[882] In 2010, an amendment to the Constitution removed the requirement of a previous period of judicial or de facto separation, making it possible for married couples to directly initiate a divorce proceeding.[883] Since 2007, judicial procedures are only required for separation and divorce should the parties be incapable of reaching an agreement or if they have a child who is underage or incapacitated; otherwise, they can simply sign a deed before a notary public to divide their common assets.[884]

456. Divorce is solely regulated by law. Decisions of religious tribunals do not bind and are not recognized by the state – except when they are rendered abroad, in countries in which Family Law jurisdiction falls within the scope of denominational bodies (*see* Part X, Chapter 1, §6, *infra*). In any case, the parties cannot prevent a divorce by invoking religious precepts about, e.g., the indissolubility of marriage.[885]

§6. Religious Decisions on the Dissolution of Marriages

457. In Brazil, religious authorities cannot dissolve or nullify marriages. Whatever effects their decisions may entail from a religious point of view, they are non-binding on the state and, for legal purposes, marriages can only be dissolved, declared void, or be voided according to the law.[886] That is not the case throughout the world, and there are countries where decisions of religious ministers in relation to marriages are legally binding. If that is the case, Brazil will grant exequatur to such decisions upon request of the parties due to their official recognition in the

879. Law No. 6515 of 26 Dec. 1977, Art. 3.
880. Law No. 6515 of 26 Dec. 1977, Arts 24–33.
881. Law No. 6515 of 26 Dec. 1977, Arts 4 and 5, *caput* and pars 1 and 2.
882. CC, Law No. 10406 of 10 Jan. 2002, Arts 1579–1582.
883. Const. (1988), Art. 226, para. 6, amended by CA No. 66 of 13 Jul. 2010.
884. Law No. 11441 of 4 Jan. 2007; CPC, Law No. 13105 of 16 Mar. 2015, Arts 733.
885. *See*, e.g., TJMG, *7ª Câmara Cível* [7th Civil Panel], Ap. 1.0145.09.537812-4/001, Rapp. CAJ Washington Ferreira, *DJ* 13 Jun. 2012; TJSC, *5ª Câmara de Direito Civil* [5th Civil Law Panel], Ap. 2011.042037-8, Rapp. CAJ Henry Petry Junior, 28 Feb. 2013.
886. Dias, *supra* note 631 at 151.

countries of origin.[887] However, decisions of religious authorities seated in Brazil cannot be enforced, even by means of exequatur because these are not foreign judgments.[888]

458. This was once the general applicable regime until an exception came about: the 2008 Agreement Between Brazil and the Holy See provides that Catholic judgments in matters of marriage can be granted exequatur, as foreign decisions, if they are confirmed by the superior oversight body of the Holy See.[889] This provision means that by forging a connection with a foreign power – the Holy See, a subject of international law – Catholic religious bodies in Brazil can have their judgments recognized within the country. That is something that no other denomination can claim, raising serious doubts as to the validity of this provision. However, the STJ – responsible for granting or denying exequatur to foreign judgments – upheld this part of the Agreement, declaring it valid, and allowing the enforcement of a religious decision that annulled a marriage.[890]

887. *See*, e.g., STF, SE 7170/Israel, Rapp. Min. Marco Aurélio (President), *DJ* 24 Apr. 2003.
888. *See*, e.g., STF, Full Court, SE 2838 AgR/Lebanon, Rapp. Min. Xavier de Albuquerque, *DJ* 18 Dec. 1981.
889. Brazil-Holy See Agreement (2008), Art. 12, para. 1.
890. STJ, *Corte Especial* [Special Panel], SEC 11962/Vatican, Rapp. Min. Felix Fischer, *DJ* 25 Nov. 2015.

Chapter 2. Legal Position of Religious Family Law

§1. Introduction

459. Family Law in Brazil falls under federal exclusive jurisdiction. Civil marriages are conducted by public officials after legal requirements have been met and a licence has been issued. Religious ministers and representatives are also authorized to perform marriage ceremonies, but the legal validity of said acts – i.e., their acquiring civil effects – depends on compliance with the conditions set forth by federal law, including proper registration in the public records. Unregistered religious marriages can be considered proof of a stable union (common-law marriages), but they do not possess the civil effects of a marriage.

§2. Prenuptial Agreements with Religious Norms

460. The Civil Code provides for prenuptial agreements, especially in Articles 1639 and 1653–1657. They require a public deed, become effective after the marriage, and are enforceable against third parties if they are registered in the public records.

461. The law is laconic when it comes to the content of these agreements: it simply states that an agreement (or a provision thereof) shall be void should it contradict a mandatory legal rule.[891] There are scholars who limit the role of prenuptial agreements to matters related to the matrimonial regime (i.e., the choice between the regime options set by the law and the regulation of other issues involving assets, such as donations from one spouse to the other).[892] Other scholars, however, defend that these agreements can also be signed to regulate the common life of the couple, including duties related to their offspring.[893]

462. In fact, some of the spouses' duties seem to be clearly, or almost unanimously, regarded as unnegotiable, such as those pertaining to the mutual respect owed to each other, and the responsibilities in relation to their children's sustenance and education. Nonetheless, there are other duties which spark controversy, such as those concerning fidelity, because the very law that prescribes these also forbids any person or entity from 'interfering in the communion of life instituted by the family'.[894] As noted by Gustavo Tepedino, one should bear in mind the family's role in promoting the dignity of its members, whose fundamental liberty to organize their

---

891. CC, Law No. 10406 of 10 Jan. 2002, Art. 1655.
892. 5 Fábio Ulhoa Coelho, *Curso de Direito Civil*, 57, No. 4 (2020).
893. Dias, *supra* note 631 at 314; Nelson Nery Junior & Rosa Maria de A. Nery, *Código Civil Comentado*, 1899 (2014); Gustavo Tepedino, Controvérsias sobre Regime de Bens no Novo Código Civil, *in Anais do VI Congresso Brasileiro de Direito de Família*, 10–12 (2007), https://ibdfam.org.br/assets/upload/anais/186.pdf.
894. CC, Law No. 10406 of 10 Jan. 2002, Arts 1513 and 1566, I.

'communal life' manifests in a 'plurality of choices'.[895] It means that the state should respect the different perspectives and preferences people may uphold concerning their life as a family.

463. Brazilian courts have yet to discuss the validity of prenuptial agreements with a clear religious characteristic. However, a clause assuming, or resulting in, a wife's inferior or subordinate status, for example, would likely be considered illegal because of gender equality being a fundamental right, and the rights and duties of the couple are to be exercised in equal terms.[896] If the said clause had a religious basis, the party(ies) could invoke freedom of religion, but this does seem improbable that such a claim would prevail in court. In less sensitive contexts, nonetheless, resorting to religion may in fact reinforce claims of the parties. For example, the fact that the spouses were Muslim and that their religion conferred upon a woman the exclusive right to manage her dowry was recognized as a legitimate reason for them to amend their matrimonial regime.[897]

§3. Religion-Based Alternative Dispute Resolution

464. Alternative means of dispute resolution include arbitration, mediation, and conciliation. Arbitrations are decided by an award, issued by a private person (arbiter) or a panel (arbitral tribunals), chosen by the parties to determine mutual disagreement. Conversely, mediation and conciliation do not involve a decision rendered by a third party; they seek to resolve the issue by means of a settlement or an agreement between the parties. The role of conciliators and mediators is to assist the parties, either by actively proposing solutions or without interfering in party decision making.[898] Mediation is primarily governed by Law No. 13.140 of 26 June 2015, whilst conciliation is principally regulated by Articles 165–175 of the Code of Civil Procedure, which also addresses mediation. As for arbitration, it is the subject of Law No. 9307 of 23 September 1996.

465. Conciliation and mediation are encouraged by the Judiciary, and some courts have elected to train religious ministers and representatives to act as mediators, thus benefiting from their experience as community leaders, with whom people often rely on to discuss issues and quarrels. For example, in 2016, the State Court of Appeals of Goiás initiated a programme known as *Mediar é Divino* [Mediating is Divine], which later expanded to the Federal District and to the states of Paraná

895. Tepedino, *supra* note 893 at 11.
896. Const. (1988), Arts 5, I, and 226, para. 5; CC, Law No. 10406 of 10 Jan. 2002, Art. 1567.
897. TJSP, *7ª Câmara de Direito Privado* [7th Private Law Panel], Ap. 1064065-88.2017.8.26.0002, Rapp. CAJ Luis Maria Galbetti, *DJ* 30 Oct. 2019; TJSP, *10ª Câmara de Direito Privado* [10th Private Law Panel], Ap. 1048106-77.2017.8.26.0002, Rapp. CAJ JB Paula Lima, *DJ* 31 Oct. 2019.
898. *See*, e.g., Scavone Junior, *supra* note 448 at 9; Mauricio Vasconcelos Galvão Filho & Ana Carolina Weber, Capítulo I – Disposições Gerais sobre a Mediação Civil, *in Teoria Geral da Mediação: à Luz do Projeto de Lei e do Direito Comparado* 3, 38 (Humberto Dalla Bernardina de Pinho ed., 2008); Carlos Eduardo de Vasconcelos, *Mediação de Conflitos e Práticas Restaurativas*, 54–60 (2014).

and Mato Grosso do Sul.[899] In the State of Rio de Janeiro, Catholic parishes have organized mediation centres, with their personnel being trained by the State Court of Appeals.[900] However, religion should not be the basis for the actions of mediators and conciliators', who are required to remain impartial and to encourage the parties to freely decide on how best to handle or resolve conflict.

466. Any conflict can be submitted to conciliation or mediation, but that is not the case with arbitration. Under the law, the latter can only be applied to resolve disputes regarding *direitos patrimoniais disponíveis* – i.e., negotiable rights involving property or contracts.[901] A person's marital status, capacity, and parental authority, for example, are thus excluded from arbitration procedures,[902] making Family Law a less suitable domain for them. It could be argued, however, that matters that can be settled by mutual agreement, being negotiable,[903] are also arbitrable.[904]

467. Arbitration can be settled by law or equity,[905] being the latter referred to as the arbiters' sense of fairness.[906] Within the limited scope of arbitration involving Family Law, it is, therefore, possible that religious precepts and values be considered and enforced by the arbiters. Parties are free to choose the law to be enforced, so long as they do not violate common decency (*bons costumes*) or public order (*ordem pública*),[907] so it may be the case that they opt to submit their controversies to religious norms. But this scenario would probably be inadmissible, for violation of the public order, e.g., the choice of religious law when it completely deprives the

---

899. Vera Batista, *Justiça Treina Religiosos para a Mediação de Conflitos*, Correio Braziliense, 29 Jun. 2017, https://blogs.correiobraziliense.com.br/servidor/justica-treina-religiosos-para-mediacao-de-conflitos/.
900. Pedro Zuazo, *Atolado de Processos, TJ do Rio Cria Centros de Mediação em Paróquias*, Extra, 20 Nov. 2016, https://extra.globo.com/noticias/rio/atolado-de-processos-tj-do-rio-cria-centros-de-mediacao-em-paroquias-20502821.html.
901. Law No. 9307 of 23 Sep. 1996, Art. 1.
902. CC, Law No. 10406 of 10 Jan. 2002, Art. 852.
903. According to the Superior Court of Justice, parties can freely negotiate and decide, e.g., about: (1) their intent to divorce; (2) the division of common assets; and (3) the renunciation of alimony (for themselves). But they cannot decide (but merely submit an agreement to a judge) on matters involving their children, for example. *See* STJ, *3ª Turma* [3rd Panel], REsp 1756100/DF, Rapp. Min. Marco Aurélio Bellizze, *DJ* 11 Oct. 2018.
904. Arguing for the possibility of arbitration in this limited context, *see* Francisco Cláudio de Almeida Santos, A Arbitragem no Direito de Família, *in Famílias: Pluralidade e Felicidade – Anais do IX Congresso Brasileiro de Direito de Família* 361, 364–365 (Rodrigo da Cunha Pereira & Maria Berenice Dias eds., 2014), https://ibdfam.org.br/assets/upload/anais/231.pdf; Fabiana Domingues Cardoso, *Pacto Antenupcial no Brasil: Formalidades e Conteúdo*, 172–174 (2009). Conversely, *see* TJSC, *5ª Câmara de Direito Civil* [5th Civil Law Panel], Ap. 2015.068323-3, Rapp. CAJ Luiz Cézar Medeiros (stating that, as a rule, arbitration has no place in controversies involving Family Law).
905. Law No. 9307 of 23 Sep. 1996, Art. 2, *caput*.
906. Scavone Junior, *supra* note 448 at 12.
907. Law No. 9307 of 23 Sep. 1996, Art. 2, para. 1.

woman of the couple's common assets, since equality between women and men – being a fundamental right – is enshrined in the Federal Constitution,[908] and as such, part of the public order.[909]

908. Const. (1988), Art. 5, I.
909. Convention on Private International Law (Bustamante Code) (20 Feb. 1928), Art. 4. The Convention was adopted in Havana, in 1928. *See* Dec. No. 5647 of 8 Jan. 1929 and Dec. No. 18871 of 13 Aug. 1929.

Part XI. Religion and Culture

Chapter 1. Religion and Art

§1. Introduction

468. Art in colonial Brazil was deeply influenced by religion. In Indigenous art, religion and spirituality are frequently on display, as creativity itself is associated with inspiration by deities and other non-human forms, and artistic representation is often thought to possess cosmological meaning and connections.[910] At the beginning of European colonization, Catholic priests and friars were among the few literate people. It is far from surprising, then, that the most notable name in literature is that of Antônio Vieira, a Catholic priest. Even the Jesuits, however, adapted and incorporated elements of Indigenous cultures for their own purposes of evangelization.[911] The major works in architecture and visual arts were devoted to Catholicism: churches were built and sculptures and paintings portraying Jesus, saints, and martyrs were crafted at that time. Music was also connected to religious events and masses. The height of this movement appears to have been the style called *Brazilian Baroque*, in the seventeenth and eighteenth centuries, developed at a time when precious metals were discovered in the colony.[912] Antônio Francisco Lisboa, known as 'Aleijadinho', was probably the most important artist of this era. He was a sculptor, who worked in the rich mining area of Minas Gerais. Aleijadinho is particularly known for his work 'The Twelve Apostles', a set of sculptures in Congonhas/MG, which was appointed by UNESCO as a World Heritage site. In literature, the most notable name appears to be that of Antônio Vieira, a Catholic priest.

469. Religious art was subject to regulation under the 1707 First Constitutions of the Archbishopric of Bahia, the main religious codification at that time in Brazil.[913] But it was impossible to downplay the influence of other cultures present in

910. Els Lagrou, *Arte Indígena no Brasil: Agência, Alteridade e Relação*, 22–28 (2013).
911. Gabriel Pereira Cunha, O Ensino da História do Brasil Colonial por Meio da Arte Sacra, *in O Ensino da História Local na Sala de Aula: Fontes, Objetos e Metodologias* 44, 48 (Jackson dos Santos Ribeiro ed., 2021); Donald Bueno Monteiro, *Música Religiosa no Brasil Colonial*, 14 Fides Reformata 75, 83 (2009).
912. Alfredo Bosi, *História Concisa da Literatura Brasileira*, 34–35 (2006).
913. Danilo Pinto dos Santos, *Critérios para Produção de Arte Sacra Imaginária no Brasil Colonial, a Partir das 'Constituições Primeiras do Arcebispado da Bahia'*, 11 Temporalidades – Revista de História 444 (2019).

Brazil: one finds references to African-Brazilian themes in Catholic sites[914] and popular Christian festivities usually combined Catholic, African-Brazilian and Indigenous traditions and art.[915]

470. The repression of African cultures and religions was robust, and despite the inability to prevent their survival, the severance of bonds to Africa led to the development of a highly particular manifestation where African-Brazilian religions share artistic images and references with Catholicism.[916] Racism and Eurocentrism most surely contributed to an idea of African-Brazilian art as being 'inferior', 'primitive', or 'naïve'. But this notion could not thwart the holistic shaping of Brazilian culture to the point where it is impossible to ignore its incredible influence. Obvious examples include music genres (e.g., samba), cuisine (e.g., *feijoada*, *acarajé*), festivities (e.g., Carnival), and martial arts (e.g., capoeira). However, it was only in the 1930s and 1940s that African-Brazilian art began to progress out of the shadows and cast off repression, as mainstream artists and artistic movements slowly embraced its content.[917]

471. Censorship was present largely throughout Brazilian history. In fact, it predates to Portugal, where it was enforced by religious and temporal institutions. In the colony, books were rare, especially because, until the early nineteenth century, it was forbidden to instal printing presses in Brazil. The first newspaper legally published in the country was created at the request of the Portuguese Prince Regent John – later King John VI – who brought a press with the royal family when they fled Europe during the invasion of Portugal by Napoleon. After Independence (1822), imperial authorities retained censorship, as did later the Republic, founded in 1889.[918] During the dictatorial periods of the twentieth century (1937–1945, 1964–1985), it was employed to repress opposition and to enforce the values promoted by the ruling elites. Protection of morals, through a Catholic perspective, was incumbent on the censors, who later became a part of the police.[919] Some examples illustrate the reach of censorship: a soap opera had to re-shoot numerous episodes and amend the plot so that a character could not marry for a second time – even though he believed that his previous wife had died, viewers knew that she was alive,

914. Vagner Gonçalves Silva, *Arte Religiosa Afro-Brasileira: as Múltiplas Estéticas da Devoção Brasileira*, 9 Debates do NER 97, 98 (2008).

915. Montes, *supra* note 40 at 48–60.

916. Silva, *supra* note 914 at 98.

917. Kabengele Munanga, *Arte Afro-Brasileira: O Que É Afinal?*, 6 Paralaxe 5, 8–9, 11, 14–18 (2019); Rita de Cássia Alves Lotti Silva, *A Arte Afro-Brasileira*, 18 Fragmentos de Cultura 313, 317–325 (2008).

918. Lino Geraldo Resende, A Censura contra a Cidadania: o Caso do Brasil, 3–4 (2005), http://bocc.ufp.pt/pag/resende-lino-geraldo-censura-cidadania.pdf.

919. Miliandre Garcia, *A Censura de Costumes no Brasil: da Institucionalização da Censura Teatral no Século XIX à Extinção da Censura na Constituição de 1988*, 6–15 (2009), https://www.bn.gov.br/sites/default/files/documentos/producao/pesquisa/censura-costumes-brasil-institucionalizacao-censura-teatral/miliandregarcia.pdf.

and that was enough to make it improper. Another soap opera had to exclude scenes suggesting the romantic involvement of people of the same sex.[920]

§2. Public Displays of Religious Art and Religious Symbols

472. The laicity principle forbids the state from identifying with any specific orientation in matters of religion. Although it is far from unusual to find crucifixes adorned in courtrooms, for example, it is unlawful to display religious symbols in public buildings, such as schools and courthouses. The private chambers of officers and public servants, however, as more personal spaces, may be regarded as exceptions. As for streets and sidewalks, despite being owned and managed by the state, they are public fora, places of gathering and demonstrations, in which 'one does not find, nor expects to find, the impartiality of the state, but the spontaneous vibration of a plural society'.[921] Whilst streets are not properly 'places of worship', they can be the set for religious manifestations, under the freedom of assembly.[922] *See* Part II, Chapter 2, §3, *supra.*

473. Religious monuments and messages, placed in the streets by individuals or private entities, usually do not ascribe to the government any kind of endorsement, and thus can be deemed acceptable. Also, a state-sponsored monument celebrating a religious minority is admissible because rather than being proof of endorsement, it merely provides visibility and shows respect to a marginalized group.[923]

§3. Religious Buildings and Architecture

474. Architecture is an art, being, therefore, protected by the freedom of expression. Devoted to religious purposes and, sometimes, infused with religious meaning, churches, temples, and other religious monuments are also under the protection of the freedom of religion. They are required, nonetheless, to comply with laws and regulations concerning, e.g., safety, health, and environmental requirements. The freedom to construct temples was not always present in Brazil. Under the country's first Constitution (1824–1889), denominations other than Catholicism – the official state religion – were only permitted to engage in 'domestic worship, or in private, in houses designated for this purpose, with no exterior form of a temple'.[924]

---

920. Nilson Xavier, *20 Casos Absurdos de Censura às Novelas Pela Ditadura Militar*, Blog do Nilson Xavier (2019), https://tvefamosos.uol.com.br/blog/nilsonxavier/2019/03/31/20-casos-absurdos-de-censura-as-novelas-pela-ditadura-militar/.
921. Magalhães Pires, *supra* note 105 at 283.
922. Mendes and Branco, *supra* note 256 at 323.
923. Leite, *supra* note 109 at 375–395; Magalhães Pires, *supra* note 105 at 276–285; Daniel Sarmento, O Crucifixo nos Tribunais e a Laicidade do Estado, *in Em Defesa das Liberdades Laicas* 189 (Roberto Arriada Lorea ed., 2008).
924. Const. (1824), Art. 5.

475. Nowadays, religious buildings are, in the most, privately owned, and it would contradict the laicity principle for the state to construct or maintain a religious site. The situation of designated landmarks can differ, as the public interest in maintaining a historic or culturally relevant building may justify the use of government funds. For more information, *see* Part XI, Chapter 1, §4 *infra*. In a very particular case, however, the STJ reversed the conviction of a former mayor of Rio de Janeiro/RJ for having contributed public funds to the construction of a Catholic church. Alongside particular reasons related to the nature of the procedure, the rapporteur mentioned that 'Brazilian society is deeply religious', and 'the state is lay, but not atheist, much less impious'. He also declared that one should acknowledge the 'historical and sociological fact that the Christian Faith arrived in Brazil in the caravels of its discoverers, whose ships, by the way, displayed Christ's Cross as symbol and reason for their audacious transoceanic adventures'.[925]

476. Places of worship within public buildings may be part of the government estate. That seems to be the case, e.g., of active chapels and churches placed in historical sites or inside military bases (associated with the right of the military personnel to religious assistance). Public ownership of these sites positions them under the government's power to dispose of them. That is why the Federal Court of Appeals for the Second Region authorized the Union to demolish a Catholic chapel in an office building of the Federal Police and replace it with an ecumenical place of worship. According to the Court, creating of space 'comporting plural manifestations' was a socially relevant act, and '[t]he fact that the chapel exists in the public building since 1947 … does not prevent the state from ceasing to maintain a temple in favour of a single religion (in violation of Art. 19, I, of the Constitution)'.[926]

477. The presence of unquestionably religious sites within public buildings leads to peculiar situations. In an interesting case, a military chaplain from the Air Force was convicted of embezzlement of public funds for siphoning donations made to a chapel situated on a military base. Since the donations were gifted in support of the chapel, the Superior Military Court decided that the act of misappropriation was detrimental to government property. As a result, the chaplain was sentenced to three years in prison and was dishonourably discharged, stripped of his rank and position.[927]

---

925. STJ, *1ª Turma* [1st Panel], REsp 1536895/RJ, Rapp. Min. Napoleão Nunes Maia Filho, *DJ* 8 Mar. 2016 (excerpts from the opinion of the rapporteur).
926. TRF – 2, *8ª Turma Especializada* [8th Specialized Panel], Ap./Rem. Nec. 0012399-43.2010.4.02.5101, Rapp. FCAJ Vera Lúcia Lima, *DJ* 7 Jan. 2015.
927. STM, Ap. 0000005-16.2006.7.10.0010, Rapp. Min. José Américo dos Santos, *DJ* 14 Apr. 2011; STM, EIN 0000005-16.2006.7.10.0010, Rapp. Min. Olympio Pereira Da Silva Junior, *DJ* 13 May 2013; STM, Rep. 0000154-35.2017.7.00.0000, Rapp. Min. Odilson Sampaio Benzi, *DJ* 10 Jun. 2020.

§4. LANDMARK DESIGNATION

478. In Brazilian law, *tombamento* is the act of designating an object or a site as part of the protected historic, artistic, environmental, and cultural heritage of the country. The Federal Constitution ascribes great importance to the protection of these objects and sites, by making it a duty of all levels of government[928] and offering legal standing to sue to the Public Prosecutors' Office[929] and any citizen as a means to prevent or repair damages to protected landmarks.[930] Statutory law extends this standing to the Public Defenders' Office, public legal entities, state-owned companies, and also private associations.[931]

479. The *tombamento* does not deprive the object or site owner of property rights, but it does limit their ability to use and dispose of it. Owners cannot disfigure the object or site, and they are required to conserve and repair it, always subject to prior approval by the government. They can sell and move the object, insofar as it does not leave the national territory. If the owner lacks resources to maintain or repair the object or site, they must inform the government, so that the latter may conduct all the necessary works or seize the property by employing eminent domain.[932] In many places, sites and buildings under *tombamento* are exempted from paying local property taxes.[933]

480. As a rule, religious objects and sites cannot be built, kept or repaired with public funds, due to the laicity principle.[934] However, places and objects with architectural, cultural, or historic relevance, having been designated as landmarks, can access public funds for their upkeep or repair. In this case, the public interest rests in their cultural and historic value, and not in aiding a religious denomination or supporting its views.[935] But the preeminent place held by Christianity (especially Catholicism) over the greater part of Brazilian history may produce some imbalance, as one would probably unearth more Catholic monuments and churches from other eras, as symbols of past architecture, than places of worship of other denominations – which for a long time could not even display the external appearance of

928. Const. (1988), Arts 23, II and IV; 24, VII; and 30, IX.
929. Const. (1988), Art. 129, III.
930. Const. (1988), Art. 5, LXXIII.
931. Law No. 7347 of 24 Jul. 1985, Art. 5.
932. *Tombamento* is primarily governed by Decree-Law No. 25 of 30 Nov. 1937.
933. *See*, e.g., Law (Rio de Janeiro/RJ) No. 691 of 24 Dec. 1984, Art. 61, I; Law (Belo Horizonte/MG) No. 5839 of 28 Dec. 1990, Art. 9.
934. TJSP, *10ª Câmara de Direito Público* [10th Public Law Panel], Ap./Rem. Nec. 1000708-23.2020.8.26.0587, Rapp. CAJ Marcelo Semer, *DJ* 2 Mar. 2021.
935. *See*, e.g., TJSC, *1ª Câmara de Direito Público* [1st Public Law Panel], Ap. 2012.008632-0, Rapp. CAJ Newton Trisotto, 3 Jun. 2013, and TJSC, *4ª Câmara de Direito Público* [4th Public Law Panel], Ap. 2013.051277-0, Rapp. CAJ José Volpato de Souza, 6 Feb. 2014 (holding that a Municipality could use public funds to help in the restoration of a Catholic church declared as landmark); TJSP, *Órgão Especial* [Special Panel], ADI 2248079-02.2017.8.26.0000, Rapp. CAJ Márcio Bartoli, *DJ* 21 Jun. 2018 (upholding a local law declaring a Catholic chapel as a landmark, but declaring invalid a provision requiring the pertinent committee of citizens to engage in religious activities).

a temple. Therefore, so to avoid any undue demonstration of preference, it is important that the government adopts impartial and objective criteria in determining the sites and objects that are in receipt of public funds.[936]

§5. Art That Offends Religion

481. Freedom of speech protects criticism and even humorous portrayals of religion and religious symbols. Hate speech, nevertheless, is not protected, and practising, inducing, or inciting discrimination due to a person's religion can constitute crimes as well as civil and administrative offences. For further information, *see* Part VII, Chapter 3, §4, *supra*.

482. It is not uncommon to find cases in which religious groups seek to prevent or stop art displays or performances that they deem offensive. One of them involved two of the most famous symbols of the city of Rio de Janeiro: the Carnival and the statue of Christ the Redeemer. In 1989, Beija-Flor, a samba school, intended to include a replica of the statue, dressed as a homeless person, on one of its floats. Not long before the parade, an injunction was granted, at the request of the Catholic Curia of Rio de Janeiro, to prevent the school from including the statue in the parade. Two days later, the order was reversed by a higher court, but the samba school decided to cover the statue with black plastic, with an inscription reading: 'Despite being forbidden, watch over us.'[937]

483. Another situation involved the police seizing a statue of Our Lady of Navigators which the samba school Unidos da Tijuca intended to incorporate in its parade in 2000. In order to avoid problems, the school decided not to use the statue. In 2020, the samba from Mangueira, another school, led to protests by Christian groups: entitled *A Verdade Vos Fará Livre* [The Truth Shall Set You Free], the samba referred to Jesus as having 'a Black face, Indigenous blood, and a woman's body'.[938] In January of the same year, the Catholic Archdiocese of Rio de Janeiro and twenty other religious entities wrote a letter to the league of samba schools requesting to be consulted in the future, should they decide to choose any religiously related themes.[939]

484. The use of images seems particularly troublesome. The Catholic Archdiocese of Goiânia/GO brought legal suit against a woman who created moulds of statues of Catholic saints to produce plaster figurines painted up as pop culture

---

936. Magalhães Pires, *supra* note 105 at 269.

937. Leandro Boechat, *'Mesmo Proibido, Olhai por Nós': Liberdade de Expressão, Censura e Religião no Carnaval Carioca*, Policromias – Revista de Estudos do Discurso, Imagem e Som 819 (2020).

938. Anna Virginia Balloussier, *Com Jesus de 'Rosto Negro, Sangue Índio e Corpo de Mulher', Mangueira Atualiza Embate entre Religiosos e Carnavalescos*, Folha de S. Paulo, 13 Feb. 2020, https://www1.folha.uol.com.br/cotidiano/2020/02/com-jesus-de-rosto-negro-sangue-indio-e-corpo-de-mulher-mangueira-atualiza-embate-entre-religiosos-e-carnavalescos.shtml?origin=folha.

939. Thomas Milz, *A Polêmica em Torno do Jesus Negro da Mangueira*, Deutsche Welle, 19 Feb. 2020, https://p.dw.com/p/3XzCy.

characters and then retailed them online under the handle 'Santa Blasfêmia' [*Holy Blasphemy*]. The plaintiff viewed such figurines as an offence to the values and symbols of the Roman Catholic Church and requested for an injunction to prevent the artist from making and selling the figurines. The State Court of Appeals of Goiás ruled against the plaintiff. According to the Court, the objects did not convey any form of religious intolerance or incited hatred, simply being a manifestation of the defendant's freedom of speech.[940]

485. Another case involved an adult magazine which displayed a picture of a model with a rosary. Arguing that the photograph offended religious sentiments, a lower court ordered the publisher not to print the magazine with that image. This ruling, however, was reversed on appeal. According to the State Court of Appeals of São Paulo, the image did constitute disrespect to religious beliefs by including a symbol of faith in a sensual context. Nonetheless, it was not possible to prohibit the issue from being published: given that the magazine did not specifically offend any individual or denomination, thus removing it amounted to censorship, which is illegal.[941]

486. A theatre production depicting Jesus Christ as a transsexual woman was forbidden in Jundiaí/SP by a court order for allegedly 'mocking' religious symbols. The order further stated that 'besides being a production of indisputable bad taste and disrespectful to the extreme', one should not 'forget the religious belief in our State, which considers JESUS CHRIST as the son of GOD', so that allowing the portrayal of 'this HOLY MAN' as a 'transvestite … amounts to an offense to countless people'.[942] The State Court of Appels of São Paulo reversed the order. It emphasized that the play did not purport to offend the Christian faith, being simply a fictional work which sought to foment debate about transgender people. According to the Court, the lower court order 'fatally wounded the artistic activity of the transgender actress' portraying Jesus, violated her freedom of expression, and amounted to 'an actual aggression to culture', by depriving the public of the possibility to watch the play.[943] The same play motivated a suit in Porto Alegre/RS, but the courts refused to forbid its performance.[944] Prohibitions and limitations were attempted

940. TJGO, *6ª Câmara Cível* [6th Civil Panel], Ap. 0095844.36.2016.8.09.0051, Rapp. CAJ Norival Santomé, *DJ* 29 Oct. 2020.
941. São Paulo/SP (Foro Regional XI – Pinheiros), *1ª Vara Cível* [1st Civil Court of First Instance], Proc. 0124915-79.2009.8.26.0011, *DJ* 6 Dec. 2010, reversed by TJSP, *8ª Câmara de Direito Privado* [8th Private Law Panel], Ap. 0124915-79.2009.8.26.0011, Rapp. CAJ Caetano Lagrasta, *DJ* 22 Nov. 2012.
942. Jundiaí/SP, *4ª Vara Cível* [4th Civil Court of First Instance], Proc. 1016422-86.2017.8.26.0309, 15 Sep. 2017.
943. TJSP, *5ª Câmara de Direito Privado* [5th Private Law Panel], AI 2180296-90.2017.8.26.0000, Rapp. CAJ JL Mônaco da Silva, *DJ* 23 Feb. 2018.
944. An injunction to suspend the play was denied by a lower court and, later, by another one, after the State Court of Appeals recognized the latter's jurisdiction. After the play was enacted, the suit was dismissed for mootness. *See* Porto Alegre/RS, *2ª Vara da Fazenda Pública* [2nd Court of First Instance for Suits Involving Government Entities], Proc. 9038978-35.2017.8.21.0001, 22 Sep. 2017; TJRS, *4ª Câmara Cível* [4th Civil Panel], AI 0290860-63.2017.8.21.7000, Rapp. CAJ

also in Salvador/BA and Rio de Janeiro/RJ. In Taubaté/SP, it was performed under the watchful eye of the police due to outraged audience members attempting to attack the actress.[945]

487. In 2020, Porta dos Fundos, a comedy group, made headlines for having its Christmas special removed from Netflix by order of a judge of the State Court of Appeals of Rio de Janeiro.[946] According to the Judge, the plaintiff, a Christian association, alleged that the movie conveyed 'religious intolerance and hate speech' for portraying 'Jesus Christ as a childish homosexual man, [and] Lucifer's boyfriend, Mary as an adulterous swearer, and Joseph as an idiot, [who had been] betrayed by God'. Citing a bomb attack to the office of Porta dos Fundos by a group claiming to have acted in response to their 'blasphemy',[947] the judge suspended the special because its exhibition was 'more likely to cause more serious and irreparable damage than its suspension'.

488. The matter was taken to the Federal Supreme Court. Since it was not in session at the time, its President, Minister Dias Toffoli, granted an interim stay of the order of the State Court. Emphasizing the protection of free speech, as well as the fact that only those people willing to watch the film were exposed to its content, Minister Toffoli stated that, notwithstanding the respect owed to any creed, one could not imagine that a satire could endanger the values of a religion existing for more than 2,000 years and prevalent in the country.[948] The second Panel of the Court confirmed this order and revoked the State Court's decision, endorsing the points raised by the President. The Panel stressed the difference between 'religious intolerance and religious criticism' to note that the movie did not 'incite violence against religious groups, rather consisting of mere criticism, conveyed through satire, to elements dear to Christianity'.[949] More recently, the court of first instance followed the Supreme Court's reasoning and ruled against the plaintiff.[950]

Francesco Conti, *DJ* 26 Sep. 2017 (in chambers); Porto Alegre/RS, *1º Juizado Especial da Fazenda Pública* [1st Special Court for Suits Involving Government Entities], Proc. 9038978-35.2017.8.21.0001, 25 Sep. 2017.

945. Joana Oliveira, *'Jesus Pode Ser Tudo, Menos Travesti,'* El País, 23 Jul. 2018, https://brasil.elpais.com/brasil/2018/07/23/cultura/1532371217_501094.html.

946. The injunction was denied by the lower court (Rio de Janeiro/RJ, *16ª Vara Cível* [16th Civil Court of First Instance], Proc. 0332259-06.2019.8.19.0001, 19 Dec. 2019), but this decision was reversed by a CAJ (TJRJ, *6ª Câmara Cível* [6th Civil Panel], AI 0083896-72.2019.8.19.0000, Rapp. CAJ Benedicto Abicair, *DJ* 10 Jan. 2020; in chambers).

947. *Polícia Analisa Imagens de Atentado contra Porta dos Fundos*, Deutsche Welle, 26 Dec. 2019, https://p.dw.com/p/3VLiE.

948. STF, Rcl 38782 MC/RJ, Rapp. Min. Dias Toffoli (President), *DJ* 5 Feb. 2020.

949. STF, *2ª Turma* [2nd Panel], Rcl 38782/RJ, Rapp. Min. Gilmar Mendes, *DJ* 24 Fev. 2021.

950. Rio de Janeiro/RJ, *16ª Vara Cível* [16th Civil Court of First Instance], Proc. 0332259-06.2019.8.19.0001, 21 Apr. 2021. An appeal pends before the State Court of Appeals.

Chapter 2. Religion and Media

§1. Introduction

489. Communications media owned by religious organizations operate under the same rules applicable to other media. Under the Constitution, Congress is mandated to create a Social Communication Council to support it on these matters. The Council was established in 1991 and is comprised of representatives of communication companies and groups (e.g., journalists, artists) and of civil society at large, elected by Congress for a two-year term. The Council is tasked with studying and publishing opinions and recommendations requested by the Legislative in matters involving communications.[951] In fact, it was only in 2002 that the Council was installed. The former Catholic bishop of São José do Rio Preto, archbishop of Belém and current archbishop of Rio de Janeiro, Cardinal D. Orani Tempesta served as member and president of Council.

§2. Print Media

490. Under the Constitution, the publication of print media – books, newspapers, magazines, etc. – by religious organizations or any other person or entity cannot be submitted to prior licencing, according to the Constitution.[952] Journalism is specially protected, as 'no law shall contain any provision which may represent a hindrance to full freedom of press in any medium of social communication'.[953] The Press Act,[954] passed during the Military Regime (1964–1985), was declared incompatible with the Constitution by the Federal Supreme Court.[955]

491. That does not mean that written statements are free of any consequence. Defamation suits and even criminal proceedings – e.g., against hate speech – can serve as limitations on what is published, including when it comes to religious media. Publications of *Folha Universal*, a paper published by the IURD, for example, have led to damages awarded to individuals in a few cases. In one such article, *Folha Universal* falsely stated that a minor had died of dengue fever and, moreover, included a picture of her.[956] In another, the said paper published a deceased minor's photograph without the consent of their parents in a piece relating to a 'suicide pact'.[957]

951. Law No. 8389 of 30 Dec. 1991.
952. Const. (1988), Art. 220, para. 6.
953. Const. (1988), Art. 220, para. 1.
954. Law No. 5020 of 9 Feb. 1967.
955. STF, Full Court, ADPF 130/DF, Rapp. Min. Carlos Ayres Britto, *DJ* 6 Nov. 2009.
956. TJRJ, *13ª Câmara Cível* [13th Civil Panel], Ap. 0019930-07.2008.8.19.0038, Rapp. CAJ Gabriel de Olveira Zefiro, *DJ* 12 Jun. 2017.
957. TJSC, *4ª Câmara de Direito Civil* [4th Civil Law Panel], Ap. 0301470-79.2016.8.24.0004, Rapp. CAJ Selso de Oliveira, 3 Sep. 2020.

492. The Federal Supreme Court has examined a case in which a Roman Catholic priest wrote a book, which, according to the Prosecutors' Office, amounted to a crime as it allegedly opined discrimination against Spiritists. The Court ruled that even though the defendant had incited 'the Catholic community to undertake a religious rescue aimed at saving adepts of Spiritism', he did so 'without gesturing violence, domination, exploitation, enslavement, annihilation, suppression, or limitation of fundamental rights', despite being 'intolerant, pedantic, and arrogant'. It was, then, ruled to be within the boundaries of freedom of religious speech.[958]

§3. Broadcast Media

493. Religious organizations are permitted to own and operate broadcast media like any other private entity. Radio and television channels operate concessions, permissions, or authorizations issued by the Union, but cable channels are positioned under a different regime. *See* Part VII, Chapter 3, §5 *supra*. Whatever conditions and procedures are placed on obtaining the right to utilize these outlets, religious entities are required to follow them as is any other person or private institution.

494. Limitations on free speech are possible in this context as well in defamation suits and other cases. For example, *TV Record* was ordered to pay damages to the family of a minor who had died in a rave party. The family had consented to the broadcast of the minor's image for journalistic purposes, but four years after the facts the network continued to use it in a religious programme. The State Court of Appeals of Rio de Janeiro confirmed the lower court ruling which had found that the network had unduly exposed the minor and his family.[959] Also, *Rede TV* and the *Igreja Internacional da Graça de Deus* [International Church of the Grace of God] were enjoined by a Federal Court of Appeals to disavow previous statements made by a minister, which were deemed offensive to atheists, and to display content about religious diversity and freedom of religion and conscience.[960]

§4. Use of Public Media

495. Religious content is present in government-owned media outlets, but it does not correspond to a large share of their programming: in *TV Brasil*, run by *Empresa Brasil de Comunicação (EBC)*, a federal entity, religious programmes ran for 0.8% of the time in 2016, whereas *TV Cultura*, run by a state foundation from São Paulo broadcast religious programmes in 0.3% of the time.[961] More recently, the licencing by *TV Brasil* of a religious soap opera, *Os Dez Mandamentos* [The Ten

958. STF, *1ª Turma* [1st Panel], RHC 134682/BA, Rapp. Min. Edson Fachin, *DJ* 29 Aug. 2017.
959. TJRJ, *6ª Câmara Cível* [6th Civil Panel], Ap. 0085992-04.2012.8.19.0001, Rapp. CAJ Teresa de Andrade, *DJ* 12 Apr. 2021.
960. TRF – 3, *4ª Turma* [4th Panel], Ap./Rem. Nec. 0014396-10.2011.4.03.6100, Rapp. FCAJ Mônica Nobre, *DJ* 12 Oct. 2018.
961. Agência Nacional do Cinema, *supra* note 711 at 59.

Commandments], produced and previously aired twice by *TV Record* – connected to IURD – stirred some controversy. The apparently unprecedented move cost *TV Brasil* about BRL 3.2 million.[962]

496. In 2011, the EBC decided not to run religious programmes in the future, but it soon repealed its decision, thus creating a 'religious diversity' segment to be aired.[963] The repeal notwithstanding, in a suit brought by the Catholic Archdiocese of Rio de Janeiro, a Federal Court of Appeals declared the invalidity of the EBC's decision to stop broadcasting religious programmes. According to the Court, the laicity principle did not support the suspension of programmes that divulged 'the Christian faith, whose ethical and moral values contribute to shape the citizen in a good manner'. Also, as the relevant programmes had been on air for more than thirty years, 'one could not deny the relevance of the service [that they] provided'. The Court rejected 'the argument that religions of a Catholic or an Evangelical nature enjoy privileges' because the rights of members of other groups and denominations do not prevent 'the expression of the faith that is shared, after all, by the majority of [Brazilians]'.[964]

962. Cristina Padiglione, *Venda de 'Dez Mandamentos' da Record para a TV Brasil Não Tem Precedentes*, Folha de S. Paulo, 5 Apr. 2021, https://telepadi.folha.uol.com.br/venda-de-dez-mandamentos-da-record-para-a-tv-brasil-nao-tem-precedentes/.

963. *See* Resolution (EBC) No. 3 of 23 Nov. 2011, and Resolution (EBC) No. 4 of 6 Jul. 2012.

964. TRF – 1, *6ª Turma* [6th Panel], Ap. 0051046-62.2011.4.01.3400, Rapp. FCAJ Daniel Paes Ribeiro, *DJ* 24 Feb. 2017.

Chapter 3. Religion and Civil Society

§1. Religious Involvement in Non-profit and Charitable Activities

497. For a long time, religious denominations, especially Catholic charities, endured as protagonists in sectors such as healthcare and education, in which the presence of the state, if any, was minuscule. The role of Catholic institutions reduced as the government, secular private entities, and other denominations (especially Evangelical and Spiritist groups) began to develop activities within these sectors.[965] Even today, religious groups are very active in charitable activities, in which they cooperate with the state, and may even be entitled to receive government funding. Some of the most renowned religious charitable institutions are: (1) Catholic – *Pastoral da Criança* [Ministry for the Child] and *Cáritas Brasileira* [Brazilian Caritas]; (2) Inter-denominational Protestant – *Diaconia* [Service] and *Coordenadoria Ecumênica de Serviço (Cese)* [Ecumenical Service Coordinating Body]; (3) Spiritist – *Casas André Luiz* [André Luiz Homes] and *Mansão do Caminho* [Mansion of the Path].[966]

498. Despite the lack of current data, it is estimated that, in 2001, approximately 50% of all charitable hospitals in Brazil had links to Catholic groups, but there are also many that are connected to Spiritist and Evangelical groups.[967]

§2. Civil Religion

499. Relations between politics and religion are mediated, or involve, concepts the likes of *civic*, *civil*, and *public religion*. The first (*civic religion*) was mainly used by medievalist scholars, regarding the management of religious events by civil authorities to emphasize the unity and autonomy of the cities then in formation in Europe. *Civil religion*, as a concept, was developed with the United States in sight, as a reference to the common religious elements shared by different denominations in society and manifesting especially in political ceremonies and discourse, via references to God and values such as order, and law – it all formed a 'moral consensus' underpinning the action of the state. The main reference here is the work of Robert Bellah. Finally, the concept of *public religion*, as articulated by José Casanova, refers to the 'deprivatization' of religion: the movement in which religious denominations challenge their confinement to the private sphere to actively participate in government and in civil society and to discuss where the borders between the public and private spheres should be placed.[968]

---

965. Souza, *supra* note 388 at 243–245.
966. *Ibid.* at 244–245.
967. Ministério da Saúde, *Rede Hospitalar Filantrópica no Brasil: Perfil Histórico-Institucional e Oferta de Serviços*, 52–53 (2001), https://www.nescon.medicina.ufmg.br/biblioteca/imagem/2465.pdf.
968. Paula Montero, *Religião Cívica, Religião Civil, Religião Pública: Continuidades e Descontinuidades*, 19 Debates do NER 15 (2018).

500. In Brazil, as a colony (1500–1822) and, later, Empire (1822–1889), Catholicism was an instrument of the state, providing religious legitimation to the government. In an apparent paradox, after the Proclamation of the Republic (1889), which decreed the separation of church and state, the Catholic Church grew stronger, as it was finally liberated from government control. It even lent support to the 1930 Revolution and the government of Getúlio Vargas, reuniting Catholicism and state, albeit in an informal way. More recently, however, the hegemony of the Roman Church has been decisively threatened by the remarkable growth of Evangelical churches, which are also exceedingly visible and vocal in relation to their views in politics and civil society. Perhaps one could then say that Catholicism was the civic religion of Brazil and, later, assumed the mantle of a civil religion. This emanated from a set of elements and values that were so deeply entrenched with prevalent morals that they could (and, in fact, did) pass for non-religious references or reflections of an allegedly unified Brazilian culture. With the growing presence of Evangelicals, this idea of a civil religion appears to be advancing towards Christianity in more general terms. All of this, of course, tends to diminish the role and importance of other religions – especially those Indigenous and African-Brazilian – by identifying Brazilian society as a whole with one of its parts.

501. It is also possible to speak of civil religion as solely linked to the state – i.e., a devotion to political ideals or principles – with a pantheon of national heroes and a myriad of political ceremonies.[969] The state borrows from religion some of its symbols to appear as transcendent as a deity and to command the passionate obedience and loyalty of citizens, without taking on board a set of typically religious values. In Brazil, however, it is hard to find the presence of this form of patriotism. It requires heroes and transforming events, and both Independence (1822) and the Proclamation of the Republic (1889) proved to be poor candidates for this position: the latter because it essentially maintained the institutional and symbolic apparatus already in place; as for the former, it involved a military coup, with no relevant popular involvement. Throughout the twentieth century, the search for heroes and symbols was ever-present, especially in military governments. The only person to ever obtain unanimous support as symbol and hero was Tiradentes, a group activist in the rich mining area of Minas Gerais, who aspired to free Brazil from its colonial status at the time; the plot, however, was discovered and he was hung and quartered by the Portuguese authorities.[970] Patriotism became almost exclusively associated with the military and with ceremonies which held little popular involvement and where the separation of government and people seem to be one of the defining features.[971]

969. The most important reference here is Jean-Jacques Rousseau.
970. Carvalho, *supra* note 533 at 58–78; Sergio da Mata, *Passado e Presente da Religião Civil*, 23 Varia Historia 180, 196–204 (2000).
971. Roberto DaMatta, *O Que Faz o brasil, Brasil?*, 81–93 (1986); Mata, *supra* note 970 at 201–202.

§3. Government Relations with Religion

502. In Brazil, religions are not overly regulated by the government. It is somewhat easy to incorporate a religious organization and public agents are hardly ever concerned with what denominations actually do. Judicial intervention does occur, but it is usually related to intra-religious disputes over management, internal procedures, and assets. It is in fact debated that the government should be more present and proactive in protecting religious groups – especially those in the minority – from acts of intolerance and hate speech.

503. The principle of laicity does not require a complete separation between state and religion, but it does demand that positions in government are not employed to promote sectarian views on religious matters. Cooperation between government departments and religious denominations are lawful (and quite common), so long as they serve public interest purposes, e.g., education, healthcare, assistance to the destitute.

504. Nevertheless, it is hardly unusual to find ministers serving as elected officials, and the defence of Christian values is a perennial keynote around election time and afterwards. Christian churches are keen on securing those positions which allow them to pronounce their opinions on issues involving morality, family life, and children. For example, according to a recent article, Evangelical denominations 'dominate' child protection councils in the country's two largest cities, São Paulo/SP, and Rio de Janeiro/RJ. In 2020, this situation was highlighted when two councilmembers allegedly forwarded privileged information to the Minister for Women, Family, and Human Rights, who intervened personally to attempt to convince a 10-year-old girl not to undergo an abortion after suffering sexual violence. Another case involved a mother who temporarily lost custody of her daughter for allowing her to take part in a Candomblé ritual – her Evangelical grandmother reported it as physical and sexual abuse, and the council allegedly accepted her claims without determining factual support.[972]

972. Gil Alessi, *Igrejas Evangélicas Neopentecostais Dominam Conselhos Tutelares em São Paulo e no Rio*, El País, 15 Dec. 2020, https://brasil.elpais.com/brasil/2020-12-15/igrejas-evangelicas-neopentecostais-dominam-conselhos-tutelares-em-sao-paulo-e-no-rio.html.

Chapter 4. Religion and Public Debate

§1. Legal Framework

505. The relationship between religion and public debate is, on one hand, mediated by the freedoms of expression and religion, and on the other, by the laicity principle and ultimately the principles of democracy and equality. It is widely acknowledged that, like anyone else, religious individuals and organizations are entitled to express their views on political matters and, moreover, on legal controversies. For example, the Federal Supreme Court has admitted religious organizations as *amici curiae* in many cases and has heard them in public audiences convened before decisions. The CNBB was admitted as *amicus* in the case involving research with embryonic stem cells (ADI 3510/DF). It was also heard – as was the IURD and two associations of Spiritist physicians – in the public audience in relation to the interruption of pregnancy of anencephalic foetuses (ADPF 54/DF).

506. According to the Superior Electoral Court, 'public statements of endorsement of, or preference towards, a certain candidacy are protected by the constitutionally guaranteed freedom of expression'.[973] However, the risk that this poses to democracy and to laicity – by means of exploiting religious affiliation for partisan purposes and colonizing public debate with sectarian worldviews – remains an issue of concern for academics and various public actors. Ministers Rosa Weber and Edson Fachin of the Superior Electoral Court have advocated for some restrictions regarding elections, but the Court has not admitted them, so to avoid what it viewed as a restriction on religious speech that was not supported by statutory law. For more on this, *see* Part V, Chapter 1, §2, II, *supra*.

§2. Historical Background

507. Christianity has always been a part of the public sphere in Brazil. At first, the Roman Catholic Church and the state were intertwined, with the former providing the latter with ideological, transcendent, legitimacy and the bureaucratic capillarity it lacked. Later, after the separation of church and state in 1890, the Church could profit from its strength and presence in a country that was still under construction, whilst benefiting from an autonomy it had never experienced before. As a result, Catholic views on morality, family, sexuality, and customs in general were not only standard measures but, in many instances, a part of statutory law. It is still very common to find crucifixes in public buildings: one of the most conspicuous of them being the crucifix displayed in the courtroom of the Federal Supreme Court, behind the seat of the President of the Court, placed higher than the Arms of the Republic. Over time, Catholic numbers began to decline, whereas Protestant numbers – especially Evangelicals – exhibited impressive growth.

---

973. TSE, RO 537003 – Belo Horizonte/MG, Rapp. Min. Rosa Weber, *DJ* 27 Sep. 2018.

508. All of this serves as confirmation that formal separation between state and religion has never been complete in Brazil. It did result from a widespread distrust of religion or a strong conviction in the convenience of its separation from the state, but in fact appears to primarily derive from the notions of an elite, obviously detached from reality. The laicity principle does not rest on a strongly secular society; on the contrary, 'the Brazilian state is not grounded on laicity, nor can Brazilian society be viewed as secularized'. The former can be classified as secular to the extent that it 'guarantees legal and legislative procedures free from religious institutional control' and 'has constitutional or similar provisions that secure religious neutrality'.[974]

509. The most important change to the religious domain in Brazil was not secularization of society, but diversification within Christianity: the dominant pattern ceased to be that of an informal syncretism under Catholic hegemony (with people adhering to Kardecism and African-Brazilian religions whilst also affirming a Catholic identity), to become one of pluralism and 'market dispute', with an astounding growth of Protestantism.[975] This rise has been accompanied by an increasing influence of these churches and their leaders in public debates, particularly those involving private morality, sexuality, and family life. Their weight in elections is also relevant, as candidates strive to be endorsed (or, at least, not condemned) by famous ministers, and many are either religious leaders or have strong ties to Protestant churches. As a response, explicitly Catholic candidacies – advocating for Catholic values or addressing Catholic voters – also rose,[976] in what appears to be a struggle for power because their political agenda is at par with that of Protestants.

§3. Contemporary Debates about Religion and Politics

510. The apparent surge in influence of religion in politics strikes academics as a setback or, at the very least, a stalemate in the process of constructing a political sphere that is independent of sectarian groups, and respectful of all people, regardless of their religious affiliations. In fact, religious interference in politics seems to be a direct reaction to modern values, particularly laicity and secularism, thus deriving from an explicit desire to 'return' to Christian values. Not only is there a disconnection between a lay state and a religious society, but also parts of the latter are engaged in a struggle against laicity.[977]

511. As a result, 'the very dynamics of laicity tends to remain in an undefined situation, where the direction depends on the social action of lay and religious

974. Marcela Tanaka, *Secularização, Laicidade e Espaço Público: Como Pensar a Política Contemporânea Brasileira à Luz da Religião?*, 40 Religião & Sociedade 169, 180 (2020).
975. Mariano, *supra* note 126 at 248.
976. *Ibid.* at 249.
977. João Felippe Cury Marinho Mathias, *Estado Laico e Não Secularizado no Brasil: Uma Reflexão à Luz da História do Protestantismo*, 17 Transversos: Revista de História 12, 25–26 (2019).

groups, but principally the latter, who are protagonists of the religious and political spheres in Brazil'.[978] As Ricardo Mariano explains:

> National political culture and, especially, party, political, and governmental leaders have contributed, in a decisive way, to reinforce the mutual instrumentalization between religion and politics and to legitimize and stimulate partisan political activism in religious groups and a religious occupation of the public sphere. This close connection between religion and politics indeed constitutes a mighty obstacle to the secularization of public sphere in Brazil.[979] (internal citations omitted)

§4. Public Reason

512. John Rawls's *public reason* does resonate in Brazilian legal scholarship: there are those who defend it as a principle of constitutional interpretation,[980] but also some who are not in total agreeance.[981] However, it is not a widespread concept in case law, despite a few noteworthy mentions in STF opinions. The idea of constitutional and supreme courts as *fora* of public reason was invoked by Minister Luís Roberto Barroso in an in-chambers opinion involving the creation of a parliamentary inquiry committee in the Senate:

> There is reasonable consensus, nowadays, in that the concept of democracy transcends the idea of government by the majority, so as to demand the incorporation of other fundamental values, including equality, liberty, and justice. That is what truly transforms it into a *collective self-government endeavor*, in which no one is deliberately left behind. More than the right to equal participation, democracy means that those who lose in the political process, so as minority groups in general, are not helpless and left to fend for themselves. Quite the contrary, they retain their status as equally dignified members of the political community. In almost all of the world, the guardian of these promises is the supreme court or the constitutional court, due to its capacity to be a forum of principles – i.e. of constitutional values, not of politics – and of public reason – i.e. of arguments that can be accepted by all those involved in the debate.[982]

513. In a notorious case involving the interruption of pregnancy of anencephalic foetuses – which was strongly opposed by religious groups – the rapporteur, Minister Marco Aurélio, did not expressly mention 'public reason', but did state that the

978. Flávio Munhoz Sofiati, *Perspectivas da Laicidade no Brasil Contemporâneo*, 5 Contemporânea 327, 347 (2015).
979. Mariano, *supra* note 126 at 251.
980. *See*, e.g., Souza Neto and Sarmento, *supra* note 150 at 447–450; Magalhães Pires, *supra* note 105 at 93–97.
981. *See*, e.g., Ana Paula de Barcellos, *Direitos Fundamentais e Direito à Justificativa: Devido Procedimento na Elaboração Normativa*, 159–166 (2016).
982. STF, M. Seg. 37760 MC/DF, Rapp. Min. Luís Roberto Barroso, *DJ* 12 Apr. 2021(in chambers).

laicity principle prohibits that 'dogmas of faith determine the content of state acts', even when some religions are supported unanimously or by the majority within the country. 'Faith and moral orientations derived thereof cannot be imposed to anyone and by anyone'. He went on:

> The Brazilian state is absolutely forbidden from promoting any religion. However …, the guarantees of the secular state and of religious freedom do not stop there – they are more comprehensive. Besides imposing a position of distance towards religion, they prohibit the state from endorsing religious moral conceptions, so to, even indirectly, coerce the citizens into following them. … [Religious freedom and a lay state] mean that religions shall not guide the treatment dispensed by the state to other fundamental rights, such as the right to self-determination, the right to physical and mental health, the right to privacy, the right to freedom of speech, the right to freedom of sexual orientation, and right to freedom in the field of reproduction.[983]

983. STF, Full Court, ADPF 54/DF, Rapp. Min. Marco Aurélio, *DJ* 30 Apr. 2013 (opinion of the rapporteur).

Selected Bibliography

Books, Dissertations, and Theses

Alfredo Bosi, *História Concisa da Literatura Brasileira* (43rd ed., Cultrix 2006).

Allyne Andrade e Silva, *Direito e Políticas Públicas Quilombolas* (D'Plácido 2020).

Aloisio Cristovam Santos Junior, *A Liberdade de Organização Religiosa e o Estado Laico Brasileiro* (Mackenzie 2007).

Ana Paula de Barcellos, *Curso de Direito Constitucional* (Forense 2018).

Ana Paula de Barcellos, *Direitos Fundamentais e Direito à Justificativa: Devido Procedimento na Elaboração Normativa* (Fórum 2016).

Ari Pedro Oro, Intolerância Religiosa Iurdiana e Reações Afro no Rio Grande do Sul, *in Intolerância Religiosa: Impactos do Neopentecostalismo no Campo Religioso Afro-Brasileiro* 29 (Vagner Gonçalves Silva ed., Edusp 2007).

Arthur Phillipe Pereira, "Uma Neocristandade no Brasil: A atuação do Cardeal Leme para tornar o Brasil um país Católico," Doctoral thesis, Theology department, Pontifical Catholic University of Rio de Janeiro, Rio de Janeiro (RJ), Brazil, 2018.

Boris Fausto, *História do Brasil* (14th ed., Edusp 2015).

Camila Mendonça Pereira, "Abolição e Catolicismo: A Participação da Igreja Católica na Extinção da Escravidão no Brasil," Masters dissertation, Institute of Human and Social Sciences, Niterói (RJ), 2011.

Carlos Eduardo de Vasconcelos, *Mediação de Conflitos e Práticas Restaurativas* (3rd ed., Método 2014).

Celso Antônio Bandeira de Mello, *Conteúdo Jurídico do Princípio da Igualdade* (3rd ed., Malheiros 2005).

Celso D. de Albuquerque Mello, *Curso de Direito Internacional Público* (15th ed., Renovar 2004).

Cláudio Pereira Souza Neto & Daniel Sarmento, *Direito Constitucional: Teoria, História e Métodos de Trabalho* (Fórum 2012).

Clèmerson Merlin Clève & Alexandre Reis Siqueira Freire, Algumas Notas sobre Colisão de Direitos Fundamentais, *in Estudos de Direito Constitucional: em Homenagem a José Afonso da Silva* 231 (Eros Roberto Grau & Sérgio Sérvulo da Cunha eds., Malheiros 2003).

Daniel Sarmento, *Direitos Fundamentais e Relações Privadas* (Lumen Juris 2006).

Selected Bibliography

Daniel Sarmento, O Crucifixo nos Tribunais e a Laicidade do Estado, *in Em Defesa das Liberdades Laicas* 189 (Roberto Arriada Lorea ed., Livraria do Advogado 2008).

Dermeval Saviani, *A Política Educacional no Brasil*, *in III Histórias e Memórias da Educação no Brasil* 29 (Maria Stephanou & Maria Helena Camara Bastos eds., Vozes 2005).

Eduardo Bueno, *A Coroa, a Cruz e a Espada: Lei, Ordem e Corrupção no Brasil Colônia* (4th ed., Objetiva 2006).

Els Lagrou, *Arte Indígena no Brasil: Agência, Alteridade e Relação* (C/Arte 2013).

Emerson Giumbelli, *O Fim da Religião: Dilemas da Liberdade Religiosa no Brasil* (Attar 2002).

Fabiana Domingues Cardoso, "Pacto Antenupcial no Brasil: Formalidades e Conteúdo," Masters dissertation, Law School, Pontifical Catholic University of São Paulo, São Paulo (SP), 2009.

Fábio Carvalho Leite, *Estado e Religião: A Liberdade Religiosa no Brasil* (Juruá 2014).

Fábio Ulhoa Coelho, *Curso de Direito Civil* (9th ed., RT 2020).

Flávia Piovesan, *Direitos Humanos e o Direito Constitucional Internacional* (17th ed., Saraiva 2017).

Gabriel Pereira Cunha, O Ensino da História do Brasil Colonial por Meio da Arte Sacra, *in O Ensino da História Local na Sala de Aula: Fontes, Objetos e Metodologias* 44 (Jackson dos Santos Ribeiro ed., Atena 2021).

Gilmar Ferreira Mendes & Paulo Gustavo Gonet Branco, *Curso de Direito Constitucional* (14th ed., Saraiva 2019).

Guilherme Madeira Dezem, *Curso de Processo Penal* (7th ed., RT 2021).

Heloísa Pagliaro, Marta Maria Azevedo & Ricardo Ventura Santos, Demografia dos Povos Indígenas no Brasil: um Panorama Crítico, *in Demografia dos povos indígenas no Brasil* (Heloísa Pagliaro, Marta Maria Azevedo, & Ricardo Ventura Santos eds., Fiocruz 2005).

Humberto Ávila, *Teoria dos Princípios: da Definição à Aplicação dos Princípios Jurídicos* (5th ed., Malheiros 2006).

Humberto Dalla Bernardina de Pinho, *Direito Processual Civil Contemporâneo* (5th ed., Saraiva 2018).

Ingo Wolfgang Sarlet, Luiz Guilherme Marinoni & Daniel Mitidiero, *Curso de Direito Constitucional* (RT 2019).

Instituto Superior de Estudos da Religião, *Pescadores de Homens: O Perfil da Assistência Religiosa no Sistema Socioeducativo do Rio de Janeiro* (ISER 2010).

Instituto Superior de Estudos da Religião, *Religiões e Prisões* (Ana Maria Quiroga et al. eds., 2005).

Jane Reis Gonçalves Pereira, *Interpretação Constitucional e Direitos Fundamentais* (2nd ed., Saraiva 2018).

Jane Reis Gonçalves Pereira, Apontamentos sobre a Aplicação das Normas de Direito Fundamental nas Relações Jurídicas entre Particulares, *in A Nova Interpretação Constitucional: Ponderação, Direitos Fundamentais e Relações Privadas* 119 (Luís Roberto Barroso ed., 3rd ed., Renovar 2008).

Jayme Weingartner Neto, *Liberdade Religiosa na Constituição: Fundamentalismo, Pluralismo, Crenças, Cultos* (Livraria do Advogado 2007).

Joaquim Nabuco, *O Abolicionismo* (Vozes 2012).
João Bosco Bezerra Bonfim (ed.), *Palavra de Presidente: Os Discursos Presidenciais de Posse, de Deodoro a Lula* (LGE 2008).
João Capistrano de Abreu, *Capítulos de História Colonial (1500–1800)* (7th ed., Edusp 1988).
João Henrique Santos, Existentes, mas Não Cidadãos: o Status Jurídico dos Judeus no Brasil Holandês (1630–1654), *in Judaísmo e Modernidade: Suas Múltiplas Inter-relações* 47 (H. Lewin ed., Centro Edelstein de Pesquisas Sociais 2009).
José Afonso da Silva, *Curso de Direito Constitucional Positivo* (35th ed., Malheiros 2012).
José Antônio Pimenta Bueno, *Direito Público Brasileiro e Análise da Constituição do Império* (Senado Federal/UnB 1978).
José Murilo de Carvalho, *A Formação das Almas: O Imaginário da República no Brasil* (2nd ed., Companhia das Letras 2017).
Kaká Werá Jecupé, *A Terra dos Mil Povos: História Indígena do Brasil Contada por um Índio* (2nd ed., Peirópolis 2020).
Laurentino Gomes, *Escravidão* (Globo 2019).
Luis Nicolau Parés, *The Formation of Candomblé: Vodun History and Ritual in Brazil* (The University of North Carolina Press 2013).
Luís Roberto Barroso, *Curso de Direito Constitucional Contemporâneo: os Conceitos Fundamentais e a Construção do Novo Modelo* (4th ed., Saraiva 2013).
Luiz Antonio Scavone Junior, *Manual de Arbitragem: Mediação e Conciliação* (7th ed., Forense 2016).
Luiz Regis Prado, *Tratado de Direito Penal Brasileiro* (RT 2014).
Luís Roberto Barroso, *A Americanização do Direito Constitucional e Seus Paradoxos: Teoria e Jurisprudência Constitucional no Mundo Contemporâneo*, *in IV Temas de Direito Constitucional* 121 (Renovar 2009).
Manoel Maurício de Albuquerque, *Pequena História da Formação Social Brasileira* (2nd ed., Graal 1981).
Maria Berenice Dias, *Manual de Direito das Famílias* (10th ed., RT 2015).
Maria Cecilia Domezi, *Religiões na História do Brasil* (Paulinas 2016).
Maria Goreth Santos, Os Limites do Censo no Campo Religioso Brasileiro, *in Religiões em Conexão: Números, Direitos, Pessoas* 18 (Christina Vital da Cunha & Renata de Castro Menezes eds., ISER 2014).
Maria Lucia Montes, *As Figuras do Sagrado: entre o Público e o Privado na Religiosidade Brasileira* (Claro Enigma 2012).
Mauricio Vasconcelos Galvão Filho & Ana Carolina Weber, Capítulo I – Disposições Gerais sobre a Mediação Civil, *in Teoria Geral da Mediação: à Luz do Projeto de Lei e do Direito Comparado* 3 (Humberto Dalla Bernardina de Pinho ed., Lumen Juris 2008).
Mons. Maurílio Cesar de Lima, *Breve História da Igreja no Brasil* (Loyola 2004).
Nachman Falbel, *Judeus no Brasil: Estudos e Notas* (Edusp 2008).
Nelson Nery Junior & Rosa Maria de A. Nery, *Código Civil Comentado* (11th ed., RT 2014).
Paulo de Assunção, *Negócios Jesuíticos: O Cotidiano da Administração dos Bens Divinos* (Edusp 2004).

Pontes de Miranda, *Comentários à Constituição de 1967: com a Emenda n. 1, de 1969* (2nd ed., RT 1967).
Rachel Mizrahi, *Judeus: Do Descobrimento aos Dias Atuais* (Companhia Editora Nacional 2005).
Raymundo Faoro, *Os Donos do Poder: Formação do Patronato Político Brasileiro* (3rd ed., Globo 2001).
Roberto DaMatta, *O Que Faz o brasil, Brasil?* (Rocco 1986).
Rudolf Zinnhobler & Idade Moderna, *in História da Igreja Católica* 205 (Josef Lenzenweger et al. eds., Loyola 2006).
Sergio Rego, Marisa Palácios & Rodrigo Siqueira-Baptista, *Bioética para Profissionais da Saúde* (Fiocruz 2009).
Sidney Nogueira, *Intolerância Religiosa* (Sueli Carneiro/Pólen 2020).
Thiago Magalhães Pires, *Entre a Cruz e a Espada: Liberdade Religiosa e Laicidade do Estado no Brasil* (Lumen Juris 2018).
Thiago Magalhães Pires, Notas Sobre a Objeção de Consciência, *in O Direito Público por Elas: Homenagem à Professora Jane Reis* 345 (Lumen Juris 2018).
Thiago Moreira Silva, "Para Além de Esquerda e Direita: A Multidimensionalidade das Crenças no Brasil Contemporâneo (1989–2014)," Doctoral thesis, Institute of Politics, University of Brasília, Brasília (DF), 2017.
Virgílio Afonso da Silva, *Direito Constitucional Brasileiro* (Edusp 2021).
Virgílio Afonso da Silva, Colisões de direitos fundamentais entre ordem nacional e ordem transnacional, *in Transnacionalidade do direito: novas perspectivas dos conflitos entre ordens jurídicas* 101 (Marcelo Neves ed., Quartier Latin 2010).
Wallace Corbo, *Discriminação Indireta: Conceito, Fundamentos e uma Proposta de Enfrentamento à Luz da Constituição de 1988* (Lumen Juris 2017).

Articles and Periodicals

Adilon Passinho Koury, *A Objeção da Consciência do Médico em sua Relação com o Paciente* (2015), https://www.cesupa.br/MestradoDireito/dissertacoes/ObjecaoConscienciaMedico_A_Koury.pdf.
Adriana Campos & Daniela Rezende de Oliveira, *A Relação entre o Princípio da Autonomia e o Princípio da Beneficência (e Não-Maleficência) na Bioética Médica*, 115 Revista Brasileira de Estudos Políticos 13 (2017).
Ailton Camargos, *Educação no Brasil: Da Colônia ao Início da República*, 17 Revista Brasileira de Educação e Cultura 129 (2018).
Alceu Ravanello Ferraro & Daniel Kreidlow, *Analfabetismo no Brasil: Configuração e Gênese das Desigualdades Regionais*, 29 Educação & Sociedade 179 (2004).
Alceu Ravanello Ferraro, *Analfabetismo e Níveis de Letramento no Brasil: O Que Dizem os Censos?*, 23 Educação & Sociedade 21 (2002).
Ana Maria Cavaliere, *O Mal-Estar no Ensino Religioso nas Escolas Públicas*, 37 Cadernos de Pesquisa 303 (2007).
Anderson José Machado de Oliveira, *Igreja e Escravidão Africana no Brasil Colonial*, 10 Cadernos de Ciências Humanas – Especiaria 355 (2007).
André Ricardo Souza, *Determinados Contornos Jurídicos, Assistenciais e Econômicos de Organizações Cristãs*, 18 Civitas – Revista de Ciências Sociais 237 (2018).

Andréa Depieri de Albuquerque Reginato, *Regulamentação de Uso de Substância Psicoativa para Uso Religioso: o Caso da Ayahuasca*, 17 Tomo 57 (2010).
Antônio Flávio Pierucci, *O Crescimento da Liberdade Religiosa e o Declínio da Religião Tradicional: A Propósito do Censo de 2010*, 1 Anuac 87 (2012).
Ari Pedro Oro, *Religião e Política no Brasil*, 48–49 Cahiers des Amériques latines (2005), http://journals.openedition.org/cal/7951.
Blasius Silvano Debald, *A relação da Igreja Católica com o Estado Brasileiro – 1889/1960*, 1 Pleiade 51 (2007).
Carlos Roberto de Siqueira Castro, *O Princípio da Isonomia e as Classificações Legislativas*, 16 Revista de Informação Legislativa 89 (1979).
Carmen Izabel Rodrigues, *Caboclos na Amazônia: a Identidade na Diferença*, 9 Novos Cadernos NAEA 119 (2006).
Claudio Santiago Dias Junior & Ana Paula Verona, *Perfil Religioso da População Indígena no Brasil: Considerações a Partir do Censo Demográfico de 2010*, 12 HORIZONTE – Revista de Estudos de Teologia e Ciências da Religião 1140 (2015).
Cristina Maria de Castro & Elaine Meire Vilela, *Muçulmanos no Brasil: Uma Análise Socioeconômica e Demográfica a Partir do Censo 2010*, 39 Religião & Sociedade 170 (2019).
Cristina Pompa, *Profetas e Santidades Selvagens: Missionários e Caraíbas no Brasil Colonial*, 21 Revista Brasileira de História 177 (2001).
Daniele Ferreira Evangelista, *'Emoção não é Coisa de Equede': Mudanças de Status e Relações de Poder no Candomblé*, 4 Intratextos 93 (2013).
Daniele Ferreira Evangelista, *Fundando um Axé: Reflexões Sobre o Processo de Construção de um Terreiro de Candomblé*, 35 Religião & Sociedade 63 (2015).
Danilo Pinto dos Santos, *Critérios para Produção de Arte Sacra Imaginária no Brasil Colonial, a Partir das 'Constituições Primeiras do Arcebispado da Bahia'*, 11 Temporalidades – Revista de História 444 (2019).
Debora Diniz, *Objeção de Consciência e Aborto: Direitos e Deveres dos Médicos na Saúde Pública*, 45 Revista de Saúde Pública 981 (2011).
Dermeval Saviani, *A Expansão do Ensino Superior no Brasil: Mudanças e Continuidades*, 8 Poíesis Pedagógica 4 (2010).
Dermi Azevedo, *A Igreja Católica e seu papel político no Brasil*, 18 Estudos Avançados 109 (2004).
Donald Bueno Monteiro, *Música Religiosa no Brasil Colonial*, 14 Fides Reformata 75 (2009).
Duina Porto, *Mononormatividade, Intimidade e Cidadania*, 14 Direito GV 654 (2018).
Emerson Giumbelli & Jorge Scola, *Marcos Legislativos de Regulação do Religioso no Brasil: Estatuto da Igualdade Racial, Acordo Brasil-Vaticano e Lei Geral das Religiões*, 19 Numen: Revista de Estudos e Pesquisa da Religião 65 (2016).
Emerson Giumbelli, *O 'Baixo Espiritismo' e a História dos Cultos Mediúnicos*, 9 Horizontes Antropológicos 247 (2003).
Emerson Giumbelli, *O Acordo Brasil-Santa Sé e as relações entre Estado, socie dade e religião*, 13 Ciencias Sociales y Religión/Ciências Sociais e Religião 119 (2011).

Selected Bibliography

Emiliano Unzer Macedo, *Religiosidade Popular Brasileira Colonial: um Retrato Sincrético*, 7 Ágora 1 (2008).

Eni de Mesquita Samara, *A Família Negra no Brasil*, 120 Revista de História 27 (1989).

Erico Tavares de Carvalho Junior & Ari Pedro Oro, *Eleições Municipais 2016: Religião e Política nas Capitais Brasileiras*, 18 Debates do NER 15 (2017).

Fábio Fonseca Castro, *A Identidade Denegada. Discutindo as Representações e a Autorrepresentação dos Caboclos da Amazônia*, 56 Revista de Antropologia 432 (2013).

Fernando Arlettaz, *La Libertad Religiosa en el Sistema Interamericano de Derechos Humanos*, 1 Revista Internacional de Derechos Humanos 39 (2011).

Flávio de Araújo Willeman, *Recusa de Tratamento da Saúde com Fundamento em Crença Religiosa e o Dever do Estado de Proteger a Vida Humana. O Caso da Transfusão de Sangue em Testemunha de Jeová*, 5 Revista de Direito do Estado 483 (2010).

Flávio Munhoz Sofiati, *Perspectivas da Laicidade no Brasil Contemporâneo*, 5 Contemporânea 327 (2015).

Francisco Cláudio de Almeida Santos, A Arbitragem no Direito de Família, *in Famílias: Pluralidade e Felicidade – Anais do IX Congresso Brasileiro de Direito de Família* 361 (Rodrigo da Cunha Pereira & Maria Berenice Dias eds., 2014), https://ibdfam.org.br/assets/upload/anais/231.pdf.

Frederico Batista Pereira, *'Non Causa pro Causa': O Voto de Direita e Esquerda no Brasil*, 26 Opinião Pública 154 (2020).

Geraldo Pieroni, *'O Ar de Portugal faz os Judeus?' A Inquisição e os Cristãos Novos Degredados para o Brasil-Colônia*, 3 Locus: Revista de História 7 (1997).

Gilson Ciarallo, *O Tema da Liberdade Religiosa na Política Brasileira do Século XIX: Uma Via para a Compreensão da Secularização da Esfera Política*, 19 Revista de Sociologia e Política 85 (2011).

Gleidson Silva & Simone Silveira Amorim, *Apontamentos sobre a Educação no Brasil Colonial (1549–1759)*, 18 Interações 185 (2017).

Gustavo Binenbojm, *Autonomia Privada e Direito à Recusa de Tratamentos Médicos Invasivos: o Caso das Testemunhas de Jeová*, 5 Revista de Direito do Estado 475 (2010).

Gustavo Tepedino, Controvérsias sobre Regime de Bens no Novo Código Civil, *in Anais do VI Congresso Brasileiro de Direito de Família* (2007), https://ibdfam.org.br/assets/upload/anais/186.pdf.

Hélio Augusto de Moura, *Presença Judaico-Marrana Durante a Colonização do Brasil*, 18 Cadernos de Estudos Sociais 267 (2002).

Ilka Boaventura Leite, *Os Quilombos no Brasil: Questões Conceituais e Normativas*, 4 Etnográfica 333 (2000).

Inácio Strieder, *A Igreja e a Escravidão no Brasil*, 28 Ciência & Trópico 219 (2000).

Ingo Wolfgang Sarlet & Jayme Weingartner Neto, *Liberdade de Expressão: Algumas Ponderações em Matéria Penal à Luz da Constituição Federal do Brasil*, 18 Espaço Jurídico: Journal of Law 637 (2017).

Instituto Nacional de Estudos e Pesquisas Educacionais Anísio Teixeira, *Censo da Educação Básica 2020: Resumo Técnico (Versão Preliminar)* (2021).

Ítalo Domingos Santirocchi, *O Matrimônio no Império do Brasil: uma Questão de Estado*, 4 Revista Brasileira de História das Religiões 81 (2012).

Ivo Pereira Silva, *Do Casamento Misto ao Casamento Civil no Brasil: Debates Parlamentares em Torno do Matrimônio na Segunda Metade do Século XIX*, 46 Revista Portuguesa de História 391 (2015).

Janaine Sibelle Freires Aires et al., *Quando Religião, Política e Mídia se Confundem: As Estratégias Políticas e Midiáticas do PRB, da Record e da Igreja Universal do Reino de Deus*, 19 Revista Eptic 88 (2017).

Jane Reis, *A Aplicação de Regras Religiosas de Acordo com a Lei do Estado: um Panorama do Caso Brasileiro*, XIII Revista da AGU 9 (2014).

João Felippe Cury Marinho Mathias, *Estado Laico e Não Secularizado no Brasil: Uma Reflexão à Luz da História do Protestantismo*, 17 Transversos: Revista de História 12 (2019).

Jurandir de Almeida Araújo, *Educação e Desigualdade: A Conjuntura Atual do Ensino Público no Brasil*, 2 Revista Direitos Humanos e Democracia 125 (2014).

Kabengele Munanga, *Arte Afro-Brasileira: O Que É Afinal?*, 6 Paralaxe 5 (2019).

Katia Mika Nishimura, *Conservadorismo Social: Opiniões e Atitudes no Contexto da Eleição de 2002*, 10 Opinião Pública 339 (2004).

Laura de Mello e Souza, *O Nome do Brasil*, 145 Revista de História 61 (2001).

Leandro Boechat, *'Mesmo Proibido, Olhai por Nós': Liberdade de Expressão, Censura e Religião no Carnaval Carioca*, Policromias – Revista de Estudos do Discurso, Imagem e Som 819 (2020).

Leandro Mahalem de Lima, *Pajelança nas Adjacências do Rio Amazonas: Dimensões Sociopolíticas e Cosmológicas*, 3 Revista Ciências da Sociedade 61 (2019).

Lilia Moritz Schwarcz, *Do Preto, do Branco e do Amarelo: Sobre o Mito Nacional de um Brasil (Bem) Mestiçado*, 64 Ciência e Cultura 48 (2012).

Luis Gustavo Teixeira da Silva, *Religião e Política no Brasil*, 64 Latinoamérica. Revista de Estudios Latinoamericanos 223 (2017).

Luís Roberto Barroso, *Legitimidade da Recusa de Transfusão de Sangue por Testemunhas de Jeová. Dignidade Humana, Liberdade Religiosa e Escolhas Existenciais*, 5 Revista de Direito do Estado 507 (2010).

Luís Roberto Barroso, *Liberdade de Expressão versus Direitos da Personalidade. Colisão de Direitos Fundamentais e Critérios de Ponderação*, 3 Temas de Direito Constitucional 79 (2008).

Luís Roberto Barroso, *Razoabilidade e Isonomia no Direito Brasileiro*, 1 Temas de Direito Constitucional 153 (2006).

Luís Roberto Barroso, *Responsabilidade Internacional de Estado-Membro da Federação. Eficácia Jurídica das Recomendações da Comissão Interamericana de Direitos Humanos da OEA. Possibilidade e Meios de Seu Cumprimento pelo Estado do Rio de Janeiro (Parecer nº 01/2008 – LRB)*, 65 Revista de Direito da Procuradoria-Geral do Estado do Rio de Janeiro 269 (2010).

Manuel Martin Pino Estrada, *Panorama Jurídico da Escravidão Indígena no Brasil*, 18 Argumenta 207 (2013).

Marcela Tanaka, *Secularização, Laicidade e Espaço Público: Como Pensar a Política Contemporânea Brasileira à Luz da Religião?*, 40 Religião & Sociedade 169 (2020).

Maria das Dores Campos Machado, *Religião e Política no Brasil Contemporâneo: Uma Análise dos Pentecostais e Carismáticos Católicos*, 35 Religião & Sociedade 45 (2015).
Mariana Lins de Carli Silva, *Curandeirismo: O Bem Jurídico Saúde Pública a Serviço de uma Política Criminal Racista*, 152 Revista Brasileira de Ciências Criminais 145 (2019).
Marta Maria Azevedo, *Diagnóstico da População Indígena no Brasil*, 60 Ciência e Cultura 19 (2008).
Mírian de Araújo Mafra Castro & Rubia Maria Farias Cavalcante, *Saberes de Cura e Práticas Corporais: Pajelança na Feira da Manaus Moderna*, 3 Marupiara: Revista Científica do Centro de Estudos Superiores de Parintins 153 (2018).
Nachman Falbel, *Dos Cristãos-Novos na Capitania de São Vicente e a Formação da Etnia Paulista*, 41 Revista da USP 112 (1999).
Oracy Nogueira, *Preconceito Racial de Marca e Preconceito Racial de Origem: Sugestão de um Quadro de Referência para a Interpretação do Material sobre Relações Raciais no Brasil*, 19 Tempo Social 287 (2006).
Paula Montero, *Religião Cívica, Religião Civil, Religião Pública: Continuidades e Descontinuidades*, 19 Debates do NER 15 (2018).
Paula Montero, *Religião, Laicidade e Secularismo. Um Debate Contemporâneo à Luz do Caso Brasileiro*, 7 Revista Cultura y Religión 13 (2013).
Paula Montero, *Religião, Pluralismo e Esfera Pública no Brasil*, 74 Novos Estudos CEBRAP 47 (2006).
Paulo Rennes Marçal Ribeiro, *História da Educação Escolar no Brasil: Notas para uma Reflexão*, 4 Paidéia 15 (1993).
Paulo Vitor de Souza Pinto, *As Alterações Políticas da Igreja Católica entre 1967 e 1971*, 9 Social Review 217 (2020).
Ralph Della Cava, *Igreja e estado no Brasil do século XX: sete monografias recentes sobre o catolicismo brasileiro, 1916/1964*, 12 Estudos CEBRAP 5 (1975).
Reginaldo Prandi, *O Brasil com Axé: Candomblé e Umbanda no Mercado Religioso*, 18 Estudos Avançados 223 (2004).
René Daniel Decol, *Judeus no Brasil: Explorando os Dados Censitários*, 16 Revista Brasileira de Ciências Sociais 147 (2001).
Ricardo Mariano, *Expansão Pentecostal no Brasil: o Caso da Igreja Universal*, 18 Estudos Avançados 121 (2004).
Ricardo Mariano, *Laicidade à Brasileira: Católicos, Pentecostais e Laicos em Disputa na Esfera Pública*, 11 Civitas – Revista de Ciências Sociais 238 (2011).
Ricardo Mariano, *Mudanças no campo religioso brasileiro no Censo 2010*, 14 Debates do NER 119 (2013).
Riolando Azzi, *A Influência do Pensamento Liberal no Clero Brasileiro (1789–1824)*, 11 Síntese 27 (1984).
Rita de Cássia Alves Lotti Silva, *A Arte Afro-Brasileira*, 18 Fragmentos de Cultura 313 (2008).
Robert M. Levine, *Brazil's Jews During the Vargas Era and After*, 5 Luso-Brazilian Review 45 (1968).

Romualdo Portela de Oliveira, *Da Universalização do Ensino Fundamental ao Desafio da Qualidade: Uma Análise Histórica*, 28 Educação & Sociedade 661 (2007).

Ronaldo de Almeida & Paula Monteiro, *Trânsito religioso no Brasil*, 15 São Paulo em Perspectiva 92 (2001).

Roney Cytrynowicz, *Além do Estado e da Ideologia: Imigração Judaica, Estado-Novo e Segunda Guerra Mundial*, 22 Revista Brasileira de História 393 (2002).

Roque de Barros Laraia, *As Religiões Indígenas: o Caso Tupi-Guarani*, 67 Revista USP 6 (2005).

Sergio da Mata, *Passado e Presente da Religião Civil*, 23 Varia Historia 180 (2000).

Simone R. Bohn, *Evangélicos no Brasil. Perfil Socioeconômico, Afinidades Ideológicas e Determinantes do Comportamento Eleitoral*, 10 Opinião Pública 288 (2004).

Sonia Apparecida de Siqueira, *Multiculturalismo e Religiões Afrobrasileiras: o Exemplo do Candomblé*, 9 Revista de Estudos da Religião – REVER 36 (2009).

Thiago de Azevedo Pinheiro Hoshino & Vera Karam de Chueiri, *As Cores das/os Cortes: Uma Leitura do RE 494601 a Partir do Racismo Religioso*, 10 Direito e Práxis 2212 (2019).

Thiago Magalhães Pires, *Lei 13.796/2019 é Avanço no Tratamento da Liberdade Religiosa nas Escolas*, Consultor Jurídico, 31 January 2019, https://www.conjur.com.br/2019-jan-31/thiago-magalhaes-avanco-liberdade-religiosa-escolas.

Vagner Gonçalves Silva, *Arte Religiosa Afro-Brasileira: as Múltiplas Estéticas da Devoção Brasileira*, 9 Debates do NER 97 (2008).

Valdemar Sguissardi, *O Que Será das Instituições de Educação Superior Comunitárias e Confessionais?*, 25 Comunicações 27 (2018).

Vânia Maria Losada Moreira, *Casamentos Indígenas, Casamentos Mistos e Política na América Portuguesa: Amizade, Negociação, Capitulação e Assimilação Social*, 19 Topoi 29 (2018).

Vera Irene Jurkevics, *INRI Cristo e a Escatologia Tupiniquim*, 1 Relegens Thréskeia: Estudos e Pesquisa em Religião 130 (2012).

Vinicius Parolin Wohnrath, *Duas Dinâmicas, Dois Resultados: A Igreja Católica na Assembleia Nacional Constituinte 1987–1988*, 28 Pro-posições 242 (2017).

Virgílio Afonso da Silva, *O Proporcional e o Razoável*, 798 Revista dos Tribunais 23 (2006).

Xiomara Lorena Romero Pérez, *La Libertad Religiosa en el Sistema Interamericano de Protección de los Derechos Humanos (Análisis Comparativo con el Ordenamiento Jurídico Colombiano)*, 29 Revista Derecho del Estado 215 (2012).

Electronic Sources

Agência Nacional do Cinema, *TV Aberta – Informe Anual 2016 (01/01/2016 a 31/12/2016)* (2017), https://oca.ancine.gov.br/sites/default/files/repositorio/pdf/informe_tvaberta_2016.pdf.

Alan Rios, *Religiões de Matriz Africana são Alvos de 59% dos Crimes de Intolerância*, Correio Braziliense, 11 November 2019, https://

www.correiobraziliense.com.br/app/noticia/cidades/2019/11/11/interna_cidadesdf,805394/religioes-de-matriz-africana-alvos-de-59-dos-crimes-de-intolerancia.shtml.

Alba Valéria Mendonça, *Apesar de Criação de Delegacia, Templos de Religiões de Matriz Africana São Atacados até Durante a Pandemia no RJ*, G1, 22 November 2020, https://g1.globo.com/rj/rio-de-janeiro/noticia/2020/11/22/apesar-de-criacao-de-delegacia-templos-de-religioes-de-matriz-africana-sao-atacados-ate-durante-a-pandemia-no-rj.ghtml.

Alessandra Schmitt, Maria Cecília Manzoli Turatti & Maria Celina Pereira de Carvalho, *A Atualização do Conceito de Quilombo: Identidade e Território nas Definições Teóricas*, Ambiente & Sociedade 129 (2002).

Ana Flor, *Igrejas Defendem a Rejeição de Acordo entre Brasil e Vaticano*, Folha de S. Paulo, 23 March 2009, https://www1.folha.uol.com.br/fsp/brasil/fc2903200912.htm.

Ana Melo, *Conheça Tudo Sobre o Santo Daime: Ritual, Chá Ayahuasca e Orações*, Terra, 8 December 2020, https://www.terra.com.br/vida-e-estilo/horoscopo/conheca-tudo-sobre-o-santo-daime-ritual-cha-ayahuasca-e-oracoes,f6df0ad2636c0fff35fa3cb9a9f5ff54h2g2bst5.html.

André Schröder, *A Era da Escravidão*, Super Interessante, 29 March 2019, https://super.abril.com.br/especiais/a-era-da-escravidao/.

Anna Virginia Balloussier, *Com Jesus de 'Rosto Negro, Sangue Índio e Corpo de Mulher', Mangueira Atualiza Embate entre Religiosos e Carnavalescos*, Folha de S. Paulo, 13 February 2020, https://www1.folha.uol.com.br/cotidiano/2020/02/com-jesus-de-rosto-negro-sangue-indio-e-corpo-de-mulher-mangueira-atualiza-embate-entre-religiosos-e-carnavalescos.shtml?origin=folha.

Áreas Territoriais, Instituto Brasileiro de Geografia e Estatística, https://www.ibge.gov.br/geociencias/organizacao-do-territorio/estrutura-territorial/15761-areas-dos-municipios.html?t=acesso-ao-produto&c=1 (last visited 17 January 2021).

Associadas, Associação Brasileira de Instituições Educacionais Evangélicas, https://www.abiee.org.br/associadas-abiee (last visited 29 June 2021).

Associadas, Associação Nacional de Educação Católica do Brasil, https://anec.org.br/associadas/ (last visited 15 February 2021).

CNBB Afirma que Golpe de 1964 Foi um 'Erro Histórico,' Folha de S. Paulo, 3 April 2014, https://m.folha.uol.com.br/poder/2014/04/1435249-cnbb-diz-que-golpe-de-1964-foi-erro-historico.shtml?origin=folha.

Constitution of the Federative Republic of Brazil (Supremo Tribunal Federal, 2019), http://www.stf.jus.br/arquivo/cms/legislacaoConstituicao/anexo/brazil_federal_constitution.pdf.

Cristina Padiglione, *Venda de 'Dez Mandamentos' da Record para a TV Brasil Não Tem Precedentes*, Folha de S. Paulo, 5 April 2021, https://telepadi.folha.uol.com.br/venda-de-dez-mandamentos-da-record-para-a-tv-brasil-nao-tem-precedentes/.

Danae Stephan, *Entre Universidades Particulares, Religiosas Lideram Ranking de Pesquisas*, Folha de S. Paulo, 7 October 2019, https://ruf.folha.uol.com.br/2019/noticias/entre-universidades-particulares-religiosas-lideram-ranking-de-pesquisas.shtml.

Diego Garcia, *Casamentos entre Pessoas do Mesmo Sexo Saltam 360% Após Eleição de Bolsonaro, diz IBGE*, Folha de S. Paulo, 4 December 2019, https://www1.folha.uol.com.br/cotidiano/2019/12/casamentos-entre-pessoas-do-mesmo-sexo-saltam-360-apos-eleicao-de-bolsonaro-diz-ibge.shtml.

Diretores, QEdu, https://www.qedu.org.br/brasil/pessoas/diretor (last visited 11 April 2021).

Discreto, Católico e Garantista, Saiba Quem é Kassio Nunes, Cotado para o STF, O Tempo, 1 October 2020, https://www.otempo.com.br/politica/discreto-catolico-e-garantista-saiba-quem-e-kassio-nunes-cotado-para-o-stf-1.2392992.

Discurso de Posse – 2º Mandato (Lula), Presidência da República, http://www.biblioteca.presidencia.gov.br/presidencia/ex-presidentes/luiz-inacio-lula-da-silva/discursos/discursos-de-posse/discurso-de-posse-2o-mandato/@@download/file/posse%20lula%202007.pdf (last visited 13 May 2021).

Efrém Ribeiro, *Orações Obrigatórias Afetam Ateus e Minorias Religiosas na Rede Pública*, O Globo, 23 March 2013, https://oglobo.globo.com/sociedade/educacao/oracoes-obrigatorias-afetam-ateus-minorias-religiosas-na-rede-publica-7928328.

Enunciado 143, III Jornada de Direito Civil, Conselho da Justiça Federal, https://www.cjf.jus.br/enunciados/enunciado/233 (last visited 28 March 2021).

Estimativas da População Residente no Brasil e em Unidades da Federação com Data de Referência em 1º de Julho de 2020, Instituto Brasileiro de Geografia e Estatística, https://ftp.ibge.gov.br/Estimativas_de_Populacao/Estimativas_2020/POP2020_20201030.pdf (last visited 17 January 2021).

Estudo Eleitoral Brasileiro (ESEB) 2002, CESOP/Unicamp-FGV, https://www.cesop.unicamp.br/vw/1IMHwTK0wNQ_MDA_ff413_/TF-01838.pdf (last visited 20 May 2021).

Fábio Góis, *Senado confirma aprovação do acordo Brasil-Vaticano*, Congresso em Foco, 7 October 2009, https://congressoemfoco.uol.com.br/especial/noticias/senado-confirma-aprovacao-do-acordo-brasil-vaticano/.

Fábio Marton, *Relatos Apontam Proliferação de Ataques às Religiões Afro-Brasileiras*, Folha de S. Paulo, 24 Sepember 2019, https://www1.folha.uol.com.br/ilustrissima/2019/09/relatos-apontam-proliferacao-de-ataques-as-religioes-afro-brasileiras.shtml.

Fernanda Calgaro & Guilherme Mazui, *Bolsonaro Diz que Vai Indicar Ministro 'Terrivelmente Evangélico' para o STF*, G1, 10 July 2019, https://g1.globo.com/politica/noticia/2019/07/10/bolsonaro-diz-que-vai-indicar-ministro-terrivelmente-evangelico-para-o-stf.ghtml.

Frente Parlamentar Evangélica do Congresso Nacional, Câmara dos Deputados, https://www.camara.leg.br/internet/deputado/frenteDetalhe.asp?id=54010 (last visited 19 January 2021).

Frente Parlamentar Mista Católica Apostólica Romana, Câmara dos Deputados, https://www.camara.leg.br/internet/deputado/frenteDetalhe.asp?id=54077 (last visited 19 January 2021).

Gil Alessi, *Igrejas Evangélicas Neopentecostais Dominam Conselhos Tutelares em São Paulo e no Rio*, El País, 15 December2020, https://brasil.elpais.com/brasil/2020-12-15/igrejas-evangelicas-neopentecostais-dominam-conselhos-tutelares-em-sao-paulo-e-no-rio.html.

Hanrrikson de Andrade, *Censo 2010 Aponta Migração de Fiéis da Universal do Reino de Deus para Outras Igrejas Evangélicas*, UOL, 26 June 2012, https://noticias.uol.com.br/cotidiano/ultimas-noticias/2012/06/29/censo-2010-aponta-migracao-de-fieis-da-universal-do-reino-de-deus-para-outras-igrejas.htm.

Instituto Brasileiro de Geografia e Estatística, *Censo demográfico: 2010 – Características Gerais da População, Religião e Pessoas com Deficiência*, https://biblioteca.ibge.gov.br/visualizacao/periodicos/94/cd_2010_religiao_deficiencia.pdf (last visited 17 January 2021).

Instituto Brasileiro de Geografia e Estatística, *Censo Demográfico: 2010 – Características Gerais dos Indígenas: Resultados do Universo* (2010), https://biblioteca.ibge.gov.br/visualizacao/periodicos/95/cd_2010_indigenas_universo.pdf.

Instituto Brasileiro de Geografia e Estatística, *Os Indígenas no Censo Demográfico 2010: Primeiras Considerações com Base no Quesito Cor ou Raça* (2012), https://indigenas.ibge.gov.br/images/indigenas/estudos/indigena_censo2010.pdf.

Instituto Brasileiro de Geografia e Estatística, *Sinopse do Censo Demográfico: 2010* (2011), https://biblioteca.ibge.gov.br/visualizacao/livros/liv49230.pdf.

Íntegra do Discurso da Presidente Dilma Rousseff na Cerimônia de Posse, Agência Senado, https://www12.senado.leg.br/noticias/materias/2011/01/01/integra-do-discurso-da-presidente-dilma-rousseff-na-cerimonia-de-posse (last visited 13 May 2021).

Íntegra do Discurso de Posse da Presidente Dilma Rousseff no Congresso, Câmara dos Deputados, https://www.camara.leg.br/noticias/448217-integra-do-discurso-de-posse-da-presidente-dilma-rousseff-no-congresso/ (last visited 13 May 2021).

Iuri Pitta, *Sul tem Maior Proporção de Alunos em Escolas Filantrópicas e Confessionais*, CNN Brasil, 15 December 2020, https://www.cnnbrasil.com.br/nacional/2020/12/15/sul-tem-maior-proporcao-de-alunos-em-escolas-filantropicas-e-confessionais.

Jefferson Puff, *Por que as Religiões de Matriz Africana São o Principal Alvo de Intolerância no Brasil?*, BBC News Brasil, 21 January 2016, https://www.bbc.com/portuguese/noticias/2016/01/160120_intolerancia_religioes_africanas_jp_rm.

Joana Oliveira, *'Jesus Pode Ser Tudo, Menos Travesti,'* El País, 23 July 2018, https://brasil.elpais.com/brasil/2018/07/23/cultura/1532371217_501094.html.

Leia Íntegra do Discurso de Bolsonaro na Cerimônia de Posse no Congresso, Folha de S. Paulo, 1 January 2019, https://www1.folha.uol.com.br/poder/2019/01/leia-a-integra-do-discurso-de-bolsonaro-na-cerimonia-de-posse-no-congresso.shtml.

Leia Íntegra do Discurso de Posse do Presidente Interino Michel Temer, Folha de S. Paulo, 12 May 2016, https://www1.folha.uol.com.br/poder/2016/05/1770780-leia-integra-do-discurso-de-posse-do-presidente-interino-michel-temer.shtml.

Lino Geraldo Resende, *A Censura contra a Cidadania: o Caso do Brasil* (2005), http://bocc.ufp.pt/pag/resende-lino-geraldo-censura-cidadania.pdf.

Luiz Antônio Araujo, *Quem Foi o Embaixador Brasileiro que Contrariou Hitler e Vargas para Ajudar Fugitivos do Nazismo*, BBC News Brasil, 4 August 2018, https://www.bbc.com/portuguese/internacional-45065825.

Maioria na Câmara se declara católica; número de evangélicos cresce, G1, 27 November 2018, https://g1.globo.com/politica/noticia/2018/11/27/maioria-na-camara-se-declara-catolica-numero-de-evangelicos-cresce.ghtml.

Marcelo Musa Cavallari, *Dom Paulo Evaristo Arns (1921 – 2016): Um Bispo de seu Tempo*, Época, 16 December 2016, https://epoca.oglobo.globo.com/sociedade/noticia/2016/12/dom-paulo-evaristo-arns-1921-2016-um-bispo-de-seu-tempo.html.

Márcia Vieira, *Doações de Evangélicos Superam R$ 1 Bilhão por Mês*, O Estado de S. Paulo, 11 October 2009, https://www.estadao.com.br/noticias/geral,doacoes-de-evangelicos-superam-r-1-bi-por-mes,449133.

Márcio Zeni & Adrieli Fiorani, *Justiça Devolve Guarda de Adolescente para Mãe Denunciada por Maus-Tratos em Ritual de Candomblé*, G1, 14 August 2020, https://g1.globo.com/sp/sao-jose-do-rio-preto-aracatuba/noticia/2020/08/14/justica-revoga-guarda-provisoria-concedida-a-avo-de-menina-que-passou-por-um-ritual-de-candomble.ghtml.

Mariana Schreiber, *Quem é André Mendonça, Advogado e Pastor que Será Indicado por Bolsonaro ao STF*, BBC News Brasil, 7 July 2021, https://www.bbc.com/portuguese/brasil-57744271.

Marina Ito, *Zveiter Assume TJ do Rio e Manda Retirar Crucifixos*, Consultor Jurídico, 3 February 2009, https://www.conjur.com.br/2009-fev-03/luiz-zveiter-toma-posse-tj-rio-manda-retirar-crucifixos-corte.

Mariucha Machado, *Aluno é Barrado em Escola Municipal do Rio por Usar Guias do Candomblé*, G1, 2 September. 2014, http://g1.globo.com/rio-de-janeiro/noticia/2014/09/aluno-e-barrado-em-escola-municipal-do-rio-por-usar-guias-do-candomble.html.

Miliandre Garcia, *A Censura de Costumes no Brasil: da Institucionalização da Censura Teatral no Século XIX à Extinção da Censura na Constituição de 1988* (2009), https://www.bn.gov.br/sites/default/files/documentos/producao/pesquisa/censura-costumes-brasil-institucionalizacao-censura-teatral/miliandregarcia.pdf.

Ministério da Saúde, *Rede Hospitalar Filantrópica no Brasil: Perfil Histórico-Institucional e Oferta de Serviços* (2001), https://www.nescon.medicina.ufmg.br/biblioteca/imagem/2465.pdf.

Nilson Xavier, *20 Casos Absurdos de Censura às Novelas Pela Ditadura Militar*, Blog do Nilson Xavier (2019), https://tvefamosos.uol.com.br/blog/nilsonxavier/2019/03/31/20-casos-absurdos-de-censura-as-novelas-pela-ditadura-militar/.

O Que é o Santo Daime, Santo Daime, http://www.santodaime.org/site/religiao-da-floresta/o-santo-daime/introducao (last visited 20 February 2021).

Olívia Bandeira, *Igrejas Cristãs no Topo da Audiência*, Le Monde Diplomatique Brasil, 16 April 2018, https://diplomatique.org.br/igrejas-cristas-no-topo-da-audiencia/.

Parlamentares católicos planejam frente conjunta com Evangélicos, Estado de Minas, 28 January 2020, https://www.em.com.br/app/noticia/politica/2020/01/28/interna_politica,1117561/parlamentares-catolicos-planejam-frente-conjunta-com-evangelicos.shtml.

Partidos Políticos Registrados no TSE, Tribunal Superior Eleitoral, https://www.tse.jus.br/partidos/partidos-registrados-no-tse (last visited 5 March 2022).

Pedro Peduzzi, *Brasil já Reconheceu Mais de 11 Mil Refugiados até 2018, Diz Conare*, Agência Brasil, 25 July 2019, https://agenciabrasil.ebc.com.br/direitos-humanos/noticia/2019-07/brasil-ja-reconheceu-mais-de-11-mil-refugiados-ate-2018-diz-conare.

Pedro Zuazo, *Atolado de Processos, TJ do Rio Cria Centros de Mediação em Paróquias*, Extra, 20 November 2016, https://extra.globo.com/noticias/rio/atolado-de-processos-tj-do-rio-cria-centros-de-mediacao-em-paroquias-20502821.html.

Perfil e opinião dos evangélicos no Brasil – total da amostra: PO913906 – 07 e 08/10/2016, Datafolha (2016), http://media.folha.uol.com.br/datafolha/2016/12/28/da39a3ee5e6b4b0d3255bfef95601890afd80709.pdf.

Polícia Analisa Imagens de Atentado contra Porta dos Fundos, Deutsche Welle, 26 December 2019, https://p.dw.com/p/3VLiE.

Quem são, Fundação Nacional do Índio, http://www.funai.gov.br/index.php/indios-no-brasil/quem-sao (last visited 25 February 2021).

Quem somos nós?, Igreja Católica Apostólica Brasileira, https://novo.igrejabrasileira.com.br/quem-somos-nos/ (last visited 18 January 2021).

Rafael Moraes Moura, *STF não tem Ministros Evangélicos, Maioria é Católica*, O Estado de S. Paulo, 31 May 2019, https://politica.estadao.com.br/noticias/geral,stf-nao-tem-ministros-evangelicos-maioria-e-catolica,70002851820.

Rayane Moura, *Mãe Perde Guarda da Filha após Jovem Participar de Ritual do Candomblé*, UOL, 7 August 2020, https://noticias.uol.com.br/cotidiano/ultimas-noticias/2020/08/07/mae-perde-guarda-da-filha-apos-jovem-participar-de-ritual-do-candomble.htm.

Raymond Colitt, *Oldest Synagogue in Americas Draws Tourists to Brazil*, Reuters, 12 November 2001, https://www.reuters.com/article/us-brazil-synagogue/oldest-synagogue-in-americas-draws-tourists-to-brazil-idUSN2520146120071112.

Rodolfo Torres, *Evangélicos se opõem a acordo Brasil-Vaticano*, Congresso em Foco, 26 August 2009, https://congressoemfoco.uol.com.br/especial/noticias/evangelicos-se-opoem-a-acordo-brasil-vaticano/.

Sebastião Monteiro da Vide, *Constituições Primeiras do Arcebispado da Bahia* (1853), https://www2.senado.leg.br/bdsf/handle/id/222291.

Shaena Montanari, *INRI Cristo, o Homem que se Considera Jesus Reencarnado*, National Geographic Brasil, 8 November 2017, https://www.nationalgeographicbrasil.com/fotografia/2017/08/inri-cristo-o-homem-que-se-considera-jesus-reencarnado.

Thomas Milz, *A Polêmica em Torno do Jesus Negro da Mangueira*, Deutsche Welle, 19 February 2020, https://p.dw.com/p/3XzCy.

Vera Batista, *Justiça Treina Religiosos para a Mediação de Conflitos*, Correio Braziliense, 29 June 2017, https://blogs.correiobraziliense.com.br/servidor/justica-treina-religiosos-para-mediacao-de-conflitos/.

Vinícius Lisboa, *Religiosos Criticam Decisão que não Considera Umbanda e Candomblé Religiões*, Agência Brasil, 19 May 2014, https://agenciabrasil.ebc.com.br/direitos-humanos/noticia/2014-05/religiosos-criticam-decisao-que-nao-considera-umbanda-e-candomble.

Other Sources

1983 Code of Canon Law.

CESCR General Comment No. 13 (21), UN Doc. E/C.12/1999/10 (8 December 1999).

Codigo Philippino, ou, Ordenações e Leis do Reino de Portugal: Recopiladas por Mandado d'el-Rey D. Filipe I (Cândido Mendes de Almeida ed., 1870).

Comissão Nacional da Verdade, *Relatório: Textos Temáticos* (2014).

Instituto Brasileiro de Geografia e Estatística, *As Fundações Privadas e Associações sem Fins Lucrativos no Brasil: 2016* (2019).

Instituto Brasileiro de Geografia e Estatística, *Censo Demográfico: 2000 – Nupcialidade e Fecundidade: Resultados da Amostra* (2000).

Instituto Brasileiro de Geografia e Estatística, *Censo Demográfico: 2010 – Nupcialidade, Fecundidade e Migração: Resultados da Amostra* (2010).

Instituto Brasileiro de Geografia e Estatística, *Censo Demográfico: 2000 – Famílias e Domicílios: Resultados da Amostra* (2000).

Instituto Brasileiro de Geografia e Estatística, *Censo Demográfico: 2010 – Famílias e Domicílios: Resultados da Amostra* (2010).

RFB, *Solução de Consulta* [Advisory Opinion] No. 254-Cosit of 26 May 2017.

STF, *Súmula Vinculante* [Binding Thesis] No. 14.

STF, *Súmula Vinculante* [Binding Thesis] No. 52.

STJ, *Súmula* [Thesis] No. 227.

Thiago Magalhães Pires, *Sub-national Constitutional Law: Brazil*, IEL Constitutional Law (André Alen & David Haljan eds., 2021).

UNHRC General Comment No. 19 (Article 23), HRI/GEN/1/Rev.1 (29 June 1994).

UNHRC General Comment No. 22 (48) (Article 18), UN Doc. CCPR/C/21/Rev.1/Add.4 (27 September 1993).

UNHRC General Comment No. 34 (Article 19), UN Doc. CCPR/C/CG/34 (12 September 2011).

Selected Bibliography

Table of Cases

Federal Supreme Court

1ª Turma [1st Panel], ARE 800395 AgR/ES, Rapp. Min. Luís Roberto Barroso, *DJ* 14 November 2014.
1ª Turma [1st Panel], HC 124306/RJ, Rapp. Min. Luís Roberto Barroso, *DJ* 17 March 2017.
1ª Turma [1st Panel], Pet 8824 AgR/DF, Rapp. Min. Luiz Fux, *DJ* 6 July 2020.
1ª Turma [1st Panel], Rcl 22328/RJ, Rapp. Min. Luís Roberto Barroso, *DJ* 10 May 2018.
1ª Turma [1st Panel], RE 562351/RS, Rapp. Min. Ricardo Lewandowski, *DJ* 14 December 2012.
1ª Turma [1st Panel], RHC 134682/BA, Rapp. Min. Edson Fachin, *DJ* 29 August 2017.
1ª Turma [1st Panel], RHC 169682 AgR/RS, Rapp. Min. Luiz Fux, *DJ* 12 May 2020.
2ª Turma [2nd Panel], HC 168052/SP, Rapp. Min. Gilmar Mendes.
2ª Turma [2nd Panel], HC 85718/DF, Rapp. Min. Cezar Peluso, *DJ* 5 December 2008.
2ª Turma [2nd Panel], HC 91867/PA, Rapp. Min. Gilmar Mendes, *DJ* 20 September 2012.
2ª Turma [2nd Panel], HC 93250/MS, Rapp. Min. Ellen Gracie, *DJ* 27 June 2008.
2ª Turma [2nd Panel], HC 93767/DF, Rapp. Min. Celso de Mello, *DJ* 1 April 2014.
2ª Turma [2nd Panel], Rcl 38782/RJ, Rapp. Min. Gilmar Mendes, *DJ* 24 February 2021.
2ª Turma [2nd Panel], RE 31179/DF, Rapp. Min. Hahnemann Guimarães, *DJ* 26 June 1958.
2ª Turma [2nd Panel], RHC 146303/RJ, Rapp. Min. Dias Toffoli, *DJ* 7 August 2018.
3ª Turma [3rd Panel], RMS 16857/MG, Rapp. Min. Eloy da Rocha, *DJ* 24 October 1969.
ARE 1211606/RS, Rapp. Min. Gilmar Mendes, *DJ* 5 June 2019.
DJ 1969/DF, Rapp. Min. Ricardo Lewandowski, *DJ* 31 August 2007.
Full Court, ADI 1057 MC/BA, Rapp. Min. Celso de Mello, *DJ* 6 April 2001.
Full Court, ADI 1076 MC/DF, Rapp. Min. Sepúlveda Pertence, *DJ* 7 December 2000.
Full Court, ADI 1480 MC/DF, Rapp. Min. Celso de Mello, *DJ* 18 May 2001.
Full Court, ADI 2076/AC, Rapp. Min. Carlos Velloso, *DJ* 8 August 2003.

Table of Cases

Full Court, ADI 2404/DF, Rapp. Min. Dias Toffoli, *DJ* 1 August 2018.
Full Court, ADI 2566 MC/DF, Rapp. Min. Sydney Sanches, *DJ* 27 February 2004.
Full Court, ADI 2566/DF, Rapp. Min. Edson Fachin, *DJ* 23 October 2018.
Full Court, ADI 3239/DF, Rapp. Min. Rosa Weber, *DJ* 1 February 2019.
Full Court, ADI 3421/PR, Rapp. Min. Marco Aurélio, *DJ* 28 May 2010.
Full Court, ADI 3478/RJ, Rapp. Min. Edson Fachin, *DJ* 19 February 2020.
Full Court, ADI 3510/DF, Rapp. Min. Carlos Ayres Britto, *DJ* 28 May 2010.
Full Court, ADI 4276/MT, Rapp. Min. Luiz Fux, *DJ* 18 September 2014.
Full Court, ADI 4277/DF and ADPF 132/RJ, Rapp. Min. Carlos Ayres Britto, *DJ* 14 October 2011.
Full Court, ADI 4439/DF, Rapp. Min. Alexandre de Moraes, *DJ* 21 June 2018.
Full Court, ADI 4451/DF, Rapp. Min. Alexandre de Moraes, *DJ* 6 March 2019.
Full Court, ADI 4650/DF, Rapp. Min. Luiz Fux, *DJ* 24 February 2016.
Full Court, ADI 4815/DF, Rapp. Min. Cármen Lúcia, *DJ* 1 February 2016.
Full Court, ADI 4820/AP, Rapp. Min. Dias Toffoli, *DJ* 3 December 2018.
Full Court, ADI 5240/SP, Rapp. Min. Luiz Fux, *DJ* 1 February 2016.
Full Court, ADI 5257/RO, Rapp. Min. Dias Toffoli, *DJ* 3 December 2018.
Full Court, ADI 5258/AM, Rapp. Min. Cármen Lúcia, *DJ* 27 April 2021.
Full Court, ADI 5543/DF, Rapp. Min. Edson Fachin, *DJ* 26 August 2020.
Full Court, ADI 5577/DF, Rapp. Min. Rosa Weber, *DJ* 19 December 2017.
Full Court, ADI 5816/RO, Rapp. Min. Alexandre de Moraes, *DJ* 26 November 2019.
Full Court, ADI 5852/MS, Rapp. Min. Luiz Fux, *DJ* 26 November 2020.
Full Court, ADI 6133/RJ, Rapp. Min. Ricardo Lewandowski, *DJ* 6 July 2020.
Full Court, ADI 6390 MC-Ref/DF, Rapp. Min. Rosa Weber, *DJ* 12 November 2020.
Full Court, ADO 26/DF, Rapp. Min. Celso de Mello, *DJ* 6 October 2020.
Full Court, ADPF 130/DF, Rapp. Min. Carlos Ayres Britto, *DJ* 6 November 2009.
Full Court, ADPF 187/DF, Rapp. Min. Celso de Mello, *DJ* 29 May 2014.
Full Court, ADPF 378 MC/DF, Rapp. Min. Luís Roberto Barroso, *DJ* 8 March 2016.
Full Court, ADPF 460/PR, Rapp. Min. Luiz Fux, *DJ* 13 August 2020.
Full Court, ADPF 526/PR, Rapp. Min. Cármen Lúcia, *DJ* 3 June 2020.
Full Court, ADPF 54/DF, Rapp. Min. Marco Aurélio, *DJ* 30 April 2013.
Full Court, ADPF 811/DF, Rapp. Min. Gilmar Mendes, *DJ* 25 June 2021.
Full Court, ARE 1099099/SP, Rapp. Min. Edson Fachin, *DJ* 12 April 2021.
Full Court, ARE 652777/SP, Rapp. Min. Teori Zavascki, *DJ* 1 July 2015.
Full Court, ARE 766168/SP, Rapp. Min. Luís Roberto Barroso, *DJ* 13 November 2017.
Full Court, ERE 31179/DF, Rapp. Min. Hahnemann Guimarães, 10 *RTJ* 527, 533–534 (1959).
Full Court, Ext 662/Peru, Rapp. Min. Celso de Mello, *DJ* 30 May 1997.
Full Court, Ext 795/USA, Rapp. Min. Sepúlveda Pertence, *DJ* 6 April 2001.
Full Court, HC 17118/SP, Rapp. Min. Gilmar Mendes, *DJ* 17 August 2020.
Full Court, HC 82424/RS, Rapp. Min. Maurício Corrêa, *DJ* 19 March 2004.
Full Court, HC 97256/RS, Rapp. Min. Carlos Ayres Britto, *DJ* 16 December 2010.
Full Court, MI 4733/DF, Rapp. Min. Edson Fachin, *DJ* 29 September 2020.
Full Court, M. Seg. 1114/DF, Rapp. Min. Lafayette de Andrada, *DJ* 26 January 1950.

Full Court, M. Seg. 23452/RJ, Rapp. Min. Celso de Mello, *DJ* 12 May 2000.
Full Court, M. Seg. 28178/DF, Rapp. Min. Luís Roberto Barroso, *DJ* 8 May 2015.
Full Court, Pet 3388 ED/RR, Rapp. Min. Luís Roberto Barroso, *DJ* 4 February 2014.
Full Court, Pet 3388/RR, Rapp. Min. Carlos Ayres Britto, *DJ* 1 July 2010.
Full Court, RE 1045273/SE, Rapp. Min. Alexandre de Moraes, *DJ* 9 April 2021.
Full Court, RE 1055941/SP, Rapp. Min. Dias Toffoli, *DJ* 18 March 2021.
Full Court, RE 1116949/PR, Rapp. Min. Edson Fachin, *DJ* 2 October 2020.
Full Court, RE 158215/RS, Rapp. Min. Marco Aurélio, *DJ* 7 June 1996.
Full Court, RE 201819/RJ, Rapp. Min. Gilmar Mendes, *DJ* 27 October 2006.
Full Court, RE 325.822/SP, Rapp. Min. Gilmar Mendes, *DJ* 14 May 2004.
Full Court, RE 349703/RS, Rapp. Min. Gilmar Mendes, *DJ* 5 June 2009.
Full Court, RE 494601/RS, Rapp. Min. Edson Fachin, *DJ* 19 November 2019.
Full Court, RE 578562/BA, Rapp. Min. Eros Grau, *DJ* 12 September 2008.
Full Court, RE 601314/SP, Rapp. Min. Edson Fachin, *DJ* 16 September 2016.
Full Court, RE 611874/DF, Rapp. Min. Edson Fachin, *DJ* 12 April 2021.
Full Court, RE 636331/RJ, Rapp. Min. Gilmar Mendes, *DJ* 13 November 2017.
Full Court, RE 646721/RS, Rapp. Min. Luís Roberto Barroso, *DJ* 11 September 2017.
Full Court, RE 670422/RS, Rapp. Min. Dias Toffoli, *DJ* 10 March 2020.
Full Court, RE 685493/SP, Rapp. Min. Marco Aurélio, *DJ* 17 August 2020.
Full Court, RE 767332 RG/MG, Rapp. Min. Gilmar Mendes, *DJ* 22 November 2013.
Full Court, RE 80004/SE, Rapp. Min. Xavier de Albuquerque, *DJ* 29 December 1977.
Full Court, RE 806339/SE, Rapp. Min. Edson Fachin, *DJ* 19 March 2021.
Full Court, RE 859376 RG/PR, Rapp. Min. Luís Roberto Barroso, *DJ* 1 August 2017.
Full Court, RE 878694/MG, Rapp. Min. Luís Roberto Barroso, *DJ* 6 February 2018.
Full Court, RE 888815/RS, Rapp. Min. Alexandre de Moraes, *DJ* 21 March 2019.
Full Court, RE 898060/SC, Rapp. Min. Luiz Fux, *DJ* 24 August 2017.
Full Court, RE 958252/MG, Rapp. Min. Luiz Fux, *DJ* 13 September 2019.
Full Court, RE 979742 RG/AM, Rapp. Min. Luís Roberto Barroso, *DJ* 1 August 2017.
Full Court, RHC 134682/BA, Rapp. Min. Edson Fachin, *DJ* 29 August 2017.
Full Court, SE 2004/Vatican, Rapp. Min. Thompson Flores, *DJ* 26 November 1971.
Full Court, SE 2016/Lebanon, Rapp. Min. Luiz Gallotti, *DJ* 26 September 1969.
Full Court, SE 2838 AgR/Lebanon, Rapp. Min. Xavier de Albuquerque, *DJ* 18 December 1981.
MS 37760 MC/DF, Rapp. Min. Luís Roberto Barroso, *DJ* 12 April 2021 (in chambers).
Rcl 38782 MC/RJ, Rapp. Min. Dias Toffoli (President), *DJ* 5 February 2020.
SE 7170/Israel, Rapp. Min. Marco Aurélio (President), *DJ* 24 April 2003.

National Council of Justice

PCA 0004536-35.2010.2.00.0000, Rapp. Councilmember Ives Gandra, *DJ* 25 November 2010.

PCA 0001418-80.2012.2.00.0000, Rapp. Councilmember Emmanoel Campelo, *DJ* 5 May 2016.
PP 0001459-08.2016.2.00.0000, Rapp. Min. João Otávio de Noronha, 26 June 2018.
PP 1344, 1345, 1346, and 1362, Rapp. Councilmember Oscar Argollo, 6 June 2007.

Superior Court of Justice

1ª Turma [1st Panel], REsp 1536895/RJ, Rapp. Min. Napoleão Nunes Maia Filho, *DJ* 8 March 2016.
1ª Turma [1st Panel], RMS 37070/SP, Rapp. Min. Benedito Gonçalves, *DJ* 10 March 2014.
2ª Turma [2nd Panel], REsp 1761486/RS, Rapp. Min. Herman Benjamin, *DJ* 22 April 2019.
2ª Turma [2nd Panel], RMS 54042/CE, Rapp. Min. Herman Benjamin, *DJ* 13 September 2017.
3ª Turma [3rd Panel], AgInt no REsp 1808964/SP, Rapp. Min. Moura Ribeiro, *DJ* 11 March 2020.
3ª Turma [3rd Panel], HC 632567/BA, Rapp. Min. Marco Aurélio Bellizze, *DJ* 29 April 2021.
3ª Turma [3rd Panel], REsp 1371842/SP, Rapp. Min. Sidnei Beneti, *DJ* 17 December 2013.
3ª Turma [3rd Panel], REsp 1448969/SC, Rapp. Min. Moura Ribeiro, *DJ* 3 November 2014.
3ª Turma [3rd Panel], REsp 1500999/RJ, Rapp. Min. Ricardo Villas Bôas Cueva, *DJ* 19 April 2016.
3ª Turma [3rd Panel], REsp 1756100/DF, Rapp. Min. Marco Aurélio Bellizze, *DJ* 11 October 2018.
3ª Turma [3rd Panel], REsp 66529/SP, Rapp. Min. Nilson Naves, *DJ* 19 June 2000.
4ª Turma [4th Panel], REsp 1183378/RS, Rapp. Min. Luis Felipe Salomão.
4ª Turma [4th Panel], REsp 555086/RJ, Rapp. Min. Jorge Scartezzini, *DJ* 28 February 2005.
6ª Turma [6th Panel], HC 1498/RJ, Rapp. Min. Luiz Vicente Cernicchiaro, *DJ* 16 August 1993.
6ª Turma [6th Panel], HC 268459/SP, Rapp. Min. Maria Thereza de Assis Moura, *DJ* 28 October 2014.
AREsp 1748279/SP, Rapp. Min. Francisco Falcão, *DJ* 9 April 2021 (in chambers).
Corte Especial [Special Panel], SEC 11962/EX, Rapp. Min. Felix Fischer, *DJ* 25 November 2015.
Corte Especial [Special Panel], SEC 11962/Vatican, Rapp. Min. Felix Fischer, *DJ* 25 November 2015.

Superior Electoral Court

AgInt no RO 060187690 – Porto Velho/RO, Rapp. Min. Luis Felipe Salomão, *DJ* 4 May 2021.
AgRg em AI 15028 – Campos dos Goytacazes/RJ, Rapp. Min. Dias Toffoli, *DJ* 7 November 2013.
AgRg em AI 23930 – Rio de Janeiro/RJ, Rapp. Min. Admar Gonzaga, *DJ* 3 August 2018.

AgRg em AI 781963 – Volta Redonda/RJ, Rapp. Min. Gilmar Mendes, *DJ* 3 February 2017.
REspE 61867 – Diadema/SP, Rapp. Min. Sergio Silveira Banhos, *DJ* 13 May 2021.
REspE 8285 – Luziânia/GO, Rapp. Min. Edson Fachin, *DJ* 6 October 2020.
RO 265308 – Porto Velho/RO, Rapp. Min. Henrique Neves da Silva, *DJ* 5 April 2017.
RO 537003 – Belo Horizonte/MG, Rapp. Min. Rosa Weber, *DJ* 27 September 2018.

Superior Military Court

Ap. 0000005-16.2006.7.10.0010, Rapp. Min. José Américo dos Santos, *DJ* 14 April 2011.
EIN 0000005-16.2006.7.10.0010, Rapp. Min. Olympio Pereira Da Silva Junior, *DJ* 13 May 2013.
Rep. 0000154-35.2017.7.00.0000, Rapp. Min. Odilson Sampaio Benzi, *DJ* 10 June 2020.

Labour Courts

TST, *1ª Turma* [1st Panel], RR 51400-80.2009.5.21.0017, Rapp. Min. Hugo Carlos Scheuermann, *DJ* 30 June 2015.
TST, *2ª Turma* [2nd Panel], Ag-AIRR 664-33.2017.5.12.0048, Rapp. Min. Maria Helena Mallmann, *DJ* 14 August 2020.
TST, *6ª Turma* [6th Panel], AIRR 1259-32.2016.5.12.0027, Rapp. RCJ Cilene Ferreira Amaro Santos, *DJ* 23 November 2018.
TST, *6ª Turma* [6th Panel], ARR 725-66.2012.5.04.0281, Rapp. Min. Katia Magalhães Arruda, *DJ* 15 May 2015.
TST, *6ª Turma* [6th Panel], RR 37200-77.2006.5.02.0025, Rapp. Min. Aloysio Correa da Veiga, *DJ* 13 September 2013.
TST, *7ª Turma* [7th Panel], RR 548-89.2010.5.09.0069, Rapp. Min. Ubirajara Carlos Mendes, *DJ* 7 December 2018.
TST, *8ª Turma* [8th Panel], AIRR 748-66.2014.5.03.0023, Rapp. Min. Maria Cristina Irigoyen Peduzzi.
TST, *8ª Turma* [8th Panel], AIRR 1786-76.2013.5.10.0016, Rapp. Min. Jane Granzoto Torres da Silva, *DJ* 8 May 2015.
TRT – 6, *2ª Turma* [2nd Panel], RO 0001547-97.2010.5.06.0013, Rapp. RCJ Eneida Melo Correia de Araújo, *DJ* 2 August 2011.

Federal Courts

TRF – 1, *5ª Turma* [5th Panel], No. 0047405-03.2010.4.01.3400, Rapp. Federal Judge Maria Cecília de Marco Rocha, *DJ* 12 February 2016.
TRF – 1, *6ª Turma* [6th Panel], Ap. 0051046-62.2011.4.01.3400, Rapp. FCAJ Daniel Paes Ribeiro, *DJ* 24 February 2017.
TRF – 2, *8ª Turma Especializada* [8th Specialized Panel], Ap./Rem. Nec. 0012399-43.2010.4.02.5101, Rapp. FCAJ Vera Lúcia Lima, *DJ* 7 January 2015.
TRF – 3, *3ª Turma* [3rd Panel], Rem. Nec. 0022869-77.2014.4.03.6100, Rapp. FCAJ Cecília Marcondes, *DJ* 3 March 2020.
TRF – 3, *4ª Turma* [4th Panel], Ap./Rem. Nec. 0014396-10.2011.4.03.6100, Rapp. FCAJ Mônica Nobre, *DJ* 12 October 2018.

TRF – 3, *6ª Turma* [6th Panel], Ap. 5007691-61.2018.4.03.6100, Rapp. FCAJ Fábio Prieto, *DJ* 10 September 2020.
TRF – 3, *6ª Turma* [6th Panel], Ap./Rem. Nec. 0019890-16.2012.4.03.6100, Rapp. FACJ Johonsom di Salvo, *DJ* 21 December 2017.
TRF – 3, *7ª Turma* [7th Panel], Ap. 6105867-64.2019.4.03.9999, Rapp. FCAJ Toru Yamamoto, *DJ* 27 May 2020.
TRF – 4, *4ª Turma* [4th Panel], Ap. 5004738-74.2013.4.04.7102, Rapp. FCAJ Vivian Josete Pantaleão Caminha, 7 December 2016.
TRF – 4, Ap. 5004738-74.2013.4.04.7102, Vice-president FCAJ Maria de Fátima Freitas Labarrère, 27 June 2019.
Rio de Janeiro/RJ, *14ª Vara Federal* [14th Federal Court of First Instance], Proc. 0004747-33.2014.4.02.5101, 28 April 2014.
Rio de Janeiro/RJ, *14ª Vara Federal* [14th Federal Court of First Instance], Proc. 0004747-33.2014.4.02.5101, 20 May 2014.
Rio de Janeiro/RJ, *5ª Vara Federal Criminal* [5th Federal Criminal Court of First Instance], Proc. 0490290-70.2013.4.02.5101, 23 July 2013.
São Paulo/SP, *8ª Vara Cível Federal* [8th Federal Civil Court of First Instance], Proc. 5021263-50.2019.4.03.6100, 17 December 2019.

State Courts

TJAC, *1ª Câmara Cível* [1st Civil Panel], Ap. 0006505-83.2012.8.01.0001, Rapp. CAJ Luís Camolez, *DJ* 17 February 2020.
TJAC, *Câmara Cível* [Civil Panel], AI 2007.003288-8, Rapp. CAJ Samoel Evangelista, *DJ* 9 November 2011.
TJAM, *1ª Câmara Cível* [1st Civil Panel], Ap. 0608236-47.2013.8.04.0001, Rapp. CAJ Sabino da Silva Marques, *DJ* 24 November 2015.
TJBA, *1ª Câmara Cível* [1st Civil Panel], AI 8012718-14.2019.8.05.0000 and 8013525-34.2019.8.05.0000, Rapp. CAJ Mário Augusto Albiani Alves Júnior, *DJ* 11 September 2019.
TJBA, *1ª Câmara Criminal* [1st Criminal Panel], Ap. 0502347-89.2015.8.05.0039, Rapp. CAJ Nilson Soares Castelo Branco, *DJ* 3 March 2021.
TJBA, *3ª Câmara Cível* [3rd Civil Panel], AI 0162366-04.2016.8.05.0909, Rapp. CAJ Ivanilton Santos da Silva, *DJ* 13 March 2018.
TJBA, Full Court, ADI 0021850-08.2017.8.05.0000, Rapp. CAJ Abelardo Paulo da Matta Neto, *DJ* 25 October 2018.
TJCE, *2ª Câmara de Direito Público* [2nd Public Law Panel], Ap./Rem. Nec. 0023200-29.2010.8.06.0071, Rapp. CAJ Luiz Evaldo Gonçalves Leite, *DJ* 21 June 2017.
TJDFT, *2ª Turma Cível* [2nd Civil Panel], Ap. 20070710228035, Rapp. CAJ Silva Lemos, *DJ* 5 February 2010.
TJDFT, *3ª Turma Cível* [3rd Civil Panel], Ap. 20160710021514, Rapp. CAJ Alvaro Ciarlini, *DJ* 13 September 2017.
TJDFT, *4ª Turma Cível* [4th Civil Panel], Ap. 2007.01.1.100958-8, Rapp. CAJ Cruz Macedo, *DJ* 11 October 2012.
TJDFT, *5ª Turma Cível* [5th Civil Panel], Ap. 0035652-03.2014.8.07.0007, Rapp. CAJ Angelo Passareli, *DJ* 1 September 2017.

TJDFT, *6ª Turma Cível* [6th Civil Panel], Ap. 0048970-86.2005.8.07.0001, Rapp. CAJ Ana Maria Amarante, *DJ* 31 March 2016.
TJDFT, *6ª Turma Cível* [6th Civil Panel], Ap. 0701352-70.2020.8.07.0004, Rapp. CAJ Vera Andrighi, *DJ* 10 March 2021.
TJDFT, *6ª Turma Cível* [6th Civil Panel], Ap. 0712619-82.2019.8.07.0001, Rapp. CAJ Vera Andrighi, *DJ* 3 June 2020.
TJDFT, *6ª Turma Cível* [6th Civil Panel], Ap. 0712997-83.2020.8.07.0007, Rapp. CAJ Esdras Neves, *DJ* 19 February 2021.
TJDFT, *6ª Turma Cível* [6th Civil Panel], Ap. 20080110614755, Rapp. CAJ José Divino de Oliveira, *DJ* 15 May 2013.
TJDFT, *7ª Turma Cível* [7th Civil Panel], Ap. 0703534-58.2018.8.07.0017, Rapp. CAJ Romeu Gonzaga Neiva, *DJ* 6 July 2020.
TJDFT, *7ª Turma Cível* [7th Civil Panel], Ap. 20160610123855, Rapp. CAJ Getúlio de Moraes Oliveira, *DJ* 11 July 2017.
TJES, *1ª Câmara Cível* [1st Civil Panel], Ap. 0000630-08.2010.8.08.0002, Rapp. CAJ Janete Vargas Simões, *DJ* 12 November 2014.
TJES, *2ª Câmara Cível* [2nd Civil Panel], Ap. 0015297-17.2012.8.08.0038, Rapp. CAJ José Paulo Calmon Nogueira da Gama, *DJ* 22 March 2017.
TJES, *2ª Câmara Criminal* [2nd Criminal Panel], M. Seg. 0011848-34.2013.8.08.0000, Rapp. CAJ Getúlio Marcos Pereira Neves, *DJ* 13 November 2013.
TJES, *3ª Câmara Cível* [3rd Civil Panel], Ap. 0017944-27.2016.8.08.0011, Rapp. Min. Telemaco Antunes de Abreu Filho.
TJES, *4ª Câmara Cível* [4th Civil Panel], Ap. 0079970-96.2010.8.08.0035, CAJ Paulo Roberto Luppi, *DJ* 1 June 2015.
TJGO, *4ª Câmara Cível* [4th Civil Panel], Ap. 5370617-70.2017.8.09.0043, Rapp. CAJ Carlos Escher, *DJ* 22 February 2021.
TJGO, *5ª Câmara Cível* [5th Civil Panel], Ap. 58752-10.2005.8.09.0051, Rapp. Judge Delintro Belo de Almeida Filho, *DJ* 26 August 2016.
TJGO, *6ª Câmara Cível* [6th Civil Panel], Ap. 0095844.36.2016.8.09.0051, Rapp. CAJ Norival Santomé, *DJ* 29 October 2020.
TJGO, *Corte Especial* [Special Panel], ADI 5236450-85.2016.8.09.0000, Rapp. CAJ Itaney Francisco Campos.
TJMG, *13ª Câmara Cível* [13th Civil Panel], Ap. 1.0271.11.005612-1/002, Rapp. CAJ Alberto Henrique.
TJMG, *14ª Câmara Cível* [14th Civil Panel], Ap. 3742436-31.2004.8.13.0024, Rapp. CAJ Valdez Leite Machado, *DJ* 11 May 2010.
TJMG, *1ª Câmara Criminal* [1st Criminal Panel], Ap. 1.0525.10.012754-3/001, Rapp. CAJ Flávio Leite, *DJ* 7 August 2017.
TJMG, *4ª Câmara Cível* [4th Civil Panel], Ap. 1.0518.18.007692-0/01, Rapp. CAJ Dárcio Lopardi Mendes, *DJ* 17 December 2019.
TJMG, *7ª Câmara Cível* [7th Civil Panel], Ap. 1.0145.09.537812-4/001, Rapp. CAJ Washington Ferreira, *DJ* 13 June 2012.
TJMG, *7ª Câmara Cível* [7th Civil Panel], Ap. 5669883-73.2009.8.13.0024, Rapp. CAJ Wilson Benevides.
TJMS, *3ª Câmara Cível* [3rd Civil Panel], Ap. 0832933-58.2015.8.12.0001, Judge Vitor Luis de Oliveira Guibo, *DJ* 16 December 2019.

TJMS, *5ª Câmara Cível* [5th Civil Panel], Ap. 0024340-49.2010.8.12.0001, Rapp. CAJ Sideni Soncini Pimentel, *DJ* 3 October 2018.

TJMT, *2ª Câmara Cível* [2nd Civil Panel], Ap. 0116330-59.2007.8.11.0000, Rapp. Judge Clarice Claudino da Silva, 25 June 2008.

TJMT, *2ª Câmara de Direito Público e Coletivo* [2nd Public and Collective Law Panel], Ap. 0003179-33.2005.8.11.0050, Rapp. CAJ José Zuquim Nogueira, *DJ* 20 December 2016.

TJPR, *17ª Câmara Cível* [17th Civil Panel], Ap. 0035069-06.2018.8.16.0014, Rapp. Judge Antonio Carlos Ribeiro Martins, *DJ* 25 August 2020.

TJPR, *4ª Câmara Cível* [4th Civil Panel], Ap. 937721-9, Rapp. CAJ Maria Alice Aparecida Blanco de Lima, *DJ* 19 June 2015.

TJPR, *6ª Câmara Cível* [6th Civil Panel], Ap. 857.609-2, Rapp. Judge Joscelito Giovani Ce, *DJ* 10 December 2013.

TJPR, *8ª Câmara Cível* [8th Civil Panel], Ap. 1056289-1, Judge Osvaldo Nallim Duarte, *DJ* 26 September 2013.

TJPR, *8ª Câmara Cível* [8th Civil Panel], Ap. 1056289-1, Judge Osvaldo Nallim Duarte, *DJ* 26 September 2013.

TJRJ, *10ª Câmara Cível* [10th Civil Panel], AI 0028834-77.2001.8.19.0000, Rapp. CAJ João Nicolau Spyrides, *DJ* 7 April 2003.

TJRJ, *12ª Câmara Cível* [12th Civil Panel], AgInt na Ap. 0221325-98.2007.8.19.0001, Rapp. CAJ Cherubin Schwartz, *DJ* 26 September 2014.

TJRJ, *13ª Câmara Cível* [13th Civil Panel], Ap. 0019930-07.2008.8.19.0038, Rapp. CAJ Gabriel de Olveira Zefiro, *DJ* 12 June 2017.

TJRJ, *14ª Câmara Cível* [14th Civil Panel], Rem. Nec. 0323579-81.2009.8.19.0001, Rapp. CAJ Plínio Pinto Coelho Filho, *DJ* 8 May 2014.

TJRJ, *17ª Câmara Cível* [17th Civil Panel], Ap. 0007712-43.2008.8.19.0006, Rapp. CAJ Elton Martinez Carvalho Leme, *DJ* 18 December 2009.

TJRJ, *18ª Câmara Cível* [18th Civil Panel], Ap. 0000197-57.2014.8.19.0810, Rapp. CAJ Margaret de Olivaes Valle dos Santos, *DJ* 10 April 2014.

TJRJ, *19ª Câmara Cível* [19th Civil Panel], AI 0068944-59.2017.8.19.0000, Rapp. CAJ Ferdinaldo Nascimento, 27 February 2018.

TJRJ, *19ª Câmara Cível* [19th Civil Panel], Ap. 0010402-89.2010.8.19.0001, Rapp. CAJ Lúcio Durante, *DJ* 5 September 2014.

TJRJ, *2ª Câmara Cível* [2nd Civil Panel], Ap. 0512101-19.2014.8.19.0001, CAJ Antônio Iloízio Barros Bastos, *DJ* 10 May 2019.

TJRJ, *21ª Câmara Cível* [21st Civil Panel], Ap. 0098969-25.2012.8.19.0002, Rapp. CAJ Regina Lucia Passos, *DJ* 9 November 2018.

TJRJ, *22ª Câmara Cível* [22nd Civil Panel], Ap. 0000560-80.2009.8.19.0208, Rapp. CAJ Odete Knaack de Souza, *DJ* 16 January 2015.

TJRJ, *27ª Câmara Cível* [27th Civil Panel], Ap. 0009943-53.2016.8.19.0203, CAJ Marcos Alcino de Azevedo Torres, *DJ* 13 February 2019.

TJRJ, *3ª Câmara Cível* [3rd Civil Panel], Ap. 0015421-45.2012.8.19.0021, Rapp. CAJ Cezar Augusto Rodrigues Costa, *DJ* 10 September 2013.

TJRJ, *3ª Câmara Cível* [3rd Civil Panel], Ap. 0030177-42.2011.8.19.0038, 0021171-11.2011.8.19.0038, and 0153765-86.2011.8.19.0038, Rapp. CAJ Peterson Barroso Simão, *DJ* 02 February 2018.

TJRJ, *3ª Câmara Cível* [3th Civil Panel], Ap. 0153765-86.2011.8.19.0038, Rapp. CAJ Peterson Barroso Simão, *DJ* 31 January 2018.

TJRJ, *6ª Câmara Cível* [6th Civil Panel], AI 0083896-72.2019.8.19.0000, Rapp. CAJ Benedicto Abicair, *DJ* 10 January 2020 (in chambers).

TJRJ, *6ª Câmara Cível* [6th Civil Panel], Ap. 0085992-04.2012.8.19.0001, Rapp. CAJ Teresa de Andrade, *DJ* 12 April 2021.

TJRJ, *Conselho da Magistratura* [Judicial Council], Rem. Nec. 0311880-15.2017.8.19.0001, Rapp. CAJ Sérgio Ricardo de Arruda Fernandes, *DJ* 7 October 2019.

TJRJ, *Órgão Especial* [Special Panel], ADI 0018946-93.2015.8.19.0000, Rapp. CAJ Carlos Santos de Oliveira, *DJ* 4 March 2016.

TJRJ, *Órgão Especial* [Special Panel], ADI 0057920-68.2016.8.19.0000, Rapp. CAJ Rogerio de Oliveira Souza, *DJ* 17 September 2019.

TJRJ, *Órgão Especial* [Special Panel], ADI 0066288-37.2014.8.19.0000, Rapp. CAJ Carlos Eduardo da Rosa da Fonseca Passos, *DJ* 15 October 2015.

TJRS, *10ª Câmara Cível* [10th Civil Panel], Ap. 0157805-84.2015.8.21.7000, Rapp. Min. Túlio de Oliveira Martins, *DJ* 17 September 2015.

TJRS, *12ª Câmara Cível* [12th Civil Panel], AI 70032799041, Rapp. CAJ Cláudio Baldino Maciel, *DJ* 4 August 2010.

TJRS, *4ª Câmara Cível* [4th Civil Panel], AI 0290860-63.2017.8.21.7000, Rapp. CAJ Francesco Conti, *DJ* 26 September 2017 (in chambers).

TJRS, *4ª Câmara Cível* [4th Civil Panel], Ap. 0060472-93.2019.8.21.7000, Rapp. CAJ Antonio Vinicius Amaro da Silveira, *DJ* 21 November 2019.

TJRS, *5ª Câmara Cível* [5th Civil Panel], Ap. 70027034164, Rapp. CAJ Jorge Luiz Lopes do Canto, 21 January 2009.

TJRS, *7ª Câmara Cível* [7th Civil Panel], AI 70084496934, Rapp. CAJ Carlos Eduardo Zietlow Duro, *DJ* 30 October 2020.

TJRS, *7ª Câmara Cível* [7th Civil Panel], Ap. 70069284933, Rapp. CAJ Liselena Schifino Robles Ribeiro, *DJ* 8 July 2016.

TJRS, *9ª Câmara Cível* [9th Civil Panel], Ap. 70015766371, Rapp. CAJ Tasso Caubi Soares Delabary, *DJ* 13 September 2006.

TJRS, *Conselho da Magistratura* [Judicial Council], Proc. 0139-11/000348-0, Rapp. CAJ Cláudio Baldino Maciel, *DJ* 9 March 2012.

TJSC, *1ª Câmara Cível* [1st Civil Panel], AI 0137975-36.2014.8.24.0000, Rapp. CAJ Carlos Adilson Silva, *DJ* 13 December 2016.

TJSC, *1ª Câmara de Direito Civil* [1st Civil Law Panel], Ap. 2011.089551-3, Rapp. CAJ Carlos Prudêncio, *DJ* 29 May 2020.

TJSC, *1ª Câmara de Direito Público* [1st Public Law Panel], Ap. 2012.008632-0, Rapp. CAJ Newton Trisotto, 3 June 2013.

TJSC, *4ª Câmara de Direito Civil* [4th Civil Law Panel], Ap. 0301470-79.2016.8.24.0004, Rapp. CAJ Selso de Oliveira, 3 September 2020.

TJSC, *4ª Câmara de Direito Público* [4th Public Law Panel], Ap. 2013.051277-0, Rapp. CAJ José Volpato de Souza, 6 February 2014.

TJSC, *4ª Câmara de Direito Público* [4th Public Law Panel], Rem. Nec. 0001153-65.2009.8.24.0113, Rapp. CAJ Rodolfo Cezar Ribeiro Da Silva Tridapalli, 5 September 2019.

TJSC, *5ª Câmara de Direito Civil* [5th Civil Law Panel], Ap. 2011.042037-8, Rapp. CAJ Henry Petry Junior, 28 February 2013.
TJSC, *5ª Câmara de Direito Civil* [5th Civil Law Panel], Ap. 5000432-45.2019.8.24.0091, Rapp. CAJ Cláudia Lambert de Faria, 9 December 2020.
TJSC, *6ª Câmara de Direito Civil* [6th Civil Law Panel], Ap. 0001964-76.2018.8.24.0091, Rapp. CAJ André Carvalho.
TJSC, *Câmara Civil Especial* [Special Civil Panel], AI 4017005-65.2016.8.24.0000, Rapp. CAJ Luiz Zanelato, *DJ* 10 December 2016 (in chambers).
TJSP, *9ª Câmara de Direito Público* [9th Public Law Panel], Ap. 1006914-54.2016.8.26.0438, Rapp. CAJ Rebouças de Carvalho, *DJ* 17 October 2017.
TJSP, *10ª Câmara de Direito Privado* [10th Private Law Panel], Ap. 0000460-26.2012.8.26.0629, Rapp. CAJ Elcio Trujillo, *DJ* 19 November 2014.
TJSP, *10ª Câmara de Direito Privado* [10th Private Law Panel], Ap. 1006628-78.2019.8.26.0565, Rapp. CAJ Jair de Souza, *DJ* 5 February 2021.
TJSP, *10ª Câmara de Direito Privado* [10th Private Law Panel], Ap. 1048106-77.2017.8.26.0002, Rapp. CAJ JB Paula Lima, *DJ* 31 October 2019.
TJSP, *10ª Câmara de Direito Público* [10th Public Law Panel], Ap./Rem. Nec. 1000708-23.2020.8.26.0587, Rapp. CAJ Marcelo Semer, *DJ* 2 March 2021.
TJSP, *1ª Câmara de Direito Privado* [1st Private Law Panel], AI 0247672-06.2012.8.26.0000, Rapp. CAJ Paulo Eduardo Razuk, *DJ* 22 February 2013.
TJSP, *1ª Câmara Reservada de Direito Empresarial* [1st Separate Panel on Business Law], Ap. 1011716-29.2014.8.26.0224, Rapp. CAJ Enio Zuliani, *DJ* 23 April 2015.
TJSP, *2ª Câmara de Direito Privado* [2nd Private Law Panel], Ap. 1071628-96.2018.8.26.0100, Rapp. CAJ José Carlos Ferreira Alves, *DJ* 26 October 2020.
TJSP, *2ª Câmara de Direito Privado* [2nd Private Law Panel], Ap. 1001772-69.2017.8.26.0362, Rapp. CAJ Rosangela Telles, *DJ* 23 October 2019.
TJSP, *36ª Câmara de Direito Privado* [36th Private Law Panel], Ap. 1015041-20.2016.8.26.0037, Rapp. CAJ Maria Cláudia Bedotti, *DJ* 4 June 2018.
TJSP, *3ª Câmara de Direito Público* [3rd Public Law Panel], Ap. 1003243-34.2018.8.26.0347, Rapp. CAJ Marrey Uint, *DJ* 9 March 2020.
TJSP, *4ª Câmara de Direito Privado* [4th Private Law Panel], Ap. 0045315-08.2011.8.26.0506, Rapp. CAJ Natan Zelinschi de Arruda, *DJ* 17 December 2015.
TJSP, *5ª Câmara de Direito Privado* [5th Private Law Panel], AI 2180296-90.2017.8.26.0000, Rapp. CAJ JL Mônaco da Silva, *DJ* 23 February 2018.
TJSP, *5ª Câmara de Direito Público* [5th Public Law Panel], Ap. 1005816-02.2017.8.26.0114, Rapp. CAJ Maria Laura Tavares, *DJ* 22 March 2019.
TJSP, *6ª Câmara Cível* [6th Civil Panel], Ap. 1008228-48.2017.8.26.0196, Rapp. CAJ Rodolfo Pellizari, *DJ* 22 April 2019.
TJSP, *6ª Câmara de Direito Privado* [6th Private Law Panel], AI 2067268-47.2017.8.26.0000, Rapp. CAJ Rodolfo Pellizari, *DJ* 15 August 2017.
TJSP, *6ª Câmara de Direito Privado* [6th Private Law Panel], AI 20677526-57.2017.8.26.0000, Rapp. CAJ Rodolfo Pellizari, *DJ* 26 September 2017.
TJSP, *6ª Câmara de Direito Privado* [6th Private Law Panel], Ap. 0015879-15.2011.8.26.0664, Rapp. CAJ Claudia Grieco Tabosa Pessoa, *DJ* 25 October 2012.

TJSP, *6ª Câmara de Direito Privado* [6th Private Law Panel], Ap. 1002369-76.2017.8.26.0123, Rapp. CAJ Cristina Medina Mogioni, *DJ* 19 November 2020.
TJSP, *7ª Câmara de Direito Privado* [7th Private Law Panel], AI 2251173-50.2020.8.26.0000, Rapp. CAJ Rômulo Russo, *DJ* 27 January 2021.
TJSP, *7ª Câmara de Direito Privado* [7th Private Law Panel], Ap. 1002466-71.2017.8.26.064, CAJ Luiz Antonio Costa, *DJ* 9 January 2020.
TJSP, *7ª Câmara de Direito Privado* [7th Private Law Panel], Ap. 1064065-88.2017.8.26.0002, Rapp. CAJ Luis Maria Galbetti, *DJ* 30 October 2019.
TJSP, *7ª Câmara de Direito Privado* [7th Private Law Panel], Ap. 4003115-88.2013.8.26.0071, Rapp. CAJ Luiz Antonio Costa, *DJ* 23 July 2015.
TJSP, *8ª Câmara de Direito Privado* [8th Private Law Panel], Ap. 0124915-79.2009.8.26.0011, Rapp. CAJ Caetano Lagrasta, *DJ* 22 November 2012.
TJSP, *Câmara Especial* [Special Panel], Ap. 1016664-33.2018.8.26.0625, Rapp. CAJ Lidia Conceição, *DJ* 10 December 2019.
TJSP, *Conselho Superior de Magistratura* [Superior Judicial Council], Ap. 0018134-71.2014.8.26.0071, Rapp. CAJ Xavier de Aquino.
TJSP, *Conselho Superior de Magistratura* [Superior Judicial Council], Ap. 9000012-51.2011.8.26.0590, Rapp. CAJ José Renato Nalini, 21 March 2013.
TJSP, *Órgão Especial* [Special Panel], ADI 2120132-62.2017.8.26.0000, Rapp. CAJ Alvaro Passos, *DJ* 9 November 2017.
TJSP, *Órgão Especial* [Special Panel], ADI 2219902-57.2019.8.26.0000, Rapp. CAJ Cristina Zucchi, *DJ* 15 June 2020.
TJSP, *Órgão Especial* [Special Panel], ADI 2248079-02.2017.8.26.0000, Rapp. CAJ Márcio Bartoli, *DJ* 21 June 2018.
TJSP, *Órgão Especial* [Special Panel], Arg. Inconst. 0020774-56.2020.8.26.0000, Rapp. CAJ James Siano, *DJ* 3 September 2020.
TJSP, *Órgão Especial* [Special Panel], Arg. Inconst. 0056828-94.2015.8.26.0000, Rapp. CAJ Tristão Ribeiro, *DJ* 18 June 2016.
TJTO, *2ª Câmara Cível* [2nd Civil Panel], AI 0024872-28.2018.8.27.0000, Rapp. CAJ Adolfo Amaro Mendes, 16 May 2019.
PR, *1ª Turma Recursal dos Juizados Especiais* [1st Appellate Panel of the Special Courts], RI 0009125-87.2018.8.16.0018, Rapp. Judge Maria Fernanda Scheidemantel Nogara Ferreira da Costa, *DJ* 17 December 2019.
Americana/SP, *3ª Vara Cível* [3rd Civil Court of First Instance], Proc. 1012306-97.2018.8.26.0019, *DJ* 21 November 2018.
Barra Mansa/RJ, *4ª Vara Cível* [4th Civil Court of First Instance], Proc. 0013080-15.2017.8.19.0007, 14 January 2020.
Campinas/SP, *Vara de Violência Doméstica e Familiar contra a Mulher* [Court of First Instance for Cases of Domestic and Family Violence Against Women], Proc. 1507648-71.2021.8.26.0114, 15 July 2021.
Jundiaí/SP, *4ª Vara Cível* [4th Civil Court of First Instance], Proc. 1016422-86.2017.8.26.0309, 15 September 2017.
Paulo Afonso/BA, *2ª Vara dos Feitos Cíveis* [2nd Civil Court of First Instance], Proc. 8002647-30.2017.8.05.0191, *DJ* 4 February 2019.
Porto Alegre/RS, *1º Juizado Especial da Fazenda Pública* [1st Special Court for Suits Involving Government Entities], Proc. 9038978-35.2017.8.21.0001, 25 September 2017.

Porto Alegre/RS, *2ª Vara da Fazenda Pública* [2nd Court of First Instance for Suits Involving Government Entities], Proc. 9038978-35.2017.8.21.0001, 22 September 2017.
Ribeirão Preto/SP, *6ª Vara Cível* [6th Civil Court of First Instance], Proc. 0045315-08.2011.8.26.0506, *DJ* 15 September 2014.
Rio de Janeiro/RJ, *16ª Vara Cível* [16th Civil Court of First Instance], Proc. 0332259-06.2019.8.19.0001, 19 December 2019.
Santa Luzia/MG, *1ª Vara Cível* [1st Civil Court of First Instance], Proc. 0209993-39.2013.8.13.0245, 23 September 2020.
São Paulo/SP (Foro Regional XI – Pinheiros), *1ª Vara Cível* [1st Civil Court of First Instance], Proc. 0124915-79.2009.8.26.0011, *DJ* 6 December 2010.
Sorocaba/SP, *Vara da Infância e Juventude* [Children and Juvenile Court of First Instance], Proc. 1045451-44.2018.8.26.0602, *DJ* 1 July 2019.
Vila Velha/ES, *2ª Vara Criminal* [2nd Criminal Court of First Instance], Proc. 0042520-84.2012.8.08.0024, 22 March 2013.

Reports and Decisions of International Bodies

Accordance with *International Law of Kosovo's Declaration of Independence*, Advisory Opinion, 2010 ICJ Rep. 403 (22 July).
The Word 'Laws' in Article 30 of the American Convention on Human Rights, Advisory Opinion OC-6/86, Inter-Am. Ct HR (ser. A) No. 6 (9 May 1986).
Castañeda Gutman v. Mexico, Preliminary Objections, Merits, Reparations and Costs, Judgment, Inter-Am. Ct HR (ser. C) No. 184 (6 August 2008).
Interpretation of the American Declaration of the Rights and Duties of Man Within the Framework of Article 64 of the American Convention on Human Rights, Advisory Opinion OC-10/89, Inter-Am. Ct HR (ser. A) No. 10 (14 July 1989).
Rights and Guarantees of Children in the Context of Migration and/or in Need of International Protection, Advisory Opinion OC-21/14, Inter-Am. Ct HR (ser. A) No. 21 (19 August 2014).
Almonacid-Arellano et al. v. Chile, Preliminary Objections, Merits, Reparations and Costs, Judgment, Inter-Am. Ct HR (ser. C) No. 154 (26 September 2006).
Gelman v. Uruguay, Monitoring Compliance with Judgment, Order of the Court, Inter-Am. Ct HR (20 March 2013).
Case of 'The Last Temptation of Christ' (Olmedo-Bustos et al.) v. Chile, Merits, Reparations and Costs, Judgment, Inter-Am. Ct HR (ser. C) No. 73 (5 February 2001).
Gender Identity, and Equality and Non-Discrimination of Same-Sex Couples. State Obligations Concerning Change of Name, Gender Identity, and Rights Derived from a Relationship Between Same-Sex Couples (Interpretation and Scope of Articles 1(1), 3, 7, 11(2), 13, 17, 18 and 24, in Relation to Article 1, of the American Convention on Human Rights), Advisory Opinion OC-24/17, Inter-Am. Ct HR (ser. A) No. 24 (24 November 2017).
Cristián Daniel Sahli et al. v. Chile, Case 12.129, Inter-Am. Comm'n HR, Report No. 43/05, OEA/Ser.L/V/II.124 doc. 5 (2005).

Table of Statutes

Federal/Imperial Legislation

Constituição Política do Império do Brasil (1824) [1824 Political Constitution of the Empire of Brazil].
Constituição da República dos Estados Unidos do Brasil (1891) [1891 Constitution of the Republic of the United States of Brazil].
Constituição da República dos Estados Unidos do Brasil (1934) [1934 Constitution of the Republic of the United States of Brazil].
Constituição da República dos Estados Unidos do Brasil (1937) [1937 Constitution of the Republic of the United States of Brazil].
Constituição dos Estados Unidos do Brasil (1946) [1946 Constitution of the United States of Brazil].
Constituição da República Federativa do Brasil (1967) [1967 Constitution of the Federative Republic of Brazil].
Constituição da República Federativa do Brasil (1969) [1969 Constitution of the Federative Republic of Brazil].
Constituição da República Federativa do Brasil (1988) [1988 Constitution of the Federative Republic of Brazil].
CA 108 of 26 August 2020.
CA No. 65 of 13 July 2010.
CA No. 66 of 13 July 2010.
CA No. 7 of 15 August 1995.
CA No. 9 of 28 June 1977.
Complementary Law No. 105 of 10 January 2001.
Complementary Law No. 160 of 7 August 2017.
Complementary Law No. 170 of 19 December 2019.
Código Civil (CC) [Civil Code], Law No. 10406 of 10 January 2002.
Código Civil [Civil Code], Law No. 3071 of 1 January 1916.
Código Criminal [Criminal Code], Law of 16 December 1830.
Código de Defesa do Consumidor [Consumer Defense Code], Law No. 8078 of 11 September 1990.
Código de Ética Médica (CEM) [Code of Medical Ethics], Resolution (CFM) No. 2217 of 27 September 2018.
Código de Processo Civil (CPC) [Code of Civil Procedure], Law No. 13105 of 16 March 2015.

Table of Statutes

Código de Processo Penal (CPP) [Code of Penal Procedure], Decree-Law No. 3689 of 3 October 1941.
Código Eleitoral [Electoral Code], Law No. 4737 of 15 July 1965.
Código Penal (CP) [Código Penal], Decree-Law No. 2848 of 7 December 1940.
Código Penal [Penal Code], Decree No. 847 of 11 October 1890.
Código Tributário Nacional (CTN) [National Tax Code], Law No. 5172 of 25 October 1966.
Consolidação das Leis do Trabalho (CLT) [Consolidation of Labour Laws], Decree-Law No. 5452 of 1 May 1943.
Estatuto da Criança e do Adolescente (ECA) [Statute on the Child and Adolescent], Law No. 8069 of 13 July 1990.
Decree-Law No. 25 of 30 November 1937.
Decree-Law No. 3200 of 19 April 1941.
Law No. 3029 of 9 January 1881.
Law No. 3353 of 13 May 1888.
Law No. 181 of 24 January 1890.
Law No. 379 of 16 January 1937.
Law No. 662 of 6 April 1949.
Law No. 1110 of 23 May 1950.
Law No. 3268 of 30 September 1957.
Law No. 4117 of 27 August 1962.
Law No. 4121 of 27 August 1962.
Law No. 4503 of 30 November 1964.
Law No. 5010 of 30 May 1966.
Law No. 5020 of 9 February 1967.
Law No. 6001 of 19 December 1973.
Law No. 6015 of 31 December 1973.
Law No. 6515 of 26 December 1977.
Law No. 7210 of 11 July 1984.
Law No. 7347 of 24 July 1985.
Law No. 7713 of 22 December 1988.
Law No. 7716 of 5 January 1989.
Law No. 8080 of 19 September 1990.
Law No. 8112 of 11 December 1990.
Law No. 8212 of 24 July 1991.
Law No. 8239 of 4 October 1991.
Law No. 8389 of 30 December 1991.
Law No. 8742 of 7 December 1993.
Law No. 8884 of 11 June 1994.
Law No. 8906 of 4 July 1994.
Law No. 9029 of 13 April 1995.
Law No. 9093 of 12 September 1995.
Law No. 9296 of 24 July 1996.
Law No. 9307 of 23 September 1996.
Law No. 9459 of 15 May 1997.
Law No. 9474 of 22 June 1997.
Law No. 9504 of 30 September 1997.

Law No. 9507 of 12 November 1997.
Law No. 9982 of 14 July 2000.
Law No. 10607 of 19 December 2002.
Law No. 11105 of 24 March 2005.
Law No. 11106 of 28 March 2005.
Law No. 12288 of 20 July 2010.
Law No. 12485 of 12 September 2011.
Law No. 12527 of 18 November 2011.
Law No. 12846 of 1 August 2013.
Law No. 12852 of 5 August 2013.
Law No. 13467 of 13 July 2017.
Law No. 13811 of 12 March 2019.
Lei das Sociedades Anônimas [Law on Stock Corporations], Law No. 6404 of 15 December 1976.
Lei de Diretrizes e Bases da Educação Nacional (LDB) [Law on the Guidelines and Bases of National Education], Law No. 9394 of 20 December 1996.
Lei Geral de Proteção de Dados (LGPD) [General Data Protection Law], Law No. 13709 of 14 August 2018.
Marco Civil da Internet [Civil Framework Law for the Internet], Law No. 12965 of 23 April 2014.
Provisional Measure No. 2158-35 of 24 August 2001.
1826 Reg. Int. (Imperial Senate).
Reg. Int. (CD), Resolution (CD) No. 17 of 1989.
Reg. Int. (SF), Resolution (SF) No. 93 of 1970.
Decree No. 1144 of 11 September 1861.
Decree No. 78-A of 21 December 1889.
Decree No. 119-A of 7 January 1890.
Decree No. 4120 of 3 September 1920.
Decree No. 4497 of 19 January 1922.
Decree No. 4887 of 20 November 2003.
Decree No. 7788 of 15 August 2012.
Instrução Normativa [Normative Directive] (DREI) No. 81 of 10 June 2020.
Instrução Normativa [Normative Directive] (RFB) No. 1863 of 27 December 2018.
Portaria [Ordinance] (ME) No. 430 of 30 December 2020.
Resolution (CFM) No. 2168 of 21 September 2017.
Resolution (CFM) No. 2232 of 17 July 2019.
Resolution (CFM) No. 2283 of 1 October 2020.
Resolution (CNJ) No. 175 of 14 May 2013.
Resolution (CNPCP) No. 8 of 9 November 2011.
Resolution (CNPCP) No. 8 of 9 November 2011.
Resolution (EBC) No. 3 of 23 November 2011.
Resolution (EBC) No. 4 of 6 July 2012.

International Treaties and Documents

2003 UNESCO Convention for the Safeguarding of the Intangible Cultural Heritage.

Table of Statutes

Acordo entre o Governo da República Federativa do Brasil e a Santa Sé relativo ao Estatuto Jurídico da Igreja Católica no Brasil [Agreement Between the Government of the Federative Republic of Brazil and the Holy See Concerning the Legal Status of the Catholic Church in Brazil] (13 November 2008).
American Convention on Human Rights (B-32) (22 November 1969).
American Declaration of the Rights and Duties of Man (2 May 1948).
Convention on Private International Law (Bustamante Code) (20 February 1928).
Convention on the Rights of Persons with Disabilities, GA Res. 61/106, UN Doc. A/RES/61/106 (13 December 2006).
Optional Protocol to the Convention on the Rights of Persons with Disabilities, GA Res. 61/106, UN Doc. A/RES/61/106 (13 December 2006).
Marrakesh Treaty to Facilitate Access to Published Works for Persons Who Are Blind, Visually Impaired or Otherwise Print Disabled, WIPO Lex TRT/MARRAKESH/001 (27 June 2013).
Convention on the Rights of the Child (CRC), GA Res. 44/25, UN Doc. A/RES/44/25 (20 November 1989).
Declaration on the Elimination of All Forms of Intolerance and of Discrimination Based on Religion or Belief, GA Res. 36/55, UN Doc. A/RES/36/55 (25 November 1981).
Declaration on the Rights of Persons Belonging to National or Ethnic, Religious and Linguistic Minorities, GA Res. 47/135, UN Doc. A/RES/47/135 (3 February 1992).
ILO Discrimination (Employment and Occupation) Convention 158 (No. 111).
Inter-American Convention Against all Forms of Discrimination and Intolerance, AG/RES. 2804 (XLIII-O/13) (6 June 2013).
International Covenant on Civil and Political Rights (ICCPR), GA Res. 2200 (XXI) A, UN Doc. A/RES/2200(XXI)A (6 December 1966).
International Covenant on Economic, Social and Cultural Rights (ICESCR), GA Res. 2200 (XXI) A, UN Doc. A/RES/2200(XXI)A (6 December 1966).
Universal Declaration of Human Rights (UDHR), GA Res. 217 (III) A, UN Doc. A/RES/217(III)A (10 December 1948).

State and Federal District Law

Constitution of the State of Acre (1989).
Constitution of the State of Alagoas (1989).
Constitution of the State of Amazonas (1989).
Constitution of the State of Bahia (1989).
Constitution of the State of Espírito Santo (1989).
Constitution of the State of Maranhão (1989).
Constitution of the State of Mato Grosso (1989).
Constitution of the State of Pará (1989).
Constitution of the State of Paraná (1989).
Constitution of the State of Pernambuco (1989).
Constitution of the State of Piauí (1989).
Constitution of the State of Rio de Janeiro (1989).
Constitution of the State of Rio Grande do Note (1989).
Constitution of the State of Rio Grande do Sul (1989).
Constitution of the State of Rondônia (1989).

Constitution of the State of Sergipe (1989).
Constitution of the State of Tocantins (1989).
Organic Law of the Federal District (1993).
Law (AC) No. 1352 of 29 December 2000.
Law (AM) No. 4916 of 12 September 2019.
Law (BA) No. 13182 of 6 June 2014.
Law (DF) No. 2230 of 31 December 1998.
Law (DF) No. 3979 of 29 March 2007.
Law (DF) No. 6466 of 27 December 2019.
Law (GO) No. 19046 of 13 July 2016.
Law (MA) No. 10489 of 13 July 2016.
Law (MA) No. 8197 of 6 December 2004.
Law (MG) No. 15434 of 5 January 2005.
Law (MS) No. 5272 of 26 May 2000.
Law (MT) No. 11229 of 15 October 2020.
Law (PB) No. 11288 of 29 December 2018.
Law (PE) No. 14484 of 21 November 2011.
Law (PI) No. 5356 of 11 December 2003.
Law (RJ) No. 1814 of 24 April 1991.
Law (RJ) No. 6483 of 4 July 2013.
Law (RJ) No. 6956 of 13 January 2015.
Law (RJ) No. 6998 of 8 May 2015.
Law (RJ) No. 7041 of 15 July 2015.
Law (RJ) No. 8113 of 20 September 2018.
Law (RJ) No. 9210 of 11 March 2021.
Law (RO) No. 834 of 21 September 1999.
Law (RR) No. 432 of 27 April 2004.
Law (RS) No. 11872 of 19 December 2002.
Law (RS) No. 14159 of 20 December 2012.
Law (SE) No. 1396 of 14 September 1966.
Law (SP) No. 10066 of 21 July 1998.
Law (SP) No. 10948 of 5 November 2001.
Law (SP) No. 17157 of 18 September 2019.
Law (SP) No. 17346 of 12 March 2021.
Law (SP) No. 17346 of 12 March 2021.
Reg. Int. (ALEAM), Legislative Resolution (ALEAM) No. 469 of 2010.
Reg. Int. (ALECE), Resolution (ALECE) No. 389 of 1996.
Reg. Int. (ALERGS), Resolution (ALERGS) No. 2288 of 1991.
Reg. Int. (ALERJ), Resolution (ALERJ) No. 810 of 1997.
Resolution (ALERGS) No. 2978 of 2006.

Local Law

Organic Law of the Municipality of Aracaju/SE.
Organic Law of the Municipality of Cuiabá/MT.
Organic Law of the Municipality of Curitiba/PR.
Organic Law of the Municipality of Goiânia/GO.
Organic Law of the Municipality of João Pessoa/PB.

Organic Law of the Municipality of Macapá/AM.
Organic Law of the Municipality of Maceió/AL.
Organic Law of the Municipality of Manaus/AM.
Organic Law of the Municipality of Porto Alegre/RS.
Organic Law of the Municipality of Rio de Janeiro/RJ.
Organic Law of the Municipality of Salvador/BA.
Organic Law of the Municipality of São Luís/MA.
Organic Law of the Municipality of São Paulo/SP.
Organic Law of the Municipality of Teresina/PI.
Código Tributário [Tax Code] (Fortaleza/CE), Complementary Law (Fortaleza/CE) No. 159 of 23 December 2013.
Código Tributário [Tax Code] (Recife/PE), Law (Recife/PE) No. 15563 of 27 December1991.
Código Tributário [Tax Code] (Rio de Janeiro/RJ), Law (Rio de Janeiro/RJ) No. 691 of 24 December 1984.
Código Tributário e de Rendas [Tax and Revenue Code] (Salvador/BA), Law (Salvador/BA) No. 7186 of 27 December 2006.
Complementary Law (Porto Alegre/RS) No. 113 of 21 December 1984.
Law (Belo Horizonte/MG) No. 5839 of 28 December 1990.
Law (Goiânia/GO) No. 9986 of 27 December 2016.
Law (Recife/PE) No. 18274 of 25 November 2016.
Law (Rio de Janeiro/RJ) No. 1936 of 30 December 1992.
Law (Rio de Janeiro/RJ) No. 2687 of 27 November 1998.
Law (Rio de Janeiro/RJ) No. 691 of 24 December 1984.
Law (São Paulo/SP) No. 13250 of 27 December 2001.
Law (São Paulo/SP) No. 17092 of 23 May 2019.
Reg. Int. (CM) (Campo Grande/MS), Resolution (CM) (Campo Grande/MS) No. 1109 of 2009.
Reg. Int. (CM) (Goiânia/GO), Resolution (CM) (Goiânia/GO) No. 26 of 1991.
Reg. Int. (CM) (Rio de Janeiro/RJ), Resolution (CM) (Rio de Janeiro/RJ) No. 679 of 1992.
Reg. Int. (CM) (São Paulo/SP), Resolution (CM) (São Paulo/SP) No. 2 of 1991.

Index

The numbers here refer to paragraph numbers.

www.ingramcontent.com/pod-product-compliance
Ingram Content Group UK Ltd.
Pitfield, Milton Keynes, MK11 3LW, UK
UKHW020137290926
15471UKWH00003B/554

9 789403 548814